LAST ROCK

THE VICE SQUAD STORY

LAST ROCKERS:
THE VICE SQUAD STORY

★ACM ЯETRO

SHANE BALDWIN

Published by www.acmretro.com
Cover and book design by Sam Giles.

Shane Baldwin asserts the moral right to be identified as the author of this work.
A catalogue record for this book is available from the British Library.

ACKNOWLEDGEMENTS

In memory of my brother Clay, my dad Mike, Dave Bateman, Jon Chilcott, Merv Woolford and John Peel.

Dedicated to my wife Jo, my mum Valerie, my sister Trayci, my niece Eloise, my sons Jake and Louie, their wives Tomomi and Phuong…and just in time, my beautiful granddaughter Lyria, born on 2 August 2015.

Thanks to the interviewees:

First and foremost Mark Hambly, who has tirelessly worked with me on this book since I first started it in the mid-90s. We've spent countless hours, in a variety of hostelries, sweating over a hot tape/voice recorder. Now we'll have to find another excuse to spend countless hours in a variety of hostelries.
Beki Bondage, Dave Bateman, Mark 'Sooty' Byrne, Julia 'Lia' Rumbelow, John 'Igor' Burchill, Simon Edwards, Ian 'Cliff Dangerous' Minter, Tim 'H' Clench, Nick 'Dr Dunglust' Quarry, Al 'Al' Rees, Shawn Stern, Rich Walters, John Peel, Garry Bushell, Charlie Harper and Alvin Gibbs.

Thanks also to Suzanne Lewis and Nicki Ratcliffe at EMI, Mark Brennan at Captain Oi!, Lol Pryor, George Marshall, Iain McNay, Matt Bristow and Matt Ingham at Cherry Red, Dave Spiller, Dave Lown, Dave Patton and Sam Lovell. And of course…Bill White.

CHAPTER 1

IT WAS GOD SAVE THE QUEEN that really did it for us. I'm a little ashamed to admit that as it was so late in the day to discover punk. Londoners and Northerners who'd been in on the Pistols and Buzzcocks since '76 would no doubt scoff, but to be fair, me and Dave Bateman were only 15 in 1977 and it took Dave some effort to find a shop near where we lived, in Hanham, on the outskirts of Bristol that would even stock it.

We'd first met when our mothers sat next to each other in the baby clinic. I was there for my two week check-up, Dave for his six months. Later, at the age of about eight or nine, we shared a passion for Bristol City FC and the likes of Slade, T.Rex, Gary Glitter and Sweet. Around the mid '70's the glam scene went quiet and music took a back seat (with the notable exception of Thin Lizzy) and football took over completely.

When we sat down in Dave's back room and actually listened to God Save The Queen we didn't know what to make of it. We'd read all the lurid tales about the Pistols in the tabloids, and I suppose partly believed them, so we probably expected the worst. At this point it would be nice to say that as the music thundered from the speakers a blinding light filled the room; that we instantly saw the folly of our meaningless existences and knew that this was indeed the answer. Actually we just played it twice and said 'Erm, well, the music's good...not sure about the vocals though.'

What we did understand, fairly quickly, was that this was something quite radical (though in retrospect all the Pistols' influences were readily available, and perhaps it was only a matter of time before someone, anyone, did what badly needed to be done) and we took it on board with a vengeance. Throughout 1977 we bought as many punk records as we could, but not being particularly well informed this meant that for every classic Models single, we got stuck with some bloody awful crap by Venus & The Razorblades or whoever. It was very hit and miss.

The next step was to go to a gig. Frankly we were a bit scared. The football terraces were at a peak of mindless violence at this point, but though we weren't fighters ourselves (though Dave became quite a well-known face in the '80s) we knew our way around. It was our territory, and we were reasonably safe. It didn't help that many of the early punk gigs that happened in Bristol took place at Barton Hill Youth Club. This was an extremely dodgy area to visit for outsiders, but the Youth Club played host to the likes of Siouxsie & The Banshees, Sham 69 and Slaughter & The Dogs, and we were tempted. But not that tempted. We weren't bloody stupid.

The first punk gig I went to was the Jam, supported by New Hearts, at the Bristol Locarno, on 4 December 1977 and it cost £1.50 to get in. I know because I still have the ticket. It would be much more cool to say the Clash or someone incredibly obscure that went on to form a huge stadium band, but that's who it was. And it was absolutely amazing. They came on ridiculously late, Weller's dad introduced them, and the whole place just erupted at the first chord. A life altering experience, and maybe not a healthy one, but certainly unforgettable.

With all the talk of the punk ethic 'Anyone can do it' flying around, we got to thinking that we should be doing something ourselves. The 'we' in this case encompasses an unlikely group of friends that had somehow fallen together, loosely based around Gays Road (harde-har) where I lived. We were an unlikely group in that we comprised of roughly 50% Comprehensive educated (The Grange and Kingsfield) and 50% Public School (Bristol Grammar), and had we not lived so far out in the sticks, we probably wouldn't have mixed so much, even having all attended junior school together. As it was, those of us at the Comprehensives had friends there, most of whom lived miles away, and it was the same with the Grammar School crowd. So we stuck together, only noticing the differences in our status when any of our school-friends met any of theirs, and cooked up a series of increasingly hair-brained schemes to amuse ourselves.

Firstly we decided to launch a fanzine, called *Graffiti*, on the grounds that none of us could play an instrument, but we could just about read and write. I tried to get it printed on the school photocopier, with the backing of my English teacher Mr Price, who was quite impressed by the fact that we'd produced something vaguely readable, even if he was unimpressed with the subject matter. The headmaster, a doddery old bigot, proclaimed it disgraceful, though he was a little thrown when he demanded to know the author of a particularly scurrilous Clash live review. It was a chap called Bob Hulmes who taught Dave and Mark History at Kingsfield School (I attended the Grange School, just down the road). Bob was a Mancunian that we sometimes went to gigs with, not as any kind of school trip arrangement, just 'Going to see the Adverts tonight Bob?' 'Aye lads, I'll be in the Hatchet about seven.' At a later Clash gig to the aforementioned (the *Sort It Out Tour,* I think) the band threw badges into the audience and people risked life and limb fighting to get one, and being a skinny little runt I ended up black and blue and totally badge-less. Bob, tanked up on gin, had steamed in like a man possessed and several people must bear the scars today, but he did get one. Observing that I was the only member of our crowd to fail in this endeavour he casually handed it to me with the words 'There yah go lad, ah can face life without a Clash badge.' A credit to the teaching profession.

Bob's involvement with our fanzine meant that the repercussions from the headmaster were minimal (though he only ever spoke to me once more, and that was to call me an animal for fighting on the bus stop) but of course we had to look elsewhere to get the thing printed. A relative of mine, Roger, got some copies done at work, and we did sell a few, but after two issues we began to wonder whether a band really was out of the question.

The only one of our crowd that had ever played a musical instrument (unless you count my juvenile piano lessons, which I kept schtum about, partly out of embarrassment, partly because Schubert's Unfinished Symphony was unlikely to be included in our repertoire, but mostly because the only punk band I was aware of with a keyboard player were the Stranglers, who I hated) was Dave. He'd been taught the rudiments of the Spanish guitar by an uncle and from there, surely, it was but a small step to Guitar Heroism *a la* Steve Jones and his brother Mick.

At first I was to have been the singer, but my tenure as a budding John Lydon was short lived when it became patently obvious that I couldn't carry a tune in a bucket. For reasons long lost in the mists of time (a line that will no doubt crop up often in this missive) it was decided that I should be the drummer; I couldn't play the drums either, but we rarely strayed into the realms of logic.

The first line-up of the Spam, as we were first known, (after a brief spell as The Proletariat, ditched when we started to spray it on the side of the local Midlands bank, then realised none of us could spell it) ran thus: Ian 'Cliff Dangerous' Minter, vocals, Dave 'Boring' Bateman, guitar, Tim 'Howard Exciting' Clench, bass, and Shane 'Benson Orb' (don't ask) Baldwin, drums. Among the honorary members were Nick 'Doctor Dunglust' Quarry, who was to have joined on second guitar when he mastered it (he's nearly there now) and Al Rees who did eventually join for a short period on bass.

Ian Minter was at the Grange School, along with Nick and myself, and I for one had never met anyone like him. Highly intelligent, knowledgeable, and with, by our standards, hugely eclectic tastes in music. While we'd all been into Slade and T.Rex, he'd been immersed in Captain Beefheart, Frank Zappa and the like. I was introduced to him by Nick, who was convinced that he'd found our singer. 'I knew him all the time I was at the Grange, and he was a very smart guy, very intelligent,' says Nick, 'I learnt how to make bombs from him, which to an 11 or 12 year old was the height of intellectual satisfaction. I mean, it was better than sex, it really was. You were growing up and you had your first lot of hormones switched on, so it was either sex or doing something destructive like making bombs. He was always either building something or destroying it...blowing it up.'

Ian was obviously the man for the job then. He was also a capable singer and lyricist, and his experience of the punk phenomenon preceded ours as he explains. 'My brother brought home Anarchy In The UK and gave me some amphetamines, and that started if off really. I took amphetamines for about six years afterwards.'

Tim 'Howard Exciting' Clench, or H as he shall be referred to hereafter, lived a few doors up from me, and was in some ways a surprising choice for our bass player (or any other position come to that). A Bristol Grammar School boy (as were many of the proper movers & shakers on the Bristol punk scene), he was, not to put too fine a point on it, a hippy. Of course his credibility rating rocketed when, on one of our interminable shopping trips round the record, clothes and music shops of Bristol, Simon Cartledge, bass player with Social Security, who had once supported the mighty Cortinas at the Locarno, and even had a record out, *nodded* to H as we passed him in the street, him being a fellow Bristol Grammar type. Were we fucking impressed or what? This type of hob-nobbing with the hierarchy you simply could not argue with, and though on our monthly London trips to buy tacky Kings Road clothes and over-priced Sex Pistols bootlegs from Portobello Road market, we were often embarrassed by his cries of things like 'Look at this guys, it's *The Doors Live In Paris in '68*!' he was a more than capable bass player, and a good mate. Still is. He did have some empathy with the punk movement though, as he explains: 'I definitely liked the attitude and politics, yeah, and I liked some of the music, it kind of grew on me, which is how music tends to affect me anyway. I liked the Vibrators, I liked them a lot, and I liked Siouxsie and the Banshees, and I liked the Pistols, eventually. Somebody lent me a a copy of Anarchy in the UK, the original EMI single, and I played it once and thought it was dreadful. But then, I didn't know what to expect. I'd heard a lot of media rubbish beforehand.' I suppose the real surprise is that he let us push him around, making him playing Sham 69 covers for as long as he did. Once described by the local listings magazine as 'Taciturn and cynical,' H tended to go with the flow, at least as long as it suited him. But we'll come to that later.

With our initial line-up completed it was down to the more mundane complications of acquiring equipment and finding somewhere to rehearse/learn. In an ideal world we'd have simply nicked entire back-lines and PA systems from David Bowie, having got the tip-off from Steve Jones, but Bowie rarely played Hanham or Kingswood, so it was all second-hand and hire-purchased tat for us. I first bought a second-hand drum-kit for forty quid from a bloke in a wheelchair who was obviously playing for the sympathy vote, as it turned out to be worth naff-all once I had an idea what I was talking about. I traded that in for a slightly better (but not much) kit of dubious Japanese origin and struggled along with that until Dad stood as guarantor for a decent Premier job much later. The others had similar problems, but this is my book so these will go unreported.

Rehearsal space was a serious problem, and remained so until quite an advanced stage of the Vice Squad era. There simply wasn't anywhere local and we couldn't afford to pay for a proper rehearsal room in central Bristol, even if we'd known where to look. Until a better proposition presented itself (which it never did) we decided to make use of the garage at H's house. We'd spent a lot of time plotting our rise to fame and fortune in the back room there, so re-locating to the garage some 10 yards away seemed a natural progression, and hey!, it was a garage: 'We're a garage band...Ooooh Ooooh Ooo!'

Romantic, in that sense, it may have been, but as these tentative rehearsals took place in the deep winter of 1977/78, most of those involved now just remember it being incredibly cold. I mean trying-to-play-guitar-with-gloves-on fucking cold. Musically, it must be said, the gloves probably didn't make a great deal of difference as we still couldn't actually play, and our early disdain for some of the poorer bands we'd seen lessened somewhat. We were sure we had a better idea of what we should be doing than they did, but at least they knew some chords 'n' stuff.

I remember our first chord well. Ah... he was a lovely little feller. Dave had a Sex Pistols poster on which Steve Jones' finger positions on the fret-board (we were getting technical now) could be clearly seen. Armed with what was obviously a sign from The Master, we hastened to our garage to try it out. It sounded shite; obviously Dave wasn't playing it properly. 'Pull yourself together man, and try it again. It's a Steve Jones chord for Christ's sake!' He did, often, and it still sounded shite. Eventually, when we'd made some progression down the road to musical virtuosity (about two doors down, on the whole) we realised that The Master must have been playing a duff chord at the time the photo was taken, as no such chord exists. Ho hum.

After a while though, we were able to turn out rough 'n' ready covers like Sham 69's I Don't Wanna, the Cortinas' Television Families, the Lurkers' Freak Show, the Ramones' Headbanger and almost anything by the Pistols. Dave and Ian also made their first attempts at songwriting, which initially amounted to plagiarism on an impressive scale, though eventually they provided the bulk of our set, much of which survived through to Vice Squad. Our next task, then, was to find a few unsuspecting folk to act as an audience to our rapidly expanding talents.

As we were rehearsing in H's garage, and as H had already demonstrated his close intimacy with the Bristol Grammar cognoscenti, it was suggested that he throw a party and invite a few of these along. The plan being, obviously, that we would play an impromptu set in the garage, impress these terribly hip people, at least one of whom must surely be sleeping with the odd Cortina or two, and then it would only be a matter of time before we were signed to Step Forward and on tour with the Cortinas. Fool proof. The day of the party arrived, and H welcomed his esteemed guests with all the effusiveness he could muster, which, as usual, amounted to bugger-all. The atmosphere was strained to say the least, with them marking all of us down as the uncultured yokels we undoubtedly were within seconds, and our crowd feeling more than a little intimidated. It must have been even worse for H, being firmly stuck in the middle. We settled down into two distinct groups and the party progressed with little in the way of gaiety and merriment, and nothing in the way of contact between the two camps other than polite enquiries after the location of the bottle opener and/or lavatory. The impromptu set idea looked more and more like a non-starter, particularly when we noted their disapproving reaction to our selection of records. It seemed that Sham 69 were now considered passé, and those in the know were now into the avant-garde sounds of Magazine and Gang Of Four, which they proceeded to play at us for the rest of the evening, having gained control of the record player when our guard was down. We half-heartedly played the set anyway, but once a couple of H's closest Grammar School mates had listened to a couple of songs for appearances sake before making their excuses and leaving, we were all on our own, freezing to death as usual.

Our days as a genuine garage band were, it turned out, drawing to a close. We now encountered what was to become a recurring theme in our lives, the Irate Neighbour Syndrome. H lived opposite one Councillor Cox, whose daughter Nicola had been at Hanham Abbot's Junior School with most of us. This connection was probably the reason why he pussy-footed around for some time before really kicking up a fuss about the din we were making. Once the bit was in his teeth, however, his powers of hyperbole made impressive listening. According to the good Councillor, the ferocious sonic assault of the Spam was capable of moving his sofa several inches eastwards during one rendition of Freak Show. This was obviously untrue; he must have been thinking of Shadow. We tried turning things down and padding the drums, but this didn't seem to pacify him, and anyway, while playing punk rock at low volume is technically possible, it is debilitating to the soul and saps morale. For the sake of H's parents' social standing and our own mental well-being, it was time to move on.

The gardens in Gays Road are narrow and long. H's garage was, naturally, next to the house, whereas my Dad's shed was at the bottom of the garden, at the furthest possible point from the neighbours. Beyond it lay only a disused slag-heap, known as The Tip, and

Hanham Woods. Perfect, we thought. How wrong we were. Surprisingly, the nearest neighbours viewed our presence philosophically; as long as we knocked it on the head at a reasonable hour, they put up with it and reasoned that at least we weren't out raping and pillaging with the rest of our generation. A chap two doors down, Jim Bishop, even used to come round and tune the drums for me. We did, however, have a hardcore of detractors, who launched a long-term campaign to oust us from our cosy nest. It got to the point where a representative of the local council was summoned to zap us with his decibel-meter-thingy, but we'd spotted him lurking in the undergrowth, and cranked it right down for his benefit. The next night it was business as usual, and thus thwarted, The Anti-Spam League sent my parents to Coventry. As if they gave a flying fuck.

Surprisingly, while all this tomfoolery was going on, we actually managed to clock up our first gigs. The first Spam gig took place at a Hanham Abbots School reunion in 1978, an inauspicious start you may think, but then all our gigs were to be inauspicious. We didn't know that at the time though, and we were all fired up for it, this was the start. It was a gig, with a stage and people and everything! It was organized by the afore-mentioned Nicola Cox and a swatty-type called Deborah, and they were dubious about our idea of regaling the assembled throng of our peers and former teachers with our newly acquired talents. In the end it didn't matter what they thought, as I rather sneakily talked Mr Bennett, our recently retired Headmaster and guest of honour at this love-fest into giving his approval before they had the chance to put the case for the opposition.

After our initial euphoria at securing this prestigious engagement, the reality of the thing began to sink in. The gear we had was barely adequate as a back-line, and the only time any of us had even seen a proper PA system was at the Locarno or Colston Hall. For rehearsal purposes Ian sang through any old guitar amp and speaker set-up that was available, but that clearly wouldn't be adequate to carry his dulcet tones across a large school hall. Here, Ian's electrical expertise came to the rescue. Sort of. He came up with an ingenious contraption assembled from, it appeared, old wire, chip-board and sticky-backed plastic, but it bloody well worked. During our sound-check (as we liked to call it, while those laying out the buffet looked on disapprovingly) his tones had never sounded so dulcet.

Come show-time, we were as nervous as hell, but we needn't have worried. No one took the slightest bit of notice of us, as if we were an embarrassing relative at a family function who'd hit the dry sherry too early. They just pretended we weren't there. The only people to show any interest at all were a bunch of local thugs who'd gate-crashed (the shape of things to come) that no-one had worked up the nerve to throw out. They seemed to appreciate our increasingly frantic efforts, which was gratifying, and later, we noticed that the rest of the gathering was beginning to sit up and cast an interested eye over us. We were winning them over, obviously, and not before time. Wrong. What they had spotted, and we hadn't, was that Ian's PA system was emitting billows of smoke and in danger of razing the whole building to the ground. Oblivious, and spurred on by this show of interest, we really went for it, until Ian finally cottoned on and disappeared into a mass of wiring and smouldering wood to turn the thing off.

It says something for our resilience that we weren't put off by this rather humiliating debut; quite the opposite in fact. Those few fleeting moments when the thugs had set aside their bottles of Newcy Brown to watch us, and the even fewer and more fleeting moments when we were under the impression that the rest of the audience were showing an interest, had been enough. We'd caught the bug good and proper, and we wanted more.

Trouble was, there were no more on the horizon. For all our efforts, our engagement diary remained empty (along with our social diary, as it happens, but that's another story). In desperation, I approached my parents, who were both active members of the local railway preservation society at Bitton (Dad was one of the founder members, a fact I'm quite proud of), known as the Bristol Suburban Railway Society (these days it's the Avon Valley Railway, trainspotters) hoping to get a gig at one of their many fund-raising events. Of course, this was far from ideal from the point of view of either party. They'd rather have had a decent covers band and we were hankering after a few genuine punks in the audience, preferably female and of the type sporting fishnet stockings and little else. As it was, we came cheap, ie free, and at least they were all alive and obliged to watch us for that reason (us playing for free, I mean, not them being alive. Ahem...). The exact number of gigs we played at Bitton has been lost in the mists of time (told you we'd be seeing that little beauty again) but it probably ran to three or four. They all took place in the goods shed, and on the posters for the first one we were second on the bill to the Soundsominous Disco. We were, however, placed above both the barbecue and the raffle. Like the garage/shed rehearsals, all anyone seems to remember now is being incredibly cold all the time (we took advantage of the free rehearsal time that could be had by pretending that all bands took six hours to sound-check, and that's a long time in a draughty goods shed in the middle of winter as I'm sure you all know) and the constant battle to keep our shoddy gear from giving up the ghost altogether.

One of these shows was attended by Ian's older brother, who brought along a friend of his called Pete Moxham. They were fairly impressed, or at least they said so, and as they knew their stuff when it came to punk, we were pleased. In fact Pete even offered to manage us, and we jumped at it. It never occurred to us that the man was a biscuit salesman with no more idea of how to operate in the music business than Harvey Goldsmith would if he found himself saddled with the task of shifting a consignment of McVities Digestives. In the event his sole act as our manager was to change our name to the TV Brakes. After that we never saw him unless we happened to bump into him at a gig or in a pub, but we kept up the pretence that we had a manager for some time.

Another gig we managed came thanks to a friend of my mother. The exact circumstances are lost in the mists of time (told you) but we somehow ended up playing at the local borstal's Christmas party. This of course was absolutely brilliant. After all, the Pistols had played at a prison, and we were just getting to these budding felons early in their careers. It was an experience I'll never forget. The people in charge seemed kindly souls, but some of the inmates were serious offenders, as Ian recalls: 'One of them was that kid that killed a little girl. He got her body in a trench then put a sheet of corrugated iron over her.

He was in there then, apparently.' This we didn't learn until later, and at the time some of the procedures struck us as a little draconian. As well as playing the gig we were also invited to their Christmas meal beforehand, and before we met the lads for the first time the officials talked us through a long list of do's and don'ts regarding our conduct when we met them. We also had to hand over all smoking materials and anything that could conceivably be used as a weapon to be locked in the safe until after the gig.

The meal passed without incident, and after some initial shyness on both sides we got chatting to a few of the lads, who struck us as decent enough sorts. The food though, according to Ian, tasted a little strange: 'I remember the food having potassium bromide in it. I think it was to quell the sex drive, and of course it tasted tainted, it tasted really awful.'

The gig itself, which took place in the sport-hall, was great, and though we knew that this was about as captive an audience as you could get, and their appreciation was as much down to the fact that we'd bothered to come along at all as the performance, it went down a storm, and we were really glad to have done it. Later I received a very nice letter from the governess thanking us for our efforts, which I still have.

Our only other gig, apart from the continuing Bitton shows, took place in the back room of the Maypole pub on Hanham High Street, which I'd found out you could hire for a nominal outlay. In a way this was the test, as all our other gigs had come with a built in audience and we were coincidental. This time we were the main event and people had to buy tickets and make the effort to show up just for the pleasure of seeing us. Much arm-twisting, emotional blackmail and bribery ensured that it wasn't the total embarrassment it could have been, with a reasonable showing of friends and a few people who'd seen us at Hanham Abbots School. There was also a contingent of younger members from the Railway Society whose musical tastes extended to the Jam and Rose Tattoo, but sadly this is the closest we came to attracting a proper punk following.

As if we didn't have enough problems, with rehearsal space, equipment, gigs and being complete and utter failures, sometime in late 1978, H announced that he was leaving. Just why this came as such a shock cannot, in retrospect, be easily explained. He'd never made any secret of the fact that, much as he admired the attitude and politics of the punk movement, musically it left him cold. The fact of the matter was that, though we knew this, he was so laid-back and had gone along with our wishes for so long that we rather took him for granted. As well as the three facets of H's character already mentioned, (taciturn, cynical and laid-back, for readers with short memories) we can now add a fourth - stubborn. Having made his decision no amount of bullying and nagging would change his mind. He had his reasons though, as he explains: 'I suppose I wanted a bit more than we were doing at the time, which is bit ironic considering what happened later. I wasn't wildly enamoured by Ian's singing style, I must admit. As for the music, that was developing, but I think I was a bit impatient, I wanted things to go a bit quicker than they had. Living in Bristol was also a handicap, which is why I moved to London and did absolutely nothing.' Cynical? H? Nah. Anyway, a replacement had to be found.

H, however, was already on the case as Al Rees remembers: 'H went off to do his own band, and I sort of got the nod from him. He spoke to me, he felt guilty about leaving you, so he asked me if I was interested and I jumped at it, never having played an instrument in my life. You went for it and I joined for a while. The only actual live performances were at the Bitton Railway Centre. I came along and did backing vocals on a couple of songs, Pretty Vacant was one, and I did bass on some songs and vocals on others. I think I did about three songs in all of my career as a live showman.'

Here, our mate H gives his account of events: 'I never really left. I announced that I was going to leave, cos I didn't think you were going to get anywhere. And I felt so guilty about leaving that I offered to replace myself, which is where we got Al Rees from. I thought, well, I picked it up really easy, so anybody can play bass. So I asked Al if he wanted to join the band, and he did. I started trying to show him how to do it, then I realised he couldn't do it, and I think what we did was we actually played a couple of gigs where he played the bass for three or four songs then I played the bass for three or four songs. I played the more complicated ones and he played the easier ones. Eventually, you started writing songs that he could play the bass to, and I played less and less, but I don't think I ever really left until you got Mark and Beki in. Al was officially the bass player, but I don't think he ever played a gig when I wasn't there.'

As our rehearsal to gig ratio was about thirty to one, Al's involvement in the TV Brakes story ran to months rather than days, but it was short-lived, as we soon received another blow to our already fragile project. Ian now announced that he too was leaving.

As with H, we failed to see this coming, though all the signs were there, with one incident in particular having a significant effect. After a rehearsal, Ian, Al and myself went for a drink at the Chequers pub next to the River Avon in Hanham. It's quite a long walk to the Chequers from Gays Road, through a series of country lanes, but it was a pleasant evening, the rehearsal had gone well and we felt like celebrating. As we were still under-age we sat outside on the balcony and sent in Al, who, despite being the same age as us, was big and sported a beard, to get the drinks. We got a few funny looks from the rest of the clientele due to our clothes, but that was nothing unusual, and we thought nothing of it. Some of them, though, obviously took more exception to our dress sense than others, as on the way home, as we reached the darkest and most isolated part of the road that led away from the pub, a van screeched to a halt beside us. A group of men - as opposed to boys - got out, calmly muttered 'We'll give you punk rock,' and systematically beat the shit out of us. As soon as Al and I went down, which we did almost immediately I must admit, we instinctively assumed the foetal position, and though it was quite a beating we didn't come out of it too badly. Ian, on the other hand, kept trying to get back up, which must have pleased them no end. He came off much worse than us, and afterwards you could actually make out the Doc Martens imprints on his face where they'd booted him every time he raised his head. 'I had a microphone in my pocket and they stamped so hard they broke the metal grill off it,' he remembers. Once they got bored with putting the boot in, one of them went through our pockets taking all we had, which amounted to nothing more than some small change and a few cigarettes. As they walked away one of them said something about teaching us a lesson for insulting the queen, which under different circumstances would have made us laugh quite a lot. Battered, bruised and covered in blood, we eventually managed to limp home.

This incident shook me badly, and I was a bag of nerves for some weeks afterwards. I'd experienced violence before of course, and had become used to gigs going up in the air and getting the odd slap at football when I failed to move fast enough, but this was the first time I'd taken such a prolonged beating. It affected Al in the same way, but after a while our confidence returned and we just chalked it up to experience. It was a different matter with Ian though. This is pure speculation really, but to me he changed overnight, and I don't think he was ever the same bloke again. The nervous reaction which is common when someone has been subjected to a violent assault, and which we all experienced, went deeper with Ian and lasted for a considerable time. He became insular and disillusioned, and the first things he became disillusioned with, apart from the human race, were punk rock in general and the TV Brakes in particular. Having experienced it first hand, the violence, or at least perceived violence that punk embraced and had at first seemed so exciting, now disgusted him. His taste in music reverted back to his avant garde pre-punk days, and he even discovered new purveyors of weirdness like American odd-balls the Residents and Snakefinger. Ian, though, cites a different reason for this change of direction: 'I didn't really want you to say that I was interested in a different type of music to the rest of the band and that's why I packed it in, but I suppose it's inevitable really. I think it was drugs, though, because as soon as I got into drugs I then started liking the Residents, and my musical outlook changed.'

Whatever the reason, Ian left to pursue this new musical direction, and as Al was still only at a very early stage of learning the bass, Dave and I found ourselves without a band to speak of. When Dad reclaimed his shed for essential house repairs it was the final straw and we joined Ian in the disillusionment stakes. We jacked it in and went back to football.

CHAPTER 2

THE END OF THE TV BRAKES was bitterly disappointing, but for a while at least it was quite a relief not having to struggle to sustain a band that, for all our efforts, had never showed the slightest sign of getting anywhere.

Dave and I still had the football, though, and it was an interesting time to be a supporter of Bristol City Football Club. In 1976 we'd been promoted (finally, after a struggle of several seasons, and then by the skin of our teeth) to the old first division. We'd won our first game in the top-flight, beating Arsenal 1-0 at Highbury with a goal from the great Paul Cheesley, winning two and drawing two of the first four games, and at one point the league table on *Match Of The Day* showed BCFC occupying top place in the league. I should have taken a picture, 'cos from there onwards it was backs-against-the-wall time. By 1978 it was one constant struggle just to stay in the first division, with just the odd little victory to keep our peckers up. It was a struggle that almost saw the demise of the club as it plummeted from the first division to the fourth in successive seasons, and by 1982 was on the brink of bankruptcy. But that's another story. Though hardly a bundle of laughs, then, the football was something for me and Dave to focus on while we licked our musical wounds.

Not that we'd been neglecting the punk scene, of course. While the likes of the Bromley Contingent snootily insist that it was all over before the end of 1976, let alone 1977, for the likes of us it really happened in 1978. During the course of that year, virtually every punk band that hadn't prematurely imploded came to Bristol. The Locarno put on punk bands every Sunday and Tuesday, which we attended whether we liked the bands or not, just to mix with the crowd (it was still the same 'we,' even though we were no longer a band, incidentally), and we also frequented other venues that put on the major bands like the Colston Hall, Tiffany's, the University Anson Rooms, Romeo and Juliet's and Trinity Church. We also went to smaller venues like the Green Rooms, the Granary, Bower Ashton Technical College and the Stonehouse to see the newer, up-and-coming acts.

I don't care what anyone says, it was a great year to be a punk, and it wasn't long before Dave and I were up for another go at forming a band.

Towards the end of the TV Brakes saga, a friend of Dave's from Kingsfield School, Mark Hambly, had come along to rehearsals and acted as roadie at some of the Railway Society gigs. He was just getting into punk and came along to a lot of the gigs we went to, soon becoming a permanent fixture in our little gang. Mark was tall and skinny, with a quiet, dry sense of humour, and for reasons that we could never adequately explain, to Dave and I he just *looked* like a bass player. It goes without saying that he couldn't play a note. But Dave spent, ooh, ten minutes or so showing him all he knew about the bass guitar, seven of which were spent drumming in the most important rule of punk rock bass-playing: 'The guitar must at all times be slung as low as humanly possible, at least around the knees and preferably brushing the ankles. This may, of course, hinder your playing, but, hey, it looks good.' He was then banished to his bedroom and told not to come back until he could bang out a reasonable rendition of Pretty Vacant. We didn't see him for weeks.

Our next problem (we had scores of others, most of which have already been outlined, but to dwell on them would have been too depressing, so we took one at a time) was to find a singer. Or at least this is how I remember the order of events. Mark places these talks slightly earlier, and perhaps he's right. Anyway, he sums up the gist of them nicely: 'Before I was in the band I was in on discussions, and there were these bands like the X-Certs, and it was 'How are we ever, or how are *you* ever gonna compete.' And that was the female singer decision, 'cos you were a year or perhaps two behind these other bands who were getting quite good sets together. It was a conscious gimmick.' It was indeed. Shame on us.

We placed an advert in the Revolver record shop in Bristol, and awaited the floods of replies from budding Debbie Harry's and Pauline Murray's. As it turned out, there was but one reply, and that was from one Rebecca Bond who had lately taken to going under the name of Beki Bondage.

After Dave had spoken to her on the phone, we met Beki and her boyfriend John Burchill in the Swan. We were highly impressed straight away. She looked great, and despite being slightly younger than us (she's almost a year younger than me) she seemed very worldly compared to us. John, who was a few years older (and still is, I believe) seemed even more so, and regaled us with magical tales of seeing the Ramones at the Roundhouse in London on one of their first visits to these shores, and other such historic events. Once we all got over our self-consciousness, we seemed to hit it off okay, and then it was crunch time.

We repaired to my bedroom to give them the only demonstration we could of our talents, which was a very poor quality tape of the Spam at Hanham Abbots School. This had seemed a good idea when we'd first thought of it, as we'd expected, at best, some impressionable young girlie who'd be easily impressed and just happy to join a band. These two, however, clearly knew their stuff. There was nothing for it though, but to play the tape, cringe throughout, and await their derisive laughter. To our surprise, as the muffled and distorted din played woefully on, they listened with interest. Then, eventually, John asked me to stop the tape. I assumed he'd heard enough. It was halfway through our rendition of the Cortinas' Television Families and I'd just murdered the drum solo. He asked me to wind it back and play it again, which I did. By a happy accident of imperfect acoustics and poor quality microphones, the snare part of the solo produced an excruciatingly loud machine gun affect, which he seemed highly impressed with, as did Beki. As far as they were concerned, that was that. If we were happy with the arrangement, she'd join.

It never entered our heads that a prospective member should have to impress *us*, other than on a personal level, and anyway, we had nowhere to hold an audition, so now we had a band.

Later, Beki told me that she'd responded to several ads placed by other bands, but no matter what influences they claimed when she rang up, they always turned out to be hippies. It got to the stage where she'd turn up at the appointed meeting place, poke her head cautiously round the corner, and at the sight of long hair and denims, run like hell before they spotted her. The truth of the matter was that as soon as she'd clocked our spiked hair and Pistols t-shirts, she was in.

The next thing to be sorted, to take our most minor problem first, was to decide on a name. It can be easily deduced from our earlier choices of names that in this respect, Dave and I were about as much use as a chocolate fire-guard and Beki wasn't a lot better. Mark just kept quiet, of course. In the end, a friend of Beki's, a rather gorgeous girl called Ange (who later took up modelling, first for the sleeve of a Heartbeat record by the Letters, and later still for a variety of smuts including a memorable cover for a Christmas issue of *Fiesta*) came up with the name Vice Squad. We liked it from the start, and with Beki's image it was of, course, entirely apt.

That was the easy bit. Now, of course, Beki had to learn of all our myriad difficulties in the way of equipment and rehearsal space. She took the news philosophically, and for a long time we merely hung-out together, making outlandish plans, watching other bands and drinking. There was a one-off rehearsal in Mark's Dad's garage, while I was at work (by now I'd left school and started a sign-writing apprenticeship, while Dave and Mark were in sixth-form and Beki was on the dole). It didn't last long though, as the wiring wasn't earthed properly and they narrowly escaped being fried on the spot. Served them bloody well right for starting without me.

Our first proper rehearsal, again a one-off, took place in a church hall in Tabernacle Road, Hanham. By now, the spring of 1979, the TV Brakes were but a fond memory, as were the vestiges of musicianship that Dave and I had acquired at that time. I remember the rehearsal as an unmitigated disaster, but again I'm contradicted, this time by Nick Quarry: 'I remember it being excellent at the time, cos Beki was there. That's what it was.' After all the red faces (mine, mainly) we did emerge with a new song that Beki had penned the words to called Nothing, and a clutch of photos, and now, at least, we did feel like a proper band.

What our next step was going to be, we had no idea, but help was on its way. The previous summer, Al Rees and I had gone to the Brillig Arts Centre in Bath to see the Lurkers. The night before, they'd appeared on *Top Of The Pops*, so we knew it would be packed and turned up a couple of hours early, just in case. When we got there people were already queuing up (it was a tiny venue) so we resigned ourselves to a vigil. We got chatting to a bloke called Bruce Gilling, who was in front of us in the queue, and he was a good laugh, so we stayed with him for the duration of the gig. The place was packed to the rafters, and the Lurkers were fantastic, of course. We had a great night, watching the skins tearing the place apart and literally swinging from the lampshades (the Brillig never put on another gig, as far as I know) and vowed to keep in touch.

By the time Beki joined the band Bruce was a permanent fixture in our happy throng and seeing our difficulties, reluctantly admitted that there was a possibility of rehearsing at his place. He lived in Redland, which is the wrong side of Whiteladies Road to be able to call

Taff (bass) and Neil Mackie (drums) and got on fine with them from the start. I struck up a rapport with, not surprisingly, their drummer Neil, and we all decided to go for a drink at the nearby World's End pub. The entire party came with us, which was a mistake, as for reasons lost in the mists of time (I was wondering where you'd got to) we were soon ejected from the pub by an irate landlord and a number of disgruntled locals. Once outside, someone put a brick through the window, and we legged it back to Whittle's place. The locals, however, wouldn't let it lie, and positioned themselves outside with the intention, as far as I could ascertain, of pulling our heads off. Strangely, no one seemed that worried, as Mark remembers: 'We were just a bunch of kids really, no one over 20 or 21 there. So we barricaded ourselves in and shouted out of the windows and stuff, and then the police came round. Everybody hid up in the attic. Then there's me, you and Mackie left downstairs playing cards, trying to look innocent, and a huge pile of coats in the corner, which was a bit of a giveaway. And then a Karen came down to meet the police in her nightie, still with her jeans and DMs underneath. By all accounts we had the good deal. We'd only have got arrested, whereas the rest of them had Dale Greenham farting and stuffing fibreglass down people's trousers.' As it turned out, the police weren't all that interested, and if they realised they were involved in a Brian Rix farce, they played along for the benefit of the locals. Once they and the vigilantes had left, the party continued, and by the end of the night the X-Certs were making rash, not to mention drunken, promises of support slots on a tour of Youth Clubs that Clive was in the process of organising. They were, eventually, as good as their drunken word, but in the meantime we managed to clock up a few gigs of our own.

By 1979, Socialist Worker's Party sponsored Rock Against Racism gigs were in full swing. They took place all over the country, and we found out that a Bristol show was to take place at the Bristol University Anson Rooms on April 12th, featuring John Cooper Clarke, Crisis, Iganda and The X-Certs. Dave and Mark spent the day at the venue, helping to set the gear up, the deal being that although crew were unpaid, they all got in for nothing. Being at work, I didn't have the option, and made my way down later. At a fairly advanced stage in the proceedings, it became clear from the agitated expressions on the organiser's faces that something was amiss. Dave takes up the story: 'It did come out over the speakers, after much rumour, 'John Cooper Clarke is pissed-up in a pub in Tottenham, and he is not going to be here,' and the basic gist of it was 'What are we going to do now?' We didn't just immediately walk up to the nearest strange organiser...it was someone we'd bought guitar equipment from, I think he was called Rich, who was working on the PA. There was some kind of introduction to some lunatic from the SWP and the next thing you know, we're the opening act.'

Everyone else moved up one on the bill, making Crisis the new headliners, and in our still fledgling state, we were about to make our debut. During the next couple of hours, much panic ensued, as you can imagine. For a start, neither Beki or I knew anything about this miraculous turn of events. We were to show up at some stage, but nothing definite had been planned. Would we get there in time? Frantic phone calls were made, but other than the fact that we'd both set off from home intending, at some stage of the evening, to show our faces at the Anson Rooms, nothing more definite could be ascertained. Luckily, both Beki and I had decided, independently, to get to the venue early to catch the X-Certs' set. The first I knew about the situation was after I'd paid in, when some kindly soul, I forget who, presented me with my sticks in the foyer and informed me that I was on in twenty minutes. With my customary inner calm and philosophical outlook on life, I burst into tears and cried 'Mother!' Not really, but you get the drift. According to Mark, Beki took the news in much the same way: 'We saw a few people we knew and said 'If you see Beki, tell her we're on.' Deb Payne or somebody bumped into her on the street and said 'You're playing tonight' and she went straight into the Richmond Springs and drank as much as she could.' Somewhat the worse for wear, Beki did make it to the church on time, and using reggae band Iganda's gear, which was hardly ideal for anyone apart from Mark: 'That's still the best bass rig I ever used, this huge great Ampeg stack, an 8x12 cabinet and a big 200 watt valve amp,' we somehow got through it. Actually, that's a pretty lame excuse. Crisis and The X-Certs used the same gear, and they sounded okay.

Fully aware of our ineptitude (we even had the classic punk rock cliché of Beki reading the lyrics from a scrap of paper) we ploughed through most of the set in a state of nervous hysteria, only pausing occasionally to gauge the reaction of the audience. When we'd taken to the stage, the crowd already numbered around 300 (expecting the X-Certs to be on first, obviously) and as we progressed this swelled to around 500. Quite a jump from Bitton Station. Amazingly, we seemed to be going down quite well. A few people danced, and each number received a decent round of applause. It would be an exaggeration to say we took the place by storm, more a fairly heavy shower, really, but emboldened by this totally unexpected show of approval we actually enjoyed the last few numbers. We left the stage feeling hugely relieved, and something approaching triumphant.

The day's wonders weren't over yet, however. As we graciously accepted the congratulations of a few sycophantic toadies while exiting stage-right, we were intercepted by a sinister looking character, who introduced himself as one Simon Edwards. This rang no bells whatever, until he explained that he was the proud owner of Heartbeat Records. Heartbeat had clocked up a fair number of releases by this time, mostly arty post-punk stuff by Clifton types, but I did have a couple of his records by Social Security (you know, I mentioned them in Chapter 1. H's mate, remember? Do try to keep up) and the Europeans. A more shameless writer would say he 'Had his finger on the pulse,' and I've no doubt Simon himself used that line more than once, but I'll just say that in Bristol, in 1979, Simon was your best bet as far as getting yourself on vinyl.

Not that we'd even considered such an eventuality arising, of course. And yet, as he liberally applied the oil like the old smoothy he was (and is) it gradually dawned on us that this was what was being offered. After the success of Brighton's Vaultage '78, regional compilations were very much in vogue, and Simon was in the process of putting together a South West version, to be called *Avon Calling*, which would be recorded later in the summer. On the strength of what he had just witnessed, we were being given the chance to contribute a track to this illustrious project. After making him repeat the offer in front of witnesses, lest his hearing should return unexpectedly, we headed to the bar to drink the health of John Cooper Clarke.

CHAPTER 3

HAVING MADE OUR DEBUT at the prestigious Anson Rooms, which was, and is, one of the largest venues on the Bristol circuit, our second gig was rather more modest.

Our Hanham local, the Swan Inn, on Conham Hill, was run by a character called Big Ron Irwin, to distinguish him from his son Little Ron Irwin. Big Ron was a pub landlord of the old school, large of stature and ruddy-cheeked, taking no nonsense and not given to suffering fools gladly. A plain speaking man, at closing time he would let out a deafening bellow of 'Geddum-down-yer-ruddy-neeeeeecksssss-aaaahhh!' and anyone still clutching a glass 30 seconds later would be forcibly ejected from the premises.

For all his gruff exterior though, Ron had the proverbial heart of gold, and partly because his son Little Ron had been at school with my mother, Medium Sized Valerie, but mostly because we were no trouble, he had let us drink in his pub since we were about 15. The law wasn't a problem as one of the locals was a copper who often drank with us. It was that sort of pub, a family run establishment, with Ron and his wife May at the helm, and a close-knit local clientele. Some of the regulars not familiar with our families were a little bemused at our appearance at first, but eventually, people who otherwise wouldn't have been seen dead in a ditch with the likes of us came to accept our presence.

Sometime in May 1979, the Swan held a charity do, and as we'd long been telling all and sundry that we were a band (it was the only explanation they'd accept for our wilfully looking, to their eyes, like we'd all been pulled through a hedge backwards) we were of course nominated to provide the live entertainment.

Just what the charity was has long been lost in the mists of time etc etc. The gig took place in the skittle-alley, and as if the surroundings of a cosy provincial pub weren't incongruous enough for our second outing as an up-and-coming punk act, the locals all dressed up in fancy dress for the occasion. Probably, as they saw it, we already were, so they were just joining in.

Later in the evening, things took an unexpected turn when several X-Certs turned up with a fair number of their entourage. This flummoxed the locals more than somewhat. They'd grown used to us, but this bunch of misfits were positively bizarre. One in particular stood out a mile, a black homosexual punk known as Princess Malcolm. For some reason he formed an attachment to me and spent most of the evening trying to undo the zips on my bondage strides, which, once the locals had got over the shock, provided them with a great source of amusement.

Basically, though, we were immensely gratified that a crew of genuine punks had made the effort just to see us. By the time we went on, the skittle-alley was packed and the landlady May later complained that she'd only managed to get a glimpse of us by dragging a beer barrel into the car park to stand on and peer through a window. She was a strong woman.

I doubt if the performance was much to write home about, but it went down well, and the 'Punk Invasion' was a talking point in the Swan for some time afterwards.

All in all, then, things were looking up. In a short space of time we'd sorted out rehearsal space, made some invaluable contacts, were about to make our vinyl debut, and had picked up a small following, albeit on loan from the X-Certs. These were things we'd only dreamed about in our Spam/TV Brakes days, and as if all this wasn't enough, the next turn of events was positively bewildering.

At this point, two characters that have a big part to play later in this story make a brief appearance, only to disappear completely before re-appearing, possibly around Chapter 5 or 6. I haven't decided yet. The two characters are Mark Byrne and Ken Lintern, who in 1979 both worked for a promoter called Kevin Draper.

Kevin Draper was the big Bristol promoter who twice weekly, on Sundays and Tuesdays, filled the Locarno to bursting point with punters for his punk shows. And they were bursting as well. Today, any Fire Officer worth his salt would weep openly at the spectacle of Kevin's minions virtually crowbarring potential victims through the already heaving Mecca doors.

When the Damned re-formed in that year, after dipping their toes in the real world and finding it not to their liking, Kevin Draper was the obvious choice to promote the Bristol leg of a lengthy Damned tour. The mighty Ruts were pencilled in as main support for the tour, and someone hit on the idea of placing advertisements in the music press inviting local bands to write in and state in no more than twenty words why they should be given the opening slot in their home town. Actually, I made that last bit up; I can't remember what the requirements were, but I know for a fact we had nothing in the way of a demo at the time, so all we could have supplied to support our claim would have been a few blurred photos and some typewritten bullshit.

For the price of a stamp we'd have been stupid not to at least give it a go, but the clever money was all on the X-Certs, ours included, and it was theirs by right.

What was supposed to happen, according to the music press, was that the promoter in each city would simply tip all the entrants into a bag, and pick out the winner at random. No one believed this for a second, hence our resignation. In every city, surely, the promoter would go through the procedure for appearances sake, pick out that city's equivalent of Vice Squad, say 'Bugger that, they couldn't pull a muscle!' and get on the phone to their equivalent of the X-Certs.

What actually happened, in our case, was that Kevin Draper couldn't even be bothered to give the matter any thought, what with all his time being taken up with raking in the dough, let alone going through the tip-all-the-entrants-into-a-bag bit, so he merely sought the opinion of Ken Lintern, who in turn passed it on to Mark Byrne. Mark was, at the time, a member of a band called St. Vitus Dance, who were managed by the same people that dealt with XTC, but the money wasn't too good so he made ends meet by helping out in Kevin's office. St. Vitus Dance were in no way a punk band, more a quirky off-shoot of the cleaned-up version known as New Wave, but at least Mark was au fait with what was going on in the lower stratum of the local scene. He was aware of the X-Certs, of course, but possibly under the influence of some mind-altering drugs, when asked the question 'Well, who the fuck do we give the Damned gig to?' he came up with a name he'd merely heard on the grapevine: ours.

The X-Certs themselves took the news okay, and ever gracious, even wished us luck with it. Some of their fans, though, were highly indignant, and I could see why. This worried us greatly for, ooh, several minutes, before the reality of just what we'd let ourselves in for sank in.

The Anson Rooms gig shrank into insignificance compared to this. We weren't particularly big Damned fans, but there was no doubt that a re-formed Damned, with their first hit single, the wonderful Love Song, riding high in the Top 20, and the equally wonderful Ruts in tow, would mean that Kevin's minions could leave the crow-bar at home. Everyone and their mother would be fighting to get in.

If I had been nervous about the Anson Rooms gig, it was nothing compared to the naked terror I suffered in the days leading up to 17 June. Mercifully, at the Anson Rooms, I'd had only minutes to think about it, and had managed to quell the nausea that swept over me by concentrating on practical matters like re-arranging the drum kit. This time we had several weeks to whip (yes, I know, 'whip', 'bondage.' You're so childish) ourselves into a state of near hysteria. One positive aspect of this advanced warning, though, was that it gave us a chance to get in some serious practice. Before the written confirmation had fluttered to the carpet in Dave's hallway we were already half-way to Bruce's place.

But it was too little, too late. We emerged from Bruce's basement with the sickly pallor and mad staring eyes of cave-dwelling hermits that really should get out more, but had we improved noticeably? No, not really. For all our efforts, 2,000 rabid Damned fans would be getting the same show as the assorted Widow Twankies and Incredible Hulks of the Swan Inn.

We blew any chance of looking cool by arriving at the Locarno, with all our gear, far too early. The only people around were the cleaners, who grudgingly let us in, and we busied ourselves getting the gear in. Then, for want of anything better to do, we explored the place. We'd been there many times, of course, but never in daylight. Like most venues, it seemed fairly glamorous in the dimmed lighting and charged atmosphere of a gig, but the cold light of day revealed it to be a bit of a shit-hole. It was hard to believe that some of my most cherished memories, of seeing the Clash, the Ramones, and the Adverts etc had taken place in this rather tatty and slightly unsanitary building.

Never mind. Just think, soon we would be treading the same boards as the Clash, the Ramones and the Adverts. Oh fuck.

We had quite a little crew with us already, though I forget who apart from Igor, Bruce and pair of rather nice blonde twin punkettes that Bruce and I had been trying, without much success, to chat up for some time. After a while, even the cleaners buggered off, leaving us to our own devices, so Bruce immediately broke into the kitchens and tucked into the only food he could find, a few stale bread rolls. He was just settling down to this hearty repast when a representative of the management showed up and went berserk. When we finally calmed him down, made Bruce put back his wretched bread rolls and convinced him that we were the support band, he ushered us backstage to the dressing rooms.

This, again, was a novelty. We could hardly believe that we were actually backstage at the Locarno, mere punters no more. Feeling, by now, positively light-headed, we broke out the guitars and had a bit of a sing-along. When the guitars weren't plugged in they didn't sound that bad.

Our first mistake (or second if you count turning up at the venue when the other bands were probably still in bed in Leicester, where they'd played the night before) was that when Dave Vanian came backstage we were bellowing out a robust barber-shop version of Anarchy In The UK. Since being kicked off the Anarchy tour in 1976, the Sex Pistols were, understandably, not the Damned's favourite band. A theme developed as, like the management-type before him, Vanian went berserk.

The management were summoned and we were immediately ousted from the backstage area and re-located in the Conference Room, behind the balcony, as far from backstage as was physically possible without finding yourself out on the street.

To say we were disappointed would be a vast understatement. As I've said, we weren't huge fans of the Damned, but we were looking forward to meeting them - they were the authentic '77 article after all. Worse still, it seemed that rather than joining in the backstage antics of the Damned and the Ruts and getting a glimpse of the life of proper Rock Stars, we would actually be stuck at a point even farther from the action, in feet and inches, than we would usually have been as punters.

There is some dispute over the next development. I believe my version to be correct, though I would prefer to believe Dave's. As I remember it, I was told (I forget by whom) that there had been a series of pranks played on the Damned by the Ruts, and vice versa, all the way through the tour. By this advanced stage, the pranks had got more and more extreme, culminating in an incident on the previous night, when the Ruts had somehow got hold of a large quantity of manure and pelted the Damned with it all through their set. This much was certainly true, as even after the road-crew had cleaned up as much of the foul smelling stuff as they could, the PA still stank the place out. In my rather mundane version, this was deemed by the Damned to be taking things too far, and for this reason the Ruts, like us, were banished to the Conference Room. In Dave's more heart-warming version, the Ruts, on hearing of our plight, decided that Vanian was out of order and elected to join us in the Conference room, though even then, it's possible that some ulterior motives were also involved: 'The Ruts and all their road-crew must have been diamond geezers to come out of the backstage dressing rooms in solidarity with us, apart from the fact they probably knew it would be easier to get a shag up there.' I'll come back to that last point later.

Whatever the reason, as we were listlessly sitting around in our dressing room feeling sorry for ourselves, the door suddenly burst open and in trooped the Ruts and entourage. They introduced themselves, and as Dave says, they were indeed 'diamond geezers.' They immediately took over the place, of course, but they were friendly enough and I had a bit of a chat with Malcolm Owen and Paul Fox before heading out front to check that my family had got in okay.

When I finally tracked them down, they'd found a table on the balcony and were quite happy, though, as predicted, the turn-out for the gig had been huge and they'd had a hell of a job getting in. What had happened, they told me, was that so many people had been crammed onto the escalator that led up to the Locarno from Frogmore Street that part of the thing had actually caved in, leaving a gaping hole. It was a miracle that no-one had been killed. This left them with two choices: be sensible and turn back, or be foolhardy and leap the abyss. We Baldwins are made of the right stuff, so Mum and my sister Trayci gathered up their skirts, Dad and various Railway Society types transferred their ciggies to safe pockets, and they jumped. Silly sods. I wouldn't risk life and limb to see me.

Family responsibilities fulfilled, I headed for the bar to see who had turned up and apply some alcohol to my badly frazzled nerves. My stomach was churning so much that when a Good Samaritan offered me a drink, I thought I'd just start with a half. I took a sip and was suddenly overcome with a desire to throw up. I didn't, but every time I took another sip, the same thing happened. This was extremely frustrating, as I'd decided from the start that the only way I was going get through this thing was with a few beers inside me. Not legless, of course, just nicely numbed, but it appeared that this was no longer an option. I would have to face the ordeal stone cold sober. Isn't life a bitch?

In the days before the gig, we'd tried to console ourselves with the thought that as we were only third on the bill (a strange character called Auntie Pus was also featured somewhere, but I think he mainly acted as compere), surely not that many people would be in when we went took to the stage. I walked around repeating this to myself as a kind of mantra, and it helped a little, but in the back of my mind I knew very well that I was fooling no-one but myself. This gig was such a sure-fire sell-out that even the most jaded punter would get there early to secure a decent place.

This proved to be the case. We stumbled nervously onto the hallowed Locarno stage at around 8.00, greeted with laughs and cat-calls from a crowd already several hundred strong and growing all the time. To make matters worse, the Damned and Ruts had taken up 90% of the stage with their gear, so all ours, including the drums, was jammed into a small space at the front. Nowhere to hide.

We prevaricated for some time, plugging in guitars, adjusting cymbals, positioning drinks, re-positioning drinks, re-adjusting cymbals, all the while listening to the laughs and cat-calls, unable to decide if they were friendly or hostile. It was difficult to tell with a punk audience. Finally, we could put the moment off no longer. We launched into our set with gusto, which was really the only thing we had to offer, and ploughed through it with all the ferocity we could muster. We kept pauses between songs to a minimum, all of us realising, without actually saying so, that to stop too long and think about what we were doing would be fatal. As the gig progressed and the crowd swelled to even greater proportions, two things made me aware that, while not exactly holding them in the palms of our hands, the audience did seem to appreciate our efforts. The first was the smattering of polite applause that greeted the end of each song, and the second was the gobbing. It was unusual for a band third on the bill to be awarded the ultimate punk accolade, but as the history books have it that the Damned initiated the ritual, we should have realised that your average Damned fan would spit at anyone with a pulse. Or without, given the chance. By the time we were half-way through our set, Dave and Mark were looking more than a little soggy and Beki was absolutely dripping in the stuff. (Later, in the bar, my mother shrieked 'Oh, Beki, what have they done to you? You look like a Christmas Tree!') I hid under my cymbals.

One moment, a few songs in, that did lighten the mood a little, was when H turned up. H, for reasons already outlined, didn't go to that many punk gigs, but felt honour-bound to give us his moral support for this one. It was most welcome, but H, being of a practical, if eccentric nature, had considered the gobbing possibilities more thoroughly than we and taken precautions. Though concentrating intently on trying not to make utter fools of ourselves, we couldn't help but become aware of a bright yellow object making its way patiently, yet determinedly, through the crowd, with the front of the stage its apparent destination. When he finally arrived, we saw that it was indeed H, clad in a huge yellow sou'wester and oilskin, obviously intent on keeping the phlegm from his flowing locks of hair. We pissed ourselves laughing, especially when someone in the crowd shouted 'Fuck me, it's Captain Birdseye!'

We were mightily relieved when it was finally all over, and gratified at the applause we received, then legged it. Now we could enjoy the rest of the evening. Or so we thought. The Ruts were absolutely brilliant in every department, of course, and we looked on green with envy. Great songs, a real 'Fuck you' attitude, and fine musicians to a man. Truly awesome.

The Damned, though, were a totally different proposition. They were completely shite. I was staggered. We'd had some evidence of their arrogance with Vanian banishing us from the backstage dressing room, and, as Mark remembers, an earlier conversation with Rat: 'Scabies came up to us in the bar, and told us what-was-what. He was very pompous.' How they played, or for that matter were received in other cities, I don't know, but in Bristol they hardly even bothered to play the songs. They seemed to believe that their mere presence was something of a gift, and that the punters should be grateful. They weren't, and as the Damned stumbled pitifully from one desecration of a great song to another, the mood of the audience turned gradually from disbelief to open hostility. A chant of 'We want the Ruts!, We want the Ruts!' went up, which seemed to shake them a little. Then, unbelievably, a chant of 'We want Vice Squad! We want Vice Squad!' Obviously we knew that this was intended as irony, and that this was, for the audience, the best way they could think of to piss off the Damned, but we enjoyed it all the same. My mother, having little or no sense of irony, took it at face value and went home more than happy.

When this debacle was finally over, we had to wait for the crowd to leave before we could start getting our gear out, so we went back to the dressing room to wait. The Ruts were still there, and it's possible that they'd sensed our earlier disappointment at not getting to witness all those wild backstage antics that we'd heard so much about. Eager to please, they went through the card.

We hadn't been back long when a very attractive blonde punkette, who's name escapes me (honestly, it does!) came into the room. I'd long admired this girl from afar, but had never worked up the nerve to speak to her. She came in with one of the road-crew, and obviously had the hots for the Ruts. As she flirted with them I wondered, jealously, which one she'd choose. After a while, the guy she'd come in with, a particularly loud-mouthed

Cockney, said 'Why don't you let us all fuck you?' I was outraged. As I'd confidently expected, she of course said 'Fuck off!' What did he expect, the cheeky Cockney git. He then said 'Oh, go on, I'll give you me jacket.' It was a nice jacket, I must admit, really nice leather and tastefully adorned with studs, but fancy insulting one of our girls like that, the bastard. Only cowardice prevented me from hitting him. She paused for a few seconds, shrugged, said 'Okay then,' and led him into the toilet. You could have knocked me down with the proverbial feather.

As they queued up outside the toilet, my relatively innocent 16-year-old mind reeled. I tried to block it out and pretend it wasn't happening, but of course it also held a strange fascination. Once when I looked over, the door was open and I could see her, led on the floor with her head against the toilet, with some bloke banging away at her. Her eyes were closed and she seemed to be in a kind of trance, just letting out the odd murmur.

When they were all finished someone, I think it was Paul Fox, asked me if I wanted a go. This was probably deliberate, as I was obviously the most horrified of all of us. Mark, for one, took it in his stride much better than I did: 'I was a fairly liberal-minded sort of chap, but I was a little surprised.' I blushed to my roots and muttered something pathetic like 'Eh, what? Um, no thanks. It's my time of the month.'

When she came out, she asked the Cockney for his jacket. He laughed in her face, nastily, and said 'Nah, you were a shit-hole fuck anyway.' She ran out of the room.
To complete our education in rock 'n' roll etiquette, they then systematically smashed every fixture and fitting in the room to smithereens. This apparently necessary chore completed, they then took their leave, wishing us all the best and hoping to work with us again in the future. Nice boys.

After we'd sat, shell-shocked, in the debris for a few minutes, it began to dawn on us that, much as we'd liked the Ruts, they'd left us in a potentially dangerous situation. Mark explains: 'We took the door handle off the dressing room, 'cos the Ruts smashed the dressing room to bits, then disappeared. And of course we were still packing up, and knowing what the bouncers were like there, we didn't want to take the blame for something we didn't actually do. So we unscrewed the door handle and took it off so they couldn't get in, a good move I think. I remember waiting outside for whoever was supposed to be picking us up, and wishing they'd hurry up before the bouncers found the dressing room and came out and killed us.'

When we next visited the Locarno, a few weeks later, we were a little apprehensive to say the least. I forget who we went to see, but we were mightily relieved when rather than being torn limb from limb, we just got a few arched looks from the bouncers. They obviously had us down as the big-girls-blouses we so patently were and blamed the Ruts. If I hadn't felt so relieved I'd have felt, on reflection, insulted.

As we'd hoped, the Damned gig brought us to the attention of a wider local audience, and on that same night I encountered a guy who was to become one of our staunchest allies. He frightened the shit out of me at first. I was walking along the Locarno balcony minding my own business, when I noticed this big skinhead bearing down on me, with mad, staring eyes, and a crazed smile playing around his thin lips (take no notice, I've been reading a lot of Raymond Chandler recently). When he stopped in front of me I involuntarily took a step back and assumed I was in for a kicking, but he just laughed maniacally and said something like 'You're in Vice Squad ain't you? I saw you with the Damned, you're alright.' It was the start of a long and beautiful friendship (God, it's *Casablanca* now), and Brian Badman, for it was he, introduced us to his equally mental brothers, Phil and Tim. They were a curious trio. All staunch Bristol City supporters, and all dedicated hooligans, yet with starkly differing personalities. Brian was, as I've said, mental and looked it. Phil was rather reserved, and I never got to know him that well, though he tended to make his presence felt in other ways, but the most curious of all was Tim. He had a perpetual butter-wouldn't-melt-in-the-mouth grin on his face, which almost always kept him out of trouble with the law, but if the truth be told, he was the maddest of the three. He habitually carried a lump hammer at football matches, but looked so angelic that he never seemed to get searched.

As most of the Fishponds Mental Mob and the X-Certs crew were Rovers fans, Dave and I were pleased to have some City fans among our following, and we saw the brothers often at matches. They were so close that they came to be referred to as a single entity, the Brianphilandtim brothers. If you turned up at a gig and asked someone who was in, the reply would usually be something like 'Rudge, Riddle, Neil, Dean Fry, Andy Whittle and Brianphilandtim.'

Apart from Da Brudders, quite a few other people started to come to our gigs after seeing us with the Damned, and it was good to have at least a section of our audiences that we could call our own, i.e. not on loan from the X-Certs.

Another result of the show was a that we acquired a degree of notoriety that was completely out of proportion to our status.

I first became aware of this when, on 24 June, we went to see a band called the Under Fives at Trinity Church in Kingswood (not the much larger venue of the same name in town). The Under Fives were school-mates of Dave and Mark from Kingsfield, and had been the only other fledgling Hanham punk band in the Spam/TV Brakes days. There had been some rivalry, but nothing serious, and we sometimes went to gigs with Tim, Paul, Sadge and Graham.

We just turned up to see how they were faring these days (and I suppose we were probably feeling a little smug at recent events, to be honest). A few people in the audience suggested that we played a short set as we were all there anyway, and what surprised me was the promoter's reaction. We'd tried crashing other people's gigs in the past with no success whatever, and this time we weren't even trying, but the bloke buckled immediately. He got really nervous and said we had to play or our fans would tear the place apart, which was utter nonsense, and just begged me to be careful not to trash the drum-kit. Suddenly we were a mixture of the Pistols and the Who, and this poor deluded guy was frightened to death of us.

We played a short set, as requested, and, of course, nothing untoward occurred, but it turned out to be the shape of things to come.

Our next gig, on 11 July, was also in Kingswood, at the Summit Youth Club. Kingswood isn't so far from Hanham, and it was a pleasant summer's evening, so ever the healthy outdoor type, I decided to walk to the gig. Also, we didn't own a bloody car, so I didn't have much choice. As I reached the top of Hanham Road, just around the corner from the Summit, I noticed a line of police vans parked up on the corner, filled to bursting point with agitated looking coppers. I assumed they were on a drug bust or something, and wondered, vaguely, who the potential target might be. As I passed they looked me up and down with more interest than I seemed to warrant, and did the same with other people in punk garb making their way to the club. It dawned on me that this police presence was all for our benefit, and I wondered what the hell they'd heard about us. It was ludicrous really, as apart from anything else, Kingswood Police Station was only about 30 second's drive from the Summit. They were obviously just making their presence felt. The Summit had a reputation as a pretty rough club, it's true, but the gig would probably have passed without incident, had it not been for the police. Most people, no doubt, just turned up out of curiosity, to see this local band who'd played a couple of fairly big gigs and had got in the local press (we'd had a small piece, our first, in a local free paper, the Bristol Journal). The fact that the police were there, and in such force, was like a red rag to a bull as far as the local nutters were concerned, and fights broke out sporadically, in and around the club, for the whole evening. As usual, the gig itself was nothing much to write home about, as far as I remember. The snare stand broke, so I had to play the last song with the thing gripped between my knees, and my idea of wiping the sweat from my body afterwards with some blue crepe paper that was hanging from the walls proved a bad idea as the colour came out and dyed my torso a vivid turquoise. Took me days to get that off.

Little...well, nothing in fact, is remembered about our next gig on 3 September at Flannagans in Weston-Super-Mare. I expect there were some fights, and we drank too much, and didn't play very well. It's a fair assumption.

The next two Vice Squad gigs were on consecutive nights, and outside Bristol (just) and to us, this constituted a tour. The first took place on 14 September at Trowbridge Town Hall, supporting the Angelic Upstarts. This was another big gig for us, and we later found out that, like the Damned slot, we got it through Mark Byrne, though this time he'd passed it on to us as he'd been offered it for his band but reckoned it sounded like trouble. Wise man.

We'd secured a van for the weekend, and packed ourselves, our gear, and as many of the usual crowd as we could cram in, while the rest of the nutters made their own way to Trowbridge.

On arrival, we were told, in no uncertain terms, that the Upstarts had brought their own support band with them, the Wall, but if some yokel promoter had seen fit to book us then we were welcome to open the show. We were disappointed, of course, as that meant going on even earlier, but if we had any thoughts of claiming our right to the main support slot, these were quelled when we watched the Wall's soundcheck. They were shit-hot, and we had no desire to follow that, thanks very much. Our only worry was that some of our crew, not knowing the change in circumstances, might not arrive in time to see us. Oh, the heartbreak!

We hung out in the car-park, checking in late arrivals like worried parents. Then I noticed a large red van, bouncing up and down rhythmically, and from the grunts and groans that it emitted, it was obvious what was going on within. After a while the grunts and groans subsided, and the bouncing up and down ceased. Eventually, the doors opened (by now a little crowd had gathered) and Upstarts singer Mensi got out with an extremely attractive brunette to much jeering and piss-taking. Personally, I was highly impressed. How did an ugly git like him get a girl like that? What a naive boy I was.

When we went on, the place was still fairly empty, but we went down quite well, and at least with the Wall taking the main support slot the pressure was off of us, so we just enjoyed it. We watched the other bands and had a few drinks, and though things were getting a little boisterous when we left, I assumed the evening would pass without anything in the way of serious incident. I later learned, though, that after our departure a lot of fights broke out, and some of our crowd not travelling with us caused a lot of trouble. Big Karen and Little Karen, who you may remember from an earlier chapter, apparently trashed our dressing room after we left and got themselves arrested.

We were oblivious to all this as we made our way to the next gig, our only concern being Al Rees, who had unwisely entered into a Pernod drinking contest with Brianphilandtim, and looked in danger of throwing up. We didn't care about him; some of us had to sleep in that van.

The next gig, on the 15 September, was at Cricket St Thomas Wildlife Park. It was a biker's festival, and whoever had been in charge of the bookings must have either been very stupid or very lazy. I'm inclined towards the latter, as the bands heading the bill were metal bands, and therefore perfectly acceptable to the assembled throng. After that he or she must have lost interest, and just booked any local-ish bands that appeared in the local press. In 1979 that meant mostly punk or post-punk arty types (round our way, anyway) and we had an idea how that was likely to go down. The fact that we did it anyway just goes to show how desperate we all were for gigs.

We drove straight to the festival site from Trowbridge, the idea being that some of us would sleep in a tent that, in a rare moment of foresight, we had chucked in the van with the rest of the gear, and the others would kip in the van. Al Rees, as I've said, was out of his face, but the rest of us weren't in much better shape. After me and Mark had spent what seemed like hours trying to erect the tent, we finally gave up and emerged from the tangled mess of rope and canvas, covered in mud, with our hands bruised and bloodied from our drunken attempts to hammer in the pegs. There wasn't really room for everyone to sleep in the van, so Mark pointed out a large camp fire in the distance and suggested we kipped down there to keep warm. I said it was too far, I was shagged out, but he went and I barged my way into the van and spent an extremely uncomfortable night.

The next morning, it turned out that what had, to our alcohol-blurred eyes, seemed a large fire in the distance had actually been a small fire in the immediate vicinity, and Mark had spent a pleasantly warm night under the stars, while I suffered the farts and belches of a van full of pissed punk rockers. The bastard.

With the resilience of youth, slight hangovers didn't impair our appetites in the least, and we set off in search of food. When we got to the restaurant it was closed, so ever thirsty for knowledge and experience, we went for a look at the animals. It was very interesting, for a while, but we were fucking hungry, and when we saw the seals getting fed we were quite indignant. As someone pointed out: 'They'll feed those fishy bastards, but what about us starving artistes?' Eventually, the restaurant opened (reluctantly, with us lot stood outside) and we managed to stuff ourselves full of artery-clogging foodstuffs before getting down to the business of the day.

There were some other bands booked that we knew, to a greater or lesser degree, so we looked for the promoter to find out where everyone had been placed on the bill. Among those bands were: the Review, a mod band who now had our old friend Taff, late of the X-Certs on bass (who of course later joined Disorder); Joe Public, some of whom went on to back Vic Goddard as a later line-up of the Subway Sect before forming Joboxers, and at one point working as Sandie Shaw's backing band (I kid you not), then later still forming Earl Brutus; Double Vision, who were decidedly Clifton types, but all good eggs, so we got on well with them; and most importantly, from my point of view, the Groove.

The Groove were H's new band, and comprised of H (bass, obviously) Keith Dunne (vocals/harmonica), Tim Galley (guitar) and Tim Burgess (drums). They were a frankly weird outfit, musically, with influences so diverse that I can't begin to describe them. But Keith was a real character, a northern Jack The Lad, and what he lacked in musical proficiency he more than made up for with energy and mouth. He was a perfect partner for H, who had plenty of ideas but no front, and the Tims Burgess and Galley ably filled their roles. I really hoped something would come of it, but as Keith was only in Bristol doing the sandwich year of a degree course and had to return to his native Manchester to complete it, the band eventually came to nothing, though they played many great local gigs.

Back in Cricket St Thomas, we were not happy chappies. When we found the promoter, we were informed that we were allocated the opening slot at 1pm. Of course, we were as sick as pigs after all the trouble we'd been to, knowing that we'd end up playing to virtually nobody, but this turned out to be a blessing. As I've said, we'd had a feeling that the opening acts at this accident-waiting-to-happen might not go down too well, and this proved to be the case. It worked in our favour because, though the bikers couldn't stand what any of the non-metal bands were playing, they had a certain tolerance level, and treated the first few bands as a joke. After a while though, the joke wore thin. It was a nightmare anyway, for purely practical reasons, as the ground was very boggy and as the day progressed, the stage gradually sank. We noticed it and we were first on, and in fact the stage was already tilting so much during our set that Tim B from the Groove had to hold my floor-tom steady towards the end.

We were just glad to get it over with, collect our £25 fee, and head for home. The unfortunate bands that were left, weren't so lucky, and the situation got a little hairy, as it were, as H explains: 'We played at about half three or four o'clock, and didn't go down that badly. We went down better than I expected, except when one of the leaders of the bike club came up to the front of the stage and pointed a gun at Keith. Being dead cool we finished the song anyway. Then he wandered up to the stage and gave Keith this piece of paper, and it was all about 'The cops are after people with guns, so watch it bro's,' or something like that. The police were trying to bust people with shotguns; it was all a bit stupid really, there was a lot of attitude involved, but they let us finish, which was more than they did for the bands that were on later. The band after us, who I think were Double Vision, got bricked off after about three numbers.'

As we left the site, our impression that we'd really be better off elsewhere intensified, as Mark remembers: 'As we were driving out, there was this big guy coming in on a chopped Harley, and obviously his favourite accessory was the shotgun holder down the forks, with the shotgun still in it.'

The ironic footnote to this episode is that though we left Cricket St Thomas several hours before the other bands, we broke down on the motorway, and as it was a Bank Holiday weekend, spent hours on the hard-shoulder waiting for the AA. We were the last ones home. Ho hum.

By late September, it was time for Clive from The X-Certs' famous youth club tour. He'd worked really hard on this, and initially we were to have played most of the youth clubs in the South West, but in the end all but three got cold feet and dropped out. Actually, the ones that dropped out were probably wise, as those that went ahead experienced a lot of trouble. No change there then.

The 'Tour' went to Clevedon Youth Club on 27 September, Portishead Youth Club on 5 October, and Sea Mills Youth Club somewhere in between (the date has been lost in the mists of time, etc), and the whole the thing was a bloody debacle. Strangely, the level of violence in these quiet seaside towns was much higher than we'd experienced in more urban areas, and it was surprising that we even managed to finish three shows.

At this point, dear reader, (around early October) the Avon Calling compilation that I made such a fuss about at the end of the last chapter finally hit the shops. Before I go into the details of Vice Squad's involvement in this project, however, I thought it might prove mildly diverting to devote a little space to the story of Heartbeat Records, the label on which said album appeared. With the first and, hopefully, last sub-heading of this book, Simon Edwards tells us how he got into all this music-biz malarkey.

The Story Of Heartbeat Records

'It goes back to the Pub Rock days I suppose, when I started buying all these singles by bands like Ducks Deluxe and Dr Feelgood. I remember I used to buy their records not from record shops, but there were all these little ad's in the back of NME from Rock On in Camden. I bought all these singles and they were great, and it made me think.

Around that time I was managing bands and recording bands and stuff like that, local bands. As this went on and more and more of these records came out I thought, well, this is really exciting, and obviously punk started at the later end of it, and over that period I started to wonder how they did it, how they made records.

I'd been recording bands, mostly live, and it all escalated from there. I was inevitably going to make a record from one of them.

I was doing folk clubs at the time as well, doing solo spots with a guitar, clearing everyone out at the end of the evening, and there was a bloke there called Stan Arnold who had his own label that did folk stuff. So I asked him, 'How do you do it? How do you go about making records?' He gave me some addresses of people that did the cut and the pressings and the sleeves and labels and stuff, so I just followed that up. I think it came to the grand total of about £380 to press a thousand records, so I decided to do it. There was a band currently doing the rounds in the punk clubs called Social Security. The bass player, Simon Cartledge, had a lovely cellar under the house where he lived, and they used to practice down there. I took me gear down there, my reel-to-reel tape recorder and my desk, and I just recorded a practice. Obviously they did a few songs three or four times and we just chose the best ones, and we cut it from that.

The only thing I recall about the end result was that John Peel played it and he called it 'Charmingly rustic,' which indeed it was.

The Europeans was the second single, and that did about 4,000 copies, which blew me away, because I'm pretty sure Social Security only did 1,000. The Europeans was more of a studio effort. I knew a guy called Steve Street who was a studio engineer and ran a little studio called SAM Studios where bands like the Pop Group used to practice and even bands like the Slits used to come down now and again... and the Cortinas used to go there, obviously. It was all that scene. Steve was the bass player [with the Europeans], and Johnny Kline was the guitarist, who went on to play with Specimen and Siouxsie and the Banshees.

It got really good reviews in NME, Melody Maker and Sounds, which was nice, but we only did one single with them. They went on to sign with Rialto Records which was a subsidiary of a major label.

For that record we used proper studios, we used a bloke called David Lord who had Crescent Studios, but in those days Crescent Studios was in his flat.

After the Europeans he bought a bigger studio in Bath, in Walcott Street, and about that time I got mixed up with a band called the Glaxo Babies, which was the third record that I released, a 12" called *This Is Your Life*. But before the Glaxos actually came on to record, a bloke in London called Iain McNay, from Cherry Red Records, got in touch with me and basically offered me a production deal whereby Cherry Red paid all the production costs of manufacturing and promotion and I would go out and find the bands, record them, get it produced and basically present him with the master tape.

The Glaxos were the next thing, and that was a great success because it got a lot of critical acclaim and a John Peel session as well. Peelie really liked it and played it a lot. Then things started going a bit odd. The session was broadcast for the first time quite without incident, but when they broadcast it again, before the show started, there was a very straight-faced BBC announcer saying 'The following programme contains music by the group known as the Glaxo Babies. The BBC would like it to be known that the Glaxo Babies are in no way connected to the Glaxo Corporation.' It was obviously a disclaimer that the BBC had to announce. We received a letter from the legal department of the Glaxo Corporation saying that if we used the name any more, we would be cut up into small pieces and put into medicine bottles. So we obviously thought we'd better change the name. All we did was put an asterisk where the 'a' was in Glaxo, and they became the Gl*xo Babies. And no more was said.

Then I did the *4 Alternatives* EP, which included the X-Certs, Joe Public, the Numbers and 48 Hours. At the time, the Brighton compilation *Vaultage 78* had come out, and I had mentioned to Iain McNay that there were a lot of bands around Bristol and wouldn't it be a nice idea to do something similar to that. He was a bit reticent, and said maybe you ought to do an EP first and see if that sells.

The *4 Alternatives* EP was like a prelude to the *Avon Calling* compilation album that I did a few months later, and which turned out to be one of my most successful things, actually. It was a good showcase for various stuff, and oddly enough it brings this story to its proper start really for what I'm doing here, because it was the first time I'd worked with a bunch of hoodlums called Vice Squad.

Since I'd done *4 Alternatives* and the other stuff which was quite garagey, I wanted to use Crescent Studios more, because they had a good studio and I just wanted to make the recording better, which is what we did.

The task was to get all these bands that I'd decided I'd like to use for Avon Calling, which I might add wasn't an easy decision. The punks and the trendies didn't get on. Some bands that maybe should have been on the album... they all refused when they discovered that Vice Squad were going to go on there. Gardez Darkx, the Colourtapes and the Spics were the three that were not going to go on, they were of the opinion that they didn't want their music to be on an album that was gonna portray stuff like Vice Squad were playing, which they thought was pretty awful. And maybe it was! So I said, in my wisdom, 'Well, fuck off then, 'cos I want Vice Squad to be on there. I think they've as much right to be on there as you have, and I think you should all be on there together, personally.' And that's how it ended up. But it was a lot of fun and the end result was great, I thought, a really good package with a great big fold-out poster.'

Riveting stuff, I'm sure you'll agree, but if I am to keep this humble tome in something approaching chronological order we'd best return to the Heartbeat saga later and concentrate on *Avon Calling.*

For the recordings, Simon booked every weekend from May through to July at Crescent Studios in Walcott Street, Bath, which was a very plush establishment boasting state-of-the-art equipment and ideally suited to scaring the shit out of novices like us.

The place obviously didn't come cheap, and the system Simon adopted was to place two bands per day in there, one to record in the morning and the other in the afternoon, sharing gear wherever possible. Given the animosity from some quarters (even some of those that still appeared on the album were far from happy), it came as no surprise to learn that Simon had wisely teamed us up with the X-Certs.

Strangely, the X-Certs, though undoubtedly coming under the 'Yob' heading, didn't come in for the same flack as us from the trendies, perhaps because they were more competent than us, but more likely because they came from Barton Hill. The Clifton types tended to make an exception in such cases as Mark explains: 'There was a lot of Barton Hill kids that were accepted into the Clifton 'scene' when the punk thing first happened because of Barton Hill Youth Club, where a lot of the more credible gigs happened. Clifton kids had to go to Barton Hill Youth Club to be cool. So therefore a lot of the Barton Hillbillies, as they were known, used to go up into Clifton drinking at the Dugout or wherever. So that crossover was always there.'

The session took place on June 19, a gloriously sunny Sunday, and we finally arrived with our motley selection of equipment, having bribed various friends and relations to forgo their Sunday lie-in to drive us and our equipment to the studio (Beki's dad cost £7 I seem to remember) having no idea at all what to expect.

Though we didn't know it at the time, Crescent gave us a very misleading idea of what your average recording studio is all about. Later we got used to studios that were based above panel-beaters shops or in glorified dungeons, but this was a sprawling ranch-style building with a garden and silver discs on the walls (okay, they were for the likes of the Korgis, but I was still impressed).

The X-Certs were already underway when we arrived, and though it was nice to be amongst friends, the fact that their track already sounded shit-hot at this early stage just deepened our gloom. We had to follow this.

I sat out in the garden with their singer Clive as the engineers Glenn Tommey and David Lord mixed the X-Certs' track. As it was such a nice day all the doors and windows were open and most of Bath must have heard it. What worried me was that most of Bath would soon be listening to us.

After lunch we set our gear up, and to their credit, if Glenn and David realised that we had no idea what we were doing, they never let on. The only sign of exasperation that I noticed was when, after spending a very long time tuning the tom-toms on my kit, we ran through our song Nothing and they realised that I only actually used them for one drum-roll in the whole song.

The backing track went down relatively quickly, as it should have because there's bugger all to it, and then it was Beki's turn.

Listening from the control room we were highly impressed when she delivered the whole lead vocal in one take, note perfect. Even Glenn and David seemed impressed. When one of them suggested that she go for a 'Double-track' and she said 'Yeah, okay' we were mightily impressed. This girl was remarkable. Not only could she turn out a vocal track in one take, but she even seemed to know what these boffins were talking about. It was all gibberish to us.

They explained to us, in words of no more than three syllables, that this meant Beki was to sing the song again and the two takes would be mixed together to give a more robust vocal track. Fair enough, we thought. They started the tape off again, and we waited with anticipation, but nothing happened. Eventually, Beki coughed nervously, and asked 'Erm, what does double-track actually mean?' Ah, she was one of us after all.

When the record was actually released, I had very conflicting feelings. Of course it was fantastic to have something on vinyl, and as Simon has said (no, I'm refraining from the Simple Simon Says gags, in case you were wondering) it was a rather good package and we were proud to be included. On the other hand, our track sounded rather weedy compared to most of the others. If you held the record up to the light and inspected the grooves, the fact that we occupied so few seemed to me ample evidence of our song's lack of substance.

The album was well received by the music press, and our track, on the whole, got the reception we were expecting. *Record Mirror* declared us 'Forgettable,' *BACUS*, the Bristol University paper, 'The worst track... definite barrel-scraping here,' and *Sounds*, in their 20 October issue, 'Vice Squad are derivative of Penetration or X-Ray Spex, especially the vocals. It says nothing and goes nowhere.' Earlier in the *Sounds* review Nothing was described as 'Rabid minimalism,' and I couldn't decide if that was a compliment or an insult. I still can't. We took some consolation from the fact that, even though reviewer RAB was obviously not exactly bowled over by our contribution, *Sounds* printed a photograph of Beki and Mark taken at the Summit Youth Club.

It wasn't all bad though. *NME* reckoned that 'Vice Squad make archetypal buzzsaw music at twice the speed of gun-powder, while their voluptuous chanteuse Becky Bondage bewails the fate of her generation from the uppermost parapet of the Clifton Suspension Bridge.' Must have been on drugs, you know what these journalists are like. The only other voice in the wilderness, from our point of view, was the late and greatly missed Radio 1 DJ John Peel. He liked the album and played all of the tracks on his show. What is more surprising is that he played the Vice Squad track several times.

John kindly agreed to be interviewed for this book when I first started it in the late '90s, and I asked him what he liked about *Avon Calling*. 'In those days if you got a compilation of local bands, as with demo tapes, really, the expectation was that three out of ten tracks would be pretty good, whereas now it's very rare if there's a good track on it. You know, they're all kind of okay, because technology has improved so everybody sounds okay. But with *Avon Calling* more than half the tracks were well worth playing on the radio.'

But why, I wondered, did he seem to favour our track so much when the kindest thing I could say about it was that it was, erm, basic? 'Well, that's what I like. I've never been a fan of that studio sound where engineers spend a great deal of time and a great deal of money on getting the top 10%, or top 3 or 4% of the sound absolutely spot on. Basic is what I'm after. Teenage Kicks still, after all these years, I maintain that no one's made a better record.'

Given the, ahem, mixed reception to our vinyl debut, we were hardly expecting CBS to come a'clamouring for our signatures, but of course there was always the chance that something might have resulted from the modest media exposure.

As you can see, logic had but a small part to play in this sudden surge of optimism, but with hindsight I reckon we needed it, because on the gig front things weren't getting any easier.

The next item on our fun-packed itinerary was a gig on 11 November at St Matthias College, Fishponds, home of the afore-mentioned Mental Mob, whose habitual drinking-hole, the Full Moon, was a mere stone's throw away. That we were playing on the Mental Mob's home turf was cause enough for concern, but there was also the fact that one of their main hobbies was beating up the students attending the college. But what the hell, we did it anyway.

We got to the venue mid-afternoon, suffering more than a little from a party that Bruce had held on the previous night, but it was only twenty minutes or so before our razor-sharp minds perceived what was lacking in the way of facilities. There was no bloody stage.

So, we hurriedly built one, and for a make-shift job it proved quite durable and was used for some time afterwards. The fact was, the thing managed the seemingly impossible combination of being both dangerously rickety and yet so sturdy that the students couldn't dismantle it afterwards, so they just left it, as Dave explains: 'It was desks with chipboard on the top and we just nailed through them using double 6-inch nails. John Cooper Clarke, Wilko Johnson, they all 'Trod the desks.' With the total disrespect and disdain that we gave to St Matthias College, coming from the Full Moon, we just thought, well, we can't play without a stage. It was really well made, considering, but there were gaps.'

There were indeed, and how we chuckled, later, watching John and Wilko risking life and limb trying to avoid serious injury on our assault course of a stage.

The support bands for the gig were the Under Fives and our old friend and colleague Ian Minter's new band, the decidedly weird Pus Trams. Purely by chance, while editing this book, I bumped into the Trams' trumpet player, Rich, in the Trout Tavern in Keynsham, and he supplied me with the information that the Pus Trams' line-up, all comprising of old school friends of ours, was: Jon Holli (vocals), Mike Dykes (bass), Rich Walters (trumpet), Ian Minter (guitar), Phil Baber (drums) and Geordie (home-made organ/synthesiser). He remembers that: 'The crowd just watched us in disbelief. Probably the discordant racket we were making and the fact that Paul Gravell (great bloke) of Under Fives had retuned the guitars just before we went on. The problem was that we hadn't done that before and my trumpet was out of tune for our whole set as a result. Under Fives went down really badly due to Graham Viney's ballet shoes and demeanour. I escaped through a window with my trumpet because the atmosphere was getting a bit tasty! Dad picked me up a hundred yards up the road.'

He also remembers, strangely, that 'We used to practice over a cess pit in an outside room at Geordie's Dad's house!' Just thought you might like to know that.

The rest of the gig was, surprisingly, relatively free of trouble apart from one of the X-Certs' crew, Dean, breaking a local kid's jaw on the way out. For some reason he tended to consider that an appropriate way to round off most evenings, and I for one wasn't prepared to argue with him about it.

The only other notable thing about this gig is that we booked a PA system owned by one Ian Tadd, who later became our manager. Mark explains: 'We used Tadd at St Matthias for the first time. He'd done one of the X-Certs youth club gigs and said 'If you need a PA, I'm your man. You pay for any broken mikes though.' He probably made a few bob out of that over the years.' For the non-muso types among you, Mark means that one of the oldest tricks in the book is to charge a band for replacement of damaged equipment, then take the old one home and repair it. We fell for it though. We fell for a lot of things with Ian, but we'll come back to him shortly.

The final Vice Squad gig of 1979 took place at the Athenaeum Arts Centre in Warminster, on 14 November, supported by Rupert and the Dufflecoats and the Mental. The Mental were fronted by Dick Lucas who later went on to form the Subhumans and Citizen Fish, and they had already released an EP called God For A Day. What they were like on the night, I've no idea, as I missed both support bands' sets and very nearly our own.

It was arranged that the van would pick up me and my girlfriend Mandy outside the bus station on Hanham High Street. After a spot of tea, which we ate while watching an episode of *Laverne and Shirley* (why do I remember that fact with such clarity when I often can't recall something of real importance that happened only yesterday? I don't know. Spooky isn't it) we got to the appointed spot in plenty of time.

We waited, and waited, shivering in the sleet and biting wind, until the truth became obvious. The bastards had forgotten us. Luckily, I had the 'phone number for the Athenaeum on me, so I found a functioning 'phone box and finally got through, to be told that they'd noticed we were missing (I should bloody well think so) and that the promoter was on his way to pick us up in his car. By the time he arrived, we looked like something out of *Scott Of The Antarctic*, and gave him hell all the way to Warminster, the poor sod. It was hardly his fault after all.

When we arrived, I insisted on going into the nearest pub for a life-restoring couple of pints, and the promoter positively quivered with fear at the very idea. He reckoned the squaddies from the nearby army base were out in force, beating up any punks they could lay their hands on, but by this stage I just didn't care. The pub we went to seemed quiet enough to me, and I got enough down me for normal service to resume before he virtually dragged me to the venue.

As it turned out, he was quite right, and I'd just been lucky in choosing, at random, probably the only pub in Warminster that wasn't full of rampaging squaddies gagging for a fight.

The first thing to meet our eyes, on entering the Athenaeum, was Paul Riddell, usually referred to as Riddle, an erstwhile member of the Fishponds Mental Mob, covered in blood and being dragged out by two St John's Ambulance men. When we found the rest of the crew, we learnt that the event had been a blood-bath right from the start. There had been a lot of trouble inside the gig, apparently, but outside the really serious stuff had been going off in a big way between the squaddies and the braver punks and skins.

It goes without saying that Brianphilandtim were in their element here, along with a small crowd of a similarly psychopathic nature, like Riddle and his mate Steve Rudge. It seemed to me that the latter two consistently came off worse during the skirmishes, but, once patched up by the long-suffering St John's Ambulance chaps, they still went back for more. You have to admire perseverance and tenacity, don't you? Beki remembers that: 'That was when Steve Rudge pulled out a cut throat razor; luckily he didn't use it. I think they were somewhat harder than we were.' You can say that again.

The gig itself was a farce, obviously. Everyone inside the venue spent more time listening to the carnage outside and worrying about how they were going to get home in one piece than listening to us, and I can't say that my own mind was fully on the job in hand.

Once the sorry affair was finally over, we waited for things to quieten down a little, then started to load the gear into the van. As we did so, there were still sporadic fights breaking out just around the corner, and at one point Rudge and Riddle came charging up and rifled the tool-box for weapons. Riddle found a hammer, Rudge a knife, and off they went yet again. They arrived back, minutes later, clearly having got the worst of the exchanges, yet again. Just how successful Riddle had been with his hammer, we couldn't be sure, but the knife had been a bad idea for Rudge, as he'd steamed in with it, jabbing and slashing for all he was worth, but had only succeeded, somehow, in cutting his own hand to ribbons. I considered suggesting that he should only eat with plastic cutlery in future, but though no match for a bunch of highly trained squaddies, he'd have beaten the shit out of *me*, so I let it lie.

To round the evening off nicely, once the van was packed, there wasn't room for me and Mandy, and we had to rely on the promoter to drive us home. By the time he'd pacified the local constabulary and taken an inventory of the damage to the hall, it was very late indeed, and I for one had had enough.

It was all a very long way from the fabulous Locarno, only months before.

CHAPTER 4

1980 - A BRAND NEW AGE (apparently).

If you had been wondering, reading the previous chapter, why we were allowed to roam the countryside spreading alarm and despondency wherever we went for so long, I don't know. I suppose the plod were just a little slow on the up-take, but once they'd cottoned-on to the fact that we were bad news, they kicked in with a vengeance.

Suddenly, our engagements diary shrank to nowt as promoters around the region were warned, in simple terms, that if they booked us, they were in big trouble. This isn't paranoia, the promoters told us straight - they had to explain themselves somehow, and this was an argument we couldn't hold against them. You could argue that they just didn't want to book us and that was just an excuse, and that's possible. It's unlikely, though, as we were pulling good crowds by this time and no promoter would willingly turn down a full house.

The methods employed by the police were crude, but effective. I've no record of the gigs that were cancelled, but they were many and we managed just six gigs during the whole of 1980.

At the start of the new year, though, what with none of us being psychic and crystal balls being pretty thin on the ground, we decided to enter the sparkling new decade on an optimistic note.

Here we must, reluctantly, re-introduce Ian Tadd, our future manager. Ian was an unashamed hippy who ran a PA company called Bertie Dugga, a rather lame joke name that amused him greatly for years after he thought of it. How we became so embroiled in Ian's schemes I'm not sure, but he ran a reliable enough PA and we used him regularly.

As the offers had somehow failed to flood in after *Avon Calling* (I expect they all lost our phone number or something) we decided that the next step in our, ahem, career, was to record a demo (Mark had read in a book that real bands did that) and Ian said he could accommodate us.

We booked Trinity Church, in Old Market, on a night that it wasn't in use, and Ian assured us that we could achieve a satisfactory result if we played in one room while he mixed us, through his PA desk, in another. It sounded like a reasonable idea, mainly because we hadn't a clue what he was talking about. We just wanted one of them demo thingies, and as cheap as possible. Looking back on it, the only advantage this plan had over using a straight-from-the-desk live tape was that we could use a second tape deck for some very crude over-dubs, which we did.

It made no difference though; the end result was embarrassingly bad. In our hearts-of-hearts we knew this, but we persevered, partly out of desperation, and partly because we had this romantic vision of some high-flying Record Company Executive muttering reflectively to his sycophantic lackeys 'It's crap, I agree, but it's crap with promise. There is something in this band that I have not heard before. Gentlemen, with the right treatment, I believe we have the next Beatles. Or UK Subs anyway.'

It came as no surprise at all when the tape got zero response from the record companies lucky enough to receive a copy, as Mark remembers: 'We sent out as many as we could afford, which was probably twenty or thirty I suppose. We put in 'Please return this tape if you are not interested' and we got about two back in envelopes without even a compliment slip. It failed dismally.'

By this time, Bruce's dad had succeeded in ousting us from his basement, after many weeks of threats, alternated with heart-felt pleading. We got back from a gig one night to find the locks changed, the doors and windows barricaded, the house swathed in barbed wire and a huge slavering dog chained to the gate-post.

Okay, that's not strictly true. I can't remember how the poor bloke got rid of us, but he did, and our next little home-from-home would have pleased Dave Vanian greatly. I can't remember how we found it, but we managed to hire a church on Coronation Road, in Ashton. The downside was that we had to practice in the crypt, and we could only use it on Saturday nights.

The bit about using the crypt wasn't so bad, though it was a little spooky, but having to rehearse on Saturday night? That was a bit of a blow. It goes without saying that our social diaries were full to bursting point and we were fighting off the girls with sticks, so this presented difficulties. I wish.

After a few rehearsals in the crypt, with gigs being so few and far between, Beki and Igor stopped turning up altogether. They came up with an impressive array of excuses, of the dog-ate-my-homework variety, in an attempt to conceal the fact that they preferred to spend their Saturday nights in the Full Moon rather than a dusty crypt, and I can't say I blame them. I did at the time, of course, but had to concede that we needed the practice more than she did. Igor, it must be said, was always in perfect shape for picking things up and putting them down again. As a roadie, he was at the peak of his powers.

The first Vice Squad gig of the sparkling new decade took place at yet another Trinity Church, this time in Bath, on 16 February.

We were supported, again, by the Mental, and as we drove into Bath we were pleased to see the usual crowd already gathering, drinking cider and intimidating passers-by.

The gig went off, by our standards, with little in the way of serious trouble. Our old friend Dean Fry got a little lairy, as usual, but just as he was pinning some poor innocent to the wall by his neck, a fearsome lady of the Church Committee, all tweeds and moustache, stormed in and bawled him out in no uncertain terms. He sheepishly returned his intended victim to terra firma, and was quiet as a mouse for the rest of the evening. We seriously considered offering her a job.

There were a couple of broken windows that I found the Vicar mournfully sweeping up, but he cheered up considerably when we agreed to pay for the damage. The fact was that we had, for once, actually made a few bob from this gig, and were more than happy. We'd have been even more happy if Dave, in an uncharacteristically altruistic mood, hadn't told the doormen, Al Rees and Nick Quarry, that they could keep the change and just give us the notes. What he'd overlooked was the fact that many punks, even by this time, secured their entrance and beer money by spending the day begging for change. We did very nicely, yes, and were able to pay for our rehearsal space for some time afterwards, but Al and Nick could barely walk for the coins weighing them down. They made a fortune!

Our next outing was not such a happy event. Though we didn't know it when we accepted the gig, the Bournville Estate in Weston-Super-Mare was a very rough place indeed. We'd never heard of it, and just assumed that if it was in sleepy Weston, it couldn't be that bad. It was organised by a band called Red Alert (not the north-east one, obviously, this lot were locals) and took place at the Bournville Community Centre on 24 April.

It got a bit hairy, as Mark remembers: 'We thought Weston was, like, a nice seaside town. I don't think that any of us even knew that the Bournville Estate existed. We drove into it, and it was like, 'Shit! What's going on 'ere?' It was very much of a surprise I think. I got pulled offstage. There was a load of big skinheads down the front and I thought 'I'm not being intimidated by these wankers,' moved down the front of the stage and they just dragged me straight off. Then they didn't know what to do really, 'cos obviously the music just stopped, and everyone looked, and they thought 'Shit, maybe we shouldn't have done that,' and I climbed back onstage. There were fights breaking out the whole time and I was very dubious about getting out of the place alive.' Always a master of the understatement, Marks adds: 'It was not very friendly at all.'

When we'd arrived at the venue and met the promoters, we'd been slightly indignant to learn that we were expected to go on before Red Alert. We were under no illusions that we were major league players, but we certainly had more claim to the headlining spot than this bunch who, as far as we knew, had never played outside the estate. We put this argument forward and it was conceded that, under normal circumstances, we had a point. On the other hand, they argued that this was a close-knit community and that almost all the assembled lunatics were related to each other, not to mention Red Alert. One look at the squinting crossed-eyes and hare-lips of the crowd seemed to bear this out, and we gave in. They'd have torn us limb from limb if we'd tried to usurp their brethren.

This turned out to be a blessing, as Mark had not been the only one with misgivings about our chances of survival. Rather than wait for the end of the gig, we loaded up our gear while Red Alert were still playing and headed for home before anyone noticed we'd left.

As was so often the case, this gig had an unhappy footnote. As we were loading the gear back into the crypt, we realised that although we'd double-checked that our dressing room was empty before hastily leaving Weston, all the cymbals were missing. Just to rub it in, some up-and-coming hardcore band on the Bournville Estate now boasted a new set of cymbals. I had the last laugh though. They were really crap cymbals.

By now we were at our lowest ebb since forming the band. We had no gigs at all in our diary, and no prospects of any; our hopes of securing some kind of record deal on the back of *Avon Calling* had come to nothing; we had nowhere satisfactory to rehearse. And we had no cymbals, of course, crap or otherwise.

What we really needed was an organisation with a greater experience than us of being treated as Public Enemy No.1 (we were new to the game), and consequently knew, and had contacts with, the few venues that couldn't give a toss about the law. Enter the Socialist Workers Party, stage right. Oh sorry, left.

Dave, Mark and I had first come into contact with the SWP through a pair of Scouse brothers who were at Kingsfield sixth form, and we went to a couple of meetings. As we were all staunch socialists, we expected to find ourselves in the company of kindred spirits, but we had our differences, as Mark recalls: 'We were all generally socialists in our beliefs, but the SWP were a bunch of lefty nutters, basically, 'We're gonna break things up with hammers,' rather than a reasonable discussion. I was never an advocate of that sort of thing. I think we sussed fairly early on that they were all completely barking fucking mad.'

Having said that, we quickly found out that the real nutters among them were the most fun, especially a bloke called Alan, who the last time I met him, in the late 80s, was a leading figure in Class War. As seems to be the case in most political groups that I've encountered, it's the well-meaning anoraks that tend to be the drag. Alan, whose chosen weapon on marches was his trusty claw-hammer, began his political career as a legitimate card-carrying member of the Labour Party, but they found him a little too hot to handle, as in turn did the SWP. He told me once that when he joined Class War, one of his former Labour colleagues congratulated him on 'Finding your spiritual home, Alan.'

One of my fondest memories of Alan is visiting his home in one of the more salubrious parts of Hanham (for all his beliefs, Alan had a successful building firm and wasn't short of a few bob) to find his kids eating tea in front of the telly and his very pleasant wife intent on her sewing. After I'd been chatting with Alan for a while, his wife shouted with immense satisfaction 'It's finished!' and proudly held up her work for our approval. Given the surroundings, I'd assumed that the black mass she'd been struggling under must be a set of car-seat covers or something. It turned out to be a massive banner depicting a yuppie with a brick bouncing off his head and the legend Class War - Kill The Rich. Alan loved it, and announced 'We'll stick it in the front garden to piss off those fuckin' dentists an' doctors.'

I didn't blame him. It was a lovely bit of needlework.

Back in 1980, as we were wallowing in our slough of despond, as I believe the gag goes, we were approached by Alan, the Scouse brothers, and a few of their anorak-adorned chums with a proposition. Having given the matter their most serious consideration, they had decided that the most effective way to overthrow the Thatcherite junta that constituted our government was to send Vice Squad on a tour of Britain. We would, they said, play all the venues sympathetic to the cause, and when those four were out of the way we would play the rest of the major cities from the back of a truck.

The idea was preposterous, of course, but we had nothing to lose, so we went for it. Apart from providing us with some much-needed gigs, the deal offered other possibilities, as Dave remembers: 'We had this discussion with them, that went along the lines of 'Yeah, yeah, we're right behind you, right on, right on,' etc. But we needed a new set of cymbals. And the conversation, every time it went away from the cymbals, came right back again. 'Yeah, yeah, but what about these cymbals? 'Oh, that's excellent, you reckon we'll be able to take you up north and then come around and then you'll be able to do some stuff off the back of a wagon...' 'Great, yeah. But we haven't actually covered the cymbals yet.' We got the cymbals, and the tour consisted of about two dates.'

As a prelude to the tour, the SWP, thinly disguised for reasons best known to themselves as Red Rebel, proposed three local gigs to seal our unholy alliance. The first Vice Squad gig under the Rock Against Thatcher banner was at Trinity Church, in Kingswood, on 12 July, supported by the Under Fives. It's a sad reflection on human nature that, because there was no trouble at all, no-one now remembers anything much about it. As with the previous Kingswood gig, there was a heavy police presence, but this time they kept their distance. We were quite surprised that they'd made no attempt to stop it. Perhaps they decided to take a more reasoned approach than other forces in the area, and just make people aware that if they insisted on turning up to listen to these weirdos making their god-awful racket they were welcome. But cause any trouble and you'll regret it, boy. If that was the case, it worked. Doesn't make for much of a story though, does it?

The next, on 16 August, took place at the Crown in Old Market. The Crown was the favoured watering-hole for Bristol punks and skins, being just down the road from Trinity Church and a mere stones-throw from Barton Hill. It was a predominantly Irish pub for most of the week, but the locals were quite happy to squeeze themselves into one of the two bars on Friday and Saturday nights, while the other was packed to the rafters with us lot.

Just how this became the accepted meeting place has been lost in the mists of time, but certainly there was a point when it was virtually impossible for punks to get served in city centre pubs, so the Crown, which was within walking distance of central Bristol (if you had a pair of stout walking shoes, ample provisions and a detailed route map) was probably, for a while, the only option. By the time the Posh Pubs calmed down and relaxed the rules, it was too late. The Crown was the place to be.

It's a little strange, then, that although the Crown had a back room that could be utilised as a gig, it was rarely used. Perhaps it was considered bad taste to mix business with pleasure, I don't know.

Again, I'm ashamed to report that as no-one got killed, no-one remembers a thing about it. Especially Mark, who consumed his own body weight in 6X Bitter and had to be carried off the stage by H, who had fed him the stuff in the first place. The scamps.

The third gig, at Carwardines on Park Street on 30 August was cancelled at the last minute by the management with no explanation, but of course we were used to that. Like either of Bristol's famous football clubs, two results on the trot was something to celebrate, while to expect a third was verging on the ridiculous.

As the plans for the famous tour filtered through from Loony Central Office, complete with what we had to admit was a pretty impressive schedule of dates, we started to get quite excited. If only half what they were proposing came off, this would amount to a major tour.

I proudly told my boss, Mike Williams, that we had a full UK Tour in the offing, and requested unpaid leave for it. Despite all the piss-taking I'd had to endure over the years from the lads at work, they were quite impressed by this turn of events, and Mike kindly agreed. I just had to give him the confirmed dates. This I did, as soon as we got them, and Mike entered them on the firm's calendar, as 'Ben's Gigs' (some spiteful bastard told them that in the Spam days, when it was fashionable to have a stupid name, I called myself Benson Orb. All these years later, I was still Ben at work).

Walking into work on a morning, I got a glow of satisfaction from seeing those words on the calendar, but it didn't last.

As time went on, the SWP informed us of minor changes in the itinerary, which Mike duly recorded on the calendar. These soon became major changes, and the whole tour was moved around, first by weeks and then months. The firm's calendar eventually became a massive illegible scrawl, before Mike gave up and just said 'Fuck it, let me know the day before you go.'

Sadly, that day never came. The tour was supposed to begin with a series of dates in Wales, but in the event we played just one, at Bridgend Sports Centre on 23 September. It was a total disaster. The audience were openly hostile (the relationship between Bristolians and the residents of South Wales has long been fraught, to say the least, especially among the young folk), and after a few numbers we gave up trying to win them over. We treated it as a rehearsal, with Beki, Dave and Mark playing with their backs to the audience (I tried it but nearly gave myself a hernia) and of course that just infuriated them all the more. We left the stage, hurriedly, to screams of abuse and just wanted to get out of the wretched place as soon as possible.

We loaded the van as fast as we could, and headed for home thankful that the other Welsh dates had been cancelled, if this was the reception we could expect.

But the evening, it turned out, was far from over. On the M4, near Cardiff, we were pulled over by the police, who breathalysed our driver, Geoff Gayden. The test proved positive 'He said he'd had two pints, but was somehow over the limit,' says Mark 'but he had three blood tests, all positive, so he was probably lying.'

We were all hauled into Cardiff Central Police Station, where Geoff was banged up in a cell, and the van was impounded. We were told that he could continue driving when the alcohol was out of his system and he tested negative, which was fair enough, if a pain in the arse. Some of us had to be up for work in the morning.

We resigned ourselves to an uncomfortable night bedded down in the police station reception area, and asked if we could get some blankets from the van. At this point, they got nasty, refusing to give us access to the van and, worse still, turfing us out of the Station. It was pissing down with rain, and surprisingly cold for September, so what, we wondered, did they suggest we do for shelter? They pointed us in the direction of the nearest subway.

Apart from our being English *and* punk rockers, some unwise behaviour by some of our party at the time of the arrest probably accounts for Jones The Plod's hostility, as roadie Nick Quarry recalls: 'When we got pulled by the police, Beki and Igor were in the back of the van chanting 'Sheep, sheep, sheep shaggers!' as they were arresting Geoff. They wouldn't let him out until he passed a breathalyser, so we spent all night wandering around Cardiff Central. There was nothing open, and it was, like, a concrete jungle. Actually, it was quite good fun. He never got prosecuted, he was just on the limit, but I don't think they took kindly to the 'Sheep, sheep, sheep shaggers!' bit. Police harassment, ha!' We eventually got home at about 7am, and I got an hour's kip before going to work. Dave and Mark were on flexi-time at Sun Life, so they probably got two hours, the big girl's blouses.

One of the many complications with the supposed tour, was that selected dates were intended to coincide with certain points on a march by the SWP from South Wales to London. Logistically, this would have been a nightmare for any organisation, but for the SWP it was doomed from the start.

For our first proposed link-up with the march, we were to play at a rally in Avonmouth on the morning of 28 September, then meet up with the marchers again for a gig at Trinity Church, Old Market, in the evening.

This seemed reasonable enough. It's not so far from South Wales to Avonmouth, at least for the seasoned marchers that we assumed the SWP faithful to be. Nor, for that matter, is it a great distance from Avonmouth to Old Market. Not if you're barking mad, anyway.

But they weren't as daft as we thought, as Mark recalls: 'The Sunday we were up early, and the lorry came round to get us down to Avonmouth, which is where they [the march] were supposed to be meeting us. The march was late so they [the SWP] gave us twenty quid and sat us in the Royal, which having worked there since, is, like, the second roughest pub in the universe.' If you ever meet Mark, you can ask him which is the first roughest pub in the universe, I can't be bothered. He continues: 'We spent lunchtime in the pub down there, then came back up to Trinity and got all the gear back off the lorry. The march was late and they ended up having to bus them all to Bristol. They just hadn't covered enough ground.'

The gig itself, actually went very well indeed. We were supported by the fine Gloucester band Demob and Zyklon B who'd supported us before at the Crown, and it was a happy event all round. The march had received some media attention, and there was a good turn-out. We went down gratifyingly well, and this led to a rather important turning point for us.

We had been badgering Simon Edwards, ever since the all-but-forgotten *Avon Calling* days, to let us put out a single. He was dubious, and understandably so, but he'd kept in touch, and we'd always harboured a vague hope that he might one day give in.

As we've seen, Vice Squad gigs that went down well and were trouble-free were as rare as hen's teeth during this period, so it was lucky that Simon chose this one to check us out. On the strength of it, he offered us a cautious one-off single deal. What Simon proposed was that we would set up a new label for the single, with us paying for the studio time and him stumping up for the pressings and sleeves.

By this time, Simon had also released fine singles by bands like Private Dicks (She Said Go) and Apartment (The Car/Winter) but circumstances had changed in the Heartbeat camp, and I'll let Simon explain in the second thrilling instalment of...

The Story Of Heartbeat Records

'*Avon Calling* had got good airplay and good press, but there's always that thing, to this day, that people think that anyone who comes from anywhere near Bristol has got straw coming out of their ears and talks through cow-pats and lives off the land. But for all that it got a good reception I thought.

Onwards we went and the Glaxos did a single called Christine Keeler which got a lot of attention, and then we did a couple of Glaxos albums and then an album by the Transmitters. Rob Chapman, the singer, went on to form the Transmitters when he left the Glaxos. We did some stuff with the Art Objects, [who evolved into the Blue Aeroplanes], an album and a single, which were good. The single, Showing Off To Impress The Girls was a great song.

It was about this time when Iain McNay called me to a meeting and actually asked me, you know, 'What's happening, what's the future?' So I went to this meeting and Iain basically said 'What bands have you got coming up, what tapes have you got?', and I had recently had a visitation from Vice Squad who'd brought me a demo tape. I played the tape to Iain McNay and he basically thought it was crap, and he said 'No, we can't do that, I don't think you should be doing that,' and I said, 'Well that's what's happening at the moment.' And he said 'Well, this actually ties in quite well with what I was going to ask you when I called this meeting.'

And then he said that because of the way his business was going that he wanted to stop the production deal that he had with Heartbeat Records. And I thought 'Oh Shit!', 'cos obviously he was paying all my production costs, so I wasn't used to forking out to manufacture records. So when he said that I was basically left up in the air, just holding a Vice Squad tape.'

It was hardly the record deal of our dreams, then, but it was still too good to turn down. The bottom line was that we had to come up with £300, and we simply didn't have it. We assured Simon that something could, no doubt, be arranged, and agreed to a meeting as soon as the SWP debacle was finally over.

From the start, the SWP had been particularly excited about a huge rally that they intended to hold in central London as the crowning glory to both the march and the Vice Squad tour. The tour had of course come to virtually nothing, and the march hadn't fared much better, but they persevered with the rally idea right up to the last minute.

My girlfriend, Mandy, had started a university course in London only a week or so before, so the plan was that we'd meet up at the rally and I'd be able to spend the rest of the weekend with her. Brilliant.

The rally was due to take place on Saturday 4 October, and as the date got closer and closer, the information we got from the SWP became more and more vague. They weren't entirely sure where it would take place, but it definitely would, and we were to enthral the assembled throng with our heady combination of social comment and biting satire from the back of a truck. By now we couldn't give a fuck, we just wanted to get it over with.

Increasingly frantic phone calls from the SWP continued right up until late on the Friday night, when they finally admitted that they would be holding some sort of rally, somewhere, but there was no chance of us playing.

This wasn't a huge surprise, but after giving our eager troops the order to Stand Down, I then had to send Mandy and her mates a telegram (they weren't on the phone, bloody students) to stop them making a fool's errand on our behalf. It cost me a fortune, and I never sent another. I should have billed the SWP for it.

It was a relief to get all that nonsense out of the way, and now the main priority was to meet with Simon. We did, and he still maintained that the offer of a single was open, but we still had to come up with £300, which was far beyond any of our pockets.

For a while the problem seemed insurmountable, which was incredibly frustrating as it seemed the only way ahead. Playing live was all but impossible, so what else was there? If our so-called career tended to be dogged by misfortune, we did, every now and again, balance this with the occasional timely stroke of luck, and at this point probably the most fortuitous so far swung into view in the shape of one Bill White.

Bill was an old friend who drank in the Crown, an outrageously camp gay man who owned a cafe in the St Werburghs area of Bristol and had other business interests that seemed to give him a reasonable income. He was a flamboyant dresser and drove a huge white Jaguar that impressed us peasants greatly.

On hearing of our plight, Bill immediately offered us the cash with no strings attached. We were most grateful of course, but it seemed only fair, with the risk he was taking, to offer him a share in the project as well as a promise to pay him back as soon as we could. He politely refused the offer of a share, his only stipulation being that he would like a mention on all our subsequent record sleeves, which was very generous, not only financially, but also in his apparent belief that this would be the first of many. Though we found it difficult to share his optimistic view of our future, we of course agreed, and if you own any of our records, and have ever wondered who this mysterious character is whose name is always mentioned alongside John Peel, Garry Bushell, our mums and dads and anyone else who knows us, there's your answer.

A suitable studio then had to be found, as Crescent was far beyond our three hundred pounds budget, and Ian Tadd, who by now had become our manager, recommended Cave Studios in Cave Street, not far from his PA lock-up. It was a very wise choice. The studio was run by Bill Ferrier, a very charming man who appeared to be the business brain behind the operation, and Andy Allen, yet another hippy who was the engineer.

We had an initial meeting with Bill in his office, to talk over the project and give him an idea of what sort of sound we were after. I'm ashamed to say that we merely told him how much we had to spend, played him a Sex Pistols record and another by the UK Subs, and said that we wanted to sound like that. If he had an understandable desire to tell us to take our paltry budget and fuck off, he suppressed it admirably and his charm glands went into over-drive. We were duly booked in to record our masterpiece on the weekend of 20/21 November with mixing later in the week.

We'd been avoiding the question of what songs we were actually going to record, as initial discussions had begun as lively debates and quickly deteriorated into stand-up rows. Beki and Dave had recently come up with a new song that they were very excited about called Last Rockers, which we had played a couple of times live and, I had to admit, had gone down well. What troubled me was that, much as I liked the song, it was quite long and had a doomy, almost epic feel which was a radical departure from the style that we were known for, and my main priority was getting Bill's money back. I felt that for our debut we were on safer ground with the older, more established material, and if that had sold okay I'd have been much happier gambling with our own money at a later date.

Mark took little part in these exchanges (he once told me that despite his being established as our bassist for around 18 months by this time, he still felt like the new boy, which is curious as Beki joined after him, but we'll go into Mark's teenage paranoia another time. Or perhaps not) so it was a straight fight between the principal songwriters and me. They won, of course, but I was placated a little by the choice of the B-Sides Living On Dreams and Latex Love. Neither of these is a classic, I'm the first to admit, but I figured that they were familiar enough to our local following to guarantee some sales and hopefully enough to cover the debt.

Despite these bickerings, recording a single was of course a massive landmark for us, and we turned up on the Saturday morning, much to the consternation of Andy and Bill, with an entourage of road-crew, girlfriends, boyfriends and, erm, friends. We also turned up with our ragged assortment of equipment, and our trusty road-crew, Igor and Bambi, were pondering how to transport it down the somewhat rickety iron stairs to the studio below when Andy tactfully suggested we use the in-house equipment. 'It would be more convenient,' he reckoned, meaning 'I'm not working with that pile of crap.'

Our initial interview with Bill had taken place in a bright and airy upstairs room, but the studio itself was of the aforementioned dungeon variety, with the hordes of mostly superfluous friends and hangers-on only making the conditions even more cramped. Andy and Bill had admirable patience, however, and experience had probably taught them that once the novelty value had worn off, most people would eventually bugger off to the pub, which proved to be the case.

Once we were able to get down to business, we ran through the songs a few times before recording the backing tracks. For the non-musos among you this means putting down the basic guitar, bass and drum parts. At this stage only the drums had to be perfect. Everything else could be doctored later, but they had to have the drum track to work from. These days you work to an electronic click-track, and record what you want, when you want, but back in the dark-ages tape recorders were not capable of recording the drum track in sections. Initially then, all the pressure was on the poor drummer. Beki sang a guide vocal which wasn't even recorded, partly to tell us where we were in the song, but mostly as moral support, and by the end of the first day the backing tracks were completed, much to our relief.

During Sunday the guitar over-dubs progressed nicely, and the general consensus was that it was all sounding pretty good. By the time Beki added her vocals we were positively hugging ourselves with glee, and that only left the minor points of the backing vocals on Last Rockers and the mix.

Here it all started to go horribly wrong. When we'd played Last Rockers live, Dave and Mark had provided the 'AAAww, AAww' backing-vocals for the chorus, somewhat self-consciously, it must be said, but it was adequate. In the studio, however, it sounded bloody awful. We tried it again with everyone to hand joining in, and that sounded even worse. Then we tried weeding out the more obviously tone-deaf among us, but that only left Beki and Bill Ferrier. Every conceivable combination and permutation of those present was given a go, but each take seemed inferior to the previous one. Bill and Andy could see that we were beginning to panic, and that nothing was going to be achieved while we were in that frame of mind, so they tactfully suggested that we call it a day and do the backing-vocals later in the week, on the day of the mix.

This made perfect sense, so Mandy and I went home, and everyone else retired to the Full Moon pub around the corner in Stoke's Croft. It later transpired that, with the pressure off and fuelled with alcohol, those that were left standing at the end of the evening returned to the studio and completed the backing-vocals in one take. So there's your scientific proof: Booze-it's good for you.

The mix passed without incident, which was hardly surprising as none of us had any idea of what distinguished a good mix from a bad one. When the record was released Vice Squad were credited as co-producers, which was very unfair on Andy and Bill as our contribution to the production consisted of playing them a UK Subs single and, when it came to the mix, screaming 'I can't hear me!' while they did the real work. Later, when we realised the complexities of the mixing process, we had to acknowledge that they'd been more than kind to us in sharing the credit.

CHAPTER 5

ALTHOUGH IT SAYS 1980 ON THE LABEL, it was actually January 1981 before the Last Rockers EP was finally released, though the reasons for this delay have been lost in the mists...etc.

The deal with Simon was that it would be on a new label, jointly owned by him and us, rather than on Heartbeat for obvious reasons. He'd already lost his deal with Cherry Red and didn't want to lose his other bands as well. After much debate we ended up with the name Riot City, which Dave claims credit for: 'As has been lost in many a record sleeve note that Simon's come up with, it was our name. I would even be so rude as to say it was my name. I'm bloody sure I remember coming up with the thing. Heartbeat didn't exactly tie-in with what we were doing and as we paid for the recording costs of our own bloody single anyway, we came up with the name of the label.'

I've heard worse, and with the riots taking place in many major cities at the time, not least in the St Pauls area of Bristol, it was at least topical.

Considering our limited budget, the final package was quite elaborate. A former school friend of Dave and Mark, Glenn Johnson, drew a suitably apocalyptic design for the sleeve depicting the four of us in the smoking rubble of a nuclear explosion, and Danica Gacesa, a friend of Simon, did a fold-out insert. I designed the 'Shatter' Riot City logo, and we chose a nice gold effect for the label.

For some reason, probably to placate me, although Last Rockers was obviously the main song, the side with Living On Dreams and Latex Love was officially the A-Side with Last Rockers the AA-side. Initially this caused some confusion, with early reviews calling it the Living On Dreams EP, which is ironic as it's easily the weakest track on the record. In fact, if I had attended the cut at Virgin Townhouse in Shepherds Bush, it might not have appeared at all. For the non-musos among you, the cut is the process where, in the production of vinyl records, the sound is transferred onto an acetate disc, and thence to the metal plates used to actually press the records. The important point here is that the cut can drastically change the sound of the finished record, and cramming two songs onto one side reduces the volume level considerably. Mark explains: 'They first cut Last Rockers with just Latex Love as the B-side. They played it [Latex Love] back, and of course they had enormous house-sized speakers there, and it was immense with the big drums and stuff, massive. If you'd been there we'd have dropped Living On Dreams, it was that good. We'd have just put out an A- and a B-side I'm sure, but because only the three of us were there we didn't feel we could.' That's Mark's way of saying that I can bugger things up without even being in the room, and he's right.

Mark also remembers that 'To Cut A Long Story Short, by Spandau Ballet, was on the other side of the Last Rockers acetate and six weeks later they were No.5 in the charts.' We, however, were not, though our ambitions were a little more modest than Spandau Ballet's. Our old friends the X-Certs had undergone a couple of line-up changes, with Taff being replaced on bass by Chris Bostock (who later turned up in JoBoxers and later still as 'Man Leaning On The Queen Vic Bar' in Eastenders and similar roles in things like The Lenny Henry Show) and guitarist Simon Justice by Kev Mills. Their long over-due debut single Together, on Recreational Records, was released at the same time as Last Rockers and resulted in a little friendly rivalry. In the end, all we cared about was clearing our debt with Bill and selling more than those bastards.

On the fabled day that the first copies of Riot 1 arrived, H and I hastened to Simon's flat to get our first glimpse of the beast. We stroked it, licked it, held it up to the light etc, and then I set about blagging as many free copies as I could, like you do. H, though, displayed the rarely seen romantic side of his nature and insisted on paying for his copy so that he could be the first person to actually buy a Vice Squad record. I was very touched by this gesture, with its implication that he was confident there would be more sales to follow, but Simon just thought 'Mug!' and took the money before he changed his mind.

Now we just had to get the thing into the shops and, hopefully, sell a few. Simon explains this part of the process: 'At the time I didn't have any distribution at all, because when I was with Cherry Red their distribution was through a company called Spartan, who I think may have gone bust, so then I had to sort out distribution. Everything I liked centred around Rough Trade who were an independent distribution company, who did everything themselves, under their own roof, so distribution was essentially set up through them for the Vice Squad EP. They had a thing called the Cartel, that was like a hub of their operation, which was in like four or five towns, York, Bristol, Birmingham and Brighton, I think, and the Bristol leg of it was part of the Revolver record shop in Clifton, which is where your distribution was done from. Which was really handy for me because it was just down the road from where I worked, and it was a nice sort of parochial operation, and I used to go in there every day in my lunch hour and there would be this hub of activity going on there.'

Promotional copies were of course sent out, but it occurred to me that as I was spending most weekends in London with Mandy, it might be worthwhile taking a Monday off work and delivering copies to the main music papers personally. We visited *Melody Maker*, *NME*, *Record Mirror* and *Smash Hits*, and as expected, they were polite but not terribly interested. I wasn't bothered by this though, as our main target was *Sounds* in general, and their Features Editor Garry Bushell in particular. Bushell was the main press champion of the early eighties wave of punk and had already launched his infamous Oi! movement (more about that later), so he was our man.

He had unwisely let it slip in the paper a couple of weeks previously that he spent his lunchtimes in a pub near the *Sounds* offices in Covent Garden called the White Lion. With that information to hand we purposely timed our visit to the *Sounds* office for that hour of the day when the drinking man can no longer fight the urge, and sure enough the receptionist informed me that he was lunching. We found the pub in question and there he was, surrounded by fawning acolytes mostly sporting little hair, Doc Martens, combat jackets and camouflage trousers. In short, they were all skins.

I had no problem with skins. Some of my best friends etc, etc. But I had expected that, had I tracked the man down, he would be with his journalistic chums of a lunchtime, and as an avid reader of *Sounds* these all appeared to me to be a bunch of big girl's blouses, an epithet that could not easily be applied to this bunch of bruisers.

Not sure how to approach the situation and stalling for time, I told Mandy there was no rush and headed for the bar. We got a couple of beers in and I adopted what I hoped would appear to be a casual, nonchalant pose. I cast the odd surreptitious glance in their direction, hoping to detect a point at which their conversation flagged so I could make my move, but the moment never seemed to arrive. After several pints and a couple of dozen glances, each less surreptitious than the last as the alcohol took hold, I realised that Bushell was now staring straight at me. Clearly, he thought that I was staring at him because: a) I fancied him, b) I wanted a fight, or c) I was a member of a struggling punk band in need of help. No doubt he had me down as a definite c), but anxious to allay his fears on a) and b), and conscious that his whole party were now looking at me, I had no choice other than to get on with it.

Nervously, I introduced myself and Mandy, and Bushell politely introduced us to the assembled throng, most of whom seemed to be members of the charmingly named Angela Rippon's Bum. Having stated our business, I produced my box of records intending to just get one out for Bushell, but the fat ginger guy from Angela Rippon's Bum, who I believe was called Tony Barker, pounced on the box and the others followed suit. I didn't have the nerve to say anything, and when I managed to claw back the remainder I asked Bushell if he might see his way clear to giving it a listen. He answered in the affirmative, asked for my phone number, and the interview seemed to be at a close.

We made our way back to the bar and had another beer in a vain attempt to give the impression that we weren't at all fazed by this meeting, then left feeling rather pleased with ourselves.

Later, in a more sober frame of mind, I put the meeting in its proper perspective and reasoned that this sort of thing must happen to him all the time. The chances of anything coming from it were obviously minimal and the best you could say was that at least we'd made the effort. Feeling much more at home with this pessimistic view, I tried to put the matter out of my mind.

The initial reviews were less than encouraging. *NME*, on 31 January, declared that 'Punk bands necessarily have a built-in obsolescence, so maybe it's time to make way briefly for Vice Squad's brash rantings. Nothing special here but there's a nice fillip in the title chorus.' To this day I've no idea what a 'fillip' is, and for reasons already explained they were referring to Living On Dreams anyway. The same week's issue of *Sounds* carried a review by Robbi Millar, which read: 'Enter a UK Subs support band. As examples of a particular genre go, this is most typical of the screaming surge of (unintelligible) punk anger circa 1977. All muscle and chains and pre-Oi! defensiveness. For what it's worth.' Ouch! This review was disturbing on two fronts. Obviously, bad reviews are best avoided wherever possible, but what worried me was that, as Robbi Millar had written it, presumably Bushell had simply chucked the single in with the rest when he'd returned to the office after our meeting.

A few days later though, I went home from work for a spot of lunch to be informed by my dear mother that 'Some bloke called Gary phoned.' My earlier mind-purging must have been pretty successful, because all pennies failed to drop and I just said, irritated, 'Well, which Gary, I know loads of bloody Garys.' 'Oh, I don't know,' she said casually, 'he said he's from *Sounds* and you can ring him before 12.45. Ooh look, it's 12.45 now. There's a phone number on the pad. Why, is it important?' I glared at her and ran to the phone. Garry was still there, luckily, and had really just phoned to say that he'd liked the record, would be giving us a mention in his column, and would be happy to inform his public of our future activities. Of course, we didn't have any, which made for a rather short conversation, but the promise of a proper mention in *Sounds*, and the fact that he'd bothered to contact us at all was great news and everyone was suitably impressed when I told them about it. We awaited the following week's issue with what can only be described as baited breath.

Sure enough, in the 5 February edition of *Sounds*, in Bushell's shamelessly self-publicising Oi!-The Column, there appeared a sizeable piece about us. The bulk of it was a picture of Beki astride what now appears to be a constipated rabbit, but was actually a children's toy in a playground where we'd taken some photos for the Last Rockers insert. With Beki displaying ample amounts of fishnet stocking and high-heeled boots, the headline inevitably read 'Vice creamer' and the short caption continued in the same cringingly pun-ridden vein. On the other hand, it was most complimentary about the record, mentioned the distributors, Revolver, and promised us more coverage in the future. We may have balked at the tone of the piece, but to complain would have been churlish. This sort of publicity you simply couldn't buy. I asked Garry, for this book, what he thought of Last Rockers at the time: 'As I remember, Last Rockers sounded like it had been recorded under a carpet but I liked the song and the spirit. An unusual structure coupled with more usual fear of war and impending doom. Spunky I'd have said.'

Our cause was furthered when cuddly John Peel began to play the record regularly, opening his show with it for a whole week. I asked him if he'd remembered us from *Avon Calling* and got this diplomatic response: 'I'm sure I did, yes, of course. There'd been quite a few bands from the Bristol area that I kept hearing of.' Until this point there had been precious little of us to keep hearing of, but whether he remembered us or not, the airplay coupled with the Sounds piece had a dramatic affect.

Back to Simon: 'We pressed the first 1,500 copies of the Vice Squad EP, which I thought might sell 7, and I just didn't know what was going to happen. To my amazement, in about three days it had sold out. I still don't know why to this day! But one of the reasons has to be that as soon as John Peel heard Last Rockers he went on to start his show with it for God knows how many nights in a row, but he was quite taken by it.

'Then we pressed another 1,500 copies, because I thought that might be enough, but it wasn't, and it went on to sell around 22,000 copies, which is fantastic, really amazing. And that, really, was the start of Riot City Records.'

It took a while for this sudden change in our fortunes to translate into anything definite on the gig front. Before the sales had begun to gladden Simon's heart, enough word-of-mouth interest had been generated by the initial release of the record to secure us our first proper out of town gig on 13 February, at the Cedar Ballroom in Birmingham. Being something of a keen Rock 'n' Roll historian or, if you prefer, anorak, I was quite impressed as I'd read somewhere that Slade and the Move had played early gigs there, but it turned out to be rather a disappointing show. We were badly out of practice having played only a handful of gigs in the previous year, and it showed. The van we had booked let us down, we arrived late, and to top it all Beki was ill and had to leave the stage halfway through to throw-up. Yet another disaster, but hey, we were getting used to those.

We cheered up a little when, in the following day's *Melody Maker*, Last Rockers was placed at No.1 on their Independent Chart, with the X-Certs at No.2 (ha ha ha!). To be honest, that was a little misleading, as these were the early days of the Indie Chart that we all later came to know and love (arf, arf). Actually, *Melody Maker's* chart was based on the sales of a single chosen shop each week, and luckily for us, for the 14 February issue it just happened to be Revolver's turn. In truth, *Sounds'* Alternative Chart was more fair being based on sales from a number of shops around the country and we had entered that at No.40 in the previous week. On 14 February it rose to No.33, then number 8, and peaked at No.7 on 28 February.

A few days after his first phone call, Garry Bushell rang again to ask when our next London date would take place, the poor deluded fool. Stifling my laughter, I told him that no such creature existed or showed any sign at all of appearing in the near future. Undaunted, he told me that he was in the process of organising a London gig himself, and if we were interested he could get us on the bill and guarantee a live review in the paper. Naturally I jumped at it, but I had misgivings when he got down to details.

The chances of anyone who hasn't heard of Oi! music picking up this book are remote (more than one person has argued that any picking-up of this book is unlikely full-stop), as for a while it was as dominant an element of early eighties punk as the traditional approach or the emerging hardcore scene. But for the benefit of, well, my mother, it was an invention of Garry Bushell's that took its inspiration from the more street-level punk of earlier bands like Sham 69, Menace, Slaughter & The Dogs and Cock Sparrer as opposed to the art-school leanings of so many of the original punks. Bushell's idea was to create a truly working class movement as, laughable though it may seem today given his later career moves, he was at this time a staunch socialist. He once even ran a full page editorial exhorting *Sounds* readers to Vote Labour! in a forthcoming election (and that's 'Old Labour,' mark you).

The movement was centred around the Cockney Rejects, who had released the rather excellent single Flares 'N Slippers on Small Wonder in 1979, produced by Sham 69's Jimmy Pursey and Bushell himself. By the end of the year the Rejects had signed to EMI and Bushell saw that this was something he could build on. There were a handful of other bands ploughing a similar furrow, mostly skinheads playing a brand of punk that was, to my ears, crude and brutal but at the same time more melodic than the hardcore direction being pursued by the likes of Discharge. It was an intriguing combination. EMI must have thought so too, as they allowed Bushell to put together a compilation, *Oi!-The Album*, which was released in November 1980. It featured the Rejects' song Oi, Oi, Oi, which gave the movement its name, the Angelic Upstarts, who had recently left Warner Brothers and signed to EMI, deceased bands like Cock Sparrer and Slaughter & The Dogs who were posthumously dubbed Oi! whether they liked it or not, and more current punk bands like the Exploited and Peter & The Test Tube Babies who, though already fairly established in their own right, somehow got trawled into the Oi! net. Apart from various spurious acts like the Postmen and the Terrible Twins, who were mostly the Rejects and friends cobbling together material to give the illusion that the album represented a veritable rash of working class rock 'n' roll rebellion, the only genuinely new Oi! band featured were the 4-Skins. I feel a BBC-style link coming on, don't you?

As a result of the healthy sales of *Oi!-The Album*, not to mention the heavy coverage that Bushell secured in the pages of *Sounds*, enough new Oi! bands like the Business and the Last Resort had emerged by 1981 to constitute a proper movement. By virtue of being the first of the 'New Breed,' the 4-Skins were top dogs among our folliclely-challenged friends, and a fearsome sight they were to be sure. Singer Garry Hodges' snarling grimace graced many pages of *Sounds*, and his equally menacing side-kick, bassist Hoxton Tom, didn't appear to be the sort of chap you'd chose to meet in an alley on a dark night either. Or a light one come to that. Yes, you've guessed it, Bushell was inviting us to support the 4-Skins at, of all places, the Bridgehouse in Canning Town, which was the unofficial home of the Oi! clan.

However, I didn't see how I could decline the offer without displaying the yellow streak that ran all the way down my back, as I'd already admitted that our forthcoming engagements diary was as bare as Gary Hodges' carefully cropped bonce. The date of this festival of love and peace, which Bushell had dubbed The Second New Punk Convention (I didn't dare ask what had happened at the first one, which Bushell described as a 'shambles') was set for 18 February, with Oi! hopefuls Anti-Establishment opening the show and Vice Squad second on the bill. This settled, I then had to tell the others what I'd let them in for. They took it better than I'd expected, and once Dave and Beki had got bored with tearing me limb from limb, and Mark had stopped crying, they reluctantly agreed that I'd had no choice but to accept the gig if we were hoping for more *Sounds* coverage.

We arrived at the Bridgehouse full, in equal measures, of Courage Best and trepidation. After a long and circuitous drive around London's East End, during which I suspected that our driver was secretly hoping that we wouldn't find the place, we got there to find the venue empty, apart from a full complement of 4-Skins. I'd rather hoped to meet Bushell first and work up to dealing with the real hard-cases later, but the option was obviously not open in the circumstances. Introductions had to be made and my ever supportive chums made it plain that this was all my fault, so get on with it, pal.

Of course, they turned out to be perfectly affable, as Mark remembers: 'The 4-Skins were fairly pleasant, friendlier than they needed to be considering our status at the time, I thought. They could see we were shitting ourselves and tried to cheer us up a bit!' They didn't succeed, though it was nice of them to try, and our trepidation grew as, once the soundchecks were completed, the audience began to file noisily in. As expected, they were all skins, and our hope that at least a smattering of punks might put in an appearance faded quickly. We did meet a young and very nervous punk couple, boyfriend and girlfriend, who were there to see us, and we had a bit of a chat with them. Surveying the crowd, they reckoned that as some rivalry had sprung up between punks and skins of late it would probably be wise to leave discreetly after our set. As our influence on the proceedings were zilch, we were in no position to help and could only agree and wish them luck. I heard later that a couple of punks took a beating not far from the venue, and I feel guilty about it to this day, even though I've no way of knowing if it was the same couple.

Anti-Establishment were a very new band and only played a short, five song set, which gave us a little confidence, and then it was our turn. Earlier, once I'd made contact with Garry Bushell, I'd felt confident enough to take a walk around the venue as long as I was no further than five yards away from him and could give the impression that I was an old and valued friend of the Godfather Of Oi! As we soon learned though, you never really get a true picture of a crowd from ground-level. Once you get up onstage, there it is in its naked glory, as Mark recalls: 'It was a sea of skinheads, it looked like baked-beans on toast. It was ridiculous, I'd never seen anything like it. I was very nervous about the whole thing before we got there, and if I'd known what it was like, I just wouldn't have gone.' He also remembers that 'Micky Geggus and Stinky Turner from the Rejects were on the door, taking the money and letting all their mad mates in,' which on the whole, was probably a good idea, as it did ensure that there was little trouble.

We delivered a reasonably competent set, which was all we were capable of in the surroundings and the crowd, though bemused and obviously more interested in the 4-Skins, at least showed no inclination toward causing us bodily harm. A few of them even clapped occasionally, which was good enough for us, and we got the hell off as soon as we felt we were trying their patience.

A lot of the evening's tension was probably due to the fact that this was the first live airing of a new 4-Skins line-up. Messrs Hodges and Tom were now augmented by Steve Pear on guitar and John Jacobs on drums, and we were as curious as anyone to see how they would shape up. The brief soundcheck had been okay, but a bit shaky, giving the impression that, for all their easy-going brashness and bravado, the men themselves were a little prone to the nervousness that plagued the rest of us. Come gig time though, they quickly shrugged it off and were absolutely brilliant.

Though a drummer of sorts myself, I just fell into the role and have never been an aficionado of the instrument, or taken any more notice of drummers than other musicians when watching bands. Over the years, the only ones that have ever left a lasting impression on me are Phil Taylor from Motorhead, Topper from the Clash, Esso from the Lurkers, Jon Johnson from Chron Gen, Dave Grohl from Nirvana & Foo Fighters, the bloke that used to be in Therapy! and John Jacobs from the 4-Skins. John Jacobs really was exceptional, and at the Bridgehouse he was, to use a much used cliche, the driving force behind the band. He seemed to be in constant contact with every part of the kit simultaneously, but unlike many overly-busy drummers, each roll and fill was used to accentuate a key change or drive the song along. Nothing he did was superfluous, and I was spellbound. They went down a storm and richly deserved the glowing review that Bushell gave them in the next issue of *Sounds*.

There are aspects of the Oi! movement that have been heavily criticised over the years, and sometimes rightly so. On the whole, I tend to put it down to naivety, mainly on Garry Bushell's part. Being a staunch socialist myself, the overall philosophy of a truly working class punk movement appealed to me greatly, and it certainly made sense that such a movement would be based around the most working class youth cult of all, the skinhead. The idea of coupling the mean and menacing image of the skin with the passion and fury of punk music was inspired. Skins were not new to the punk scene, as demonstrated by some of the bands mentioned earlier as Oi! influences, but to his credit, Bushell was the first to attempt to give them a platform of their own. Where he went wrong, in my humble opinion, was failing to anticipate that taking the skinhead into the public domain, with major label records and national music press coverage, would excite the interests of other elements of the press. To your average *Daily Mail* reader, the image of a skinhead, like it or not, is a violent racist. The violence aspect didn't worry me all that much as any kind of punk gig was prone to that at the time, as I've already shown, but the racist aspect of the skinhead cult that was established in the original movement in the 60s and 70s should have been addressed from the start. John Peel, who championed the Cockney Rejects on his Radio 1 show, had similar misgivings: 'Well, most of it seemed to be rather cartoon violence most of the time. The Oi! aspect of it used to disturb me a bit because of the right-wing involvement. Whether it was real or imagined, there was an aspect of it that I was uncomfortable about, I must admit, you know, because there were some kind of links with ultra-right-wing organisations.'

If someone like Peel, who would normally revel in something like Oi! had such reservations, it's astonishing that Bushell didn't see the potential for some sort of media backlash. Before he even approached the project, again in my humble opinion, he would have been wise to set up something along the lines of SHARP (Skinheads Against Racial Prejudice) which addressed such problems in the 90s in America and Britain, as you all know other than my mother. It needn't even have been effective, but its existence would have given Bushell some ammunition in the fight that was to come.

On 3 July the 4-Skins, the Last Resort and the Business played a gig at the Hamborough Tavern, in Southall, West London, which ended in a riot with the local Asians laying siege to the venue because of the perceived racist overtones of Oi! music. The following week Simon Kinnersley, in the *Daily Mail*, penned a double page spread which began 'Every week up to half a million youngsters read the pop music paper *Sounds*, which is on sale at almost every newsagent in Britain. What many of the readers, and certainly their parents, do not know is that *Sounds* is not merely a pop paper but a vehicle for viciously extremist and fascist views.' He also contended that '*Sounds*...glories in and glorifies the mindless racist hooliganism of the skinhead cult.' Oh dear. The piece was peppered with inaccuracies, and Bushell, *Sounds* editor Alan Lewis and the publishers Spotlight Publications Ltd / Morgan Grampian Ltd, took legal proceedings against Associated Newspapers Limited, the editor of the *Daily Mail*, and Simon Kinnersley, but the damage was already done. On the day the article appeared I spoke to Bushell on the phone, unaware of what had happened, and he gave me a brief resume of its contents. He sounded genuinely shocked, stunned even, and still seemed unable to grasp how anyone could misconstrue his vision in such a way.

It was by no means the end of Oi!, but there can be no doubt that the movement was done irreparable damage by the events at Southall and the *Daily Mail*. The bigger bands like the Cockney Rejects and Angelic Upstarts regularly achieved respectable chart positions, with both making several memorable appearances on *Top Of The Pops*. Newer bands like Infa Riot also made the charts and the Oi! compilations always sold well, but ultimately Oi! was always destined to be an underground movement, and it flourishes as such today. That's no mean feat though. When you think of later music press inventions like New Wave Of New Wave and Romo, it's difficult to imagine, in 30-odd years' time, labels set up to promote that music and new bands wanting to play it. Looking back on the whole debacle now, Garry remains rueful but positive: 'Despite the lies of the *Daily Mail* and the disdain of the hippy end of the music press, Oi! bands are now respected worldwide, Oi! bands headline every punk festival you can think of, and they influenced everyone from Agnostic Front to Green Day via Rancid and Blink. Black Flag asked to have a track on the fourth album. There are Oi! scenes in Chile, China, Indonesia, Malaysia, Israel, Brazil, India and Russia as well as the USA, Canada, Australia, New Zealand and throughout Europe. It is a global phenomenon. Why? Because people around the world realised that Oi! was working class punk, pure and simple, and its message was and is universal: 'the kids they come from everywhere, the East End's all around.''

A gig at Mount Pleasant Hotel in Malvern, on 20 March, was notable as the promoter was one Chris Berry, who had been a partner in the early days of Cherry Red. He was managing a splendid local band called the Samples, who supported at the show, and was in the process of setting up his own label, to be called No Future. I wonder whatever happened to that?

Next day we headed for the College Of Art & Technology in Gloucester, for a show with a band called Icon, but local outfit Demob turned up with their crew and bullied the promoter into letting them play as well, something they tended to do as a matter of course, the scamps. Then on 2 May we played a return gig at the Swan, supported by the mysterious Blue Turks. Mysterious only in the sense that I can't remember who the hell they were, though Mark seems to think that Tim Galley and another friend ours, Bill Edwards, were involved.

After the unexpected success of Last Rockers, the pressing problem was to follow it. Simon's eyes were all £-signs and we were keen to get another record out as well. As I'd been proved so comprehensively wrong the first time (and as we'd been easily able to pay Bill White back both his money and his faith in us) I had no problem with the idea of a new song as the next single. Clearly, Dave and Beki were on a roll, as Mark and I learned when we were presented with their latest composition, Resurrection. It's my favourite Vice Squad song, and Mark says that it's among his, so the principal songwriters could be forgiven for the rather smug expressions on their faces when they first came up with it. Like Last Rockers, it was a departure from the more standard punk material that made up the bulk of our set, and again it was quite long and the arrangement was, by our standards, fairly complex. On the other hand, Resurrection was more up-beat than its predecessor, which I got bored with fairly quickly, even though Last Rockers remained the audience favourite for the rest of our existence.

For the B-Side of Riot 2 we plumped for Young Blood, which was a song written by Dave about mindless violence, around a drum pattern that I'd worked out in rehearsal, which is why I got a songwriting credit. The second B-Side song was Humane, Beki's first attempt to highlight the animal rights beliefs that she held dearly.

Recording began at Cave Studio on 29 March, and followed almost the same pattern as the Last Rockers session, so we needn't go into all that again, with the only noticeable difference being that this time Andy spent a lot more time over the radio mix. These days most new releases come with a variety of mixes for every occasion: weddings, funerals, bar mitzvahs etc. Back in the dark ages you did two, and the finished product had to be a compromise between them. The first, and most important, was the stereo mix that determined how it would sound when the punter eagerly dropped the vinyl onto his or her turntable and stood back waiting to be impressed. The second, which at the best of times was an after-thought, was the radio mix. This determined how the record would sound when reduced to mono, which is the way that most radio listeners would have heard it at the time if the lucky record were granted air-play. At the Last Rockers session, the stereo mix through the huge studio speakers took an age, while the mono one through the puny little chap perched on the mixing desk was over in a flash. We didn't realise it at the time, but the latter had obviously just been a token gesture as Andy and Bill had, understandably, rated our chances of air-play at nil. As Last Rockers had been played incessantly on Radio 1 by John Peel, this time around the radio mix also took an age.

For the front of the sleeve we used a live photograph taken by Mandy at the Malvern gig, which was given a negative affect by, I assume, Danica Gacesa, as no one is given a credit for the finished article, and Dave made up a collage of photos for the back which were contributed by numerous friends and hangers-on.

This time I did make it to the cut, along with Simon, Beki and Bambi, at Virgin Townhouse. While it was possible to record in any manner of studio to suit one's purse, when it came to the cutting of a record there were only a handful of options, and none of them came cheap. The high-flyers of the music industry would book themselves into the Townhouse for months on end to make use of the luxurious state-of-the-art studio and accommodation facilities on offer at a staggeringly high price. It really was a beautiful place: all leather sofas, massive fish-tanks set into the walls and gorgeous receptionists.

On one memorable visit, a friend of ours returned from a visit to the lavatory to announce, triumphantly, 'Guess who I've just seen, Stevie Wonder!' Naturally, as one we replied 'Did he see you?' Oh well, I suppose you just had to be there.

Just booking the cutting room for a couple of hours was cripplingly expensive, and as the person in charge was obviously used to dealing with the likes of Stevie, I'd assumed that we would be treated like something slightly distasteful that he'd recently scraped from his boot. Nothing could have been further from the truth, however. The cutting engineer, Kevin Metcalfe, was a lovely bloke who had worked with Simon before, and seemed genuinely pleased to work on our record which was, to say the least, different from the sort of material he usually dealt with. Like Simon, Dave and I struck up a rapport with Kevin, and we used him whenever possible on later projects, usually ending the session with him taking us for a few beers in his local.

Being a pessimist by nature, I had my doubts that we would be able to match the sales of Last Rockers, but these were soon dispelled. Simon remembers the flurry of activity at Revolver Records: 'The second thing we did was the Resurrection EP. The sales were just fantastic. Before Last Rockers I never dreamed of something like that actually happening, and just seeing all these records just flying out of this little back-room of Revolver Records was just phenomenal. They couldn't believe it either, they'd never had so much work in their lives!'

A trawl through the archives gives up just one review of Resurrection, and a somewhat disparaging one at that. It's uncredited, but judging from the typeface, and applying the methods of Sherlock Holmes, I deduce that it is probably from the pages of *Sounds*. Under the heading 'The Dregs' it begins 'Ah, the bin-liners! The pins! The mucus!' and continues as a diatribe against the existence of punk bands in 1981 without the merest mention of the record itself. Hardly encouraging.

Nevertheless, it entered the Indie Chart at No.22 on 30 May and by 13 June had risen to the dizzy heights of No.4.

In an Oi!-The Column piece on 14 March, Garry Bushell had mentioned that he and photographer Ross Halfin would be paying us a visit on a country-wide jaunt intended to seek out as many up-and-coming punk acts as he could find. For some reason this never happened, and instead he despatched *Sounds*' local correspondents, or 'stringers', to cover each of the bands he had targeted.

The lucky fellow to be allocated Vice Squad was the aforementioned RAB, a frustrated would-be *NME* writer, as he freely admitted. We met RAB and photographer Andy Phillips on 5 May at the Berkeley Centre, on Park Street, where we were supporting the Angelic Upstarts. The Berkeley was a short-lived venture as a live music venue, better known before and afterwards as Carwardines, but during its brief existence it hosted some creditable gigs, like Splodgenessabounds, who were in the charts at the time and an early show by the Stray Cats. We were pleased to be invited to play there, and when the promoters suggested that we help out with publicity for the gig, we were quick to exploit the situation. They stipulated that, as the Upstarts were the headliners, obviously their name should go at the top of the posters. Fair enough, but they should have been more specific, as Bristol was soon awash with posters displaying a tiny Angelic Upstarts logo, barely noticeable above a massive Vice Squad one. They weren't best pleased, and I don't suppose the Upstarts were either, but even by this early stage we were getting cocky.

We felt we were on a roll, and the gig itself did nothing to dispel the impression, as Mark recalls: 'We were introduced by the DJ as 'Bristol's biggest-selling independent band,' and I looked at Dave and said, 'Yeah, we are!' It had never remotely crossed our minds before. We bounced up onstage full of beans, and I think we did quite a good one from what I can remember. I remember thinking 'Well, yeah, we're actually kind of doing something here,' and about the X-Certs, thinking 'This should be them.' That one brought it home.' We did indeed go down a storm, and with *Sounds* on the premises this rare occurrence couldn't have been better timed.

Afterwards we did a photo session in the dressing room and had a quick chat with RAB, arranging to do the interview proper in the trusty Swan Inn a few days later.

He made no attempt to pretend that he understood what we were trying to do, or have any real sympathy with it, but he was friendly and open-minded and that was good enough for us. Old Ron was highly amused at the idea of someone from a newspaper (for *Sounds* was registered as such) coming into his Public Bar to interview us, and took the piss out of RAB at any given opportunity. Whether this had anything to do with the fact that, when the piece was published in the 6 June issue of *Sounds*, the pub was referred to throughout as the Crown, is anyone's guess. It was a nice piece though, that in a fit of hyperbole described the audience during our set at the Berkeley as 'A pinballing, careening, cruncher of a crowd - the pogo doesn't just go vertical in Bristol any more but every which way, often on each other's shoulders. It looks like World War II on fast/forward to me but I'm assured it's all good bruising fun and nobody gets hurt who doesn't want to; just Vice Squad's loyal fans enjoying themselves as they always do, loudly and long.'

The conversation covered all the topics that became the staple diet of future interviews: Punk's Not Dead/Violence/The Kids/Vivisection. He also gave a brief band history, during which I was most interested to learn that 'Dave and Shane's earliest approach to the music biz was a little roadieing for the Cortinas, Bristol's first punk band.' Utter rubbish, of course, but we certainly never made any attempt to deny such a credibility-boosting myth.

All the quotes in the piece were from Beki and Dave, which was also in line with future interviews, and I thought they put on a pretty good show, with Beki coming across as the romantic idealist and Dave the down-to-earth working class hero. We certainly won RAB over anyway, and he concluded 'What did impress me was their straightforwardness and sincerity. They honestly want to see a better world, help it come about, and I say good luck to them.' If you ask me, the man must have been on drugs.

Under the inexplicable heading 'Vice Up The Dance,' the article was spread over two pages with two photographs, one of Beki snogging her mate Chrissy and the other a group shot taken in the Berkeley dressing room. I was a little disappointed that none of my pearls of wisdom were used, as the lads at work were quick to point out, but overall we were well satisfied.

The piece had an unfortunate aftermath, however. Beki was mortified when, in the following week's *Sounds*, a letter from one her workmates was published. It ran, in part, 'I work for the Department Of The Environment at Tollgate House in Bristol and know their lead singer Beki Bondage very well. She works here as a clerical assistant and is such a pleasant, attractive and well-dressed girl. But in the evenings, when she transforms herself into a 'punk,' I am simply horrified by her appearance!' He continued 'Please Beki, forget this Vice Squad business - your true vocation is obviously a sensible home life with a loving husband (me?) and 2.4 children. Please see the error of your ways - and don't give up your day job!'

The letter was signed Steve Trevor, and just to rub it in he enclosed a clipping from the trade paper *Environment And Transport World*. This was also published, alongside a photo of Beki taken by Andy Phillips at the Berkeley. The clipping was typical of the kind thing found in such publications; a head and shoulders photo of Beki in her work clothes, with a one paragraph caption giving a description of her job. But at the end, instead of the usual 'She enjoys squash, tennis and amateur dramatics, and we are happy to announce that Beki will be marrying Kevin Smoothbastard from Accounts in January,' it read 'She is a singer with a local punk rock band called 'The Vice Squad' which plays at discos and clubs in the city. They recently released a record, so look out for her in the charts.' Pretty cringing stuff, I'm sure you'll agree. All it needed was an exclamation mark at the end.

Being an insensitive sort of cove, I thought it was pretty funny but Beki was furious. I don't know what form of retribution was brought to bear on the hapless Steve Trevor, but knowing Beki it was swift and merciless.

Still, it did indirectly get us a feature in, of all places, *Smash Hits*. Under the heading 'Vice Girl In Civil Service Riddle,' Beki was interviewed ('Beki feels strongly about virtually everything') and a band photo was cringingly captioned 'VICE SQUAD: Dave, Beki, Mark & Shane - waiting for the leather forecast.' Boom boom!

A later *Sounds* letters page printed a similarly light-hearted attack on Dave and Mark. Possibly having heard that Steve Trevor was only now able to sit up in bed and digest watery soup and egg custard, the letter was signed Anon. Under the heading 'Confessions of a Salesman,' it ran 'With reference to Beki Bondage working in the Department of Transport (sic), so what? Big deal! Dave and Mark, guitarist and bassist respectively, are working for the capitalist insurance system in the name of Sun Life. How do you think you would feel about handing your money over to a pair of anarchistic insurance salesmen!'

Luckily, my workmates only read *The Sun*, *Golfing Monthly*, *Classic Cars* and *Fiesta*.

A major event in what we laughingly refer to as our career, came about in the shape of our first John Peel Session. We were aware that Peel's criteria, when selecting bands for sessions, was eccentric to say the least and often made on a moment's whim, as some of our detractors were quick to point out. (There's a joke about the West Country and tractors in there if you can be bothered. It might help if you work in an Italian or a Spaniard.) In his foreword to the BBC book *In Session Tonight*, by Ken Garner, Peel asserted that: 'Considering the perversely random nature of our commissioning of sessions, it is astonishing how few have turned out to be unsatisfactory.'

On being granted one, we chose to dismiss the likes of Steeleye Span and Fairport Convention from our minds, though we knew that such atrocities had graced the John Peel Show in the past. We reflected on classic sessions by the Slits, Siouxsie and the Banshees, the Lurkers and, yes, the Damned, and considered it a great honour.

The recording took place at Langham House, which if I remember rightly was near the main Radio One building, though most sessions of the period were recorded at the BBC's Maida Vale studios, on 1 June. The BBC, in their infinite wisdom, had decided to spend vast amounts of licence-payer's money on computerising Maida Vale, so those of us recording sessions at the time had to make do with the more antiquated facilities available elsewhere.

The finer points of studio equipment came pretty low on our list of misgivings, however. Once the initial euphoria had worn off, the logistics of recording a Radio 1 Session, as conveyed to us by Simon who had some experience of such things, began to sink in. We had to transport ourselves, and all our equipment to London, set up the gear, record at least four songs, mix them, and come up with something that could be broadcast to the nation in a single day. Though well aware that literally hundreds of acts had managed to perform this feat previously, our self-esteem was still so low that we doubted if it could be done. If it had taken several days to turn out the two EPs, both of which, happy though we were with them, still left room for improvement, what were we likely to come up with in a single short day?

The session was produced by Tony Wilson and engineered by Dave Dade, and it soon became obvious that they were used to dealing with the likes of us. The weak, lily-livered and downright inexperienced must have been a speciality of theirs, as the session flew by. The mix was already at an advanced stage by mid-evening, and it sounded pretty bloody good, if we said so ourselves. By around 10.30 the thing was 'In the can,' as us musos like to put it, and we breathed a communal sigh of relief.

We'd chosen Coward, It's A Sell-Out, 1981 and The Times They Are A-Changin' as being broadly representative of our vast repertoire, and were more than impressed with the final mixes. All of those songs were re-recorded later, some of them more than once, but it's only fair to Tony and Dave to admit that we never bettered their versions.

As our moods tended to swing from severe depression to extreme cockiness, depending on recent events, we were now on something of a high and demanded to know when the mighty Peel himself would be paying us a visit. During this period the John Peel Show was broadcast from 10.00 'til 12.00 every weekday evening, from the very same building, and we rather assumed that having issued the invitation in the first place, the man himself would bung on some lengthy reggae 12" and pop in for a chat. We were disappointed when Dave Dade informed us that Peel, apparently never the most gregarious of people, tended to avoid such encounters. He explained that this was no kind of snub, but experience had taught the man that these meetings tended to be full of self-consciousness on both sides and therefore best left alone. This seemed fair enough, but I for one was terribly disappointed when I bumped into Dave a few days later on Oxford Street, and he told me that after we'd left for home Peel had broken his habit and come down to speak to us.

When it was first broadcast on 3 June, I listened to, and recorded the session in my bedroom, while my parents listened to it in the living room downstairs.

My father was a big fan of John Peel, and most weekday nights, between 10.00 and 12.00, would find him hunched over the living room table with his headphones on, swigging endless mugs of coffee and smoking his foul untipped Woodbines. He even became an armchair Liverpool supporter under the influence of Mr Peel.

On the night in question, my mother, who frankly couldn't stand the din that Peel dished out nightly, relented, and dad was able to dispense with the headphones for once. After the second song, 1981, Peel read out our names: 'Dave Bateman, guitar, Shane Baldwin, drums, Beki on vocals and Mark Handly at the bass. That's Vice Squad from Bristol and 1981.' In my bedroom, callous bleeder that I am, I laughed heartily at the fact that he got Mark's name wrong, and pictured him fuming in his own room where I knew he was listening. The next song, our butchering of the Bob Dylan classic The Times They Are A-Changin' had Peel declaring 'I'm all for that, I must say,' and at the end of the session he concluded 'See, It can still be done.'

What with getting my name read out on Wonderful Radio 1, John Peel's encouraging comments, and him fucking up Mark's name, I was more than happy as I made my way downstairs to gauge the reaction of the old folk. Mum, I knew, would just be impressed that we were on the radio again, but as a regular listener to the show, dad had heard many sessions and was able to make comparisons. What with that and the fact that sons naturally seek the approval of their fathers, it was his opinion that I really wanted. Never the most effusive of people, he merely patted me lightly on the back, smiled, and said 'Good session, kid!' As I'd known him for a number of years by this time, I was aware that this was the equivalent of an after-dinner speech from a top media celeb' coming from Michael J. Baldwin, and I was quite satisfied. When he'd gone off to bed, mum took me to one side and whispered, confidentially, 'Don't take any notice of that silly old sod. When John Peel started playing your songs he grinned like a Cheshire cat, and when he read out your name I thought he was going to burst!' It was one of the proudest moments of my life, and I'm not ashamed to admit it.

Peel was obviously as keen on the session as his comments had suggested, and it was repeated so often that we lost track of just how many times it was eventually broadcast.

The next Vice Squad gig of note took place at the Lyceum Ballroom, in the Strand, London, on 5 July. The Lyceum was a big venue, and in Victorian times (you'll have to excuse me, this is one of my other anorak interests. Though I could never be one myself, I have a lot of time for the world's thespians. Stop sniggering at the back.) was a theatre run by the great actor-manager Henry Irving, aided by his assistant and side-kick, Dracula author Bram Stoker. The Lyceum was frequented by the cream of Victorian high society, and therefore it was something of an honour for any actor to tread its hallowed boards. I'm a big fan of the Sherlock Holmes stories (the label for us sad people being 'Sherlockians') and the Lyceum has special interest for the likes of me. The venue was featured in one of the stories, The Sign Of The Four, and played host to the celebrated American actor William Gillette when he brought his play Sherlock Holmes to the theatre in 1901, with the young Charlie Chaplin as Billy, Holmes' page.

Eighty years on, Henry Irving must have been spinning in his grave, as the Lyceum had gone a little down-market, being used mostly as a disco and a venue for live bands.

Sunday night punk gigs at the Lyceum, promoted by John Curd's company Straight Music, became regular fixtures, and this was our first. The line-up was the Damned, Anti-Nowhere League, our good selves and Ruts DC in, I think, that order.

The show was advertised as a '5th Anniversary Commemorative Cock-up,' which suggested that the Damned were keen on anniversaries, as at the Locarno two years previously they'd been celebrating 'Three Years Of Anarchy Chaos And Destruction' (no poofy punctuation for these wild men of rock - commas are for girls, maan.) The fact that the bill was virtually the same as the Locarno had not been lost on us, but a couple of things had changed in the two years that had passed.

On 14 July 1980, Ruts singer Malcolm Owen had died of a heroin overdose. The news had shocked and saddened us, not least because he was the first person of our acquaintance to suffer such a fate, though he certainly wasn't the last. The rest of the band carried on for a couple of years as Ruts DC, with a new member, Gary Barnacle, and we all went to see them whenever they played in Bristol. I was glad they persisted, as the new line-up was well worth the effort, but they never really shook off the spectre of Malcolm's death, and it wasn't too much of a surprise when they called it a day in 1982, though they've since reformed, to much acclaim, and I caught a great set by them at Vegfest 2014 in Bristol.

The other change was, of course, that we had sold a few records of late, hence our place on the bill above Ruts DC. Though flattering, this caused us some discomfort, as Mark remembered when we talked about the Locarno gig: 'I felt really embarrassed years later at the Lyceum when they supported us as Ruts DC. And they were just full of congratulations, 'I think it's brilliant what you've done.'' As fans of the Ruts, we couldn't have been paid a bigger compliment, and we treasured it.

The reputation of promoter John Curd went before him, and stories of his more outrageous acts were legend. Probably the most famous is an incident that apparently occurred when he was promoting an early gig by the Ramones at the Roundhouse in London. The story goes that Malcolm McLaren was keen to secure the support slot for his fledgling Sex Pistols, and though Curd was not interested, Talcy Malcy wouldn't let it lie. It seems that McLaren pursued John Curd to his lair, sorry, home, and hammered away at his front door, until the enraged promoter finally lost his patience and threw the hapless manager down several flights of stairs, causing no little injury in the process. The list of items that followed him down the stairs, like buckets of wallpaper paste, dustbins, items of furniture, a selection of valuable potted plants and a baby tortoise called Kevin, vary depending on whose version you listen to.

We were, therefore, a little wary, but it was a great gig to be offered and I was really excited about it. As most punks had stayed away from the Bridgehouse show, in a way this was our first London gig.

Once we'd negotiated our way around the Lyceum's labyrinthine backstage area, we found our dressing room, and were pleasantly surprised to find a large quantity of beer awaiting us. We'd never been given a 'rider' before, and were touched by Mr Curd's generosity. Later of course, we learned that the laying on of food and drink in a band's dressing was par for the course, and not the promoter's little way of saying he loved us. Later still, when we had an agent, we realised that we could have virtually anything we wanted on the 'rider,' but as the cost was taken into consideration when negotiating the fee, we ended up paying for it. No such thing as a free lunch etc. From then on we just asked for a crate of beer and some sandwiches and fruit. Got to think of the old complexion.

The Damned were a little more friendly when we met them (though they could hardly have been less so than the last time without ejecting us onto the streets of WC2) and Rat even came into our dressing room for a chat, but we hadn't forgotten the Locarno and were, I'm ashamed to say, less than gracious.

I don't know the capacity of the Lyceum, but it seemed huge to me, and by the time it was our turn to take to the stage it was packed to the rafters. Whatever we may have thought about the Damned, you couldn't deny that they could pull a crowd. I remember little about the set itself, other than the fact that we went down well, and that we were all amazed that most of the people at the front seemed to know all the words to all the songs on our two EPs. Even Beki didn't know all of them.

I was pleased that we'd gone on early, as it was my birthday and I fully intended to get pissed. So with business out of the way, I looked forward to getting a few down me, hopefully before the Damned went on. After the Locarno fiasco I didn't expect them to be up to much, as on the evidence of that gig one could have been forgiven for assuming that they were content to live off their reputation without making any sort of effort. In fact, I couldn't have been more wrong. They were absolutely stunning. None of us could believe that it was the same band that had put on that lazy, sloppy and arrogant show two years before. Just what brought about this transformation, I've no idea, but no one could have touched them that night.

CHAPTER 6

AT THIS JUNCTURE, which is a posh word I like to chuck in now and again in place of the word 'point' to impress people and avoid repetition, things began to move along a bit.

For much of this tome to date, a cruel and cynical world cared not a jot whether the members of Vice Squad lived or died, but recent events changed all that. Our manager, Ian, reckoned he was bombarded with calls from record labels anxious to sign us up, and though he was an inveterate bullshitter there was certainly interest from at least two or three.

We were quite happy with the way things had progressed thus far with Riot City and there was even talk of an album for the label, so we were certainly in no hurry to leave. But then another slightly shifty ginger-nut entered our lives, as if Tadd wasn't enough to be going on with, in the shape of one Ashley Goodall. Ashley, it turned out, was an A&R man for (if you're a *MaximumRocknRoll* reader I suggest you sit down and take a few deep breaths) the mighty EMI corporation. Oh, the horror!

Mark takes up the story: 'I remember meeting Ashley Goodall one lunchtime in Tadd's lock-up. We [Mark and Dave] wandered up from the Sun Life canteen, which was, like, a hundred yards away. We used to go up quite often. Have a spot of lunch together then wander up and see what the latest happenings were. By the time we met Ashley he'd seen us live once or twice. At that time there was a few people scouting around us, it may not have been companies like CBS, but there were people sniffing around. I'm sure an offer was talked about, this quarter of a million pound deal, and being, like, 19, earning £50 a week at Sun Life, a quarter of a million pounds was just a monstrous amount of money.'

Dave has some (admittedly vague) recollections of EMI's initial reconnaissance of the good ship Vice Squad: 'It was either some extravaganza at the Lyceum or a sweat 'n' spit-pit job at the 100 Club. EMI were there, the only thing is I don't think we were introduced, and probably, when you think about it, that was for the best. One of the things our management got right at that stage was to keep us well away from anyone in authority.'

Under normal circumstances, a company like EMI scouting a band like us would have seemed preposterous, but Ashley, it turned out, had been the man responsible for Oi!-The Album appearing on the label and the signing of the Cockney Rejects and Angolic Upstarts. How he got his superiors to agree to those deals is open to debate, but I suppose the guaranteed press coverage from Garry Bushell must have helped, and memories of the Sex Pistols debacle of a few years earlier, which caused the company a great loss of face within the industry, might have made them a little cautious about turning down the so-called New Punk, just in case.

They hedged their bets though, and most of Ashley's releases were put out on the Regal Zonophone label, a subsidiary of EMI that had remained dormant since the 70s. This is pure conjecture on my part, and it certainly never occurred to me at the time, but I do wonder if shifting Ashley's releases to Regal Zonophone after the first few was perhaps a way of ensuring that if anything embarrassing occurred, at least EMI's name would only appear in the small print.

The bottom line, though, was that Ashley had managed to convince his superiors that this New Punk lark was too good to miss, and we, apparently, were next on his hit-list.

After Ashley's initial meeting with Ian, Dave and Mark, the results of which we had discussed between ourselves at some length, a formal meeting for all concerned was set up.

Of course, we all had our misgivings, and Igor believes that apart from the question of signing to a major label, teaming up with Ashley did us no real favours: 'One problem was that you didn't ever really have an A&R person who believed in you. And that's what should happen, you should have an A&R person fighting your corner. It was more that John Cavanagh, the director, who liked it rather than Ashley. And that whole deal was shit wasn't it? That was Tadd as well. That was the biggest mistake.'

As Beki says, however, I suppose we did little to endear ourselves to Ashley: 'I think the fact that we called Ashley Goodall 'Ashtray Fuckall' made it hard for him to like us! Plus he let us stay in his flat and we drank all of his mead. I've no idea why he gave us mead instead of beer, he probably decided to let us have some as a treat and failed to realise that we were rampant piss heads who'd drink the last drop.'

At first we reasoned that it had been perfectly acceptable to most people (though there were objectors like Mark Perry in *Sniffin' Glue*, it must be said) when the main players in the first wave of punk signed to majors, so what was the difference? Right, we'd sign then. On the other hand, times had changed, and very few punk bands were now signed to majors. The indie network was now much more organised than it had been when, for instance, the Clash signed to CBS, and if the current situation had prevailed in 1976-77, they may have chosen one of the bigger indies instead. Plus, EMI were one of the labels that had dumped the Pistols in the first place. Right, we wouldn't sign, then.

On the other hand, perhaps the reason that most of the current punk bands were not signed to majors, was simply that they were never given the chance. EMI were the only major signing punk bands by then, and as they already had the Rejects and Upstarts, both of whom we admired and respected, who were we to turn our noses up? Right, we'd sign then.

But, on the other hand, was it right, morally? This was, like, selling out wasn't it? Selling our souls to The Man, sucking corporate cock, etc. And apart from anything else, we knew that the Crass mob would be down on us like a ton of bricks. Right, we wouldn't sign then. On yet another hand, though, as the indie labels had become more organised, hadn't the bigger ones become a far cry from the bedsit DIY indies of the past? Some were now quite large companies operating in much the same way as their major counterparts. As John Peel said: 'There's nothing to say that to form an indie label is in some way morally superior to major labels. The people running them are just as likely to be incompetent or dishonest.' It goes without saying that I didn't have Simon in mind when I decided to use that quote, but it nicely sums up one opinion voiced in the overall indie-versus-major debate that was raging in the Vice Squad camp. Ashley was of course quick to point out the advantages of having a company like EMI backing us. Their marketing and distribution was second to none, their press office was likely to gain better results than our usual policy of me phoning Sounds once a week, and money (which I'll cover in more detail shortly) would be on the table to enable us to commence recording and touring as soon as our signatures were on the document. Put like that, it was everything I'd ever dreamed of. I just wanted to make records and tour, and I didn't really care much about anything else.

Mark, being Mark, sums up the previous few paragraphs rather more succinctly than I: 'We had every intention of trying to stay indie, but as soon as EMI was mentioned that was it, we went.'

Right, we signed.

I have a copy of the contract in front of me as I write, and I'm still as baffled by it now as I was then. 28 pages of heretofor's and hereinafter's that would have the Clear English Society foaming at the mouth.

Before signing, we all perused the document at length, stroking our chins and nodding sagely, before admitting that none of us could make head nor tail of it. Not being total mugs, we decided to seek professional help (no, I can't be bothered) in the shape of a guy called Bryan Reynolds.

Bryan was already quite a high-flyer in legal circles, and later handled some really big cases like the Brink's-MAT bullion trial, but he had his Achilles Heel, and that was rock 'n' roll. Though firmly ensconced in posh offices in the salubrious business section of Bristol, nothing excited Bryan more than some scruffy band turning up on his well-scrubbed doorstep begging for help. The secretaries ran for cover, and his colleagues looked askance, but when we outlined our problem Bryan practically rubbed his hands with glee and got straight down to it.

He gleaned two things from the document straight away. The first was that, as threatening as it looked, it was just the normal contract that any band of our lowly status could expect from a company like EMI. The second was that he was certainly not going to get rich by choosing to act for us. He took us on anyway, for a nominal fee, and we were neither the first or last band from Bristol to benefit from his generosity.

He waded through endless guff about what constituted 'an album' or 'a single,' 'Eastern European Sales Provisions,' 'Local Variations in Brunei, Cambodia, Peoples Republic of China, Hong Kong, Indonesia, North Korea, South Korea, Laos, Macao, Malaysia, Philippines, Singapore, Taiwan (Republic of China), Thailand and Vietnam' and so on before giving us the gist.

I can't remember Bryan's words now, so I've just spent an agonizing hour trying to make sense of the thing myself.

As far as I can make out, what it boiled down to was this. The contract was split into 'Albums' and 'Options,' though before the 'Options' we had the 'Initial Period.' The 'Initial Period' and 'Options' lasted for one year, unless the company decided to extend them for three months. On the 'Initial Period' (or signing) we were paid £2,500 (wow!). Once they'd heard the album and were satisfied, we got another £2,500. If, at this stage, they decided they wanted to take up the 'First Option' or 'Second Album' (this is where it gets confusing), we got another £2,500.

When the 'Second Album' was completed to EMI's satisfaction, we got another £2,500. Then, at the end of the 'Initial Period,' the company had to decide whether they wanted to take up the 'First Option,' even though the 'Second Album' had to be completed by then and they'd have paid good money (although not a lot of it, granted) for it up front. On the commencement of the 'First Option' we were then to be paid £7,500.

We would then be paid another £7,500 on 'the completion to the company's satisfaction of the recording of the Second Album,' although I thought that was what we were given £2,500 for back in the 'Initial Period.'

What confuses matters even more is that the document refers to the 'First Option Album' and 'Second Album' completely separately when they were surely one and the same. If they decided to take up the 'Second Option,' we would get another £7,500 and…oh fuck it. My brain hurts.

If any of that made any sense to you then I doff my cap. Suffice to say that it carried on in the same vein with the money involved rising to £10,000, £12,500, £15,000 and so on for the various stages of the subsequent 'Albums' and 'Periods' if they chose to pick them up. These were of course advances, and in the unlikely event that we sold enough records to clear them, we would be paid a whopping 10% royalty during the 'Initial Period,' rising to 11% in the 'First Option Period,' then 12% for any further 'Options' or, if you prefer, 'Albums,' that the company required. Got that? Clear as fucking mud, I know, but it's the best I can do.

Brian explained that the royalty rate, though pathetic, was par for the course and irrelevant anyway unless we paid off the advances, so we immediately stopped worrying about that side of the deal.

We did have several objections to other aspects of the contract however. Firstly, we insisted on complete control (where have I heard that before?) over where and how we recorded, secondly we were to be consulted on all aspects of artwork and design, and thirdly we wanted to use the Riot City name on all our records. We got the idea for the last one from Stiff Little Fingers and the Specials, who'd used the Rigid Digits and Two Tone names, respectively, when they'd signed to Chrysalis. Presumably, they too had felt a little guilty about signing to a major label, and figured that this would fudge the issue. Good plan!

Once we'd fallen for the financial implications of the contract (and just where Mark got his quarter of a million from, I've no idea) I don't think EMI cared a lot about our guilt-assuaging clauses, but they played the game and disputed them all, as Mark remembers: 'Bryan Reynolds put in a huge amount of work, and I know the contract went backwards and forwards at least three times.'

Presumably, once we came to an agreement, there was a formal signing of the contract, though 'If there was, it wasn't outside the gates of Buckingham Palace, I fuckin' know that,' says Dave, referring of course to the Pistols' rather more glamorous signing to A&M with the world's press looking on. The fact is that no one actually remembers signing the thing, but when we did, on 20 July 1981, the chances are that it took place in my house with just my mother looking on. Nervously, at that.

Nevertheless, the event had to be celebrated in some way, and Ashley came up with a plan that ideally suited our status, as Mark recalls: 'We went to a Pizza-Something-Or-Other, on Milsom Street in Bath. It was an auspicious occasion, and he paid for it, so we drank as much as we possibly could. Then we had a race afterwards, me and you, both blind pissed, up four storeys of scaffolding, really stupid. We could have died, and Ashley was going 'Oh shit, what have I signed up 'ere?''

With the formalities out of the way, and having already sold our souls to the devil, so not much point worrying about that any further, there were other decisions to be made.

In the first place, Ashley assumed that on signing we would give up our day jobs, but the paltry first advance, even coupled with gig money and royalties from the Riot City records put that out of the question, so we had no choice other than to continue along the same lines as before. This was a relief in a way, as it meant that not only could we avoid having to make a difficult decision, something we all shied away from whenever possible, but it also kept up the pretence that we were just distributed by EMI rather than being actually signed to them.

We weren't fooling anyone but ourselves, of course, but I'll deal with the implications of the deal later. One of the most impending problems at this stage was just how Simon was going to fit in with our new situation.

Unsurprisingly, he hadn't been exactly over the moon on learning that we'd decided to sign to EMI, in fact as I remember it he was spitting blood for some time afterwards. But he now allows that: 'It was the obvious next step really, wasn't it, to sign to a big label... it had to be done. You'd have kicked yourselves forever if you hadn't done it.'

Full of guilt, we insisted that Simon carried on as our publisher, as well as taking care of the merchandise. When Simon had suggested, on the release of Resurrection, that we should produce a t-shirt to commemorate the event it had seemed a good idea, but we didn't have any great hopes for its success.

Our sole venture into the world of merchandising thus far had been a couple of hundred badges we'd had made up using a logo that Big Karen had designed (or rather nicked from a *Doctor Who* cartoon strip) some time earlier. It was a good design, and with the aid of an overhead projector in work, I used it to make our back-drop, whereby it became the logo on the front of the Resurrection EP. You know, the spiky, pointy one. As for the badge itself, its sole claim to fame was that the first person to buy one, for 20p, was Peter Gabriel who Dave and Mark accosted at Moles club in Bath. Fair play though, he paid up and even put it on, though no doubt it ended up in an ashtray as soon as the coast was clear.

I think we sold enough to cover the costs, but it wasn't exactly a runaway success, and we figured that in a world plentifully stocked with UK Subs and Motorhead shirts, who in their right mind would choose to walk around with Vice Squad emblazoned on their chest? All the same, it was somehow quite flattering to think of our ugly mugs on a t-shirt, so we agreed to get a couple of hundred run up. If we carted them around from gig to gig, surely we'd shift them eventually?

A photo from the Last Rockers 'posing outside Virgin' session was selected, and Dave proposed that a line from Resurrection, 'They tried to bury the legend, now it's time for the Resurrection' be used as the text. I mean, Pretentious? Moi? It worked well enough in the song, but I reckoned people would laugh their socks off at seeing it in cold screen-print. Dave, though, wisely argued that '20,000 people have bought our record and only a handful of them actually know us. Only the blokes in the pub know we're wankers really. The rest'll go for it, believe me.'

As usual, he was quite right, and as soon as they went on sale at a gig in, if I remember rightly, Malvern in March they sold like the proverbial hot cakes. Clearly this was a side of things that had to be considered seriously, as Simon recalls: 'We all sat down and had a meeting about what we needed to have, merchandise-wise. And in those days there was a lot of companies doing all sorts of stuff, like badges and hankies, and it was a real well-oiled machine 'cos of all the earlier punk stuff that had gone through from the first wave. And these people were still in business, you know, Better Badges, Acme Tee Shirts in Northampton etc.

'But merchandising was one of the most fantastic things. It was probably next to being you, playing onstage, to be behind that fucking table with literally hundreds of kids all going 'Whuurrgh! I want one of them! I want one of them!' and you just thought fuckin' 'ell, this is unbelievable!

'They bought everything, hankies, posters, badges, stickers, we did the lot didn't we?'

The fact that the merchandising went so well was pleasing not only from a financial point of view (though later it did dig us out of a few holes in that respect) but it also meant that Simon remained a part of the touring team.

The future of Riot City Records, though, was a little more complex. As I've already outlined, the label was a joint venture and was officially co-owned by Simon Edwards and Vice Squad. The fact that we could continue to use the name for our EMI/Zonophone releases was therefore never in question, but where the Specials/Two Tone comparison falls apart is that only Vice Squad were moving to Manchester Square, whereas Chrysalis had taken Two Tone wholesale.

Riot City was effectively split in two, with Vice Squad using the name for major label releases and Simon running a parallel label through the indie network for other bands. This didn't mark the end of our involvement with the label by any means, but it'll make life simpler if I return to the Riot City saga later in this missive.

With our signatures still drying on the contract, and wisely not wishing to lose any time after the success of Last Rockers and Resurrection, Ashley was keen to get us into the studio for an album as soon as possible. This wasn't a problem for us; we had easily enough material, and the sooner we got into Cave to record it the better.

Ian, though, had a cunning plan. He'd met a guy called Roger Wall, who owned a studio called The Facility in the Whitehall area of Bristol, which though spacious and well equipped, apparently came very cheap. We'd never heard of it, despite the fact that Whitehall is just down the road from Kingswood, and anyway, why not use Cave?

Now came the cunning part. Ian had worked out that the initial advance from EMI came to, more or less, exactly the amount of money that they had calculated it would cost us to record an album at Cave, which made sense. However, he argued that if we found a studio that could do the same job cheaper, we could come out with a modest profit.

Well aware that we couldn't have come up with Last Rockers or Resurrection without Andy or Bill's help, we were far from convinced, but Ian could be pretty persuasive when he put his mind to it, so we agreed to at least look at the studio and meet Roger. Mark recalls the fateful occasion: 'It was Tadd's idea, I blame him entirely. It looked like a proper studio, it was very well laid out, and I was fairly impressed with the look of the place. Bad idea.'

It was indeed, and as Simon remembers: 'The Facility was a joke in Bristol. It wasn't really the studio, it was the person on the desk that was the problem. Nothing against him personally, but it was just never renowned as a good studio to record in.'

Simon, I have to admit, made this abundantly clear at the time, but for some reason our brains seized-up and we were held in the snake-like hypnotic stare of a mad hippy. Well that's my excuse anyway.

The recording took place over a weekend in July, (the exact dates have been lost in the mists of time, naturally) and we moved the gear into The Facility on the Friday night to ensure an early start on the Saturday morning. We were a little disturbed to find Roger wandering around in what appeared to be his underwear, and vast amounts of pornography stacked on every available surface. Clearly he'd taken our name at face value, and he eyed Beki suggestively, apparently under the impression that his luck was in.

From the start, nothing sounded right. We'd run through a song, and it would sound okay through the cans or, for non-musos, headphones, but when we went into the control room to listen to the playback, it had a horrible trebly quality. Also, the guitar sound was appalling, but when we pointed these facts out to Ian and Roger they insisted that it would all be rectified in the mix. It was just, they reckoned, a different way of working than at Cave, and it would all turn out fine in the end.

Just how we swallowed that, especially with Simon making his opinion abundantly clear throughout the entire proceedings, I've no idea, but we did.

When the time came to record backing vocals, many old friends came in to help out, and they too voiced their concern at what they were hearing. Unbelievably, we actually quoted Ian and Roger's explanations to them verbatim, and they had little choice but to accept them.

On a happier note, this was the first time that Dave and I were re-united with our colleagues from the Spam/TV Brakes days on what could be, loosely, described as a musical project. Ian Minter, H, and Al Rees were all present and correct, and this seems as good a time as any to give you a brief rundown on their later musical activities.

On leaving the TV Brakes, H had formed a band called Cold, with guitarist/singer/songwriter Lucy Hunt, and played many gigs, though as H remembers: 'I think the highlight of our career was the Marshall Rooms at Stroud, supporting UK Decay. We made a couple of demo tapes, which everybody liked but nobody would do anything about.'

Apart from two spells with drummers Simon Bogle and Mark Ernest, I ended up playing drums for Cold quite often, which I really enjoyed. H and Lucy's material was a lot more complex than ours, so it was a bit of a challenge. I also played on two of their demos (Mark played on the other one) and was disappointed when the only response we got was a play on Radio Bristol and an interview with H and Lucy in Out West, the local listings magazine (the one that gave the 'taciturn and cynical' quote I used earlier). It was brilliant stuff, and I really didn't see how they could miss. Happily, when the tracks were released as a download album called *At The End Of The Hallway* by the fabulous Bristol Archive Records label in 2010 it became one of their best sellers. Fame at last!

But sadly, back then, it wasn't to be, and when Cold folded, H decided it was time to move on, as he recalls: 'Then I moved to London and joined the Reptosexuals, which was Keith from the Groove's new band, for a while, which was pretty dreadful really. We managed to play the Marquee and the Half Moon, Herne Hill, and the Rock Garden, all these places I'd heard of. I'll say one thing for Keith, he was good at getting gigs, considering how bad we were.'

There I feel H is being a trifle modest. Rough around the edges the Reptosexuals may have been, not to mention a mite eccentric, but I had a great night watching them at a gig at the Oval pub in Kennington. Keith was always an endearing front man (and to be honest, front was all he had, but he had it in buckets) while, as in the Groove days, H was the perfect foil for him.

H later joined what can only be described as a biker covers band, which again came to nothing, but he always remained, to a greater or lesser degree depending on the prevailing circumstances, a part of the Vice Squad team.

I recently asked him what he thought of what we did as Vice Squad, which I've always looked upon as an extension of what we started together as the Spam/TV Brakes. Here's his reply: 'I liked most of what you did to be honest, and I think if I'd still been in it at that point I'd have been happy to stay...I liked a lot of the songs.

'I always tell people, if they ask, that I used to be in a band called Vice Squad, who I left because I didn't think they'd do anything, and six months later they were touring America.' Which sums up my memory of it really.

'I don't regret it really, I've enjoyed all the bands I've been in since. At the time I was very aware of all the internal squabblings, nothing's ever as good as it looks from the outside. So no, I don't think I regret it, my life's gone the way it's gone and I'm quite happy with it now.'

Ian, as we've already seen, went on to form the Pus Trams with a group of friends from Kingsfield School, and later 'I had another group called the TV Brakes, that Dave came to see. That was probably the most musical thing I've ever done. That was about 1981/82 sort of time, but that all split up when the others all went to college and stuff.'

After getting married, he, like H, had moved to London, and worked under various names, though sadly with little success.

Looking back on the original TV Brakes, and his decision to leave, Ian now says: 'I've always regretted it. It was drugs I suppose, and depression at people's attitudes. At some of the gigs we went to see, loads of people would turn up, and it was just the Bristol National Front turning up all the time. So it just ruined it, 'cos they'd just shout at the band and start fights and things.'

On the subject of the first Vice Squad album, Ian sums up what most of our friends were trying to tell us: 'As regards to what I thought about Beki coming in and your musical direction, I just felt really pissed off that you couldn't get a really good producer and a really good studio to record things in, that's the main thing that's stuck in my mind.'

By now, Al Rees had given up any hopes of a career in music, and was at college in Liverpool. Luckily, he happened to be on a home visit, and was therefore able to join us. He'd also been back in Bristol in February, and I suppose I should have worked in this quote back in chapter five, but if it's all the same to you, we'll do it here: 'I went off to college with nice tidy hair, and as most people do when they get away from their parents' influence, I did what I wanted, which was to get it all cropped off. When I got back you all said 'Brilliant, we're going up to London this weekend, you'd better come with us.' You were supporting the 4-Skins, so you thought 'At least we've got one skin among us, we might get out alive.''

Incidentally, the photo of a rather shy looking skinhead on the back of the Resurrection sleeve is Al in his brief period under that guise.

Once all the backing-tracks, vocals, over-dubs and backing vocals were completed, we went into The Facility, as it says on the cover of the album, for the mix '...on the day of the Royal Wedding because there was nothing better to do.' Which with hindsight was quite appropriate, as the betrothal of Chuck and Di, like our album, also turned out to be a bit of shambles.

We listened keenly for the magical transformation promised by Roger and Ian that the mixing process was going to cast over what had, until now, sounded a right bloody mess. And of course, it still sounded a right bloody mess.

In desperation, we tried to pep it up a bit by opening the album with the Manchester Mayflower Club faithful doing a chant of 'Vice Squad! Vice Squad!' that Mandy had recorded on a portable cassette player at a gig there, and bunging a few end-of-the-world type sound effects on the end of Last Rockers to close it, but frankly, we were just pissing in the wind.

Not a lot got past the razor-sharp intellects of Roger and Ian, and it eventually dawned on them that perhaps we were a little unhappy with what so far passed as our debut album. It seemed to us that Roger's only useful contributions to the proceedings had been coming up with a name for the album, *No Cause For Concern*, which in itself had a touch of irony, and was nicked from a Margaret Thatcher speech anyway, plus plentiful supplies of porn.

Clearly, the peasants were revolting, and here Ian pulled a stroke that to this day I just cannot believe we fell for. The answer, he now said, was not in the mix but the cut. Admittedly it sounded a little ropey now, he said, but all would be resolved at the cutting stage, where astounding transformations could be performed, and these recordings had been specially prepared with these in mind. It would be brilliant in the end, honest.

As you can imagine, we were still far from convinced, but in his way Ian was pretty canny and quickly pushed the matter aside by making the sleeve artwork top of the agenda.

In another canny move, and the more I write about Ian, the more I have to grudgingly admire his nerve, he enquired whether any of us happened to know any professional artists. Of course, we didn't, and it just so happened that Ian's father was just such a creature. Now there's a thing.

I think Tadd Snr was actually an artist in the building trade, doing those rough artist's impressions of how a proposed architectural monstrosity might look in the hands of skilled and sensitive workmen, rather than the abominations that you see around you. Anyway, we knew no other artists, other than the alcoholic variety, so we went for it.

We met Mr Tadd at his home, and spent a very pleasant evening with him and his equally charming wife, looking at sketches of tower blocks and housing estates. These were, of course, entirely irrelevant to the project under discussion, but we were too polite to mention the fact, and he was duly commissioned to come up with a riot scene for the front of the sleeve and a policeman or soldier in combat dress for the back.

The finished artwork, though hardly stunning, was at least adequate, and it was despatched to EMI along with the master-tapes of the album. At this point, EMI, having heard the tapes would, under the terms of the contract, have been quite at liberty to turn them down, but to our surprise they accepted them without a murmur. Simon, who had been unhappy about the project from the start, now says: 'EMI have got to take responsibility for putting the fucking thing out. They should have said no, that's crap, go out and do it again. All the playing was alright, it was the production, the way it was recorded. It just needed to be reworked, which is very sad...it was one of the saddest points of my being in music, really...it was just...shit!'

It's nice of Simon to shift the blame like that, and I accept that EMI could have stepped in and sorted out the sorry mess, but it was we who insisted that EMI had no involvement in the recording, and we who allowed Ian and Roger to walk all over us. Being a stiff-upper-lipped Englishman, I tend to side with Mark when he says that, at the end of the day, Brian, 'It was mostly our fault, however you look at it.'

Though hearing the finished product appeared not to put EMI off us totally, it did calm their ardour somewhat, and the release date was put off until October, which suited us just fine. If they could have made it October 2050, all the better.

In the meantime, we were shown around our new home-from-home, EMI Headquarters, in Manchester Square, West London, and introduced to numerous employees, including our newly appointed Press Officer (impressive, eh!) Suzy Rome, who also worked with another up-and-coming outfit, from Birmingham, called Duran Duran. Huh, stupid bloody name or what?

Hands were shaken, and backs were slapped, and we were then taken to Ashley's office, which we were delighted to discover contained a fridge full of Heineken. Obviously, this was going to be a regular stop-off point whenever we were playing in London.

We were also amused to find every available surface stacked with carrier bags full of Dennis Waterman singles, which EMI must have been hyping at the time, and a copy of our own demo tape from a couple of years before that no-one had ever bothered to listen to. Alright, no-one in their right mind would have signed us on the strength of that, and they'd got us for £2,500 anyway, but we couldn't resist teasing Ashley that, at that time, he could have had us for nothing. Jesus, we'd have paid him!

Everyone we met at EMI was courteous and apparently anxious to help, but they couldn't hide the fact that they had no more idea of what we were actually doing there than we had. This was a massive corporation, all geared up to furthering the careers of Queen, Cliff Richard, and um, Bow Wow Wow. Not to mention that Erika bird that used to get her tits out at rugby matches. Yes, they even signed her up, a sure sign of desperation which went some way to explaining our welcome to the fold.

Once we'd visited Manchester Square a few times, and the novelty had worn off, it became apparent that the only real friends we had at EMI were Ashley, Suzy and some blokes from the legal department who seemed just as isolated as us. Though we had little to do with them business-wise, we used to drink with them in the Jolly Tobbold pub around the corner.

Suzy was a gem, and I was being a little glib when I dismissed her other charges, Duran Duran, in so cavalier a fashion just now, because they had already begun to have considerable success. In February, the single Planet Earth had reached No.12 in the charts, though in May Careless Memories had only reached a disappointing, in comparison, No.37. They bounced back in June, when their eponymous debut album reached the giddy heights of No.3, and by the time we showed up The Duranies, as *Smash Hits* had taken to calling them, had just reached No.5 with the single Girls On Film.

So, though we never got to meet Freddie, Bryan, Roger, the other one from Queen, or Cliff, through Suzy we were now hob-nobbing with the stars. Yes, many's the time Simon Le Bon nodded to me from the other end of the Jolly Tobbold bar, and one day I'll regale my grandchildren with tales of the magical conversations I had with the Superstars Of The New Romantics. One in particular sticks in the mind. Probably with the intention of scrounging a fag or something, I was strolling around Manchester Square looking for Beki. I stuck my head around the door of the video viewing room to find Simon and co. giving their latest bird-and-boat infested epic a once over. All casual like, I said 'Ello boys, seen Beki anywhere?' and one of them said 'Yeah, she was down by the coffee machine just now.' Really, you can't buy memories like that, now can you?

The fact that Suzy was given the task of looking after our press while also handling probably the hottest band of the moment was certainly no accident. I've long imagined the following conversation:

Music Press Journo: 'Hi, Suzy, it's Julian from Ramalamapopcrapweekly. We could really use a Duran Duran interview. You did promise!'

Suzy: 'Hi Julian, sorry I didn't get back to you, but after Girls On Film, things have gone really crazy, you know?'

Music Press Journo: 'Fair enough, but come on, when can I talk to them. I promised my editor and he's spitting blood.'

Suzy: 'Oh, this is really awkward Julian, the boys are so busy just now, I just don't know where I can fit you in. Oh, and by the way, did you give any thought to doing that piece on Vice Squad we talked about? This New Punk thing's really gonna happen you know.'

Music Press Journo: 'Oh…okay…I'll talk to the gits.'

Suzy: 'Hey, whadayaknow, I had you pencilled in for lunch with Simon next Tuesday all the time!'

Of course, we had our own contacts in the music press, thank you very much (well, all one of him) but thanks to Suzy, we began to see ourselves in practically every paper and magazine going.

On 15 August, Ms Beki Bondage graced the front cover of *Sounds* on the occasion of our second interview for said paper, this time conducted by Bushell himself. The interview took place on 1 August at the Mayflower, on Birch Street in Manchester, and Bushell attended our matinee performance.

This was the second time we'd played the Mayflower, and in case you're thinking that there was something a little strange about the likes of us playing a matinee, you could be forgiven. The first time we'd played the venue on 6 June, we'd assumed that the promoter was on a fast track to the loony-bin when he insisted on our putting on an afternoon performance for the local juveniles. In our neck of the woods, no-one under the age of 16 was the slightest bit interested in anything outside the Top 30, and we assumed that the spotty oiks of Central Manchester would follow a similar pattern.

As it turned out, we couldn't have been more wrong. When the doors were flung open, the place was immediately flooded with sprogs of every description who proceeded to strip Simon's merchandise stall bare in a matter of minutes. All in all, they were a fantastic audience, full of enthusiasm and lacking the cynicism of their elders.

On day of the interview, for reasons lost in the mists of time, Ian and Igor took the gear to Manchester in a hire-van, me and Dave travelled in Simon's Volvo, while Beki, Mark and Bambi made their own way oop north in the latest death-trap that Bambi was pleased to call a car.

This plan was not one that could be classed as an unqualified success. Simon, Dave and my good self arrived at the venue to find numerous punks and skins milling around, and as the promoter himself was among those present, we assumed that all must have been well. This was not the case however. Promoter he may have been, but the owners of the Mayflower hadn't seen fit to issue the oaf with keys, so we just had to wait for one of their chosen representatives to show up. Garry Bushell and photographer Kevin Cummins turned up not long after we did and hot on their heels, Igor, Ian and the gear also put in an appearance. So far, so good. It was a pleasant summer's day, so for a while we were content to join the afore-mentioned punks and skins in their milling around on the grass outside the venue.

As time marched on, with no sign of the key-bearer or the rest of our entourage, a little uneasiness began to creep in. It was also a mite embarrassing, with these Big City Folk tut-tutting and looking at their watches every five seconds with increasing exasperation. By the time some lackey finally showed up with the keys the promoter had been exposed to some pretty ripe abuse (in the article Bushell, in a fit of pique, dubbed him 'Rudolph The Red Nosed Promoter' after observing his boozer's conk) we were much relieved. The gear was moved in pronto, and considering the fact that we had also shipped Ian's entire PA system up from Bristol rather than using a local firm, the whole setting-up process was completed in a pretty impressive time.

This was just as well, as obviously we were anxious to impress the Big City Folk with our professionalism. There had been precious little in the professionalism stakes thus far, so when talking to Garry and Kevin we made much of our road crew's performance, and they had to admit that Ian and Igor were definitely hot stuff, especially being a man short.

The fact that Bambi had been neither toting his barge nor lifting his bale with his fellow road crew members had more significance than the increase in their work-load, however. If you have been following this story closely, you will remember that Bambi had been allocated the task of transporting Beki and Mark to the gig, and here, as the saying goes, it all went pear-shaped.

Mark takes up the story: 'Beki and I came up with Bambi in his pink 3-Litre Capri, which blew up at Knutsford Services, blew a gasket, steam everywhere. We had a matinee to do, so we rang the venue and Simon came out to get us, which took ages.'

It did indeed, and the half-hearted show of contrition that the promoter had been giving due to his earlier lack of foresight quickly evaporated when he realised that we only had half a band. He joined Bushell and Cummins in the tut-tutting corner until, to our relief, the others finally showed up. Our relief was short-lived, however, when we clapped eyes on the bloody fool Mark. I'll let him attempt to explain what has always, for me, been a blemish on his otherwise spotless copybook: 'My family were away on holiday, and my sister had all this Adam & The Ants type stuff, including this big fluffy shirt with frills and laces, and I thought I'd borrow it for the night. She'd never know. I'd get it washed, ironed and back on a hanger; they weren't back for a week, lovely.

'I remember walking into the venue and it was rammed. It was all these kids under 16, and there were a lot of young kids, 8,9,10 year-olds. As I walked to the stage I took me jacket off, and you and Dave, your faces just said 'You bastard!' I played the gig, but no noise came out 'cos all the strappy bits off the sleeves got tangled up in the strings.'

But despite all the cock-ups, and Mark wandering around like a cross between a Duran Duran roadie and Barbara Cartland, the Mayflower Rug-Rats didn't let us down. We went down the proverbial storm, and it would have been a churlish Sounds Features Editor that could have reported otherwise.

After a hasty photo session with Kevin Cummins in the Mayflower dressing room, the interview itself took place in a nearby pub, as is nearly always the case, with journalists traditionally being second only to musicians in the alcoholism stakes. Throughout, Bushell mercilessly ripped the piss out of Mark for the stupid shirt, and while under normal circumstances we would have jumped to the defence of a fellow band-member, this was different. The berk was asking for it.

Apart from these exchanges, in a lengthy discussion which covered all the usual subject matter, I was impressed to observe that Bushell took down our comments in short-hand rather than using a tape recorder, though he now says that 'That wasn't short-hand. It was just a scrawl! I stopped using a tape recorder after interviewing the Skids. They were young; I think Jobbers was just 16, with really heavy accents. I understood them face to face but the resulting tape proved as hard to decipher as alien hieroglyphics. If a haggis could talk it would have sounded like Richard did back then.' I feel strangely disillusioned! Anyway, after the interview he caught an early train back to the Big Smoke, missing the evening show, but reading between the lines I gathered that we'd won him over and the finished article proved this to be the case.

Typically, for Garry, it began with a surreal fantasy scene:

> 'Yyyyeeeooowwwwwll!! Sorry if that's spelt wrong chums, but that's about the closest approximation I can get to the noise I'm sure I can hear emanating from mon gob, something approaching what experts would describe as an agonized scream of pure unrelenting pain.
>
> The reason for this strange outcry is almost certainly the rhino hide cat-'o-nine-tails eating into my stinging flesh like Buster Bloodvessel chomping into a three-quarter-pound Wendy Burger.
>
> The hand that holds the lash lifts up again as if to deliver another blow. I strain to break the ropes that bind me but they're too strong, the knots too tight.
>
> The face of my tormentor, Beki Bondage, the Vice Squad chanteuse (for it is she), twists into a sadistic smirk.
>
> "Now repeat after me," she orders. "Women are not inferior to men, men are inferior to women. Say it! Women are not inferior to men, would you like coffee or sandwiches, sir?"
>
> Do what?
>
> "Would you like coffee or sandwiches sir?"
>
> I blink the face above me back into focus and am more than a little surprised to see not Beki's mess of rainbow hair but a noble son of the desert bedecked in British Rail

uniform proffering a veritable cornucopia of cardboard sarnies in his sweaty palms. Not only that but close inspection of my shirt reveals not one speck of spilt red corpuscles, my flesh bears not one scar...

Bloody hell, these Rock Dreams have sure got a way of getting on top of a chap, 'specially on a long train journey up to Manchester for a Vice Squad gig at the Mayflower Club, and would you believe Desolation Row?'

'Noble son of the desert'? Jesus. I hadn't noticed that before. I wheeled that bit in to demonstrate the man's eloquence, but I suppose there we see the early stirrings of his later tabloid style already showing its face. Mind you, the fact that I obviously took no notice of it at the time and possibly had a little giggle at his wit doesn't reflect too well on me either, does it?

Bushell went on to give us the kind of write-up that most bands pray for:

'...the whole place is transformed into a pulsating pogo paradise with the breathless arrival of the AWOL Beki Bondage and bassist Mark Docile disguised as a Spandau Ballet roadie in a ridiculous frilly shirt. A quick coke and the band are up on stage launching into the sprightly bounce of their super-punk opener Still Dying to the instant approval of the rabid matinee audience.

I blink (again, - must be something wrong with me eyes) and double-take: this don't sound like the same band I saw supporting the 4-Skins at the New Punk Convention all them moons ago. There they'd been fun but they'd sounded maybe a touch old-fashioned and untogether. Now they're transformed, stronger, harder, tighter than the last pensions rise, totally explosive and all-together more convincing.

Skinny Shane Baldwin (as in Stanley) belies his pigeon-with-anorexia frame to hammer home the powerhouse drumming; Dave Bateman delivers the stinging six-string goods; Mark, well Mark, oh sod it I can't get over that shirt; while Beki is overflowing with confidence and good humour, dodging the gob, dancing, laughing and dominating the stage - a true star.'

Blimey. I had to live with that pigeon-with-anorexia crack for years afterwards though. Nevertheless, it would be a churlish *Sounds* Features Editor interviewee that had any complaints.

Incidentally, I'm happy to report that Mark got his just desserts for that Ridiculous Shirt Incident: 'The next Thursday morning I was tucked up in bed when my sister stomped in carrying a copy of Sounds, and there I am in her shirt. She wasn't at all impressed.' Assuming this to be the same sister that was in the habit of attacking our hapless bass player with sharpened gardening implements (that's another story, you'll have to take my word for it) his punishment was no doubt swift and brutal. Ha! If she'd invited Beki, Dave and myself around we'd have been there like a shot, wielding trowels, spades and scythes, eager to get stuck in. But she didn't. Some people have no consideration for others.

Still on the media front, a second Radio 1 session now beckoned. Though Peel was still our main man at Wunnerful Radio 1, we were quite surprised when Richard Skinner, who occupied the early evening slot, offered us a session on 9 August. These days, within reason, it's not unusual to hear an out of the ordinary single on daytime Radio 1 or a chart record late at night, but in the period under discussion here, the borders were pretty rigid. By day it was all chart fodder, and late at night, when all decent law-abiding folk slept the sleep of the good and deserving, the rampaging hordes were unleashed.

Richard Skinner had the thankless task of bridging the gap. He couldn't play anything too offensive as a lot of the daytime crowd were still listening in driving home from work, and to make matters worse, if Mandy and her mates were anything to go by, this was the time of day when all the students were most likely to tune in, whilst preparing themselves for all-night orgies of casual sex and drug-taking. So the poor bloke had to offend no one and be hip at the same time.

This was a problem that had dogged what the BBC planners called the 'in-fill' period since its relatively recent inception in autumn 1978. Previously Radio One had shut down at 7.30, then came back on for Peel at 10.00, and the new slot lurched from one identity crisis to another until producer Mike Hawkes took over in September 1980 to give what was now called the *Evening Show* some sense of stability. It was never easy though, as he recalls in Ken Garner's book *In Session Tonight*: 'Because of all the changes, the slot was barely established when I took over. Peel had a clear identity and a reputation built up over years. The *Evening Show* then didn't - it had already had a variety of presenters, who didn't quite have the authority of Peel.'

The *Evening Show* eventually became an important show for up-and-coming bands in the 1980s, but as we recorded our session during its embryonic stage, at the time we regarded it as far less important than a Peel session. A Peel session was always the big one for any band, but as the breakfast show was never on the cards, the Evening Show, with its early evening slot, was the closest the likes of us were ever going to get to daytime exposure.

The session was recorded at Studio 4 in Maida Vale, North London, which you may remember was in the process of being computerised at the time of our Peel Session, hence our having to use the rather out-dated (but perfectly functional, if you ask me - we'll come to that later) Langham House on that occasion.

But for all my Luddite leanings, I couldn't help being impressed by Maida Vale. I know about as much about architecture as your average town planner, but even I could see that the building's beautifully ornate exterior had been carefully preserved by the BBC, which endeared me to them more than a little. Once inside, though, it was like taking a stroll through Dr Who's Tardis, in more ways than one. Firstly, they'd taken the computerised business as far as it was humanly possible in those days, to the extent that you were afraid to take a crap in case the bowl measured your excreta, diagnosed its contents, and gave you a printed readout. Secondly, once the gear was loaded in and the backroom boys were doing their stuff, I decided to explore the place. After I'd given a few broom-cupboards a thorough once-over (computers can't do everything, even now) I peered through another door and assumed that I must indeed have found the home of the late William Hartnell. Imagine it: one pokey little room, another pokey little room, another pokey little room, then BAM! The interior of the Royal Albert Hall. It turned out to be the room where all the classical stuff for BBC Radio 3 was recorded, and that's why they needed so much space, but I'm not kidding you, it was huge, and looking at the outside of Maida Vale you wouldn't have believed the building capable of housing such a monster. After all those broom cupboards, it fair shook me, I can tell you.

Back in Studio 4, we met the engineer, Mike Engles, who was kind enough to talk us through all the new-fangled technology (though to be honest, he might as well have been talking in some particularly obscure Japanese dialect for all the sense we could make of it) before introducing us to producer. He seemed a nice enough bloke, but after we'd run through a few numbers he'd apparently heard enough and disappeared for most of the day leaving Mike to guide us through the donkey work. The most likely explanation for this is that he just thought we were pretty crap, and if that was the case then fair enough, but it was disappointing as we'd recognised him as Dale 'Buffin' Griffin, drummer with the mighty Mott The Hoople. Still, we were pleased that we'd managed to refrain from tugging our fore-locks and saying 'Fuck me! You played drums on All The Young Dudes...we are not worthy! etc.'

However, even if he had shown more of an interest, I'm inclined to doubt that the session would have been any more satisfactory. The fact is that this was by far the worst session of the four we eventually made for the BBC, but I always tend to put it down to the fact that the staff were still coming to grips with all the new technology.

Sure, it was fun watching the pretty patterns on the monitors jump about in time to the music, as Mike whizzed around the space-age mixing desk apparently in full control of things, but with a sense of deja vu, we had to come to the conclusion that, for all his efforts, it sounded dreadful. After the No Cause debacle, his assertions that it would all come out okay in the mix left us unconvinced, but with the time constraints inherent with a BBC session there was nothing we could do.

Sure enough, when Buffin (which we never had the nerve to call him to his face) returned for the final mix, we listened with interest, and were less than impressed. A horrible, muddy guitar sound swamped everything else, and the vocals, bass, and drums, when audible, sounded like they were recorded in a cheap four-track studio. All-in-all, it amounted to a right bloody mess.

The five songs, Living On Dreams, Evil, Coward, Still Dying and Resurrection, were first broadcast on 21 August, and it may say something about my social life at the time when I reveal that, like the earlier Peel Session, I listened to it in my bedroom. After Still Dying, (the last line of which, incidentally, was changed from 'We're not fucking dying' to 'We're not Simon Edwards,' presumably because you can't say 'fuck' on the BBC unless you're on an arty programme on Radio 4) Skinner read out the following: '...we're playing all their session tracks tonight for the Sex Aids, the Vice Squad Road Crew, all the groupies that follow the band, the crusty Bristol punks, especially the two Bambies, and the, quote, incredibly beautiforous Igor...say no more!' Igor goes on about that last bit to this day, but personally I doubt the existence of any such word as 'beautiforous.'

Skinner seemed pretty bemused by the session, but battled on gamely, mustering all the enthusiasm he could, and at the end read out a lengthy list of forthcoming gigs and releases, almost none of which actually took place, but that was hardly his fault.

Thanks to all this media exposure, the gigs began to come in thick and fast (by our standards, anyway), and we moved into a period of playing a lot of venues that would soon become old favourites for the first time.

On 10 August Vice Squad graced the stage of Bristol's famous - or perhaps infamous is nearer the mark - Granary Club. The Granary was a former, erm, Granary, and donning my anorak once again, I can tell you that during the sixties and seventies practically every rock luminary that drew breath played there. We're talking about the likes of Jimi Hendrix, the Who, Led Zeppelin and Thin Lizzy.

The Granary's manager, Les, was a real character, and though that word has been bandied around to the extent that much of its meaning has become lost, here we are dealing with the genuine article. A large, robust man, ruddy of cheek and loud of voice (come to think of it, he'd have got on well with Old Ron at the Swan, but I suppose they moved in different circles) Les ruled his little empire with a rod of iron. He was quick to see the potential of the New Punk, as Bushell would have it, and booked early gigs by the likes of the Cockney Rejects, the Business, Infa Riot and the Exploited. As we were the local exponents of the stuff, he moved in on us smartish and we played his club regularly. I got quite friendly with Les, but it soon became clear that no matter how attentive he appeared to be during conversations, he was never actually listening to a word you were saying. And in case you're wondering if he just tended to glaze over when confronted with my less than arresting personality, I can assure you that he was the same with everyone. On one occasion, my mother turned up at one our gigs, said hello to Les, who she had met several times before, and stated her business, ie 'Hello Les, I've come to see my boy and I should be on the guest list.' Les nodded sagely, apparently devouring her every word, then led her into his office and interviewed her for the post of barmaid that he'd been advertising. When mother pointed out his faux pas (bit of French, classy eh?), he didn't turn a hair and offered her the job anyway.

This lack of communication with Les made negotiations extremely hard work, and though I liked playing there I dreaded the end of the evening, when I would have long and rambling conversations with him, forever trying to drag him back to the all-important topic of our fee.

The 100 Club at, funnily enough, 100 Oxford Street in London was our next new adventure, and, of course, in punk circles, this place was legendary.

It had begun as a traditional jazz venue in the 1940s, under many names including the Feldman Jazz Club and Jazz Shows, before changing its name to the 100 Club in 1964 and opening up to a wider range of bands to pay the bills. It remained jazz based, but the likes of the Who and the Animals played early gigs there and it became a renowned launching pad for all manner of dreadful hairy gits who would go on to stadium super-stardom.

Roger Horton, who had taken over the ailing Jazz Shows and changed both its name and booking policy, though only with the aim of keeping as much jazz as possible at the venue, was quick to see the potential of punk. In the Radio 2 documentary *100 Not Out*, he says: 'I was at the forefront of the emergence of punk music, and we decided we would stage the first punk festival. This was in August 76. We put on a three day festival running three days, and afternoons, I think. The emergent punk bands were the Sex Pistols, the Clash, the Damned... I've got to be honest and say I found the music to be absolutely horrific... but the emergence of punk was enormously colourful. The club was packed every night we put it on, with young people. We know they had shaven heads, we know they dyed their hair green, we know they had safety pins dangling out of their ears, and all the punk paraphernalia. But the thing is, that it was no different than any other music cult that we've seen over the years. Even going back to the trad boom, it was a case of young people dressing up, except in those days the dress was long sweaters and beards and duffel coats. It was just another facet of young people's music and there have been other facets since, and there always will be. The punk thing, it paid the rent at the time. I didn't like it personally, but it kept me going through part of the 70s, which were tough years for promoting jazz, very tough indeed.'

By the 80s, the 100 Club was operating along the same lines, still a major jazz venue but on other nights quite happy to book any band that could pull a crowd, punks welcome.

We first played there on 1 September, our minds full of all the stories we'd heard, mostly apocryphal, no doubt, of the famous '76 punk festival. You know, the one where Sid Vicious gobbed at Rat Scabies, who promptly invented the pogo and trod on someone's foot who then thrashed Nick Kent with a handy bike-chain and bumped into a member of the audience who stabbed a pillar in the eye with a glass thrown by Captain Sensible. Or something like that.

To us, this was the stuff of legend, fuck George Melly and Kenny Ball. In the early days the 100 Club had apparently been a rather dingy basement, but by 1981...it still was. We dragged our gear down the steps into the gloom, or more likely stood by and laughed at Igor and Bambi dragging it, then surveyed our surroundings. For a start there were no dressing rooms. Two minutes in the Big Time and we were already prima donnas (bit of Italian, classy, eh?).

We were brought to earth pretty sharpish. Our enquiries after the whereabouts of the dressing rooms caused the bar-staff to grin and roll their eyeballs toward the ceiling, and when we mentioned the rider they dissolved into helpless laughter. They poured us each a half of bitter, warned us not to ask for another, and told us we could get changed in a broom cupboard. It didn't even have a door on it.

Another problem was that the stage was dominated by a rather large piano, obviously there for the use of the jazz merchants. We asked if there was any chance of it being moved, and were told in no uncertain terms to 'Fuck off!' When we played the club at a later date, we were flattered to turn up and find the piano moved and the stage bedecked in red carpet, until we learned that the Rolling Stones had played a secret gig there the night before. Next time it was all back to normal.

We were supported by the Dark, which, as Mark remembers, caused us no little disquiet: 'When we played at the Granary, the DJ put this record on and Dave and I walked upstairs, leant over and asked, 'What was that record you just played?' He said 'It's Einstein's Brain by the Dark.' So when we get to the 100 Club and the Dark are supporting, sheer terror! 'Cos they were from Islington and we were playing the 100 Club and everyone there is going to be there to see the Dark and they're all going to walk out as soon as they finish. In my eyes, you know, it was going to be a complete and utter nightmare. The Dark were very, very good, but luckily people didn't go home straight after and we went down pretty well, it turned out to be a really good gig.'

They were indeed very good and I watched their set as the punters began to file in. Before long, the place was pretty packed, and getting quite warm. By the time the Dark finished, the place was really packed, and the atmosphere almost unbearable. Because it was a basement, there was simply nowhere for the heat to escape.

By the time we went on, it was almost impossible to breath, a problem made worse by the fact that, as Mark said, we went down very well. Normally, of course, this was a Good Thing, but all those pogoing lunatics were consuming oxygen and generating heat. Bad Thing. Being a totally untrained drummer, my technique was all over the shop and as a consequence I could sweat off several stone in rehearsals. In this atmosphere I was in danger of wasting away altogether. We later played hotter venues, and I sort of got used to it (at least when I bought an industrial-sized fan out of band funds) but this first time I found it difficult to cope. By the last number I was drenched in sweat and struggling to keep up. There was absolutely no fucking way I was doing an encore.

Of course, I had no choice, not wanting to look like a big girlie, and I somehow managed a couple more numbers before virtually passing out over Simon's merchandise stand. It was at this point that I resolved to jog to work and back every day. And make Igor buy me a fan. A big one.

Despite its drawbacks, we became fond of the 100 Club and played there often, though Dave reckons it was never quite the same after the first sweat-sodden experience: 'The first time we played there we were the best thing since sliced bread and the second time we were old hat. To the same people. In London, I always had the impression that people had somewhere better to go to later, which of course they often did.'

On a purely gratuitous note, I remember one 100 Club gig when Igor came rushing up to me, full of indignation, to report that two girls had been giving blow-jobs in the toilets for 50p. I agreed that this was hardly the sort of thing we wanted happening at our gigs, particularly given the name of the band. The music press would have had a field day. He soon put me straight: 'Nah, you twat, they'd finished before I got there!' You had to love him.

Vice Squad's first foray into Yorkshire, a county that really seemed to take to us in a big way, was at Sheffield Marples on 14 September. Marples was a big pub in the centre of the town that put on bands on its first floor. As usual, the gear went up during the day and the band were picked up from work in Simon's Volvo.

We arrived at around 8.00 and made straight for the bar, of course. Dave describes the sight that met our eyes: 'Three quarters of the audience were women, three quarters of the women were well shaggable, totally unheard of in punk rock circles in those days, and the quarter of the audience that were blokes all looked like undernourished rodents or reptiles. To my mind it was heaven.' One track mind that bloke.

His day was really made when we went into the venue proper to take a look at the local support band, Debar. They were, to be honest, pretty awful, but they had one redeeming feature. They were all girls. We got to know Debar quite well, some of us more than others, and soon found out that they had something of a reputation for their, erm, friendliness, to visiting male band members. Rumour had it that one of them had given Captain Sensible a dose of what was then called 'The Clap.' How we laughed.

Upstairs at Marples turned out to be another sweat-box, and a few songs into the set I was grateful that Igor, with his native cunning and ingenuity, had had the sense to place the drums somewhat off stage-centre, next to an open window. It was still unbearably hot, but at least I could gulp down a few breaths of fresh air between numbers.

Though we'd only been in the county for a few hours, we'd found the locals to be friendly (in the normal sense of the word - the other would come later), and helpful. They seemed eager to please, and around halfway through our set, seeing that we were suffering a little from the heat, they kindly came to our aid by slinging pints of beer at us. In keeping with the Yorkshire stereotype, when it dawned on them that ale costs money, they switched to slinging pints of water.

As we were going down very well, we could only assume that this was their way of showing their appreciation. It was certainly more sanitary than gobbing. After a while, though, the sheer volume of liquid being propelled stage-ward became a bit of a problem. Being struck in the face with a full pint of water does, it must be admitted, have a certain refreshing quality, but as the stuff was arriving by the gallon and we were surrounded by electrical equipment, there was also an element of danger.

But help was at hand, as Dave, dripping with sarcasm, remembers: 'When we came off our manager was ashen-faced, shell-shocked, having just bridged himself on a 240 Volt mains and formed a human chain between one bit of live and another bit, otherwise all the mic stands and everything else would have gone live and we'd have died. But he took the belt for about forty minutes, as, funnily enough, no other human being on earth would be able to do. I forget what the end result of that was, but I'm sure it cost us a lot of money.'

On 14 September we made our first visit to the Porterhouse, in Retford, which became known as both the Swealterhouse and the Slaughterhouse, due to the intense heat and occasional outbreaks of violence.

The Porterhouse was a three storey building, with a pub on the first floor, a disco on the second and gigs on the third. It was quite a plush venue, really, the sort of place that in a major city wouldn't have dreamed of putting on the likes of us, but as Retford is somewhat off the beaten track they relied on punters from the surrounding areas and booked anyone capable of pulling a crowd. The toilets seemed to get trashed with stunning regularity, but obviously they did their sums and considered it worth the extra expense.

The main disadvantages from our point of view were that, firstly, being above both a pub and a disco, the top floor was always steaming hot regardless of the time of year, and secondly that as the owners had a full club licence they weren't about to let the punters go until they'd shed their last drop of beer money.

What this boiled down to was that the main band wasn't allowed to take to the stage until 1.00am. This was a little awkward, as Dave recalls: 'We were known to drink a bit in those days, but it was impossible to drink until you were due on because you wouldn't have been able to get on the stage. The punters were still there, though, and bearing in mind that Retford is in the middle of bloody nowhere, God knows where they were going on to. They must have slept in bus shelters or something. There was usually a good atmosphere, a good gig, very hot and sweaty, and the only place where we all managed a shag in the dressing room, on separate occasions, or quite a lot of the time on the same occasions. We were going to erect a plaque, but we never got around to it.'

He always drags things down to his own level, doesn't he? It's quite true though, and we always looked forward to playing the Slaughterhouse. Oh, you want details? Briefly, then, I got to know a girl from Grantham that worked in a pea-packing factory; Mark was caught with his trousers down, as it were, with a groupie that Igor dubbed Honey Bane, even though she looked nothing like her, Beki got friendly with Glynn from Chron Gen (more of that later) and Dave went through most of the female population of Lincolnshire. Satisfied? I'm sure Dave was, ffnarr, ffnarr

The next two Vice Squad gigs stick in the mind for no other reason than the fact that for the first time we were afforded the luxury of staying in an hotel.

We played at the Central Hall, Grimsby, on 3 October, 'Where the men were men, and so were the women,' as Dave ruefully remembers, and stayed in Cleethorpes before travelling down to Stevenage the next day.

As the AA had a department that booked hotels for its members, Simon was given the task of arranging one for us. For some reason no hotel in Grimsby took kindly to the idea of a punk band gracing their premises, so after the gig we drove down to one in Cleethorpes that had proved more accommodating, fully intending to sample the heady nightlife of that glittering seaside resort.

It was quite a novelty to play so far from home and not have to drive straight back afterwards, so we quickly checked into the hotel, had a wash and brush-up and set out to paint the town red.

By now the pubs were all closed and most of Cleethorpes seemed to have followed suit, but eventually we found a rather gaudy looking nightclub and made our way to the door. Then, as now, it was a matter of routine for the penguins on the door to search people on the way in for offensive weapons, and dressed as we were, we knew that our ritual humiliation would be more thorough than most. We were used to that though, and as we were all clean as the driven snow, we just wanted to get it over with and head for the bar. The routine over with, much to their obvious frustration, the doormen had to concede that there was no reason not to let us in. They were on the point of doing so when one particularly eagle-eyed and vindictive penguin glanced at Dave's Doc Martens. He noticed that the toes rose slightly at the front and stamped on them hard. If our erstwhile fretboard wizard had had his wits about him and screamed, we might have got away with it, but he simply stared at the man with a puzzled and slightly hurt expression on his face. He had us. The penguin grinned widely and said 'Out chum, no steel toe-caps in here. Rule of the house.'

Back at the hotel, we had another wash and brush-up, Dave put on some carpet slippers which for reasons best known to himself happened to be the only other footwear he had with him, and back we went.

From steel toe-cap Doc Martens to cuddly carpet slippers; was there ever a more clear statement of peaceful intentions? We couldn't fail, surely.

By the time we got back to the club it was getting quite late, and we were gasping for a beer. We hauled up to the door and looked beseechingly at the bouncers. Mr Vindictive had a quick conference with his chums, gave us a kindly smile, and wandered over to us. He stopped in front of Dave, looked at his slippers, smiled even wider and said 'Sorry mate, you're improperly dressed for this establishment,' then burst out laughing.

Back at the hotel, we had another wash and brush-up, then went to bed. Rock 'n' Roll eh? At breakfast, we were all still feeling a little morose, and the hotel staff seemed to sense this, as Mark recalls: 'They were very nice to us at breakfast the next morning, we had to sign some napkins; they were actually mildly impressed that we were, like, pop stars and stuff. 'Cos nobody ever goes to Cleethorpes, do they?'

A little bucked by this fawning adulation, we headed down to the beach for a photo session with Simon, some of which were later used on various record sleeves and fan club newsletters. I forget which, but if you can see sand and people freezing to death, it's that session.

We checked out of the hotel, and roared down the drive in Simon's trusty Volvo, as the hotel staff no doubt asked each other 'Who the fuck were they anyway?' and chucked their napkins in the bin.

Onward and, well, downward really, geographically speaking, to Stevenage Bowes Lyon Hall. If I remember rightly, which is unlikely, the Bowes Lyon Hall was part of a community centre, but it certainly hosted many gigs at the time.

We were supported by Erazerhead, and a number of friends had made their way up from Bristol for the gig, including Dave's girlfriend, Jane. Igor, Bambi, Jane and myself had been dabbling in a side project called the Sex Aids for a few weeks, with Igor on vocals, Jane on guitar, Bambi on drums and yours truly on the bass. None of us could actually play our appointed instruments, but that was part of the fun.

In a fit of enthusiasm and unjustified ego, we decided to open the show, and had a hasty rehearsal in the dressing room. Hey, let's do the show right here! Right now! etc.

We went down like a lead balloon, which is unsurprising as we were crap, but I was more bothered by the unhealthy smell that Ian's PA was emitting. The Sex Aids crept off-stage to a deathly silence, and I hurried up to Ian to find out what was wrong, though I had my suspicions.

During the Vice Squad sound check it had become clear that Mark's bass stack had given up the ghost. We immediately assumed that the only option was to hire one for the night, but Ian, quivering at the thought of the cost, insisted that we could get away with putting the bass directly through the PA system. Though no technical wizard, it occurred to me that perhaps the PA couldn't cope with the extra punishment, hence the smell.

Whether through a misguided sense of loyalty to his beloved PA system, or a total inability to admit he was wrong is open to argument, but Ian was having none of it. The show had to go on.

During Erazerhead's set, the smell got worse, and other people began to voice their doubts, but it was to no avail.

Around three quarters of the way through our set, things came to a head. Just how we were received by the Stevenage faithful, I've no idea, as I spent most of time staring, bemused, at first the monitors on Mark's side of the stage, then various sections of the PA, as they began emitting billows of smoke. Hanham Abbots School all over again.

Ian started having kittens, as it were, and we had to draw the set to a hasty close with a version of Last Rockers that had a more apocalyptic feel to it than usual. If the audience felt a little short-changed by the briefness of the set, they seemed mollified by the spectacular special effects that we'd provided. Most of them thought it was all part of the show.

As Dave would no doubt put it, I forget what the end result of that episode was, but I'm sure it cost us a lot of money.

CHAPTER 7

IT WAS AT THIS POINT (have I used 'juncture' yet? Oh yes, so I have. Bugger) that a problem we had been putting off for some time appears to have come to a head.

As explained earlier, though signed to a major record label our position, financially, (yes, I know it's a dirty word, but one has to eat y'know) was less than secure and it had seemed prudent to carry on working as long as we could.

A glance at the list of gigs at the end of this book will show that we weren't playing, usually, more than two or three a week at this time, but the problem, as Simon explains, was that most of them were in the north: 'I used to drive you up to bloody Sheffield after work, I remember doing that a lot. At least twice a week we'd be travelling to some town Oop north, be it Hull, Middlesbrough, Sheffield or wherever, and I would be driving the band up. The lorry would go up separately and I'd pick all the members of the band up after work and we'd arrive about 7 or 8 o'clock. Often we never did soundchecks, we'd do the gig and then I'd drive back with a car full of fucking snoring punks. We'd get back to Bristol at about 3 or 4 in the morning and I was up again at 8 o'clock to go to work and of course this took its toll on me and I collapsed one day in the canteen at work. My doctor said I was suffering from exhaustion.'

The rest of us had had similar experiences of late, mine occurring after sitting in on drums with H's new band, Cold. Although I'd only just got back from one of Vice Squad's northern jaunts, and been to work, I didn't see how one more gig could do any harm, so I did it. When we came off-stage, several people commented that my skin had turned a rather nasty shade of grey, which I laughed off, but then a purple mist of the type described in fanciful Victorian novels came over me and I came as close as I ever have to passing out without the aid of alcohol. When I mentioned this to Dave and Mark, they admitted that after one of our Sheffield gigs they had both managed to clock in at Sun Life only to fall asleep in the toilets for the rest of the day. Only sympathetic workmates had saved them from the sack, and clearly this state of affairs couldn't continue.

We still had some misgivings though, as Mark recalls: 'I was very, very close to not doing it. I agonized for quite a long time. It was a difficult decision, because although Sun Life was a real no-head job, you could go in, do your time, go home again and it was easy money. The only thing that made me do it was... it's like doing the Lottery syndicate at work... it's not whether you win, it's that if all the other bastards win you've got to be there as well. If I'd have been sat in Sun Life and you were all around some pool in Hollywood... my fear was that you'd all be having much more fun than me!'

As far as I remember Beki, to her credit, had no misgivings at all and was keen to go for it from the off, but Dave, Igor and I had similar fears to Mark (it went without saying that if we 'went professional,' as it were, Igor would come with us on the same wage, being our erstwhile fifth member). Dave's situation was, of course, identical to Mark's, but like Igor, who was a civil servant, the chances were that if it all went horribly wrong they could all pick up the threads of their careers at a later date. The main pain in the arse, as usual, was yours truly.

By now I was about three years into a five year apprenticeship, and, basically, if I threw in the towel at this stage, that was it. My boss, Mike, was a good bloke, and his advice was 'Give it a go, get it out of your system, then come back and get on with the job,' which was more than fair of him.

I knew, though, that to properly fuck up a career in the music industry takes at least a year with major label backing, and though my absence was hardly likely to result in his business collapsing around him, he would have to fill my position long before then.

Also, according to Mike, the unions were making conditions so difficult for prospective employers that signwriting apprenticeships were now as rare as rocking-horse droppings, so if I went for it, there was no going back.

As if all this wasn't bad enough, I had to consider that my parents, who were old friends of Mike's, had pulled a few strings to get me the job in the first place.

In the end, Ian suggested that we have a formal meeting at our house to weigh up the pros and cons with my parents, which we did. To be honest, despite all of the above, I suppose I knew that there was no way I was going to back out. As far as I was concerned, this was my band; me and Dave were the founder members and I'd have died rather than see some other bastard at the drum stool.

I only admitted that to myself much later, after talking to Dave, who remembered the meeting thus: 'I think that we were already sort of halfway there weren't we? Because you were the only one with anything, really, to lose, I think that was semi-stage-managed. For the sake of you and your parents, it was laid out what was on offer and what wasn't.'
So I had, in fact, already made up my mind?

'That's what I mean by stage-managed. As much on your part as anybody else.'
What a crafty little git I was. I broke the news to Mike, and my guilt was assuaged to some extent when he said that my absence would only be really felt during a busy period immediately before Christmas, and if I could come back for a week then he'd be fine. On reflection he was probably only trying to make me feel better, but I did go back and was glad to do it.

Resigned to our fate, we chose Friday 16 October 1981 to 'go professional.' We'd chosen this date to for two reasons. Firstly we'd secured a support slot for 10 October at the Corn Exchange in Cambridge, which was easily the biggest venue we had ever played, making it, I suppose, noteworthy in itself. But secondly, the big deal for all of us was that we had been invited to support the mighty UK Subs on three dates of their current tour, with this being just the first. There being a whole week between the first gig and the second, we saw no reason to rush into things, but on the 16th we resolved to take the plunge.
It's easy, these days, with Charlie constantly playing the pub circuit, to forget just how big the Subs once were. They were a massive influence on all the punk bands of the period, and we practically worshipped them. We'd seen the original line-up of Harper/Garrett/Slack/Davies (alright, there were earlier line-ups, pedants, but that was the one that counted) many times and they were awesome.

That line-up had split back in June 1980, after recording the classic live album *Crash Course*, which ironically, turned out to be easily their best-selling album, reaching No.8 in the charts and earning them a gold disc.

Bassist Paul Slack and drummer Pete Davies were quickly replaced by Alvin Gibbs, formerly with the Users, and Steve Roberts, formerly with Cyanide, on bass and drums respectively, and the second classic line-up was born.

Before officially launching the new line-up at the Music Machine, in London, in August of that year, the band played a series of low-key 'secret' gigs, mostly in London pubs. On at least one occasion, however, they did stray a little further afield, and provided me with one of my fondest memories. If you'll allow me the indulgence, I'll share it with you.

Some eagle-eyed member of our clan had scanned the listings section of one of the local papers in the usually fruitless pursuit of finding something interesting to do at the weekend, other than drink ourselves stupid. He came across a curious advertisement for a charity event, apparently an annual affair, that was due to take place in a field behind a pub just outside Wells, Somerset.

Most of the acts appeared to be local amateur pop bands, but at the top of the bill, in letters no larger than the others, it said 'UK Subs.' Weird.

Numerous phone calls to friends in London were made, but they could neither confirm or deny that the Subs would be gracing this inauspicious event, so we decided to take a chance.

The gig was billed for the Saturday, and most people made their way into deepest Somerset that morning, but Mandy and I packed a tent into my trusty Ford Anglia and headed down on the Friday night. We found a place to pitch said tent, then went into the pub to find out if the Subs really were playing, and if so secure our tickets.

It was a quiet country hostelry, and the landlord looked us up and down, suspiciously, as we made our way to the bar. I bought a couple of drinks, then pointed at a poster on the wall advertising the following day's festivities, and asked, 'Have you really, like, got the UK Subs playing here tomorrow?' He consulted the poster. 'Yeah, that's them. Every year I phone this agency in London, and they get me a band that's been on *Top Of The Pops*. We mostly have local lads playing, y'know, but it's nice to have somebody who's been on the telly as well. As long as they come cheap, of course.'

It turned out that he hadn't the faintest idea of who the Subs were, but their agent had obviously sold him the gig on the fact that they were a chart band and had been on *TOTP* several times. As they were only playing warm-up gigs the fee was probably only minimal, and the landlord got a bargain. We chatted to him for a while and had a few more drinks, being careful not to alert him to the fact that he was shortly to be invaded by every punk and skin in the south-west of England and beyond, but as we, or at least I, staggered drunkenly in the direction of our tent, I could see he was beginning to have second thoughts.

As dawn broke the next morning a glorious sun rose to cast its majestic rays over the Somerset countryside, while birds rose chirping from their nests and butterflies flitted playfully from rosebud to bluebell. Well, I expect they did anyway, I was fast asleep at the time.

By the time we emerged from our tent and made our way to the pub, things were well underway, and the bar-staff were looking a little flustered. As predicted, the field beyond already showed a healthy turnout of punks and skins, with more arriving all the time, and the locals seemed more than a little perturbed.

The landlord seemed in two minds. It was barely midday and his pub was already rammed with thirsty punters, and to that extent he was quite happy; he just wished it was rammed with other thirsty punters.

When we finally got some drinks in, we made our way to the 'festival site' to gauge the mood of the crowd and it soon became clear that the landlord's misgivings were groundless. I wouldn't go so far as to say that known psychopaths were strolling the fields sniffing flowers and reciting poetry, but there was no doubt that the surroundings did seem to suffuse all assembled with an unnatural feeling of peace and tranquillity. Apart from the odd punch-up, of course.

As the day wore on, the locals eventually realised that they had nothing to fear from these weirdos and a great time was had by all.

Most of the bands, as the landlord had said, were local acts, but Demob turned up with their crew and, as usual, blagged their way onto the bill.

The Subs, never the types to play the pop star role, spent most of the day drinking with the great unwashed in the beer tent, and only returned to the backstage area when their set was imminent.

By the time they were due onstage, late in the evening, we were all full of anticipation and quite thrilled that we were to be among the first to see the new Subs line-up.

I forget if we had any qualms about two of our heroes being replaced by relative unknowns, but if we had, these were soon dispelled. Messrs Gibbs and Roberts were shit-hot and the whole band seemed anxious to prove that they were back and they meant business.

I've never seen a better UK Subs set, and believe me, I've seen a few. Gibbs and Garrett charged around the stage like men possessed, Roberts beat the shit out of his kit without missing a beat and Harper sounded like he was tearing his vocal chords to shreds. The crowd, as the cliché goes, went wild.

All too soon it was over, and for a couple of minutes we just stood there, slightly stunned. No doubt about it, the Subs were back alright.

Earlier in the day we'd met Charlie in the beer tent, and astonishingly, when I interviewed the Subs for a feature in *Record Collector* magazine in 2012, he remembered the fact: 'The first time I met you was at a little open air thing down in Devon. We got in a van down in Tooting Broadway and shunted all the way down to Devon somewhere. That's when me and Nicky crawled under the stage and got under the drum riser, and strained with all our might and tipped the drummer off the drum riser! Who was actually Steve Roberts, so that must have been 1980.

I remember having, not a picnic, but we had some beers, and Beki was lying on the grass with her boyfriend.' Okay, it was Somerset, not Dorset, but what a memory!

And when I asked him, the same went for Alvin: 'Yes, I recall that show too. I remember Nicky at one point disappearing before then coming up through stage from underneath it having kicked out one of the podium panels. He quickly reunited himself with his SG guitar and we went into a ramming speed version of Left For Dead. It was a good gig.'

When Mandy moved to London that September I'd fully intended, when visiting her, to see as many new bands as I could, but nine times out of ten we went to see the Subs at the Marquee, Lyceum, or the Music Machine. I just couldn't resist it.

Given the above, you can imagine how we felt when offered the chance to support them not only at Cambridge, but two further dates at Birmingham and Manchester. On top of the dates that we already had in our diary, it was these that forced the decision to quit work.

As much as we looked forward to the Cambridge gig we were, as usual, pretty nervous about it. Luckily we had no idea of just how large a venue the Corn Exchange actually was and, as far as I know, still is. We were just a bit twitchy about getting to meet the Subs properly. Looking at a photo taken by Simon from the back of the hall during our set it looks like we're playing a stadium gig of the type much bemoaned by Steve Jones before he started playing stadium gigs. It was fucking huge.

When we first arrived we just wandered around the back of the venue waiting for someone to come and tell us what to do, though no one seemed particularly bothered by our presence, or indeed keen to acknowledge it. Steve Roberts ambled by and said hello, which bucked me up no end, then Alvin Gibbs came over for a chat, which I thought was nice of him. Now that I'm old and cynical, the thought strikes me that they may have been trying to ascertain whether we had any legitimate business being where we were, or should be thrown out. I like to think not.

Our bona fides established, we were issued with passes and allowed backstage to meet the rest of the band. Charlie Harper, for all his vocal histrionics, was obviously a pussy cat, but Nicky Garrett seemed a pretty menacing character. He was a brilliant guitarist, but for him it seemed that a punk rock set was lacking a vital element if by the end something or someone wasn't severely damaged. Only recently I had seen a Subs show at the Marquee, where Nicky had spent the first half of the set dangling by his legs from a piece of scaffolding near the ceiling, before jumping down and trashing the drum-kit for no apparent reason. Mind you, I must admit that up until then, he hadn't missed a single note. It was with some trepidation, then, that we met the mad maestro of the six-string, as Mark recalls: 'I remember sitting around chatting to the Subs, and that was just all we'd ever wanted to do wasn't it? It was just like real hero worship. Nicky Garrett was, like, dangerous and we were a bit frightened of him. He was a lovely bloke, but I was a bit frightened of him.'

Elated at all this hobnobbing with the stars and pumping with adrenaline at the size of the audience, another that appeared to know all the words to all the songs, our set seemed to be over in no time at all. We had a few medicinal beers backstage, then headed back into the hall to see the Subs, who were rubbish. Only joking; they were brilliant, of course, and we couldn't wait for our next support slot on 16 October at Digbeth Civic Hall in Birmingham.

On the fateful day, and still with some misgivings, I washed up my brushes, packed up my gear, and said goodbye to the lads, for the time being anyway, before Simon picked me up from work for the last time. There wasn't a dry seat in the house.

Digbeth Civic Hall was another large venue, which took some filling, but Birmingham natives GBH were also on the bill, which meant that their large local following was also in attendance, and we even bumped into a small group of kids that we'd met at one of the Malvern gigs who insisted that they'd made the trip purely to lend us their moral and vocal support. If we had any doubts about this, we chose to ignore them and feel that we were adding the ticket money from, ooh, half a dozen punters to the promoter's coffers. Well, it was better than nothing.

We went on first, naturally, but went down extremely well from the start. So much so, in fact, that Steve Roberts, who was watching from the balcony, insisted that the lighting man turn on the aircraft lights that he used to illuminate the drum platform currently occupied by me. It was a kindly thought, and everyone I spoke to afterwards agreed that it looked great, but the things generated a fantastic amount of heat, and I limped off at the end with back and buttocks red raw. The man must have had the skin of a rhino to play in front of those every night.

The next gig, at Manchester Polytechnic, went even better thanks to the Mayflower crew, and we would have been feeling pretty pleased with ourselves but for one thing. Our debut album, *No Cause For Concern*, had finally been released and as predicted its reception could at best be described as luke-warm.

If most of our friends were too polite to give full vent to their feelings, an uncredited and undated clipping from one of the glossies, probably *Smash Hits*, sums up what most thought of the thing: 'Normally it would be cause for complaint if an album lasted barely half an hour; here one feels positively grateful. Basic isn't the word - badly recorded, 100mph ramalama power-chord chants with vocals from Beki ranting away in her padded cell down the corridor. It's like a cartoon parody of punk that makes you laugh at first but then simply irritates. (No points - just a Go Faster stripe).'

In *Sounds*, Garry Bushell had no choice but to inform his public that we'd delivered a turkey, but loyally fought our corner the best he could under the circumstances:

> 'What a waste. It's unbelievably annoying when a talented band make a debut album that sucks, especially when they're as strong a band as Vice Squad.
>
> Let's clarify that - the album sucks only in relation to how good an album I, and surely they, know they could make.
>
> Let's face it, many of the bands wrapped up in punk are pretty faceless, but Vice Squad are a genuinely notable exception.
>
> They've got character and flair, and they've got a fine selection of strong songs, yet on this record even their strongest numbers have to battle to overcome a real bland sound.

This is loose where it should be tight, the guitar is lost in the mix when it should be prominent, and generally the songs are sacrificed on the altar of studio lethargy.

Vice Squad owe it to their fans and to themselves to re-record all these numbers and give them away free at gigs.

If you're not a Vice Squad addict, don't judge them too severely by the monumental cock-up that filters through from the production right down to the lousy cover, they are capable of much more.

Are EMI to blame entirely? I'd like to hear the band's opinion. Sorry, this is nowhere near as good as it should have been.

Don't hit me Beki. Well, not in front of the wife, anyway.'

This was the important review, and as Mark says: 'It was better than I thought it would be, and probably better than we deserved. I remember L.A.M.F., the Heartbreakers album being mentioned quite a lot, because previously that had been the worst produced punk album ever, but I think we took the biscuit on that one.' Bushell even went so far as to give the album three stars, which counted as 'good.'

Recently, I asked him how he could be so kind as to bestow three stars on such a lousy album: 'You must be the first person who ever complained about getting a decent review!' he laughs. 'I guess I let my liking for the band over-power my critical faculties.'

The *NME* didn't even get around to reviewing *No Cause For Concern* until 2 January 1982, by which time it made no difference, but again we came off better than expected. Reviewer X. Moore, it seemed, had been following our careers with interest since the *Avon Calling* days, where he reckoned we had 'kicked some fury amongst the pile of neat, reserved pop toons.' He'd even heard us on the radio: 'When Peel played Coward at three minutes to midnight at the end of what must have been a Vice Squad session, it cheered me up, Beki's squawling vocals taking me back to Don't Dictate and focussing the guitar fuzz-blur.'

On the surface, this opening, which also mentioned our first gig '...supporting the mighty Crisis,' might have seemed encouraging, but the review also had severe doubts about us in particular and the continuation of punk in general. He continued:

> 'Most of it lives up to my expectations but one or two tracks are GOOD. Young Blood swaps drums for handclaps held high and I hear Sham, whilst Saturday Night Special frames teenage kicks Buzzcocks-style - GOOD.
>
> Floor toms thump, mounted toms roll, Evil pummels and pounds behind the drumkit. Buzzcocks meet Sham and lose - BAD.
>
> This is easy!
>
> Coward speeds-up and it's Beki's vocals that swing along the song again, 'specially when she sneers the punchline, "Easy to control", ('cept she punchlines the sneer: "E.Ze.Toucantro-ohl!") whereas Offering is Vice Squad messing up and messing in, guitar fuzz-stabbing sporadically against the unhealthy rhythm heartbeat at the close of

play - a number that is punk reduced to the four elements (you can join the dots/make the connections).

The rest? Vice Squad write seminal anthems, but with this production, they're just part of the haze.'

Though it stung at the time, I now enjoy reading that X. Moore, while listening to Sell-Out, was 'conjuring images of Vice Squad sat in EMI's offices pulling faces at The Clash 'cross the road at CBS.' He was quite right, of course, but with all the other nonsense surrounding the album, it had never occurred to us that including the song, especially with its drum intro that I'd blatantly nicked from the Clash's Tommy Gun, would amount to rank hypocrisy on a major label album. Still, you've got to laugh haven't you?

He concluded that: 'Vice Squad are nothing special, nothing extreme, no reason to drop your latest summer fashion (no reason for Oi! to be re-defined as anything but overwhelmingly flaccid) but listening to *No Cause For Concern* I remembered how good punk can be. 'Course I wanted to hate it and pretend the punk I had was more vital - what I want to know is who'll be playing punk for Phil and Joanne's kids?'

Not what you'd call a rave review, but like Bushell, X. Moore did seem to be attempting to focus on the album's few good points, while understandably keeping the tone flippant lest he should alienate the NME faithful, who on the whole were totally against the whole New Punk/Oi! movement. Again, better than we had any right to expect.

Two things strike me though: when did I change my name to Evil, and who the hell are Phil and Joanne? Those two out of the Human League? Do we care? No, I suppose not.

The provincial press were no more encouraging. The *Bath & West Evening Chronicle* declared us 'Chainsaw rock from the most notorious Bristol band doing their level best to prove that punk ain't dead - but in so doing, digging a deeper grave for it. In fact one or two of the songs aren't at all bad. If only they didn't always rely on guitar feedback.'

According to the *Basildon Evening Echo* (I'm not making this up, honest) 'Vice Squad, from Bristol, are a riot of spluttered female vocals, buzz-saw guitars and whirlwind songs full of protest - if you could only hear the words. They spend the entire record pretending to be crazed one-chord wonders and then sign off with something devastating and depressing called Last Rockers. But that's punk.'

In a bizarre twist, the reviewer on the *Swindon Evening Advertiser* mistook the woeful production for a whole new concept in the record making process, hailing us as the new messiahs of the left-field and accurately predicting our influence on the much later industrial scene.

No he didn't, he thought it was shit as well: 'It's the so-called 'Oi' brigade - they're either brashly attempting to pump life into the rotting carcass of punk, or cheerily keeping alive the spirit of '76. Decide for yourself. Suffice to say that this is crashing, crushing, bloody-fingered rock, all force, no subtlety, combined with angry young lyrics (if you can catch 'em).'

Any hopes we may have had that the reviews would effectively bury the album and save us some embarrassment, disappeared when it entered the national chart on 24 October at the surprisingly high position of No.32, and stayed on the chart for five weeks.

Of course, it felt good to walk into Virgin and see our name up there with Cliff, Blondie and Randy Crawford, but then I'd see some poor sucker buying the bloody thing and be overcome with guilt. I'd feel like taking it out of his hands, replacing it in the rack, and handing him Cliff's latest. It might have been rubbish, but at least it was properly produced rubbish.

But it wouldn't have made any difference. The fans, it seemed, had enough faith in us to overlook the reviews and give us the benefit of the doubt. Having listened to the album though, the feedback we got from them confirmed what we already knew all too well. We had let them down, badly.

The only thing we could do, by way of damage limitation, was get out on the road as soon as possible and prove our worth, and through our recently acquired London agent, we secured a slot on Anti Pasti's Six Guns tour.

Anti Pasti, from Derby, had had a head start on the likes of us, releasing their Four Sore Points EP on Dose Records in November 1980. Will (bass), Dugi (guitar), Kev (drums) and Martin Roper (vocals) had also toured with the UK Subs and had been given heavy coverage, including a front cover of *Sounds*.

Their *The Last Call* album had reached No.31 in the national chart on 15 August, and the Six Guns single which this tour was promoting was destined to be an indie chart No.1.

I'd spoken to Martin on the phone once, when he'd found that they were double-booked on a gig somewhere, and he'd rang to ask if we'd like to fill in for them. It turned out that we already had a booking for the night in question, but I thanked him for the offer, like you do, and we had quite a pleasant chat, so I foresaw no difficulties with working with the band now.

Where I did see a possible difficulty was with Chron Gen, who were booked as the opening act on the tour. They'd been going a year longer than us, having formed in 1978, and earlier in 1981 had played on the highly successful and heavily publicised Apocalypse Now tour, along with Discharge, the Exploited and Anti-Nowhere League and Anti Pasti. Their debut single on their own Gargoyle Records, Puppets Of War had sold in large numbers, going to No.4 on the indie chart, and their latest, Reality, on Step Forward, had also sold well, reaching No.2.

Chron Gen were a high profile band, and though they had little choice but to play second fiddle to their Apocalypse Now comrades Anti Pasti after the success of *The Last Call*, I could have fully imagined them resenting us for coming in from nowhere to take second spot on the bill.

I owned a copy of Anti Pasti's *Four Sore Points*, and frankly didn't think much of it. It seemed pretty turgid and unoriginal to me, but as they were headlining this little jaunt, it hardly mattered what I thought. I didn't, however, own anything by Chron Gen, so with the express intention of checking out the opposition, I went out and bought Reality. I soon wished I hadn't. It was a bloody marvellous record.

Chron Gen were Glynn Barber (vocals/guitar), John Thurlow (guitar), Pete Dimmock (bass) and Jon Johnson (drums), and I was particularly concerned about the last named. If this record was anything to go by, Jon was shit-hot, and this proved to be the case.

This brings me, in a roundabout way, to something that I suppose I should have mentioned earlier. By now Beki and Igor had split up as a couple, though Igor continued to work with us, and her current beau was none other than Glynn from Chron Gen. This meant that in the time leading up to the tour, Beki spent some time in the Chron Gen camp, and was in a position to confirm or allay my paranoid fears about having to follow the Jon Johnson act. Kindly, she told me that Jon was good, but that I had nothing to worry about. She had every faith in me, apparently, and had even got into an argument with Glynn about who had the best drummer, bless her.

Getting down to the logistics of the tour, we'd assumed that transport would be taken care of in the usual way, ie crew and gear in a hired van and band travelling with Simon and the merchandise. But here Ian pulled what I have always considered to be his master-stroke, and, with hindsight, explained why he'd been so keen for our album to come in well under budget. He argued that we were just throwing money away by hiring vans all the time, so why didn't we buy one? We had money in the bank after all, and if we splashed out on a massive furniture van that he just happened to know that Gulliver's Vehicle Hire had for sale, when the time came for our own headlining tour, this could be converted to transport not only the band, but also the backline and PA.

Here it is no doubt clear, even to readers of the meanest intelligence, that we were being done over good and proper, but we went for it. Let's pause for a moment and go over the facts:

Under Ian's guidance, we had unleashed a truly awful album onto an unsuspecting world.

The only thing to be said for this album was that it had left us with some cash to spare.

This happened to be precisely the amount that Gulliver's were asking for a second-hand furniture van.

The only reason we needed a van of this capacity was to accommodate a PA system.

Ian not only managed the band, but also owned the PA company.

Geddit? Yes, not only was Ian raking it in from both his manager's percentage and PA costs, but we were actually paying for his transportation out of our own pockets. Once or twice we'd questioned whether it was strictly necessary to haul his rig up and down the country, rather than using a local firm, but he always insisted that, wherever our destination happened to be, the native keys-dangling-from-belt and backstage-pass-festooned-jacket brigade were the most incompetent in these isles.

He managed to convince us that it would be a luxury tour bus, with a comfortable, heated living section looking out over the cab, boasting sumptuous seating and plush bunks.

Probably staggered by the fact that he'd actually got away with such patent nonsense, and before we had chance to come to our senses, Ian wisely didn't wait for our first headline tour, but bought and converted the van in time for the Anti Pasti jaunt.

The Six Guns tour was pretty impressive, 13 dates with only a few days off, and most of them in good sized venues. It kicked off at the Leeds Bierkeller on 29 October, and when we arrived late in the afternoon Anti Pasti were already sound-checking. The first person I clapped eyes on was the dreaded Jon Johnson, lounging nonchalantly in the corner with his feet up against a pillar, apparently without a care in the world. The git.

Nervous as hell, but feigning a similar line in nonchalance, we pretended we hadn't noticed Chron Gen and introduced ourselves to the evening's promoter, Nick Toczeck. He seemed a decent enough bloke, in fact he was, and we worked with him often later on. He was one of the dreaded punk poets, and made several records, but we took the lenient view that those thus afflicted should be more pitied than scorned.

Once we'd been shown our dressing room and the gear had been brought in, it was time to meet the other bands, no matter how much we would have liked to put it off.

The fact that Beki was going out with Glynn, and I'd at least spoken to Martin on the 'phone, resulted in these meetings being not quite as stilted as first nights on tour can be, but clearly it would take some time for any sort of real camaraderie to kick in. Actually, the only hostility came from the Anti Pasti road crew, who made no attempt to hide the fact that, as far as they were concerned, we had no right to be there at all, having not paid our dues on the Apocalypse Now tour etc. With the rapier-like wit of Oscar Wilde and Noel Coward, we hit back with 'Oh fuck off, you're just roadies, go hump something.'

I don't suppose that helped, and subsequent events only heightened their hostility. Once the gig was over, and while the equipment was being dismantled, various members of the bands decided that this was where the traditional touring hi-jinks should commence, and began chasing each other around the building pelting anyone in lobbing distance with the remains of the rider. Jolly good, I thought, keeping well out of the way. Quite out of character, Mark featured heavily in these exchanges, lobbing and pelting for all he was worth and generally displaying more animation than I'd ever witnessed on stage. I was proud of the boy; somebody had to do it and it certainly wasn't going to be me. I might have spilt my drink.

It all ended in tears though, as these things so often do. As the frivolities seemed to be reaching their peak, Martin managed to put his arm through a pane of glass in the door leading down to the stage. I forget what his actual injuries were, but he was rushed to hospital where his arm was put into a sling and he was advised to skip the next few dates entirely. Their most optimistic view was that if the arm healed quickly, he might be able to re-join the tour somewhere towards the end.

After hurried consultations with the tour promoters it was decided that on the following day Anti Pasti had to drop out, and we were now to headline at the Cedar Ballroom, Birmingham. After that, we were given no indication what was likely to happen.

If it wasn't for the fact that we were obviously weeping copiously over Martin's frustration at being excluded from his own tour, this could have been viewed as something of a promotion. We sympathetically scribbled 'You tit!' or something similar on Martin's plaster-cast entombed arm and resolved to get on with the job. As someone once said: 'The show must go on!'

Anti Pasti's road crew had to attend the sound-check, as part of their duties included some work on the PA, but if they'd been hostile the previous day, by now they were positively seething. Eventually, sick of the snide remarks and thinly veiled insults, I asked them straight just what their fucking problem was. They reiterated their earlier opinion of us, which was water off a duck's back; I mean, come on, all that paying-your-dues crap went out with Led Zeppelin, surely. And anyway, after all we'd been through to get ourselves this far, I for one felt we had no apologies to make. Seeing that they were failing to get to us, their leader added a final point, and this one hit home: 'The fact is mate, you're just not fuckin' big enough or good enough.' Ooh, the bitch!

We couldn't deny that though we were, on the whole, unimpressed with Anti Pasti, they were a lot more experienced at this touring lark than we were. We had no idea how long we were expected to take over the headlining slot, and it certainly wasn't a responsibility we'd anticipated. If everyone thought like this lot, and our inexperience showed, we could be in for a hard time.

As it turned out, the Birmingham audience accepted Anti Pasti's absence philosophically, as did the Manchester University crowd the next day, and we went down pretty well, on the whole.

By the time the tour made its uneasy way to Rotherham Civic Hall on 1 November, the remaining members of Anti Pasti had had enough of sitting around in the wings and elected to carry on for the time being as a three-piece. I forget who sang, but it seemed to go off well enough, and again we were reduced to support act status. This didn't concern us particularly, however, as it had been made clear from the start that if a decent sized audience showed for a gig headlined by us, they were obviously only there for Anti Pasti, but if one man and his dog put in an appearance, the others had obviously heard about Pasti pulling out. We couldn't win.

The only real downside was, predictably, Ian's van. The 'luxury' side of things turned out to be a cramped area right at the front of the van, with two sets of seats that Harry Houdini would have struggled to convert into bunks, let alone sleep in, a tiny gas heater that spewed out toxic fumes but little in the way of heat, and an intercom that mysteriously broke down whenever we felt like swearing at Ian. Which was most of the time.

Now we are talking deep winter, and Ian's 'Luxury Tour Bus' had more leaks than a leaky thing. We spent a substantial part of every day freezing our balls off, frankly, apart from Beki of course, who had other bits to worry about.

Bearing in mind all of the above, it was actually a much more enjoyable tour than one might imagine. The main reason for this was that, contrary to our expectations, Anti Pasti and Chron Gen didn't fall into one camp and alienate us into another; quite the reverse. It seemed that they hadn't got on particularly well on the Apocalypse tour, and helped no doubt by the Beki-Glynn connection Chron Gen teamed up with us, and we had a great time.

The only way to survive on tour is to develop a completely obnoxious Jekyll & Hyde persona, one that your mother wouldn't recognise unless she thought back to your puberty years, and Chron Gen, bringing us their wealth of experience, were our teachers. Before long we learned that any sentence uttered that wasn't liberally dosed with expletives was a sentence wasted, and that any opportunity to fart in someone's face should be seized upon with glee. All pretty standard stuff really.

We later realised though, after touring with other bands, that some of Chron Gen's habits were peculiar to them alone. They had a constant running gag, whereby they would go out of their way to convince people that they were all gay, despite all the evidence to the contrary, and feigned massive drug habits when in fact, they were what would now be termed 'Recreational Users,' Why they did these things, I don't know, but they certainly made life entertaining.

The most disturbing trait, though, was Glynn's, and funnily enough, it was one that I never felt like imitating. Glynn, it seemed, liked nothing better than getting his cock out in public, to put it crudely (and if you can think of a genteel way of putting that, you're a better author than I), and we could see why. He had every reason to be proud of it. As time went on, we learnt that Glynn's member was legend in punk rock circles, and it truly was a monster. Any excuse for airing the beast was seized upon, and if none were forthcoming he invented one. At one gig, I forget which, I was sat in the dressing room, leaning over and rummaging through my bag for clean socks or something, when someone apparently attacked me with a blunt instrument. I felt a huge blow to the side of the head, saw stars for a few seconds, and when I came to my senses, there was Glynn, cock in hand laughing uproariously.

As Dave says: 'He could put dents in doors with it...you haven't seen anything like it in your life. He could take your fuckin' eye out with it. Funnily enough, Beki was quite amused with Glynn for quite a while.'

Anyway, back to business. Martin did turn up for the next date, at St George's Hall, Bradford, but didn't participate, just hung around backstage looking pissed off, which was understandable. St George's Hall is a large and prestigious venue for a band to play (I once saw Motorhead there at the peak of their powers, when only the best venues were good enough for them, to give you some idea) so it must have been pretty galling for him. In the dressing room afterwards, the clever money was saying that, Doctors or no Doctors, Martin would be back in the fold for the next gig. There were three perfectly good reasons for this train of thought: 1, he really had looked very pissed off hanging around backstage like a spare thing at a wotsit: 2, after Blackburn there were two clear days off for him to nurse his damaged limb, but most importantly: 3, the next gig, on 5 November was at Derby Assembly Rooms.

Derby was of course Anti Pasti's home town, and the Assembly Rooms was another big venue where they were expecting the local populous to give them a hero's welcome.

All of the above occurred as predicted, Pasti went down the proverbial storm, and Martin played the rest of the tour, albeit hampered by several pounds of plaster-cast.

The next day saw us at the good old Slaughterhouse in Retford, and on 7 November the tour took in West Runton Pavilion ('The arse-end of the universe,' according to Mark) before we returned home. The reason for this was that there were two more days off after West Runton, and the next gig on the itinerary was Cardiff Top Rank on the 10th, practically a local gig for us. This couldn't have worked out better; a good chance to get some kip and wash our smalls.

Suitably refreshed, and sporting gleaming underwear, we made our way to Cardiff. Somewhat reluctantly as it happens, what with it being in Wales, but there seemed to be little choice in the matter. There are only two items worth reporting with regards to this gig. The first is that the afore-mentioned Kevin Draper videoed the proceedings, using the very best video camera that modern technology had to offer in the early eighties, which of course meant that he spent the evening dodging about the stage tottering under the weight of what appeared to be a small nuclear power-plant perched on his shoulder. This footage was later released on video, and later still on DVD, which I'll come to later.

The second is that some Welsh bastard nicked my bag. This was far from a rare occurrence, things go walkies all the time on tour, and on these occasions one tried to assume a philosophical out-look and reason that, as Crass were so fond of telling us 'All property is theft' but still, it rankled. The main reason is that said bag had contained my most prized possession, a Motorhead t-shirt that Mandy had bought me for my 18th birthday.

But it wasn't only prized for that reason. To explain, and I can see this getting complicated, but bear with me, this t-shirt had gained a minor celebrity status of its own. Now, these days musical styles cross over almost as a matter of course, but in the dark ages the boundaries were very rigid. I was very fond of Motorhead, Girlschool and the like, and if the truth be told so were many other punks, but quite innocently I had worn my Motorhead shirt in a number of Vice Squad photos, not realising that this would be cause for comment. It was apparently not the done thing for a member of a fairly prominent punk band to wear a metal band's t-shirt, and my sartorial faux pas was apparently frowned upon in some quarters. Luckily, this wasn't the case in *Sounds*, as Bushell was equally as in favour of rock and metal as he was of his own Oi!/New Punk, and as a result of this, Simon's heartfelt plea for the return of my bag got me a second mention in *Sounds'* gossip column:

> 'WATCH OUT - THERE'S A THIEF ABOUT: Distressed call from sexy Vice Squad drummer Shane concerning his black hold-all that some callous tealeaf half-inched from the dressing room of Cardiff Top Rank.
>
> Seems that said kitbag contained not only stocks of Vice Squad t-shirts but also Shane's near-legendary Motorhead t-shirt, and the band are offering 'a substantial reward' for its recovery - probably a good lashing from the gorgeous Beki.'

Cost me a tenner to get him to put 'sexy,' but it was worth it. Anyway, moving swiftly along...oh, you want to hear about my first gossip column appearance? Well, alright then, but it's a bit embarrassing.

Before the Mayflower gig where we did the Bushell interview, and while, you may remember, we were waiting for someone to let us in, Bushell had not been idle with his note-pad. As well as the interview, the following had also appeared in *Sounds*' hallowed pages:

> 'VICE IS NICE: Spotted on the grass outside Manchester Mayflower Club last week - Vice Squad's drummer Shane reading *Swish!*, otherwise known as 'the hottest, sexiest spanking monthly'.
> 'It's not mine', he protested cowardly, 'the roadie bought it, I was only looking, honest.'

I spoke nothing but the truth, as anyone who knows what a rampant pervert Igor is will attest, but still, it went down pretty badly with the girlfriend and elderly relatives, I can assure you.

Anyway, and now we really must be getting on with it, after Cardiff the Six Guns tour made its merry way to Hull Tower Ballroom on 11 November, Middlesbrough Gaskins 12 November and Scarborough Taboo Rock Club 13 November, but these gigs lacked one vital element, ie, us.

It had been made clear from the start that on 11 November we had a prior engagement, and it was one that we were quite excited about.

BBC West Television had a rather dire 'Yoof' series called *RPM*, hosted by a bloke called Andy Batten-Foster (under our naming system this quickly became Andy Battered-Foreskin), that each week featured a few songs by a local band specially recorded at a gig at the Granary. These were usually quite low-key affairs, and we only bothered watching the programme if the band in question was someone we actually knew.

However, someone at the BBC had a bright idea. Hugh Cornwell and Jet Black from the Stranglers lived in nearby Bath, and noticing that several local bands were gaining ground in the current wave of punk, they decided to persuade the Stranglers to team up with one of the new groups (I feel an urge to type 'are not concerned/with what there is to be learned,' I don't know why) for a big punk night. They agreed, and we were offered the support slot.

None of us were big Stranglers fans, in fact, I couldn't stand them, but like the Damned you couldn't argue with their credentials. Also, we were going on the telly! albeit only locally.

It was BBC policy that tickets for events being filmed for broadcast were free, and for most *RPM* gigs these were fairly easy to get hold of, but with the Stranglers heading the bill our gig proved rather popular. All of a sudden, friends, relatives and strangers in the street who'd been nursing sick grandmothers/doing their homework/washing their hair or inventing a cure for cancer whenever we'd played previous gigs, found themselves free of all commitments for this one. Funny that. Even Mandy's mother, who had always loathed me with a vengeance, showed up.

All in all then, it was a bit of an event, and with our customary lack of cool we arrived at the Granary far too early. Once the gear was loaded in we divided our time between trying, in vain, to bum a few out of hours drinks from Les and discussing the Stranglers. As I've said, I hated them, mainly because of Dave Green's keyboards, which irritated me beyond belief, and I went into this prejudice at some length. As a callow youth I'd bought a couple of their singles, but I'd since seen the light, and Mark, though more tainted than I had also changed his view of them: 'I had been into The Stranglers and had stopped, I think. I might have seen them once, or perhaps not at all, I'm not sure, but I had two or three of their albums and then got rid of them, which is something I never do. I never, ever, get rid of records. I lose them along the way, but I never purposely get rid of them, but those I swapped for the first half dozen Jam singles. Which I've since lost!'

Having said that, the others just seemed mildly indifferent to the band, which in my view just wasn't good enough, and I launched into a fierce diatribe putting forward what I considered to be some pretty convincing reasons why the Stranglers should be strung from the nearest yard-arm, Mr Christian. I'd just paused for a cough and a drag, fully intending to expand on this theme, when who should walk in but The Men In Black themselves. Sweating a little, I was just reflecting how incredibly embarrassing it would have been if they'd entered the room 30 seconds earlier, when Hugh Cornwell strolled right up to me, shook me by the hand and said 'Hello, I'm Hugh. I see your album has just charted, congratulations!'

He chatted to us for some time, as Dave remembers: 'He was genuinely interested in what we'd done and knew something about us. I was very impressed with Hugh 'cos he actually did go out of his way to be sociable...sound bloke, plenty of time for him.'

Ever felt like a complete and utter? The nicer he got, the more I cringed, and the others cast reproachful glances in my direction until I began looking around for a stone to crawl under.

I went out of my way to avoid the rest of The Stranglers, worried that they might rub it in by asking if they could name their children after me, but it turned out that the others still retained some of their '77 hard-man persona, as Mark recalls: 'JJ came up and said 'Feel free to use my bass stack. Touch any of the dials and I'll kill you, but plug in there, switch on there and that's your lot.' This thing was about 12 foot high, so I thought I'd make the most of it but oh, God, what a horrible noise!'

Or, to put it another way, 'In nutshell, Hugh Cornwell, sound bloke,' says Dave, 'the other three, a bunch of cunts, simple as that.' Well, I wasn't completely wrong then.

As you can imagine, I was pretty relieved when the pleasantries were over with and we were able to get down to business. Naturally, The Stranglers soundchecked first, and if this was anything to go by, it seemed that they were planning to play mostly new material. On the whole, this proved to be a mistake as most of the audience, even if they weren't Vice Squad fans, were into the New Punk/Oi! thingy and not likely to take kindly to the plaintive, lilting material that the Stranglers were purveying at the time. There was, however, one notable exception, as Dave remembers: 'Their soundcheck was obviously the first time that any of us had heard Golden Brown, because it hadn't yet been released, and it was like, Fuckin' 'ell, that's good! But, everything else they played all night sounded like a sack of shit, and nobody was that interested in them.'

A couple of times during their soundcheck, the floor-manager asked The Stranglers to turn the volume down a little as his fellow technicians were complaining, and they were happy to oblige, while we exchanged worried glances. If Golden Brown was too rich for their blood, what the fuck were they going to make of our infernal din?

We didn't have long to wait for an answer to that one. Roughly two-and-a-half bars into our soundcheck, the technicians begged us to stop and began screaming blue murder at the hapless floor-manager. He asked us to turn down, we refused, and all Hell broke loose. Our refusal wasn't purely bloody-mindedness though. It was mostly, I have to admit, but there was also a practical reason why Dave's guitar stack couldn't be cranked down to the level they desired, as Mark explains: 'The Stranglers had a different guitar sound, it was a Telecaster or Strat sound rather than a Gibson [that Dave used, or a copy anyway], a much cleaner sound so you don't need the overdrive...you've got to drive a Marshall to get the sound out of it.'

Things went from bad to worse: 'By now the union are involved,' says Dave, 'they've got a decibel-meter in and apparently we're louder than Concorde half a mile away, or something like that. Which gives you a rough idea of the sort of set that The Stranglers were playing, because they only had to turn down a little bit and they were quite legal, but we'd have had to have unplugged and my mate Shane on drums would still have been fuckin' illegal on his own.'

He continues: 'The union at the BBC is particularly strong, so the technicians are not having any of it, the floor-manager's running around in circles, and we all adjourn to the Llandogger Trow. We drink shit-loads of cider, which was our particular poison at the time. When an irresistible force meets an immovable object...the technicians were not going to do it when we were that loud, and we weren't going to turn down, so the gig was off. 'Several hours later, Tadd comes in and the gig's back on. They'd done a deal...the Beeb were gonna bung them twenty quid in their pockets and they weren't worried about their ears any more.'

But wasn't the official line that they'd been issued with protective ear-muffs?

'Yeah, and twenty pounds, which was a lot of money in those days, you could buy a house in Yorkshire. Probably still can!'

The news that we were going on the telly after all would have been better received if those in control had reached a compromise sooner. As it was, by this time we had, as Dave has said, been left to our own devices in a public house for a considerable time, under the impression that our services were no longer required.

It was, then, a somewhat tired and emotional Vice Squad that made their way, unsteadily, back into the Granary. There was no time for a soundcheck, and anyway we all had some serious sobering up to do, so we all kept ourselves well away from the main arena and the temptation that the bar had to offer. Well, when I say all of us, I can't honestly include Dave in that statement. I'll let him tell you the sorry tale: 'This is my one case for the defence, and I'm glad to have the chance to make it. When we get back to the Granary I bump into our A&R man, the erstwhile Ashtray Fuckall; he's totally unaware of this [the fact that we've spent most of the afternoon in the pub] because he's just driven up from London, and plants a huge wad of money in my hand and tells me to get the band whatever they're drinking. I couldn't find any fucker. I didn't drink it all myself, I must have found some people or I'd have died, but you're drunk already and somebody offers you a load of free booze...Next thing you know, it's Lights, Camera, Action! and you're on the telly making a complete and utter of yourself.'

Mark seems to go along with that view: 'The over-riding memory of the whole thing is the big beginning...I can't remember which song it was, but I think it must have started with drums and two big crash chords. I was stood up on the PA and Dave, with his Clockwork Orange outfit, ran to the front of the stage, hit the big power chord, and pulled his plug out. I collapsed on me knees laughing, and I turned around and you were off the back of your drum stool with your legs in the air! We stopped and said 'Sorry, we're gonna go again on this one.''

You might have thought that Dave would have learnt from this mistake, but no, he turned it into a kind of party-piece and performed it at regular intervals throughout the set. If the plan had been to broadcast the whole performance, it would have been a write-off, but luckily the BBC only needed half a dozen or so songs and we were just about able to deliver that many reasonable renditions.

To be fair to Dave, if the cameras hadn't been there we wouldn't have had any problem with his antics. The packed audience seemed to enjoy watching this idiot tearing around the stage like a cross between Mick Jones and Norman Wisdom and on the night, at least, it was a great gig. We went down a storm.

The reality only hit home a few days later, when we were invited to the BBC's viewing room on Whiteladies Road. Most of the footage was totally unusable, but the required half dozen songs could be salvaged it seemed, though even these were slightly marred by Beki having problems with her vocals. The fact that we'd been playing live more regularly than we were used to had taken its toll on her voice, and it showed.

Despite all of the above, the BBC seemed quite pleased with the footage, and decided that our broadcast should be accompanied by a pre-recorded interview. We were given the choice of venue, and naturally went for the public bar of the Swan. (Actually, we normally drank in the lounge, but that seemed a little middle-class, so we slummed it.)

The interview took place on a weekday lunchtime, much to the amusement of the locals and Old Ron. While the BBC crew were setting up the lights and cameras, we met our interviewer, the legendary Dave Pritchard. We didn't know at the time that he was legendary, which isn't surprising as at this time his reputation was confined to the BBC, but we quickly learned for ourselves that this was an extraordinary man. Once all the introductions and pleasantries were out of the way, he asked what we were all drinking, and as usual it was Courage Best's all round and a lager for Beki. I took a sip of my pint, then looked up to see that Mr Pritchard had drained his in one gulp and was giving the rest of us a puzzled stare, wondering what could possibly be holding us back. Not wanting to look like wimps, we forced them down and he immediately did the same thing again. Only on the third pint did he seem content to slacken the pace a little, but not much, and he continued to foist drinks on us for the rest of the afternoon. I mean to say, we weren't exactly adverse to the occasional libation, but this man was clearly a lunatic.

Much later, Mr Pritchard of course found his spiritual home as the producer of Keith Floyd's cooking programmes, but more of that later.

Despite his drinking habits, Dave was the consummate professional, and as soon as the cameras switched on he magically transformed himself from bar-room drunkard to totally lucid and on-the-ball interviewer in the blink of an eye.

This took us by surprise, as we'd all assumed that the interview would descend into one of those drunken 'Yer me best mate you are. No, honest you really are, you an' me against the world mate, eh? Ha, ha!' conversations that we were all quite used to. But no. Mr Pritchard's interviewing technique would have impressed Michael Parkinson, and some of us, me and Mark to be precise, were in no condition to cope with it.

Of course, neither of us were ever up to much in interviews, but when it came to the printed word, this didn't matter too much. If either of us managed to string a coherent sentence together that was relevant to the topic under discussion, it was usually duly reported, if only to prove that we were still alive. More often, as we've seen, Mark and I just sat around scratching ourselves while Beki and Dave delivered the Vice Squad Manifesto. Well, they seemed to be quite good at it.

It was the fact that this was being filmed that made it embarrassing. Beki and Dave, as usual, answered all the questions at length, making all the points I would have liked to have made if I hadn't been struck dumb at the sight of a microphone, and I particularly liked Beki's comment on getting gobbed at: 'It's not the idea that they're spitting, it's the diseases it carries. Up north they've got tuberculosis and things half the time…'

You don't see me at all, thankfully, but Mark seems to appear with stunning regularity when you consider that the fact that he remains mute throughout. For all his reticence, people noticed him though, apparently: 'I just sat there looking like a cocaine addict, everyone seemed to think, but I just had a bad cold actually. Good hair though, I thought.' Vain sod.

All in all, when the broadcast eventually went out, it seemed to go down quite well; so much so that we were even chosen as the closing act for the end-of-series programme. If we'd had any doubts about skipping a few dates of the Pasti tour, we reckoned that, on the whole, we'd made the right decision, even if Battered Foreskin's introductions were always unpleasantly sneering.

Vice Squad finally rejoined the Six Guns tour on Saturday 14 November at the Rainbow Theatre, London, which all you rock historians out there will know can safely be referred to as legendary (yes, I'm getting bored with that word as well, but I've lost me Thesaurus). It's another of those venues that make it more difficult to name anyone of note that didn't play there in the 60s and 70s, than those that did. Everyone of a Rock-Anorak donning disposition will have a favourite, mine being that Thin Lizzy recorded *Live And Dangerous* there, while our mate H was keen to point out that Pink Floyd considered the place a virtual home-from-home. Shut up, H.

Amazingly, given that the Rainbow is so steeped in history, and given the fact that the events that I am shortly to unfold were to, um, unfold, until I presented Dave with the documentary evidence he stoutly refused to believe that he'd ever played the venue. Now we're all prone to lapses in memory; old age, alcohol etc. But how could anyone clean forget that they'd played the bloody Rainbow? Well, Dave did, until I dug out a battered itinerary, thrust it in front of his face, and said 'Well who the fuck's that then?' God, I thought I had a brain like a sieve.

I think we have safely established then, that the Rainbow was a little out of all our leagues, including Anti Pasti. For that reason, the crowning glory to the Six Guns tour, although headlined by Pasti, had a strong supporting cast, and was in fact a sort of mini one-day festival called Woodstock Revisited (no, it wouldn't have been my first choice either, but there you go).

All the gear was loaded in on the Friday night, and on the Saturday morning only Anti Pasti, ourselves, the Angelic Upstarts and Splodgenessabounds were allocated soundchecks, in that order, which seemed to me a little unfair on Chron Gen. Typically, they didn't appear to give a toss.

The fun and frolics kicked off with the Case at 1.45, and the rest of the acts appeared in the following order: Eraserhead, the Insane, the Wall, Honey Bane, Chelsea, Splodgenessabounds (and I hope I'll never have to type that word again), Charge, Chron Gen, Angelic Upstarts; then Vice Squad at 9.00 and Anti Pasti from 10.00, closing the show at 11.00. Phew. I thought it might save some confusion later if we got all that out of the way now, okay?

Obviously, it was something of an honour to be granted a soundcheck at this auspicious event, but equally obviously, as we had to get there in the morning and were the penultimate act, we found ourselves with a lot of time to kill. Naturally, we made our way to the nearest pub, which was already heaving with punks and skins, got a round of drinks in, and wandered around to see who exactly was in. Here we got our first inkling that, despite all the precautions taken by the promoters, Paradise Productions, in the way of security, the day was likely to end unhappily.

Virtually the first person we clapped eyes on was a skinhead called Nicky Crane whose claim to fame was that he was the bloke on the cover of the infamous Strength Thru Oi! compilation. But it wasn't all the controversy surrounding that fine, if misguided album, that set the alarm bells ringing, oh no. It was the fact that he was brazenly sporting a 'White Power' t-shirt and was surrounded by a massive crew of like-minded Neanderthals. And judging by their demeanour, it was more a question of when, rather than if, the shit was going to hit the fan.

The pub was of the large, economy size, so while Crane's minions were just in a surly rather than violent frame of mind, those of us unfamiliar with the contents of Mein Kampf were free to come and go for most of the day. Come to think of it, I doubt if any of those arseholes had ever read it either, but I digress. According to the beer-stained itinerary in front of me, 'There will be no pass-outs for guests or paying customers,' but as I remember it, people drifted from the gig to the pub at will, and if it hadn't been so patently obvious that this was another accident-waiting-to-happen, we'd all have had a lot of fun. We made the best of it though; we chatted to lots of people and did a couple of off-the-cuff fanzine interviews, but the feeling of impending doom couldn't fully be shaken off.

When we returned to the venue for Chron Gen's set at 7.00, most people seemed aware that there was likely to be trouble. The question was, when. The Angelic Upstarts, who were to follow Chron Gen, seemed the most likely to spark a riot, and that in itself is odd in a way. They had a strong skinhead following, and had, as we've seen, been hauled on board the Oi! train whether they liked it or not. What's odd is that Upstarts singer Mensi has always been an active anti-fascist, but then made records like England, espousing the 'English Rose' and 'A land so fair and so true.' Now, (and I'm getting into deep water here, I know, but let's persist and see how we get on) I am not what could in any way be described as a patriot. To me, the whole idea of being proud of a country that you just happened, without any form of consultation and with no choice in the matter, to be born in, is a bit weird. Nobody asked me, I'm just here. The old shack has its good points and its bad points, and when it comes to human rights and justice it would probably come reasonably high in a world-wide league table, for all its faults. But that's no reason to get a St George Cross tattoo on your arse.

No, I tend to side with Samuel Johnson, who famously said 'Patriotism is the last refuge of a scoundrel.' Mind you, he also said "Touch my pint an' I'll kick your fuckin' 'ead in.' Ah, I can see you're confused. I'm not referring to the eminent wit and lexicologist. I'm talking about Sammy 'Mad Dog' Johnson who used to drink in my local. As it happens though, the late Doctor Johnson and 'Mad Dog' were in complete accord when it came to the subject of patriotism, and both tended to use the same phrase to express their feelings on the matter. The main difference being, of course, that the good Doctor usually delivered his speech to a quiet and appreciative audience, while Boswell sat in the wings and took dictation, and 'Mad Dog' tended to grab you by the throat and spit the words through gritted teeth while smashing your head into the nearest wall. In both cases, the point was made clear to the listener.

What do you mean I made all that up. How dare you?

All the same, I would have thought it pretty obvious that patriotism needn't necessarily denote fascism, and if ever a man was the living embodiment of that fact then that man was Mensi. Try telling the Boneheads.

The Upstarts had hardly started their set when the place went up in the air for the first of many times that evening. The security managed to calm things down eventually, but the atmosphere had turned very ugly, and Ashtray, who had turned up in time for the Upstarts, was frankly shitting himself.

As was, apparently, Igor: 'It was so frightening that I had a shit in the sink in the dressing room, cos I didn't realise that they had any toilets backstage, and all the skinheads were just killing everyone weren't they? And I was so scared and I was dying for a shit, and I thought, 'If I have a shit in the sink, it'll probably wash away,' and it didn't! You lot were all out front, and there's this big turd in the sink, and then [Upstarts drummer] Decca Wade was knocking on the door cos he wanted to swap some beer? And I was going 'You can't come in here at the moment!' In the end, I found some paper, and I wrapped it up and threw it out the window onto the street in Finsbury Park, ha ha!'

For some reason, perhaps because it had been so predictable, none of the rest of us were that bothered. Like the bloke in the Monty Python sketch who was continually struck on the forehead by the ball during a cricket match, no matter how hard he tried to avoid it, we were getting used to it by now. All Beki recalls is that: 'I remember that gig because it was very dark and you couldn't see the edge of the stage and I nearly fell into the orchestra pit. Luckily I have no recollection of Igor's toilet troubles.'

The fighting continued, sporadically, for most of the Upstarts' set, and when they decided to call it a day it was our turn. Boy, we couldn't wait!

While Igor and Bambi sorted the gear onstage more fighting broke out, and Ashtray was hopping about on one leg, working himself into a frenzy.

It wasn't the most enjoyable of sets, and I couldn't help but reflect that Thin Lizzy had never had to put up with this sort of nonsense. Or Pink Floyd, unfortunately. Perhaps because we weren't a recognised skinhead band, nothing serious went off during our set, although the atmosphere certainly didn't improve, and we just ploughed through it, with even less attention to the subtleties and nuances than usual, exiting stage-left as soon as we thought was allowable under the terms of the contract and happy to still be in one piece.

Once backstage we all felt relatively safe, and had a couple of soothing beers. All except Ashtray, that is, who seemed in serious danger of wetting himself. Strange behaviour, we all agreed, for someone who reckoned he had toured with the Rejects and all that entailed. We did our best to ignore him.

When Anti Pasti took to the stage, more trouble broke out, and we suggested that if it wasn't too much trouble, and once they'd finished their drinks, obviously, it might be a good idea if Igor and Bambi started loading up the gear. Ashtray fumed for a few minutes, infuriated at our casual attitude, then exploded: 'Will tell your people to get their fucking shit together! Come on! Get your fucking shit together you bastards!' Two parts amused and one part astonished at this outburst, Igor and Bambi rolled eyeballs to the ceiling, ambled over to the gear and began packing up.

If he'd left it there, Ashtray would probably have got away with it, but he wouldn't let it lie. The boys were getting on with the job, after a fashion, and that was good enough for us. But not Ashtray. Eventually, he stormed over and repeated, virtually word-for-word, his earlier outburst, but by now Bambi had had enough. I can't remember his exact words, but the following reconstruction (some parts are played by actors) should give you the gist.

Bambi grabbed him by the scruff of the neck, and screamed something like 'Listen you jumped up little shite, I don't work for *you*, I don't even work for *them*, I'm here cos they're my mates and they asked me to come. Me and Igs will pack this gear up when we're good and ready, and if I hear one more word out of you I'll smack your fuckin' teeth in, alright?' It was alright.

Suitably chastened, Ashtray kept his trap shut after that. Once the gear was in the van we wondered, briefly, whether we should do the honourable thing and stick around to make sure that Pasti and the others were able to escape the carnage, or get out now while we had the chance. Yep, we legged it.

Although, as I've said, the Rainbow was the crowning glory of the Six Guns tour, it wasn't the final gig. Someone on the staff of the promoters obviously had a rather poor sense of humour, as the tour actually closed with something of an anti-climax at Portsmouth Top Rank the following evening, 15 November.

Or perhaps that's a little unfair. If all three bands and their road-crews had hit it off during the course of the tour, I suppose a low-key date like this one would have been a nice way to round things off. Have a party, hug and kiss each other and all that stuff. But that was never really on the cards.

However, we all recognised the gravity of the occasion, and made at least half-hearted attempts to capture that ole end-of-tour atmosphere, as Dave recalls: 'Word was that Anti Pasti and their roadies were gonna sort out our luggage, kit, and everything else. We went into their dressing room and they had all these water bombs in the sink, balloons and that, which they didn't have by the time they got back there. I mean, it was nothing extreme, I've seen a fuck sight worse on rugby tours these days, but we emptied a couple of fire-extinguishers into their gear and destroyed all their ammo; they had flour and stuff like that.'

It was pretty tame stuff, and it occurs to me that, perversely, the pranks might have been a little more Jeremy Beadle if we'd all been more friendly. Dave agrees: 'Yeah, exactly, that's a very good point. It was an anti-climax other than the fact that *we* stitched *them* up rather than *them* stitching *us* up.'

Feeling quite smug at having got the better of the buggers, and reflecting that discretion was, perhaps, the better part of valour, we decided that this was probably a good time to leave.

We did so, with our customary lack of cool and finesse, as Mark remembers: 'We all legged it to the van and made a quick getaway. We got about half a mile up the road and realised that Igor wasn't in there, so we turned around and caught him being chased up the road towards us; we had to drag him in and make another quick getaway.'

And so endeth our first major tour.

TV Brakes, 1977. *Left to right:* Me, Ian, Dave. Nice socks.

These pics were taken by our bassist Howard Exciting.
Why we didn't see the flaw in this plan for a band photo I've no idea.

The first Vice Squad rehearsal, at Tabernacle Church, Hanham, early 1979, in our best punk clobber (my shirt is from Boy in the King's Road). Safe to say we looked better than we sounded. *(Nick Quarry)*

Trinity Church, Old Market, 24 June 1979, supporting The X-Certs and The Numbers. Ian, in the background, reflects that if we wanted a singer in THAT outfit, he got out just in time.

Vice Squad's whip hand

OUTRAGEOUS Bristol punk rocker Becky Bondage doesn't just wear leather gear for kicks. . . she's deadly serious.

The 16-year-old singer loves the leather, her whip and studs and her band Vice Squad's bondage image.

Becky's multi-coloured hair and her leather clad band members give the fans plenty to shout about.

Becky of Church Road, Frampton Cotterell, who is on the dole, said: "I've worn clothes like that for 2½ years since punk started in Bristol."

The band caused a stir in the music business with their song "Nothing" from the "Avon Calling" Bristol bands's compilation album.

"We're now going to do some demo tapes and send them round the record companies, I think we've got the right image," she said.

And anyone who reckons the punk rockers are out of date can think again, says Becky. "It's the only thing that's in — the mods are 16 years out of date."

But Vice Squad have come up against opposition when trying to get gigs in Bristol because some people believe they are connected with the National Front.

"It's only because we've had a couple of skinheads hanging around at our gigs but we are definitely anti-Nazi," said Becky.

Our first press, a cringingly clichéd piece in local free rag *The Bristol Journal.*

PUNK singer Becky Bondage of Vice Squad in her leather stage gear — it's not quite the Christmas image, but she says she's sticking with it. Picture by MALCOLM ROUSE.

There's no room in that photo booth for Igor, Beki, and her cleavage...

An unused shot from the *Last Rockers* insert session, outside Virgin Records, Merchant Street, Bristol. How we laughed at the window displays behind Mark and Beki. *(Danica Gacesa)*

Beki at the 100 Club. Acker Bilk looks on approvingly.

Right: The 100 Club again. I'm about to lose that stick.

Below: After the same gig. Me talking to one of Keith Dunn's Big City Friends.

On stage in 1981. *Facing page, bottom and this page, top:* Market Hall, Carlisle, 3rd December.
Remaining shots: Cambridge Corn Exchange, 10 October. Greatly honoured to be supporting UK Subs for a
few dates of their *Endangered Species* Tour. *(Simon Edwards)*

Cleethorpes, 4 October 1981. We'd played Grimsby the night before. Oh, the glamour! The only photo in which I'm the tallest member of the band, having built a little sand hillock in advance. Mark showing his best side. *(Simon Edwards)*

Okay, he could look pretty cool. Tall with good hair. The bastard. *(Simon Edwards)*

"Be very, very, careful what you say next, Barber…" *(Simon Edwards)*

Above: Extracts from *Deathwimp II*, photo strip from *Flexipop!* magazine. So bizarre in itself that I can't think of anything to add.
(Neil Matthews / Flexipop!)

Right: Photo for a piece in the *Bristol Evening Post* on Riot City Records. Taken at Simon's flat, 4 Melrose Place, Clifton. Nice 'tache, Simon.
(Bristol Evening Post Archives)

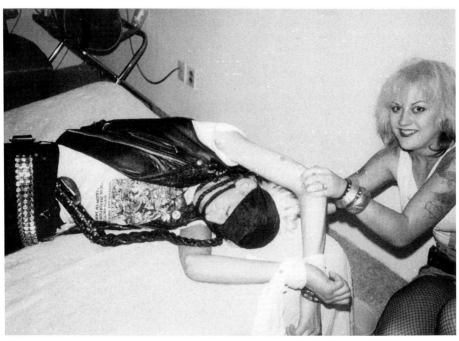

No comment!

Go on, guess where *we've* been...

Right: Unused Chaotic Dischord photo from the *Fuck Religion, Fuck Politics, Fuck The Lot Of You!* session. Michael Bill from the nearby Full Moon pub and Mitch from Dead Katss/Colonel Kilgore's standing in for me and Dave. *(Simon Edwards)*

Below: Unused photo from the Sex Aids single session.
Back row, left to right: Merv, not sure, Terry, Tim Galley.
Middle row, left to right: Bambi's girlfriend (partially obscured), Mark, Bambi, Tim Cook, Andy Payne (partially obscured), Dave, Simon Harrison-Boyle (partially obscured), me.
Front row: Igor. Someone's just told the one about the Bishop, the actress, and the stuffed aubergine. Tim Galley doesn't get it. *(Simon Edwards)*

Vice Squad second line-up with Sooty and Lia. Boots Hairspray made a fortune out of us. *(Anagram Records)*

The new line-up's first gig, at the Granary on 4 January 1984.
Backing vocals by Paul Riddell, who had recently got into a fight with a motorbike. He lost. *(Simon Archer)*

Unused photo from the *Shot Away* album shoot.
Left to right: Soot, Terry, Lia, Steve, Jon, me, Glenn, Dave, Mark, Merv. *(Ken Lush)*

Boarding the plane for Lisbon. Somehow I've already lost my shirt. *(Steve Street)*

Jon leaving our hotel in Cambridge, trying to look as if he hasn't nicked all the towels.

Dave and H, both in '80s Football Casual wear, at Yesterdays, King Street, Bristol, to see Mark playing with the Crazy Trains.

On the beach in Lisbon. The cheap wine was so acidic it burnt Sooty's eyes quite badly. How we laughed.
(Steve Street)

CHAPTER 8

THOUGH PROBLEMATIC AT TIMES, the Six Guns tour had, on the whole, been a great introduction to life on the road, and we were thirsty for more.

Simon, who had been with us manning his trusty merchandise stall, nicely sums up the way we all felt about the whole touring experience: 'I always put it down as one of the most exciting parts of my life, doing all that; being on tour was real fun. You were completely knackered, but it was so much fun, and the fact that you were playing to people who wanted to see you, and you were selling lots of records and selling lots of merchandise, and the whole thing was just working... it was fun, it was exciting.'

By the time we bade Anti Pasti and their loveable minions a not-so-fond farewell, plans for the first Vice Squad headlining tour were nearing completion, but before we move on to that most infamous of tours, this seems a good time to tackle one of the responsibilities that came with our new-found, erm, fame?

As well as the bundle of cheques and ready cash that pitched up on Simon's doorstep to gladden his heart each morning, (and I can't say it exactly depressed us either, even if most of our share found its way Tadd-wards) there also tended to be an even bigger bundle of fan mail nestling against the old pint of pasteurised.

We were a bit overwhelmed by this. I mean, it's one thing for someone to buy a record or come along to a gig and gob at you, but to take the trouble to sit down and write a letter? It was the diversity of the people that wrote that struck us most, I think. For instance, as well as punks and skins, a lot of people in the Forces wrote regularly, which seemed odd, given a lot of our subject matter, but when we got to know these kids (for they were just kids, really) they'd only joined up out of desperation. Anything to get off the dole.

Early on, while the volume of correspondence was still manageable, it was simply split four ways, and we spent all our days off writing letters. We soon had a huge list of pen-pals who we got to know quite well, and although I usually hate writing letters it was fun to do. To this day I wonder if Ratz from Nottingham has managed to pack in smoking, (I advised against it) and how Suze from Glasgow and her wayward boyfriend ended up (I said 'Chuck him, girl').

For some reason, though, the amount of mail we got seemed totally out of proportion to our lowly status. I'm not familiar with the contents of the letter boxes of the Truly Rich And Famous, but the (literally) sack-loads of mail that began to arrive soon became a cause for concern. Something had to be done, as Mark recalls: 'It was purely by demand, I think. We had loads of people writing, and I think it was Simon, actually, that said 'Look, you know, I'm getting so many letters, you've gotta start a Fan Club.' We said 'Ha! Don't be so stupid!' These days we would just have a Facebook page and a Twitter feed, but in the early eighties people and bands still had Fan Clubs and it seemed we had to have one, however ludicrous the idea may have seemed.

Mark's girlfriend, Kerry, agreed to take on the responsibility (my sister Trayci took it over eventually), and it was launched in time for the release of *No Cause For Concern*. Kerry's address duly appeared on the sleeve, leaving Simon's morning pinta relatively unmolested as the missives now pitched up on the unfortunate girl's doorstep, and almost immediately she began to see the folly of her rash decision. To her eternal credit, though, Kerry went about the task in a brisk and business-like manner, and we were all roped in to decide what form the Fan Club was to take, as Mark remembers: 'The idea was to try and get something out there to those people that other people couldn't get, so it was a little bit special. You know, they were keen enough to go to the trouble of handing over however much money it was, so we made an effort with it, made it as good as we possibly could.'

Nevertheless, it was never quite as good as I would have liked it to have been, purely due to lack of resources. The membership began at around 400 and peaked at around 700-800, but we did our best, sending out regular newsletters, advanced notice of tour dates, badges, stickers, photos, and an exclusive flexi-disc of the Radio 1 Richard Skinner session.

We still answered most of the letters ourselves, but the great advantage of having Kerry in charge of the operation was that she would systematically go through them and direct any with specific questions to the band member most likely to give a vaguely intelligent answer. Also, if the writer simply wanted to know when we would be playing Middlesbrough next, or when our next record was coming out, Kerry usually knew better than we did, so she replied. This not only relieved our workload to a small degree, but she actually got to know a lot of the kids herself and built up a correspondence with them, so if we were away on tour, and the mail was piling up, there was always someone back at base-camp that the little darlings could contact.

It was a pretty satisfactory arrangement all round, though a lot of work for Kerry, but she got her revenge. One night, when we were all drunk, she suggested that it would a nice idea if we sent out signed Christmas cards to all the members, and we agreed that it would indeed be a nice idea, burp! When we sobered up, it still seemed a nice idea in principal, but had lost a little of its shine in the cold light of day.

Ever practical, we reasoned that if we performed the task in a pub, it mightn't be so bad, but we were wrong. At the appointed hour, Kerry showed up in the Swan with what appeared to be the entire Christmas card counter from WH Smiths, dumped the lot on the table, chucked a box of ball-point pens at Mark and exited, stage-left, laughing her head off.

It was a gruelling session, as Mark remembers: 'The signatures started off as Mork, Bill, Des and Slime and ended up as, like, four squiggles by the end. It was a lot...it took *hours*.' Bear in mind that this took place in the early days of the Fan Club, but it set a precedent that lasted for its entire existence. When the membership was at its peak, the first signs of Christmas decorations in the high street shops (around Easter, usually) were enough to send fully-grown guitarists running screaming into the countryside. Kerry's revenge was swift, brutal, and enduring.

For Vice Squad's first headlining tour, Ian engaged the services of a northern agency called T.O.P., that none of us had ever heard of, but Ian assured us that they were a well-established and respected firm, and their proposed tour schedule (10 dates between 30 November and 12 December) seemed to take in most of the venues we favoured, so we chose not to worry about their lack of credentials.

By now, I ought to mention, there was a definite backlash against us on our home turf, partly due to the fact that we had signed to EMI, and partly because we were in serious danger of becoming successful, something always liable to raise hackles in our neck of the woods. Anyway, the fact that the proposed tour took in no dates south of Birmingham suited us fine at the time, and as Chron Gen were pencilled in to support we looked forward to it with relish.

In the end, Chron Gen couldn't do it, and as the tour went from being referred to by those involved as, at first, The Tadd Tour, then The Pig Tour (after we saw the tour posters which portrayed Beki's visage less than favourably) and eventually Oi! - The Absolute Fuckin' Disaster Tour, you can probably gather that it didn't go all that well.

As Beki remembers: 'The Tadd Tour was Oi!-The Absolute Disaster Tour and we were all freezing in that guy's house or sleeping in the truck. There was ice on the inside of the truck windows. I remember waking up about 5am with a hangover and me and Shane nicking two pints of cow's milk off a float, I hated milk but was so thirsty I drank it. We really roughed it, especially considering we were gobbed at in those days. It's character building though, all bands should be made to go through it, especially the X-Factor mob, then after ten years or so on the road they can say that they've paid their dues.'

But before we go into the details of the Tour From Hell, it's time to re-introduce a major character to this heart-warming story. Mark Byrne, who you may remember as the (at the time) unknown benefactor responsible for our securing the Damned/Ruts and Upstarts support slots, was drafted in by Ian, along with his mate Steve Barnett, to roadie on the tour.

Mark, as I've already mentioned, had been a member of St Vitus Dance, and was offered those gigs himself, but turned them down. Here's his explanation for this: 'We were supposed to support the Damned, but we got so badly gobbed on supporting the Dickies, it was unbelievable...we shat out of it. I can't believe I gave up the chance to support the Ruts, but there you go. I wasn't trying to do you any favours, we were just trying to get out of it ourselves: 'Ooh, I know a band called Vice Squad, they're really young, they'll do it, they don't mind being gobbed on, apparently.''

As you may have gathered from the above, Mark was a few years older than us and had already had a chequered but interesting career before throwing in his lot with the good ship Vice Squad. Here's a brief summary in his own words:

'It all started in 1979 with Vitus Dance; well, we called ourselves the Gods at first, and we were really lucky because very early on we caught up with two guys who were

'It all started in 1979 with Vitus Dance; well, we called ourselves The Gods at first, and we were really lucky because very early on we caught up with two guys who were promoting gigs at the Locarno, one called Dennis Betheridge and another guy called Ian Reid, who were from Swindon. And then we found out that Ian Reid, who never used to turn up at the Locarno - it was just a money making thing for him - managed XTC. Malcolm Young, our bass player, just thought they were fantastic, loved XTC, he was well into that kind of student-punk or new wave. I just thought Ian Reid? Yeah, that's great, a manager of a group that's got a record contract. And, you know, he came and saw us, and he thought we were great, and he said 'Yeah, I'll manage you' and that was the beginning of it really.

We started at the beginning of the year, found Ian Reid about Easter time, and by October we'd done a John Peel session, so it was really good. And that was even though we'd never had any record company interest at all, and we never did. Ian was always, like, 'You're not doing any indie stuff, you're getting a record deal, I'm getting you a record deal.' And then it was 'I tried to get you a record deal, I couldn't get you a record deal, I don't want you anymore. Bye.' We split up after that.

We lasted for a year, and we supported Toyah at the Marquee, we supported the Police, we supported Classix Nouveaux, we supported the Members at some gig in Twickenham, we got plenty of choice little gigs. But basically, the London gigs and the Peel session were the cream of it really. We were a bit late on the scene I'm afraid. We had a fine year with it, and then it was done.

'With Malcolm Young I got a band called Voice Of Nature together, and we did that for two years, but we were so totally skint, y'know. So everything just took so long. You had to save up the money to photocopy cassette covers for demos, and then get loads of cassettes off people, and then peel the labels off and stick our own on to have enough to send out. Just getting ten cassettes together to try and get gigs was a major thing.'

To bring things back to our tale, Voice Of Nature eventually decided to play one final gig, then split for good: 'We had a party, in a club just up from the Colston Hall, and you came along with Vice Squad. I'd met you at Kevin Draper's party, and you lot were always up for a drink, anywhere, anytime. So you turned up and there was just drums, guitars, and bass, and just anyone was having a pop, and then we played some stuff. Then you said you were off on tour with Taddy, and he was looking for two people to roadie, so Steve Barnett, who was our drummer, and I went off and roadied on the Absolute Disaster Tour!'

One small piece of trivia before we move on. As a result of the Vitus Dance/Toyah connection, Mark got a small part in an episode of TV detective series *Shoestring*, series 1, episode 9, entitled *Find The Lady*, with, as well as Toyah, Christopher Biggins and Gary Holton, first broadcast on 12 February 1979 on BBC1. Thought you'd like to know that.

As early as the first gig, at the Cedar Club in Birmingham on 30 November, the promoter admitted that he didn't actually have the money to back the tour properly, and suggested that we meet at the hotel after the show to discuss how we could overcome this minor hurdle. Of course, anyone in their right mind would have been on the first train home out of New Street as soon as the gig ended, but ever the optimists we waited in the hotel bar to see what Tadd and the mysterious northerner (his name is, naturally, lost in the mists of time, but you've probably already guessed that) had managed to cook up. It amounted to an ultimatum: stay in hotels until the northern wonder goes skint and disappoint your adoring fans when the tour goes bust, or freeze to death sleeping in the van most nights and fulfil your obligations to your public. Like idiots, we went for the latter.

In a vain attempt to mollify us, the Northern Wonder (I've decided I like the name, so I'll use capital letters from now on), pointed out that for any gigs within striking distance of Sheffield, from whence he came, we could kip at his place. As he lived in a converted monastery, which I must admit was pretty impressive, and as all the gigs were in the north, this actually helped quite a lot. In the end, we only had to sleep in the van for a few nights, but as that year's winter still stands as one of the worst on record, that was more than enough. Also, even when it was feasible to drive back to the monastery, this involved spending half the night in Ian's laughable luxury tour bus, freezing our bits off on the drive back. Simon, who as usual was in charge of merchandising, showed the feudal spirit by resolutely staying in hotels for the entire tour and laughing at us derisively when we showed up, shivering, coughing and sneezing, for soundchecks.

And the misery didn't end there. Oh no. Our early, fanciful notions of staying in hotels or B&Bs were soon followed out of the window by our not unreasonable assumption that we might at least be provided with a little beer money. On tour, one is traditionally provided each day with a PD, which I believe stands for something fancy in Latin, but by the time we came along had been bastardised to Per Day, i.e. pocket money paid, like, Per Day. This didn't disappear entirely (even Ian had more sense than to think we would stand for that. No food? No worries. No accommodation? Okey doke. No beer? AAAAAARRRRRGGh!) but we were reduced to a strictly regulated intake, and we weren't happy.

To make things worse, while we were all destitute, Mark and Steve were somehow kept on the wages that Ian had originally promised, as Mark recalls: 'We were on £100 a week each, in your pocket. That wasn't bad was it, in those days?' Bloody right it wasn't. It was in fact more than twice our weekly wage, and before long we were bumming drinks off the road crew.

And, believe it or not, things got worse still.

But it has just struck me, and not before time, I fancy, that as we now have two Marks involved in this missive, this is as good a time as any to relate how one of them acquired his nickname, thereby saving us from any unnecessary confusion later on. Mark Byrne not only took his change in status from budding rock star to roadie in his stride, he actually got right into the role, and bought himself a sort of light fawn boiler suit in which to perform his duties. Now, as Mark is not a big bloke ('Small but classically formed' is how he chooses to put it) and sports a cute, slightly chubby face, the overall effect was to make him rather cuddly in appearance. When he turned up, thus attired, for the first date of the tour, in a rare show of wit Tadd immediately piped up 'Fuck me, it's Sooty!' We all followed suit, and the name stuck. To this day, despite his having tried in vain to shake it, many people still know him only as Sooty or Soots. So Sooty it is from now on, okay kids?

Back to the plot where, if you remember, things got worse still. If the first thing that struck us, on clocking the tour posters, was their unfortunate tendency to portray our vocalist in a somewhat porcine light (they were nicknamed The Pig Posters), the second was the ticket price at the bottom. £2.50! It doesn't sound much now, but as tickets for most gigs by bands like us were going for £1.50 at the time, it was way over the odds. We told the promoter that the kids wouldn't (and in some cases just couldn't) pay it, and he said he'd see what he could do. In the event, despite our protestations, he stuck with it, and seemed genuinely shocked when the first thing that happened when we arrived at each gig, was the club owner screaming that he must be out of his mind charging this outrageous sum of money to see this bunch of clowns. Some of the more polite ones gave us a weak grin and said 'No offence, like.' None taken. They were dead right.

We were left in something of a quandary. As we were only too aware, we had delivered one almighty turkey of an album, and were keen to play as many gigs as we could in an attempt to prove that we could, in fact, deliver the goods, as it were. Now, despite our good intentions, it just looked like we were trying to fleece the poor suckers a second time. In hindsight, we should have pulled out, really, but we clung to the hope that the Northern Wonder would see sense eventually and saw it through to the bitter end. Unfortunately, he was as stubborn as he was stupid, and the ticket price was never reduced. (As an aside, his main reason for booking the tour at all seemed to be to raise funds to promote some band called Flock Of Seagulls, that he had a stake in. Whatever happened to them?)

On the whole, most of the fans coughed up the exorbitant entrance fee - none too happily, obviously - but as Mark recalls, to some of them that extra pound made a big difference: 'I remember in Liverpool, a couple of kids coming across and saying 'We were told it was gonna be £1.50 and it's £2.50,' and we said 'Sorry, but it's not that big a deal is it?' and they said 'Well yeah, if we pay to get in we can't afford the ferry back to Birkenhead.' We managed to blag them in, but it wasn't easy because it wasn't our money, was it? It was the promoter's money. In Liverpool, certainly, it really affected people...it was quite a downer.'

Though they were more than forthright in complaining to us about the ticket price, and who could blame them, the kids were great at all the gigs come show-time, and their enthusiasm took Sooty, for one, by surprise: 'Birmingham wasn't too bad, it had a good stage, but at Sheffield I spent most of the gig led down on the floor, with a monitor pushed against my back and my feet against the front of the stage, just to give you, or them [Dave, Mark and Beki], two foot of walking space. Just to keep all the kids back. It was just complete mayhem. That was when I realised it was all crazy...and really exciting, y'know?' Talking of mayhem, when Chron Gen wisely pulled out of this nightmare of a tour, Mayhem, a fine band from Southport, in Merseyside, stepped in to support for many of the dates. I'm a little sketchy about the band's recording activities at the time of the tour, but

Collo, Johnny, Deadcat and Mick McGee later signed to Riot City and had two EPs in the indie charts, Gentle Murder and Pulling Puppet Strings.

Much as we liked Mayhem, though, they did cause some problems, as Mark remembers: 'Mayhem turned up late all over the place. And in Huddersfield, Mayhem's back-drop was a fucking great Union Jack - in a reggae club! I thought, 'Oh God, we're not gonna get out of here alive."

In case you were wondering, no, Mayhem were not right-wing. As Mark says, bearing in mind the Oi! thing that was prevalent at the time, 'It was just a bit of a fad. Perhaps just patriotic, shall we say. They were a bit boisterous I seem to remember, things just seemed to happen around them.'

But it wasn't all bad, I suppose. There were, for instance, a couple of memorable nights off.

The first just happened to be on Dave's 20th birthday, 5 December, making it a double cause for celebration, and as we were spending the night at the monastery, we decided to paint Sheffield red. A glance through the local paper revealed that we had probably chosen the worst night of the entire year to sample the bedazzling nightlife of South Yorkshire, as there appeared to be fuck-all happening. Apart, that is, from a gig by the Bootleg Beatles at Sheffield University. 'Tribute' bands are two a penny these days, but in 1981 it was still something of a novelty, so we gave it a go. Also, student bars were subsidised, an important point given our financial situation.

On arriving, the first people we bumped into were Debar, who, for those of you with short memories, were the local all-girl band who had supported us at Marples. They and a whole bunch of Sheffield punks had reached the same conclusion as us regarding the evening's lack of possibilities, but once we got together, a pretty raucous time was had by all. The students were pretty bemused by the presence of all these loud-mouthed punks, especially when, during the Bootlegs' set, Dave (ever observant) bellowed loudly at the bassist 'Oi, Paul! Yer supposed to be fuckin' left-handed!' If looks could kill...

Towards the end of the night, Debar's guitarist, Aileen, took Dave off to the toilets for a 'birthday blow-job.' It was alright for some; I was lucky to get a card and a box of chocolates.

After that evening Dave and Aileen were an item for a while; Igor started seeing one of Debar's entourage (nice girl - we were all invited to afternoon tea in her posh house with her equally posh parents); and there were rumours about Mark and their bassist, though to be fair, these were never substantiated.

On the second night off, we made Ian drive us to the good old Retford Slaughterhouse, where the Exploited and Chron Gen were playing, with the express intention of scrounging as much of their riders as we could. We weren't proud. For some, as well as the free booze (mainly from Chron Gen; the Exploited ran for cover as soon as they saw us) the evening had some fringe benefits. Beki was of course more than happy to be meeting up with Glynn again, and Dave had arranged an assignation with Aileen.

It was a fine gig, and we all managed to get a bit pissed, but then Ian got his revenge by stubbornly refusing to drive us back to Sheffield. His plan was to park the van on some moor or other and spend the night there. Undaunted, we stocked up on booze (I 'acquired' a bottle of brandy from somewhere, apparently) and decided to make a party of it. The exact spot that Ian chose for this impromptu gathering has been long lost in the mists of etc etc. Suffice to say, it was a pretty godforsaken neck of the woods, but we made the best of it. We had a few drinks and a few laughs, and eventually things got quite lively. I'll let Dave relate the more sordid details (what a surprise): 'In the front seat, Beki's giving Glynn one. Glynn's sat there with his knob that comes up to here [points at the ceiling] and Beki gets on board, and she's happy as fuck. Now Aileen, the Vicar's daughter, is giving me a blow-job on the back seat, but you know, I was staying out of the way of them, 'cos comparisons could've been drawn!

'Shane was getting stuck into a bottle of brandy big-style. Then you fell into a bog in the middle of this moor, I seem to remember...'

Yes. Thanks Dave. Let's move on...

The tour was also made more bearable by the presence of Sooty and Steve, who as well as providers of beer, were also a good laugh. Sooty we already knew, of course, but we'd only met Steve twice, briefly, before the tour, and apart from his drumming abilities (he was brilliant, the bastard) all we knew about him was that he seemed excessively cheerful at all times and possessed a peculiarly high-pitched laugh.

He was, we learned, a proud father, and spent much of our days off searching out gifts for his offspring, which seemed kind of cute to us. He was also, however, an aficionado of certain illegal substances - as were several of our happy throng - and when these weren't readily available he was nothing if not resourceful.

Over to Dave: 'When the whizz ran out on tour, he had us going around some dodgy estate on the arse-end of Manchester or somewhere into some boarded-up chemist's shop, where he ordered about forty packets of Dodos [perfectly legal tablets, containing God knows what dodgy chemicals, that seemed to exist purely to enable lazy students to cram all night before exams]. 'Don't worry lads, if you're desperate these'll do the trick!' 'So we said 'Well, alright Steve, how many of these do you need?'

'He said 'Oh, about two boxes.' Fair enough, it did keep you awake and give you a sort of buzz, but Igor did his two boxes then came back: 'I can't piss! I can't piss!'

''Oh,' said Steve, 'I didn't tell you about that one did I?' And then there's probably half a dozen instances of Igor running back with things like 'I've turned blue,' and 'Me eyelids have turned purple.'

''Another one I failed to mention,' Steve would say. There were all these side-effects that could have left you dead on the spot, but you were awake!'

Probably the best gig of the tour was Carlisle Market Hall, on 3 December, as Mark recalls: 'Carlisle was an absolute stormer, that was our Beatle-mania one where people followed us back to our hotel and stuff. That was the one that made us carry on, 'cos it was bloody depressing up 'til then. Six hundred-odd people in that night, Simon did a bomb.'

Simon certainly did have a good tour (with money in his pocket and hotels every night, he was always going to have a better tour than the rest of us, the git) but he took particular pleasure from the following incident: 'When we left Hull and drove to Middlesbrough we went via York, because we had been told that a shop in York was selling bootleg Vice Squad t-shirts. We stopped there, and went in, and said 'Have you got any Vice Squad shirts mate?,' and he said 'Yeah, I've got these.' He showed me them, and I said 'Are you aware that they're bootlegs? We're from Vice Squad.' His face was a picture. We walked out with a pile of bootleg t-shirts, which we went on to sell in Middlesbrough, ha ha!' No flies on that boy, I can tell you.

Nevertheless, it was an awful tour, a fact that we made clear to Tadd and The Northern Wonder by having t-shirts printed with the legend Oi! - The Absolute Disaster Tour (the people at the shop refused to print the word 'Fuckin'' after 'Absolute,' the poofs) but it was water off a duck's back to them as long as the kids were coughing up the cash.

As depression began to set in properly, what had begun as an in-joke on Mark, who one night confessed that hearing the song I Go To Sleep by the Pretenders on a pub jukebox made him homesick for Kerry (aaw!) got to us all. We got into the habit of playing it repeatedly on any jukebox that had it, just to wind him up. But by the time the tour was nearing its welcome conclusion, the opening bars of that maudlin ditty had us all cuddling our jackets, dreaming of home, and weeping pathetically into our beer.

Oi! - The Absolute Fuckin' Disaster Tour was put out of its misery at Worksop Sports Centre on 12 December, and few mourned it's passing, as Mark remembers: 'Cleopatra's was horrible, Brannigan's was good, the Mayflower was always good, and Worksop Sports Centre wasn't. We were all so jarred off by then I think.'

Now, if you were paying attention, you may remember that when I left my boss, Mike Williams, to become a Famous Rock Star, I had agreed to go back to work for him for a week in the run-up to Christmas. The Worksop gig was on the Saturday, and I was due back at work on the Monday, a fact that I must confess I was in two minds about. Though hardly a battle-worn touring veteran, after two problematic tours, my time in the world of signwriting seemed to have happened a million years ago. On the other hand, they were all good blokes, even if they took the piss out me mercilessly, and I looked forward to seeing them all again.

They still took the piss out me, of course, but there was a subtle change in that I spent lunchtimes in the pub with the rest of them, rather than going home for lunch with my mother, which had been my habit in the old days (ooh, several months before). It was a good week, even if, apart from a guy called Steve Woods, who had an interest in music and had even roadied for Arthur Brown (you know, 'Fire!, doo doo doo') was the only one that had the faintest idea of what I had been up to in my absence.

All too soon the week was over, and so was my career as a signwriter. But although Mike never really approved of what I was doing, he was always gracious whenever I called in to say hello, and more than helpful when I was trying to sort out artwork for Vice Squad or some of Riot City's releases. Top bloke, in the current parlance.

Vice Squad had only one more gig in 1981, but what a gig. The Christmas On Earth Festival, at the Queen's Hall in Leeds on 20 December has passed into legend. Anybody who was anybody in punk played it, and it turned out to be the crowning glory of our wave of punk (I've given up trying to work out if we were second, third, fourth, fifth or sixth-wave - who cares?).

The Queen's Hall was a massive venue (now, sadly, a car park), and the event, which was promoted by John Curd's Straight Music, attracted around 10,000 people. Apparently, there were at least another couple of thousand punters who had purchased tickets but couldn't get there because of the appalling weather conditions.

One look at the line-up should explain why there was so much interest. As if the prospect of seeing the mighty Vice Squad wasn't enough (stop sniggering, you) for the paltry sum of £4.50 one could sample the delights of, (deep breath) The Damned, The Exploited, UK Subs, Black Flag, Anti Pasti, Anti-Nowhere League, Chron Gen, Chelsea, Trockener Kecks, The Insane, Charge, Lama, and GBH. Bow Wow Wow were supposed to appear but didn't. We all wept buckets.

Given the weather situation, which hadn't improved since our ill-fated tour, we decided that, to be on the safe side, we should make an early start. Simon, Igor and Bambi stayed at my house, to cut down on the time that Ian would have to spend picking people up, and we set off at an obscenely early hour, something like 4.00am. Beki had been staying with Glynn, and was to make her way to Leeds with Chron Gen, with dire threats ringing in her ears should she get there late.

All sorted then, or so you would have thought.

I recently wrote an account of the show for issue 15 of *Vive Le Rock* magazine, for their 'You Should've Been There!' page, so to save me writing it all out again, here it is:

> 'As the weather was so atrocious, we (Dave, Mark and I from the band, roadies Igor and Bambi, Riot City honcho Simon and our then manager Ian) all slept at my parents' place in bunks and sleeping bags ready for an early start at 4.00am. Beki was going out with Glynn from Chron Gen at the time, and staying at his place in Hitchin, so was travelling to the gig with them.
>
> The weather was every bit as bad as anticipated, with non-stop snow and the roads treacherous with ice, but the early start got us there in reasonable time, if not terribly good spirits
>
> At the cavernous venue, which, apparently, had originally been a bus and tram depot, it was freezing cold, but not freezing enough to stop the snow from melting and pouring down the steps into the hall itself, so you were wading through water and muddy slush most of the time. So, when Ian announced that he had to drive to Sheffield to pick up some parts for his PA system, I decided to tag along with him, anything to get out of that hell hole. Of course, if I'd known that we'd still be talking about this event 32 years later...
>
> Well, it was certainly warmer and drier in the lorry, and we stopped in a nice pub on the way back for a meal and a few beers, and ever the benefactor, when I noticed that the pub sold draught ale in plastic jugs I bought some for the lads and lass. The latter of whom should have been there by then, so we hastened back to the Queen's Hall.

We weren't unduly disturbed, at first, by Beki and Chron Gen's non-appearance. The weather was so bad that a lot of people were having trouble getting to the show, but as time wore on promoter John Curd and his people were getting decidedly agitated. And you were really, really, ill-advised to get John Curd and his people agitated.

Just as we were considering hurriedly drinking the rider before it was taken back due to our no-show, Beki and Chron Gen finally showed up. Although it was quite late in the day, we were informed that a 40 minute slot could be made, and that as it was Chron Gen's fault that Beki was late, we had the option of either doing the whole 40 minutes ourselves, or sharing with Chron Gen. So we said 'Tough tits Barber, you don't get to play then!' Only joking.

In fact it all worked out rather well for us. We went on considerably higher up the bill than we should have, and with only 20 minutes to fill, just played all the tracks from our first two EPs, and our cover of EMI, finishing with Last Rockers, and if I say so myself, it went like a bomb.

Earlier in the day I'd walked (or waded) around the venue, picking up, incidentally, a nice bootleg Motorhead BBC In Concert session EP from a stall, and it was obvious that plenty of people had turned up, but it was only when I got up onto the stage, and then up on to the drum riser, and looked down, that I realised how big a show this was. I've since heard that anything from 7,000 to 9,000 people were there, but anyway, when it got to my solo 'military' snare bit at the end of Last Rockers, and the whole crowd, looking like a football crowd, clapped along, the hairs on the back of my neck stood up. I saw Rammstein in a 10,000 seater stadium in Nottingham last year, and looking down on the crowd took me right back. Shame we hadn't had flame throwers and a huge foam-squirting cock, really.

Chron Gen also benefited from doing a 'mini-greatest-hits' set, before the Subs ripped the place up, as did the Exploited. For some reason the Exploited's sound man 'helpfully' 'flatted' the mixing desk, ie moved all the faders back to zero, so the Damned's chap had to start from scratch, but it made no difference, they closed the event in fine style anyway.

All in all, it was one of the best nights of my life.'

CHAPTER 9

THOUGH NOT OFFICIALLY WORKING FOR US once the debacle that was the Absolute Disaster Tour had ended, the events he had witnessed had set Sooty thinking. As he says, his opinion of Ian as a manager was luke-warm to say the least: 'For a man who didn't drink much or take drugs, he used to just disappear into a sort of fantasy land...he used to go on about all sorts of mad stuff. I can't remember what he was on about, he just used to talk drivel, and Igor was seriously worried about him. Then I said to Igor 'We've got on so well, what about if I managed you with Ken Lintern?' who was then with Rainbow Promotions. I proposed a me and Ken package, 'cos I didn't want to bullshit, and I thought I'd be a lightweight sitting in an office all day long on the phone trying to negotiate with EMI. I thought no, I want to be involved with the musical side of the management, ie the production, even from that early stage.'

Igor asked us if the idea was worth pursuing, and we had few real objections other than fear of the unknown. After all, in his own peculiar way Ian had steered us through some hazardous waters. On the other hand, he was undeniably completely hat-stand, so we gave Igor and Sooty our blessing.

They had a meeting with Ken, and he was happy with the idea, but with certain reservations, as Sooty recalls: 'Igor, Ken and I had a chat, and Ken said 'Yeah, I'll go along with it, but I'm not getting involved with any of the messy stuff. If you get rid of Ian, I'll be in with Soot, we'll do it as a partnership, but you two have got to go to him.''

Ever cautious, before the situation proceeded any further, on 4 January we all met with Sooty and Ken at the Swan to discuss the implications of the move and just how the Dynamic Duo would divide the work, not to mention the money. The deal they proposed was that, as Sooty outlined earlier, he would take on all musical duties and Ken would be the business brains of the operation. Between them they would take 15% of our earnings, as opposed to the usual 10% that a single manager would at that time have charged, but for that we got a free road manager, driver, sound engineer and producer, which seemed fair enough. And neither of them were hippies.

The next day Sooty and Igor picked Ian up from his house and brought him to a pub called the Green Dragon in Downend, where the rest of us were waiting - we couldn't in all conscience leave all the dirty work to them. We couched it in the most diplomatic way we could, but as you can imagine, he wasn't best pleased, and threatened all manner of legal proceedings, but as Sooty says, our minds were by this stage made up: 'It started off a bit fancy, and in the end we said 'Well, fuck off! We don't care what you say, or what you say you're going to do, we know you can't do it Ian, we think we know you.' Igor quite rightfully said 'I just care about Vice Squad, and I don't think you're right for 'em.''

In the days that followed, Ian came up with a few typically bizarre objections to our plans, the most notable of which was his assertion that he'd seen it coming all along and cunningly secreted his Bertie Dugga partner, the other Ian, in the next bar at the Green Dragon with a long-range microphone. He apparently had all our libellous words on tape and would pursue us through every court in the land.

For reasons that he couldn't comprehend, we rather failed to quake in our boots, so somewhat chastened he agreed to meet Mark and I on 7 January to discuss terms. As Beki, Dave and Sooty couldn't attend due to their meeting on the same day with Ashley at EMI, to discuss the future of Vice Squad, Ian saw that he was beaten, and eventually a deal was done which essentially meant that he got to keep the cursed van and received a small cash settlement, if I remember rightly. He certainly got the van anyway, which was never any use to us in the first place.

Later, he vented his spleen when someone stole the damned thing, put sugar in the petrol tank, and set fire to it, by telling the police that we were surely the prime suspects. They went through the motions and questioned us, but made it clear that they weren't all that interested, and as far as I know the true culprits were never apprehended, as they say in all the best detective novels.

To all intents and purposes, that was the end of Ian Tadd as far as we were concerned, and under Elephant Management, which Ken chose as the name for his and Sooty's partnership, we embarked on the next stage of what we laughingly referred to as our career.

Rather mundanely, their first job was to sort out a couple of rehearsals at the Impulse Cafe in St Pauls, and transport to a one-off gig at Bradford University Queen's Hall on 15 January. The rehearsals were fine, but one of our budding Brian Epsteins made an inauspicious start to his career in band management while driving us to the gig in a hire-car, as Mark recalls: 'Sooty drove us into a taxi, which took our wing mirror off, and that was the first time he ever drove us!' When asked about this crash, Sooty goes on the defensive: 'A CRASH? A scrape I'd call that...not crash was it?' Alright dear, stop breaking the crockery. Actually it was a really good gig, and we all enjoyed working together, especially as this time we didn't have Tadd or The Northern Wonder breathing down our necks. Relative sanity at last.

Our next outing was much more exciting, and we proudly told anyone in the pub who would listen that we were embarking on our first European Tour. I'd been abroad twice before, on a school trip to Scandinavia at the age of ten, and a cheap package holiday to Malta with Mandy in 1980, but most of our lot had never left this sceptred isle before, so it was quite a big deal for us. The fact that our European Tour consisted of just three dates in Holland dampened our enthusiasm not one iota.

On 21 January Sooty picked us all up in a hire-van, and we set off for the 11.30pm crossing from Dover in high spirits, but lacking one wing mirror. Yep, he did it again, the clot.

The main thing we'd all heard about cross channel ferries was the availability of cheap booze, so naturally, once the van was parked up and the formalities sorted out (the amount of paper work involved in taking equipment abroad is unbelievable) we headed for the bar. Mark's diary entry for that day reads: 'Drank all night, Shane passed out,' which is a fair summary but a little incomplete. When we got there, we found a strange and exotic brew called Stella Artois, which we'd never heard of but was cheap, so we tried it. It was very nice, so we had a few more. Now, Stella is a brew with many fine qualities, a prince among beers, but it just doesn't agree with me. I know this now, but I didn't then. To cut a long story short, from what I can piece together from my hazy memories and what the others told me the next day, in an extreme state of drunkenness I got into a row with a touring rugby team and only avoided being torn limb from limb when my trusty comrades apologised on my behalf and dragged me out of the bar. I apparently expressed my gratitude by throwing Igor down a flight of stairs before, as Mark says, passing out.

When I emerged, shamefaced, in the morning, someone said: 'My God Shane, your skin is grey!' It was nothing compared to how I felt. I've tried Stella Artois a few times since, but it always has the same affect; I just never learn.

Actually, some time after I wrote the above, Beki recalled that I'd been imbibing more than beer:

'Shane and me drank a bottle of vodka between us on the ferry and then I bought some whizz at the club and took that. I had a bad throat so Sooty gave me a half bottle of brandy. Then some guy offered me some cannabis, he opened this tin and I just pointed to the biggest bit assuming he'd break a bit off and make me a joint. He put nearly all of it in and I started smoking that, then someone else gave me a spliff. So I had a spliff in my mouth, one in my hand, brandy in the other. I threw up about seven times, the sink was cracked so most of it went on the floor. I managed to get through the gig and started to feel great towards the end and wanted to do an encore but I think that the rest of you were knackered by then. There was a guy from CBS there, EMI didn't have any representatives for some reason so they sent this CBS guy. I told him there were some really good posters in the next room and he said 'I think it is in your imagination' because he'd seen me off my head all night.

Mark's girlfriend Kerry had about a third of what I had and was unconscious in the van for several days, so I was lucky really.'

Mark has a similar tale of woe: 'I drank a large part of a bottle of gin, and I don't like gin at all. I chucked my boots up big-time, but then so did everyone else 'cos it was quite a rough crossing.' Was it? For some reason I never noticed.

There was little time for recovery though, as, as Beki says, we had a gig on the same day as our arrival in this strange land. This was at a club called Gigant, in Apeldoorn, where we were also based for the 'Tour' in an out of season holiday camp. Feeling a little jaded, we made straight for the camp with the intention of getting a little shut-eye before the soundcheck.

It turned out to be a rather picturesque cluster of log-cabins in the middle of a lot of charming woodland, covered in a layer of thick white ice that made it look like something off a Christmas card. The only downside was that the only heating provided came in the form of very cute but utterly ineffective pot-bellied stoves.

All the same, the whole trip already seemed extremely exotic to such unworldly types as ourselves, and despite feeling like the proverbial shit (especially me), after a kip we made our way to the club in good spirits.

This was more than a little dampened when we got to the venue and had a look at the PA provided. Now none of us were equipment snobs, in fact to a man and woman we found the whole technical side of making music a complete bore, but you have to draw the line somewhere, and we drew it straight through Apeldoorn. The PA was arranged by a member of the night's support band, Cheap 'n' Nasty, a lovely but clearly deranged bloke that at first thought we were joking when we told him we had no intention of playing through what looked like a cassette player wired to two shoe boxes. It didn't help his case much when he chose to demonstrate its capabilities by dancing around the stage screaming 'Is good PA! Is fine PA!' and playing a small plastic saxophone into the mike. Diplomatic as ever, we said 'Is not good PA, is shit PA. Get another or we're not playing.' He finally got the message, we got a proper PA, and the gig was fantastic, though Igor, like Beki, was now in something of a mess:

'Do you remember that Apeldoorn gig? That's the one where we all got stoned before. We got stoned before, and Beki was being sick in the sink, because some kids came up and gave us some dope at the bar, and Beki was being sick in the sink and didn't realise there wasn't a pipe attached to it, so it came straight out the bottom! And I was so stoned, that...the bar had mirrors, and it was a long bar, and there was arches to get into the bit where the gig was, and I couldn't find my way through, I kept walking into a mirror!
And you hadn't done a soundcheck, because we got there and there was a rubbish PA, and they sent the PA away, and got another PA delivered, and by then the club was open and there wasn't a soundcheck, and I had to go and do the soundcheck on my own, when the club was full of people. I couldn't play anything, but I had to go and play your drums, and I had to go and play Mark's bass, which I could do a little bit, and I had to go and play Dave's guitar, ha, ha, ha! I was stoned out of my head thinking I was playing virtuoso Jimi Hendrix stuff on Dave's guitar when I couldn't play a note.'

I still felt awful, of course, but by show time I had ceased to be grey and taken on a much healthier colouring of light puce. Ten minutes before we were due on, I realised I had left my stage clothes back at the camp, and that didn't improve my mood any, but it proved to be blessing in disguise. Stage clothes, in my case, had nothing to do with image and were a purely practical consideration. It was okay to walk around all day in heavy bondage strides and 10-hole Doc Martens, but you try playing drums in that lot. I usually wore khaki jeans and baseball boots onstage, the cheaper and crapper the better, as those were the lightest. Still, there was no choice, and though it was bloody hard work, it was worth it as by the end I had sweated out all the remaining crap in my blood stream and felt great. Welcome to Holland.

After a few bottles of Grolsch, another brew new to us (we were especially fascinated by the china and rubber stoppers on the bottles), we headed back to base.

The following night's gig, 23 January, at the Dreiluit in Zaandam, was, we were assured, the big one as it was the one that the Amsterdam punks would attend. Things didn't quite go to plan, though, as Mark recalls: 'That was the one that made all the papers wasn't it. A load of bikers turned up and they [the police] held the train back from Amsterdam...there was a lot of people on a train to Zaandam Station and they just locked them up for the duration of the gig and sent them home again. We'd heard there were going to be loads of people there and it was going to be brilliant, and then we heard all these tales about people not making it off the station. A couple had escaped and came and told everyone, but there was a load of bikers there, so I think it was probably just as well that they didn't make it, perhaps, because with the local bikers and kids from Amsterdam...ooh, it could have been a bit lively!'

Even without most of the Amsterdam punks, it was still fairly lively, what with the locals and a strange mixture of outsiders. We knew little of the squabbles and rivalries that existed between our European cousins other than the obvious things like World War 2 (you must have seen it, it was in all the papers). Mark remembers that 'This little German nutter turned up who spoke French all night 'cos he'd have got beaten up if anyone had realised he was German. He told us and made us swear not to tell anyone.'

That one was obvious, but when around halfway through the evening we heard from the dressing room what sounded like a herd of marauding buffalo entering the hall, we raised an eyebrow or two. 'Oh, that will be the Frieslanders' said one of the promoters. None of us were too hot on Geography, but it seemed unlikely that we could have failed to notice an entire country so close to home. Friesland? Where the Hell was that? We were told that Friesland was in fact part of Holland, but the inhabitants insisted that they were a separate country ('a bit like Cornwall?' one of us asked, to baffled looks all round). We never did fully understand the politics of their situation, but the Frieslanders, though completely mad to a man and woman, became a permanent fixture on our future European jaunts and in an odd way we were always pleased to see them. They tended to liven things up if nothing else.

The 'tour' wound up the following night at the Club Vera, in Groningen, about which no one can now remember anything, apart from Sooty's recollection of the long drive back to the camp. In fact, that journey is Sooty's abiding memory of the whole tour: 'I remember driving back from Groningen to that camp, that out of season holiday camp that we were given, and it was just so icy. I'd never known that sort of ice where you couldn't drive more than, like, twenty miles an hour because the van was just skating on the ice all the way back. It took us hours to get back. It was freezing the whole time.'

The next day, 25 January, we had a long lie-in before driving to Amsterdam to drop off a groupie that Igor had picked up in Zaandam (is a girl that hitches up with a roadie a groupie or a roadie-ie? Consider and discuss). On the way we stopped to pick up presents for the folks back home, which totally blew our cool rock 'n' roll image with Mareeka, or Margarine as she was referred to for reasons better known to Igor. I felt slightly embarrassed when she asked why I had bought a miniature shirt of one of the local football clubs, and had to admit that it was for my little brother Clay, who was eight years old at the time. It was the first time I'd really spoken to her, and we chatted about our families and stuff all the way to Amsterdam. Who needs cool, eh?

We boarded the 1.00am crossing to dear old Blighty, and in an ideal world that would have been the end of this largely pleasing episode in our story. However, it is not, as you may have noticed, an ideal world, and once back on British soil it was back to grim reality. A gig at the 100 Club, supported by the Fits, had been booked for 26 January some time before the Dutch tour came up, but we figured we could just get some kip on the journey home and be fresh and full of beans by the time we got there. Once off the Ferry, at 5.00am, we parked the van up and tried to get some sleep, but of course it was freezing cold, and in the end we gave up and drove straight to London.

I'd been looking forward to this gig, as our old friend Keith Dunn, of the Groove fame, now a London resident, had promised to come down and bring all his sophisticated Big City friends. He also promised to take some photos, and looking at them now reminds me just how wrecked we were by the time we took to the stage.

We always liked playing the 100 Club, and it went fine - Keith's mates were impressed anyway - but we were hardly at the peak of our powers, such as they were, and we just wanted to go home and get some sleep.

The only notable thing about the gig, in the long term, is that it was the first time we worked with SKAN PA Hire. Sooty's diary for 1982 was a purely business affair, very useful in the writing of this book, but revealing little of the inner man other than what girls he'd been shagging and when. Something in the performance of SKAN boss Pete and his assistant Jamie must have impressed him though, as in it he notes that they were 'EXCELLENT!,' as indeed they were. Though confirmed hippies, they had a firm grasp of what this punk lark was all about, and we all thought they were great. We resolved to work with them in the future as often as we could, and it was the beginning of a long and beautiful friendship.

The next Vice Squad outing, on 5 February, was unusual to say the least. Our agent got a call from one Anthony Cluett, who was on the Ents Committee at Newcastle University, and was keen to book us at the earliest opportunity. Our agent pointed out that for a Bristol band to play a one-off gig in Newcastle was sheer lunacy, logistically and financially, and that it would make much more sense to wait until the next tour when we could fit it in along with other gigs in the north east. He was adamant, however, so our man offered up the most outrageous terms he could think of in the hope that Ant would think better of it, but he bought the whole package. We were paid way over our normal fee, provided with accommodation on campus, and given everything we asked for on our hastily expanded rider. We thought it was bloody Christmas all over again.

It was one Hell of a drive, and though once in Newcastle we spotted the University in the distance almost immediately, no matter how we approached the City's traffic system we utterly failed to get any closer to the place until we threw Igor's map out of the window.

When we got there we were shown to the hall in which the gig was to take place, but couldn't do much as it also doubled as a dining room, and meals were still being served. There was plenty of activity on the stage, though, so we wandered up and introduced ourselves to the local PA crew. We'd hardly been on the stage for a minute when one of the lighting rigs that were being hauled up to the ceiling on chains suddenly broke from its moorings and hurtled back down towards us. We all dived for cover, but the roadie immediately below it just looked up casually and grinned before a fellow crew member grabbed the chain and stopped it, mere inches from his head. He then cackled a bit and just wandered off. We were all quite shaken by this if he wasn't, so we asked one of his mates who this lunatic was. 'He's Mensi from the Upstarts' cousin,' he told us, as if that explained everything. Which come to think of it, it did.

After a look around the place, I did a few sums and worked out that though the hall was pretty big, there was no way that the promoter could break even. Even if we sold the gig out, you just couldn't get enough people in to cover the costs. When I put this to Anthony, he was disarmingly honest: 'Well, I really wanted to see you and I didn't want to have to pay to travel down to London.' Bloody students, eh?

Any thoughts of a sell-out gig quickly evaporated, though, as apart from a small party of punks from Leeds early in the evening, no one else showed up. Around an hour or so before gig time, we left the bar and took a last desperate look around the hall. It was still practically empty, so suitably despondent we went back to the dressing room and consumed the substantial rider that we had been saving for a party after the show.

By the time we had to go on we were all considerably the worse for wear but it hardly seemed to matter under the circumstances. When Anthony came to drag us to the stage he was a lot cheerier than most promoters who've spent a fortune and pulled one man and his dog, but I put that down to the fact that as it wasn't his money he just couldn't give a fuck. Personally, he'd saved himself the coach fare to London, let alone the entrance fee to the 100 Club, even if he'd cost the University a packet.

In fact, there was rather more to it than that. When we got to the hall, we were fair staggered to find it packed to the rafters. It turned out that there had been a film show elsewhere on the campus, and as soon as that finished practically all the students had dutifully made their way to our gig. This was great, of course, except that as well as staggered, we were also staggering. A lot.

It didn't go so well, as Mark recalls: 'There was a lot of people there in the end...I had to be helped up onto the stage, which was about a 3ft step, but I couldn't do it 'cos I was so pissed, and Bambi just hung my guitar on me.

'We had quite a few new songs, 'cos we were just about to start recording the new album, so we were gonna try out a few new songs to see how they went down...we were running a few up the flag-pole, as it were.

'The big finale was Last Rockers, with Dave and I up on separate PA stacks, guitars out, all the bollocks...a big crash chord, lights go down, and you heard this big crash and Beki going: 'You fuckin' idiot!' He'd fallen off the PA and just missed her; as soon as the lights went off he lost his bearings and crashed off the PA and just missed her. Of course, I hear all this and freeze, and the lights go back up and I'm being helped back down by Bambi because by now I've got vertigo. Not cool!'

Surprisingly, we went down really well; it was just the sort of behaviour that the students expected from the likes of us, and the punks, most of whom we knew personally, had enough piss-taking ammunition to last them for months. Even Anthony, though still out of pocket, got away with it as it turned out to be something of a University talking point for some time afterwards. It even got a rave review in the University magazine, which stated that we were '…the most exciting band I've seen so far in the 80's.' The author? One A. Cluett, of course.

As Mark has said, by now we were already in the process of writing songs for a new album, but before that Tadd had one last bequeath from his reign to bestow on us.
Shortly after the Absolute Disaster Tour, EMI had suggested to Ian that we get straight on with a new single, which seemed reasonable enough. They also suggested, tactfully, that as the album hadn't been, ahem, quite all it could have been, that we try using their Manchester Square studio for the job. Now however you apportion the blame for *No Cause For Concern*, there was no denying that they had stuck by the terms of the contract and left us alone to come up with the album we wanted in whatever studio we chose. The results spoke for themselves, and for once I can't blame Ian for agreeing to the idea. It would have taken degrees of bullshit far beyond even Tadd's high standards to talk his way out of that argument.

Beki and Dave wrote three new songs for the release: Out Of Reach, which became the a-side, Sterile and (So) What For The Eighties, and we settled down in our new luxury (paid for by the hour) rehearsal room under some old railway arches next to Temple Meads Station to knock them into shape.

For Out Of Reach we shamelessly nicked a Slade intro which I'm sure was the sort of thing that Noddy & Co. turned out in their sleep, but we found it quite hard going. When we finally cracked it we were so childishly pleased with ourselves that we also used it for the middle-eight and ending, but it seemed to work. Sterile, I still feel, boasted Beki's best ever set of lyrics (though to this day I can't pretend that I fully understand them) so we respectfully kept the backing low-key. We upped the pace for the final track, (So) What For The Eighties, which much more akin to our usual fare, and were confident that overall it was a pretty strong package.

We had all been quite taken aback when Ian had suggested that it might make a favourable impression on EMI if we acted professional and made a demo of the songs for their perusal. Good God, pre-production? Who did he think we were, Queen? As there seemed no discernible way that Ian could make any money out of this, and indeed some would surely have to be spent, we couldn't understand his coming up with something so out of character. It all became clear when he revealed that Sooty's brother David had a 4-track studio set up in the basement of his home in Cotham and we had been offered the use of it free of charge. Sooty engineered the session, which was a pretty casual affair being just a demo, and this casual attitude wasn't helped much by the fact that Cotham boasted a fine hostelry called the Cotham Porter Stores - a cider house.

At one time the south west was awash with cider houses that served up scrumpy, a sort of real ale version of the sanitised muck that passes for cider in these dark days. The cider house is now long dead, in central Bristol at least, and even by the early eighties they were getting few and far between, so working this close to one was a treat for aficionados of the murky liquid like us. For those of you unacquainted with this noble beverage, scrumpy was cloudy, rather bitter, and as strong as fuck. Good stuff. Horrific tales abounded about how the farmers that made it chucked in dead rats and the like to give it body and flavour, and some maintained that prolonged imbibing of the drink could cause blindness. Bloody loonies. Where's me glasses?

Anyway, suffice to say that we got the demo done as quickly as humanly possible, then headed to the Porter Stores leaving Sooty to mix the thing. When we got back we all agreed that he'd done a fine job (and we loved him, and he was our best mate, and we felt a bit sick, actually, burp!) and a few days later EMI were of the same opinion.

So far, so good. All that remained was to make sure that our rehearsal room was booked for the day before the recording to ensure that we were at the peak of our powers on the big day. You're ahead of me aren't you? Yes, that's right, there was a double-booking and we couldn't get in. We phoned around, but all the other rehearsal rooms we knew were fully booked, so we gave up and went for a drink in the George and Railway pub which was our local on rehearsal days. The landlord, Geoff, was a former teddy boy that had played in rock 'n' roll bands in his formative years, and this being neither London or 1976, he was always very supportive when we told him what we were up to all day. On hearing of our sorry plight, he insisted that we bring the gear in and play in the back room. It was a kindly thought, but we had to point out that his was a quiet family-type pub, the back room was only feet from the main bar, and that rather than practising our set we really needed to just play the same three songs over and over again, which would have tried the patience of even our most ardent fans. We couldn't possibly put Geoff and his punters through that all night. Even we weren't particularly keen, to tell the truth. Geoff wouldn't let it lie, though, so we got set up and had our practice after all, much to the chagrin of the pub's regulars. What a way to prepare for a major label release.

The first day at Manchester Square was strangely reminiscent of the No Cause recording session, in that no one there seemed at all sure what to do with us or, indeed, what they were doing in general. As we played the songs over and over again, they approached the thing in many different ways, each sounding as diabolical as the last, and after a while they got a little desperate. People were drafted in from all over the EMI building and consulted, but nothing seemed to improve matters, and when Decca Wade, the former Upstarts drummer who was playing on a backing track for Honey Bane elsewhere in the building stuck his head round the door to say hello, they dragged him in too. The opinion of a man of his experience was of course valued and he duly gave it. Unfortunately, being a Geordie, no one had any idea what he actually said, but we thanked him anyway. By the end of the day we had a backing track of sorts, but it still didn't sound too hot, so it was in a rather subdued frame of mind that we repaired to the five star hotel that EMI had laid on for us. Only joking. Actually, after spending the rest of the evening in the pub we slept on Ashley's floor in Kilburn after, as Beki said earlier, drinking his supply of mead wine and laughing at his Marks & Spencer pyjamas.

As the session progressed and the guitars were recorded, it still sounded pretty awful to us, and the engineers' assurances that it would all come out okay in the mix of course just brought on gloomy sense of deja vu. Resigned to our fate, just for a laugh we decided to draft in our mascot, Fred The Milk Churn.

Fred was an, erm, milk churn that we'd nicked from one of the venues on the Disaster tour. Why? Well, it had seemed a good idea at the time. We made him eyes, a nose and a mouth out of white Gaffer tape, put one of Mandy's jumpers over him, bought him a beret and a plastic guitar and stuck him at the side of the stage every night. In a certain light he resembled a slightly better looking Captain Sensible.

Now a touring veteran, it was time for Fred's recording debut, so for Dave's guitar solo on (So) What For The Eighties? we tipped him on his side, put the mike inside and recorded what Beki has since described as 'one of the most excruciating aural experiences ever!' And she's not far wrong.

We weren't at all pleased with the final mix, which was very heavy on vocals and drums but very light on guitar and bass; something that at least one reviewer picked up on. On the whole, though, the single received surprisingly good press.

Melody Maker: '"Oi" is generally some middle class snob's idea of "the working class", like Ind Coope beer from the keg or playing dominoes in back-to-back houses with all the kids stoning cats and booting in old age pensioners. If some of the "real punk" crowd are stupid enough to fit in with those stereotypes, more fool them.
Vice Squad sound more wised-up - instead of the usual glue-sniffing drone there's a fruit of a girl singer. A surprise.'

Bushell in *Sounds*, under the heading Last Minute Entry: 'Beki's Bash Street Boys howl in on the last orders bell - but it's well worth waiting for. Vicious drums blast a path into a forcefully bubbling sulphate-pop work out that's catchy enough to chart without losing anything on the blood, guts, and beer front. Vice Squad are growing in stature at an alarming rate. But how the hell does she cram so many words into her mouth at one time?'

Smash Hits: 'By far my favourite sound of all the current punk groups, the Vice Squad could become a big pop band, but it sounds as if whoever mixed this record wants the girl singer to become a solo artist.
The band can be heard somewhere in the background, punking away for all they're worth, while she sings clear as a bell in front.'

Despite our misgivings, Out Of Reach sold quite well and became our only 'Hit' single, reaching a rather pathetic No.68 in the national chart on 13 February before bombing straight out again the following week. The only thing that can now be said about our 'Hit' is that it qualified us for the Guinness Book Of Hit Singles. Just.

It is possible that the record could have reached a higher position. There was much talk at EMI about the possibility of getting us on *Top Of The Pops*, which as well as boosting sales was just about the only proof that your granny would accept that you were a genuine Rock Star, but we were wary on two fronts.

Firstly, the Clash's decision not to appear on the programme still meant something to a lot of punks, and when the Exploited went on to promote Dead Cities they received a lot of flak from the great unwashed.

Secondly, there was at that time a certain number that you had to reach in the charts (somewhere in the forties, I believe) to qualify for the programme. Much nudging and winking went on at EMI to the affect that we could, you know, find ourselves at just such a position if we wanted, know what I mean mate?

As for the Exploited appearing on the programme, I thought it was just wonderful. As far as I was concerned, seeing bands like them, the Rejects, the Subs and the Upstarts on *TOTP* was the way forward. Alright, it was a crummy programme, but if there was any better way of recruiting new converts to The Cause than Wattie screaming and gurning at the nation on peak time television then I had yet to hear about it. The underground system of independent labels and fanzines is something that I've been involved in from my formative years to this day, but if you get a stab at the mainstream, grab it with both hands, that's my motto. Also, you got to laugh at Big John's silly haircut over your baked beans on toast.

Having already sold our souls to The Man, this was probably the next logical step, and we had many earnest debates about whether or not we wanted to appear on the programme, but one thing we all agreed on was that we didn't want to get the chance through any of the nefarious means that certain people had hinted at. If we did it at all it would be on our own merits, just like the Exploited. Of course, when the record dropped out of the chart the argument became academic, so EMI pulled out the stops to get us on *The Old Grey Whistle Test*, or *Whistle Test* as I believe it had been shortened to by then. The shortening of the name was a feeble attempt to shed the programme's hippy image that still lingered since the days when the wretched Bob Harris was its presenter, but we liked the idea as at least you played live on the show rather than miming. In fact, apparently it was having to mime, rather than anything on moral grounds, that was the Clash's main objection to appearing on *TOTP* in the first place. Sadly, again such arguments became academic, as after some initial enthusiasm the BBC went cold on the idea, and we never did get to play on national TV.

The *TOTP* episode was still on our minds when we met up with GBH for a gig at Lancaster University on 27 February. For us this was a warm-up for the next night's show at the massive Glasgow Apollo, a big date on the punk calendar billed as The Gathering Of The Clans. GBH were, of course, hardcore, on an indie label, Clay, and immensely popular. Basically they were as punk cred as you could possibly get, so it was a rather shame-faced Mark that admitted to them that we had been at least tempted by *TOTP*.

Amazingly, they said we were mugs for not going for it: 'Don't you realise it adds at least fifteen thousand to your sales?,' one of them apparently pointed out, shaking his head sadly at our stupidity. I dunno, you try to do the right thing...

The line-up for The Gathering Of The Clans was the Exploited, Anti-Nowhere League, Our Good Selves, Infa Riot and the Threats - a pretty good package that quickly sold out. We were slightly bemused when our agent pointed out an unusual clause in the contract that stipulated something along the lines of 'If any member of the band leaves the building at any point of the evening, the management accepts no responsibility for their safety, and should said member fail to perform his or her duties, as stipulated under the terms of this contract, this contract shall be rendered null and void.'

It seemed a little odd, but we'd heard that Glasgow could be a pretty rough place, so we figured they were just covering themselves and thought little more of it. We left our hotel in Carlisle and arrived at the Apollo in plenty of time for our soundcheck, which passed without much in the way of incident.

As they were above us on the bill, the Anti-Nowhere League were next up, and as I may have hinted earlier, we were more than a little suspicious about them. They were managed by John Curd, and their seemingly overnight elevation in status seemed to us, rightly or wrongly, purely down to that fact. It has to be acknowledged that they went on to sell a Hell of a lot of records, a lot more than us, and are popular to this day, but somehow I never got over that initial uneasiness. It didn't help when we almost bumped into singer Animal, who was bedecked in quite startlingly normal clothes and carrying a kit-bag, in a narrow corridor backstage, and instead of snarling menacingly and threatening to tear us all limb from limb, he politely stood to one side and said 'After you.' Now, I admire politeness in a chap at all times, but this was hardly what we'd been led to expect from The Animal. Sooty has similar recollections: 'I'm sure Dave and I have elaborated this over the years, but we remember them whacking some black grease on to make themselves look grubby. They looked quite punky, but they still had their kit in training bags...and then they came out and went 'Bleeaaargh!' They did their soundcheck, and I was up by the desk, and Wattie was up there and he grabbed the talk-back mike off the PA guy and went 'Abba! Abba!' They'd just finished a song and he went 'Fuckin' Abba!' Everyone laughed, and that was his comment on their music, that it was Abba, you know, and then he just walked off. It was great!'

While we're on the subject of Wattie-At-Glasgow anecdotes, I may as well add a couple of my own. Soundchecks over with, I had a look around the merchandise stalls that were busy setting their wares. At one I bumped into Wattie and noticed that the guy had some Partisans shirts for sale, and as I was rather a fan of said band, I asked the guy how much they were. Before he could answer, Wattie pointed out the Vice Squad shirts on offer, which were obviously bootlegs, and asked what I thought of them. As slow on the up-take as ever, I said they weren't bad, and asked again how much the Partisans shirts were. The stall-holder saw that he was bang-to-rights and gave me a shirt for nothing, but I remained totally mystified by this show of generosity until Wattie took me to one side and explained the deal.

My second anecdote may be entirely apocryphal, but I hope not, and it certainly did the rounds. At this time there was a short-lived fad for punks to keep white mice as pets and carry them around in their jacket pockets - I remember Peter from the Test Tubes walking around the Lyceum with a number of the beasts perched on his shoulders. Anyway, I wasn't there, but apparently, backstage at the Apollo one of these rodent-loving punks was chatting to the Exploited when her poor dumb chum jumped from her shoulder to the floor, and in a reflex-action, perhaps due to his upbringing on the mean streets of Edinburgh, Wattie immediately stamped on it with his army-issue boot. We all liked Wattie. By now we were all in need of a stimulating libation or two, and we mentioned this to one of the promoters, asking which of the local hostelries he would recommend. He blanched visibly at this request, then composed himself and pointed out paragraph 13 clause b), or whatever, of the contract, the one I mentioned earlier about no one leaving the building. At first we assumed he was joking, but before long he managed to convince us that he was very much in earnest, and that if we vacated the premises at any stage of the proceedings, we might as well keep going all the way back to Bristol, though he was a little vague about why he considered these draconian measures necessary.

Our frugal rider was now but a fond memory, so we asked if it would be okay to send a trusted roadie, ie Igor, out for supplies, and this was deemed okay as long as there was someone on hand to carry out his duties come show-time should anything, like, happen to him, which suited us quite nicely. However, Igor saw that this guy obviously knew something about the prevailing circumstances in the area that made this a bad idea for him personally, even if the guy wasn't letting on exactly what these circumstances might be, and steadfastly refused to go.

More than a little fed up at this turn of events, we returned to the backstage area to see what entertainment value could be had from chucking the remains of the food part of the rider at Infa Riot, who responded in kind, until one of them beckoned us to the window. We looked out to see the crowds of punks that had been gathering all day grouping together and looking not a little agitated at something. Several coaches were parking up just down the road, which was hardly unusual for an event on this scale, but this seemed to be the focus for their agitation, and we soon saw why.

When these vehicles disgorged their occupants they were revealed to be mostly mods, who proceeded to stalk down the middle of the road in a menacing manner, with their leader brandishing a large and lethal-looking sword. Being of a cowardly and squeamish disposition, I didn't hang around to witness the outcome of all this, but paragraph 13 clause b) suddenly made perfect sense and I was glad that Igor had trusted his instincts. Inside the Apollo, as the Threats kicked off the show, the atmosphere was no less menacing, as John Hamilton reported in his *Sounds* review:

> 'A venue like the Glasgow Apollo is not exactly the best place for any up-and-coming band, or any punk band for that matter, to establish any kind of link with the punky hordes. The stage is unnervingly high, and the actual venue is a cavernous affair more

suited to Abba than any band on tonight's bill.'

With the possible exception of the Anti-Nowhere League, perhaps, boom boom! During the Threats' set the bouncers attempted to keep order in a manner quite unsuited to a punk gig, as Mark recalls: 'The stage was about ten foot high, and nobody was allowed to leave their seat. One kid got up and started jumping up and down and three bouncers rugby-tackled him out through a fire-door...the bouncers were terrifying.'

The bouncers' resolve began to crumble during an excellent set by Infa Riot, during which the crowd made its present felt in no uncertain manner, and I'm happy to report that by the time we went on they had more or less given up altogether. Back to John Hamilton:

> 'A rally-rousing cry met Madame Bondage as she led her Vice Squad out into the void. The new single 'Out Of Reach' came over as powerfully as a herd of stampeding elephants, and was met by a reaction also similar to a herd of stampeding elephants. The gruesome Shane pounds away madly and 'Evil' is under way, during which Beki (in the process of cajoling her crowd) comes dangerously close to being pulled off the stage by an over enthusiastic fan, who gets roughed up and thrown out by the bouncers, as is usual with the Apollo. The Squad's anthem 'Last Rockers' bursts forth at a blistering pace, and makes an excellent finale to an amazing set.'

Oh great, so, now I am not only a 'pigeon with anorexia' but I'm 'gruesome' with it. Thank you, *Sounds*. Still, as live reviews go it certainly was one of our better ones, and not far short of the truth at that. We were fair amazed at the reception we got, and at the end, rather than the usual deluge of bottles and glasses, we were showered with gifts, including a very nice studded wrist strap which I wore for a long time afterwards. If you happen to be reading this, thank you, generous punter.

The Anti-Nowhere League and Exploited both went down a storm, and what at one point looked like an accident-waiting-to-happen proved to be a great success, and something of a showcase for the whole British punk movement of the time. Concluding his review, John Hamilton sums the whole thing up rather nicely:

> 'This year has been a great year for punk, and the Gathering Of The Clans and the Glasgow crowd prove it.'

Once we were confident that the surrounding area was now totally free of sword-wielding mods, we despatched Sooty to retrieve our van while we finished our drinks and sat around feeling rather smug with the other bands, who were also feeling a mite smug, so we were in like-minded company.

When we emerged around twenty minutes later, we were surprised to find Sooty shaken, and not a little stirred, in a previously pristine but now badly dented hire-van. Mark explains: 'Sooty went to pick the van up and a load of little kids recognized him and said 'Oi! Give us some t-shirts!' He said 'I can't!,' got in the van, and they started lobbing bricks at him. He had to drive very fast around the block and then come back when they'd gone. They were just a bunch of kids, but as hard as fuck!'

Over the next few months, John Hamilton's 'Great year for punk' continued to gather momentum, and we gigged regularly, including another of the now famous Sunday nights at the Lyceum on 28 March with the Damned and Peter And The Test Tube Babies, but let's take a brief break from all this seriousness and look at a bit of silly but fun promotional fluff that took place on 3 March. In the early 80s there was a curious magazine called *Flexipop!*, that was similar to *Smash Hits*, in that it was a light-hearted, glossy magazine, which mostly concentrated on pop but also covered a smattering of punk and metal, and the gimmick was that, as the name suggests, you got a free flexi disc with every issue. Some of them were quite good, and I still have my Motorhead one, a rollicking live version of Tiny Bradshaw's Train Kept A Rollin'.

One of the magazine's oddest regular features was a three page photo-story, the sort of thing usually found in in girls' comics like Jackie, set out like a comic strip, with photos instead of cartoons and the dialogue in speech bubbles. The twist in *Flexipop!* was that instead of the usual models posing for the photos, they used 'pop stars.' Sometimes it was real pop stars like Tight Fit, Mari Wilson and Depeche Mode, but other times it was the likes of the Rejects, the Upstarts, Blitz, and, yes, now it was our turn.

The photos were credited to Violent Neil Matthews and the words to Cruncher Collingbourne, really Huw Collingbourne, and I did once read, on the internet (though of course I can't find it now), one of these chaps saying that we had been difficult and hadn't wanted to take part, only giving in after drinks were bought and much nagging. It doesn't really sound like us, we were always pathetically grateful when any paper, magazine, or fanzine took any interest in us, so either he's mistaking us for someone else or we just got the wrong end of the stick and had expected a simple interview and photo session. We may have just been self-conscious about the idea of acting out a story, with props, in a public place. Well, whatever happened on the day, we went ahead with it, and had a great deal of fun. The story was called Deathwimp II, and the idea was that while we were all in our room (really the SAM control room) our upstairs neighbour, Sooty, was driving us mad by listening to Roger Whittaker! Beki cracks, goes upstairs and trashes his records, with the deathless prose line 'That's the last time you'll play this lot of pig's poo!,' to which Sooty replies 'Ooo, what a rough girl!' Then, over the next two pages, he pushes over Ken Lintern, and with dummy revolvers, machine guns and bazookas, kills us all, one by one. The outside photos were shot in a grass square just off Stoke's Croft, and years later I was working as a temp in a nearby office. As I knew no one, I sat on a bench in the square to eat my lunch, and it was only after I'd been there some time that I realised I was sat next to the tree that I'd been stood against when Sooty had killed me with a bazooka, my line being 'What's this thought bubble doing here? I've just had my brains blown out so how can I think?'

It was published in issue 17 of the magazine, in April, with Paul Weller on the cover, and it actually came out rather well, even if the colour processing was messed up so all the blood came out black. Interesting to note that Sooty's copy of the magazine, which I'm looking at right now, still has the Haircut 100 flexi disc firmly taped to the cover, unplayed after all these years.

On 22 May 1982 the event on the lips of the nation was the entry at number 47 in the national chart of our second album *Stand Strong Stand Proud*. Oh, and there was a war on as well, if I remember rightly.

We'd begun work on the album back in January, as soon as Sooty and Ken had taken over as our management, and written it in the rehearsal room under the Impulse Cafe in St Pauls. Most bands have a problem with that 'difficult' second album on the grounds that the songs on the first have had plenty of time to develop while the band is still farting around in the gutter. When that has been such a storming success, the band then have to follow it with all-new material conjured up in a relatively short space of time. Usually, if the aforementioned success has failed to reach the required level of storming, the question is academic as there will never be a second album. Somehow, though, we managed to fall between these two stools. Our first album had managed to chart quite successfully, despite being the proverbial crock as acknowledged by one and all, so we were granted a second, and largely undeserved chance. The point I am trying to make here is that many bands, having made the classic album fitting for their genre, feel they have to move on or progress in their future work. We, on the other hand, had had a hit punk album, but still failed to produce a good punk album, so that was our mission for *Stand Strong Stand Proud*.

The album was produced by Sooty, for his own M.B. Productions, and we booked into Cave Studios for two weeks from 11 February.

The engineer for the session was, of course, our friend Andy Allen, who had engineered (and produced, if the truth be told) our first two singles, and though he never disputed Sooty's role as producer, he was never a man to let his opinions remain unheard. Before a note had been fired in anger, he put his foot down over the cleanliness, or lack of, of my drum kit, which after the extensive live work we had been undergoing of late, was thickly encrusted with dried-up gob. His reaction is one that we all still chuckle about this day. He insisted that the thing be thoroughly washed and scrubbed before he would go anywhere near it, as Sooty remembers: 'One of the funny things was the washing of the drum kit, as though spit hasn't got a particularly good acoustic quality, so we had to scrub it off! You were really pissed off: 'Why are you doing that to my drums? If the kids see 'em all shiny they'll start spitting on 'em again!' But I remember Igor pointing out, down in the cracks on the drums, where there was some interesting mould growths on the gobs, where they'd been there for a long time. It was, like, Awwwh! Yeah, it was positively alive your drum kit, it was a rather wonderful thing really. Gaffer tape wouldn't stick to it, it would just fall off, 'cos it was just so covered in people's mucus. Great!' Once I met Andy's, on reflection, perfectly reasonable standards of hygiene, things went well as Sooty recalls: 'Beki was a bit hard to get along with, wasn't she, but she was on cracking form. You were all on cracking form, you knew exactly what you were doing. With Mark it was hard to get a good version down on the bass, but he was fully aware of that, so it wasn't a problem. He'd say 'No, that's shit, I'd better do it again,' 'No, that's shit, I'd better do it again,' 'Oh, that was a good one wasn't it?' 'Yeah, that was great Mark,' you know what I mean, so there were no egos.

'Dave was the complete workman, did what he was told for me the producer. I don't mean did as he was told - Dave had it all planned out - but I mean as producer, when I asked him to do something, and he thought he could do it, and it was a good idea, he would do it, and in that respect he was great to work with.'

Sooty's right about Dave. As the main songwriter, he had the album planned out well in advance, with copious notes and instructions on how each song was to be structured. A good many of the lyrics were Beki's, and Dave kindly included an inferior effort of mine, Fistful Of Dollars, much reworked, but the arrangements were all down to him.

Like many of the early punk records, the album had certain obvious musical reference points, as Mark recalls: 'I was quite impressed with a lot of it because I didn't have the sort of musical background, the sort of glam rock/Velvet Underground sort of thing that Dave did. So a lot of the more obvious Bowie/Velvets rip-offs that he was doing were new to me...and very good.'

For the finished article, though, Sooty justly claims his share of the credit: 'I came up with an idea that really gave the album a sound. I had this odd pedal that squashed the sound up, and we got a very clean sound on the guitar, and Dave played all the stuff clean, which would have sounded awful on its own, and then he played exactly the same part again with this dirty guitar sound. When we mixed the clean one under the dirty one it gave it that much more of a kind of colourful poppy-ness that *Stand Strong* has got.'

The whole album was mixed by Sooty and engineer Andy Allen, with the rest of us looking on and chuckling at their squabbling disagreements on matters that meant nothing to us, in one mammoth all-night session on 8/9 March. They were finally satisfied with their labours, as were we, by 4.00am, and after a couple of hours kip we took the tapes straight to EMI for the agreed delivery time of 12.00 on 9 March. Talk about cutting it fine.

Ken drove us to London for the meeting, and we listened to the tape on the way. He proclaimed himself highly impressed, and given time to stretch, yawn, and smoke a gasper or two, I had to admit that it didn't sound too bad at that. EMI were in full agreement, though I was a little miffed when Ashley, who always had his doubts about my abilities, suggested that we had used a drum machine for the new, speedier version of Out Of Reach. I was miffed firstly because I'd sweated blood to get the song both faster and perfect just to shut him up, but secondly because if I'd thought of using a drum machine, I probably would have done, and saved myself the trouble.

Once the back-slappings and Well Done's were over with, though, we reached what I believe could be termed a bone of contention with EMI. Somewhat predictably, they wanted just Beki on the cover. As far as I remember, she was as against this as the rest of us, so, as a compromise, it was agreed that a band photo taken by photographer Simon Spokes would be used for the sleeve, but we would also include an inner sleeve with photos of Beki overlayed with the album's lyrics.

With that unusually blood-less dispute over with, EMI lost no time in arranging the cut, at 10.30am on 11 March in Abbey Road. I wasn't there, but Sooty was: 'I came up with Dave, and we cut the album, and that was when Ashley was going, like, 'Ooh, McCartney's in Studio 4, McCartney's in 4, do you want to come and see McCartney?' And we're going 'What do we want to come and see Paul McCartney for? To say 'Hello, you're Paul McCartney aren't you? You're really famous and we're nobodies'? And then he went 'Oh, well, Bowie's in 2, Bowie's in 2' and all this. We went 'Oh Ashley, please, we're just having a cup of coffee in the cafe."

When the press reviews appeared, they were not the raves notices that I suppose we'd been hoping for, but on reflection I suppose they were mostly fair:

Bushell in *Sounds*: 'This isn't a great album but it is a very good one. For Vice Squad it's a crucial show of strength because their first album was such a let-down. Like the equally dodgy debuts from Chron Gen and the 4-Skins, the Squad's No Cause For Concern was fatally nobbled by lack of care and knowhow.

Thankfully, this time round they screwed their loaves and roped in professional production ears. Take a bow Mark Byrne, and tell-all ex-Ex-Pistol Andy Allen...And together they've concocted a delicious twelve track cocktail of punk sense and pop sensibility.

No fashionable Motorhead-metal abrasions here, as the title track single shows the new Squad sound is brazen punk-pop, bold, lively and infectious, with a touch of Penetration thrown in for good measure.

Beki's voice is the big surprise. Never has she sounded richer or more confident, applying her lavish larynx to a variety of tightly-played tempos including several that'd make Billy Whizz tongue-tied. The girl can SING, and in an age of shriekers that's a rare mercy.' In case you're confused about the Andy Allen reference, Bushell was mistaking our Andy Allen with another Andy Allen that had recently been working with Paul Cook and Steve Jones.

Chris Bohn in *NME*: 'Many things Vice Squad are not. Most positively they're not often wrong and though being right isn't always enough it does help.

Being right, a shade to the left of indignantly claiming to be in the right, is something very dear to Vice Squad. The accuracy of their earlier records...has strengthened their resolve and broadened their range.

They are no longer content with living out their lives using the excuses doled out to them, as did the Oi! boys, and if they're not above celebrating pyrrhic victories in random assaults on an oblivious establishment, they know how to hurt where it counts.

Vice Squad's tentative jabs at "important" targets are nothing compared to the knockout blows they deliver to the petty ones. This is both sensible and fair, as it is those niggling little things, the personal jibes, that have scarred them the most, namely, from their potential audience, and gamely, us!'

He later continues: 'Pitched somewhere between epigram and slogan, the words - by Beki or guitarist Dave - are often smart and memorable. They have the cutting edge lacking in the more mundane post-punk splutter of the group.'

And concludes: 'What could have been great ends up being not bad. Not bad at all.'

Carol Clerk in *Melody Maker*: 'Most striking are those numbers where the band reach out beyond familiar boundaries. There's tracks like No Right Of Reply with its fast/slow contrasts, Saviour Machine which sets airborne vocals over restless rhythms, and Rock 'n' Roll Massacre (the story of RIP's like Janice 'n' Jimi) with its rattling verses, emphatic choruses and quiet conclusion, a plaintive reference to the Sid/Nancy saga ("Remember the Chelsea Hotel...") and a lonely bell tolling into the silence.
An immeasurably improved band, Vice Squad offer an album for the thinking punk...'

Other reviewers were less impressed:

Mark Cooper in *Record Mirror*: 'The best a "new" punk band can hope for is to sound almost as lively as an earlier and more original punk thrash. Vice Squad don't roar or rage or exult - they go through the (now) tidy motions of punk, clipped drumming, leading bass, wall to wall guitar.'

Wigan Evening Post: 'Vice Squad are fast emerging as the latest champions of new punk. They have been held aloft as positive proof that punk is still alive and kicking, still a relevant movement with something relevant to offer.
Sadly, nothing would seem further from the truth. Vice Squad's new LP *Stand Strong, Stand Proud*, on EMI, for all its desperate exhaltations [sic], is 1977 ideals and ideas slightly polished up to hide the wear and tear...but the shabbiness is nevertheless all too evident.'

By now, though, we were beginning to take a more philosophical view of the possible effects of reviews on actual sales. You would rather read a good one than a bad one, of course, but the album's accompanying single release, the predictably named Stand Strong EP, gave us cause to wonder about the true power of the press.
In the established tradition of the music business, the single slightly preceded the album, and in the 24 April edition of *Sounds* Steve Keaton had made it our first (and last) Single Of The Week, with a photo that took up most of the rest of the page, and easily the most gushing review we ever received, even if he did refer to it throughout as '*Stand Strong Proud*':

'Whatta way to go! The first truly GREAT record Vice Squad have ever made explodes like a head in a scanning contest...Sharp and shining with more than a little pop sense, the thing rages like a leather-clad King Kong over the cowering, crumbling Empire state competition. An impressive beast.'
He continued in this rather over-excited vein for some time before concluding: 'Jeez, how much more wonderful can a record get? '*Stand Strong Proud*' is 70mm magnificence with all the trimmings. You'll dream of it at night.'

It died a fucking death.

Of course, in the great Vice Squad tradition, it goes without saying that there was more to the single's failure than that. Never the types to shy away from the opportunity to shoot ourselves in the foot or defend a totally pointless corner, we had had endless arguments with Ashley over which tracks were to be included on the, at that stage, single.

Stand Strong was of course always going to be the a-side, and we insisted that, clinging to our punk value-for-money ethics, there had to be two non-album tracks on the b-side for the die-hards that bought both records.

Ashley, however, was equally stubborn, and insisted that his favourite song from the album, Rock 'n' Roll Massacre, be included. In the end we compromised and released a four track EP with Stand Strong and Rock 'n' Roll Massacre on the a-side and two new songs, Tomorrow's Soldier and Darkest Hour, recorded at SAM, for the b-side.

Initially this seemed like a good idea, but all too soon we spotted its fatal flaw. When the record arrived we took it to Igor's local, the Full Moon, as the locals were keen to hear our latest masterpiece. It was duly installed, and the correct number selected, but when the record that was already playing and shaking the building to its foundations faded out, a rather tinny and barely audible noise limped from the speakers. What we (and EMI) had overlooked is the simple fact that, while it is perfectly possible to cram two songs on each side of a 7" record, this reduces the sound level considerably, and while this matters little on the b-side, it has certain repercussions for the a-side. In the case of a juke-box, it means that the paying punter is likely to grab the bar-person by the scruff of the neck and demand his or her money back as they can hardly hear the bloody thing, and this is what happened in the Full Moon. It was quickly removed.

More damaging was the fact that the record was effectively ineligible for radio airplay, as no DJ was likely to start mucking around with his faders for the likes of us when there were plenty of other records around that delivered the standard level of sound. Of course, as we later learned, the usual industry procedure for gaining airplay for EPs was simply to press a number of singles with just the a-side or main track to be issued to DJs, and why no one at a major label like EMI suggested this I simply can't imagine.

In the end, our main radio champion for *Stand Strong Stand Proud* was, as ever, John Peel, who had invited us back to Maida Vale to record a second session for his show on 28 April. The session, which was produced by Roger Pusey and engineered by Martin Colley, gave us a chance to air album tracks Propaganda, No Right Of Reply, and a reworked Humane, plus, for reasons that now escape me, Sterile. When the session was broadcast on 10 May, I listened to it in my bedroom, by which time all the review copies of the album had been sent out, so I was mortified when, after playing No Right Of Reply, Peel paid us a few compliments, calling us 'Terrific,' for one, then mentioned casually: 'They have an LP out shortly...well, I say shortly, I've already seen it reviewed in fact, but we haven't got a copy of it yet, he said rather sulkily.' Crimson with embarrassment at this oversight, I felt even worse when after Humane he declared that we were 'Almost single-handedly dragging punk into the 1980s.' I was on the phone to EMI the following day at the crack of dawn. Well, lunchtime anyway.

All in all, though, we were quite pleased with the album's reception. In some ways *Stand Strong Stand Proud* was an exercise in damage-limitation after the first fuck-up, and we took the chart placing as a reflection of that. It was lower than *No Cause*, but at least people were still listening.

CHAPTER 10

WHILE WE WERE BUSY trying to keep Vice Squad on an even keel with EMI, it was far from the end of Riot City, which continued and expanded under the tutelage of Simon. This part of the story is, you will not be surprised to hear, rather complex, which is why, as promised earlier, I have decided to take time out to explain as much of it as I can in a separate chapter.

As you may recall, though we were equal partners with Simon in Riot City and our EMI deal included a clause that we would continue to issue our records under the name, we effectively handed over the reins of the label to Simon when we left.

This was a mainly guilt-assuaging gesture, but there were at least two consequences that we didn't anticipate.

Firstly, though Simon carried on with Riot City as a completely indie label, many people assumed that as Vice Squad were signed to EMI, so was the entire label, which attracted much derision from the Crass mob, as Dave remembers: 'We still wanted to be on Riot City and that was part of the terms of our signing to EMI, as I remember, so that we could disguise the fact. Although I think we justified it to ourselves, genuinely, being young and idealistic people, that it would be completely separate from EMI, which we found out in a fortnight was definitely not the case.'

Secondly, once in charge of Riot City, Simon chose to take it in a direction that we didn't entirely approve of.

Initially, we continued as a partnership, with Simon consulting us about ideas for new signings, while we came up with some of our own, a good example being Wigan band the Insane. At the time Beki was going out with their drummer, Dave 'Bambi' Ellesmere, who of course had previously been a member of Discharge, so it was only natural that their Politics single became Riot 3. It was moderately successful, reaching No.18 on the indie chart in December 1981, but the band left Riot City soon after to sign to No Future.

Riot City kicked off 1982 by releasing all the tracks from our two EPs as a 12" (Riot 1/2) in a sleeve designed by Danica Gacesa with a previously unpublished front cover photo taken by Simon at the Cambridge Corn Exchange when we supported the UK Subs. On the back of the sleeve were two more unpublished photos by Simon, one of which was taken in Cleethorpes (the other I can't place) and all the lyrics, but beyond that we could see no possible reason why anyone would want to buy the thing. Simon was insistent that it was a goer, however, and he was right. The record sold over 10,000 copies and reached No. 21 on the indie. Not bad for a load of old tat in a new sleeve.

Next up were Leeds outfit Abrasive Wheels, who Dave and I had seen at the Granary supporting Slaughter, a short-lived reincarnation of Slaughter & The Dogs fronted by, if memory serves, Ed Banger. On the night, Slaughter were pretty lame, but the Wheels were stunning, and on our recommendation Simon got in touch with them. We were more than chuffed when they joined our happy throng, especially when we heard their self-released debut 7" The ABW EP (Abrasive Records ABW 1). To this day it is one of the most blistering records I've ever heard, and it's perhaps due to that fact that their Riot City debut Vicious Circle (Riot 4) was a slight disappointment - it was a perfectly respectable punk rock record, reaching No.12 on the indie in February 1982, but it lacked the bite of its predecessor. This was but a temporary blip, however, and the band went on to record some of Riot City's finest material, including a re-release of The ABW EP, on red vinyl, which as Riot 9 reached No. 24 on the indie in April 1982. Their final two Riot City releases, both of which registered pretty high on the Awesome Scale, were the single Burn 'Em Down (Riot 16) which reached No. 14 on the indie in October, and the album *When The Punks Go Marching In* (City 001) which made No. 3 in November. Both releases were produced by Mike Stone, famous for his work with the Lurkers and owner of Clay Records, and credentials like that couldn't easily be argued with, but Dave and I were still a bit disappointed as we had been angling for the producers' job ourselves. I must admit that we had a bit of a chuckle to ourselves when the band immediately jumped ship to Clay Records, (no one was ever actually signed to Riot City - all deals were on a record to record basis) and presumably Simon was none too pleased, though he doesn't seem too bitter about the betrayal now: 'They were like a cross between the hardcore and the more poppy side of punk, weren't they, and they were accepted by both sides. They were a good band; in fact, next to you guys, they were the most successful Riot City band.'

Simon came up with the next signing, a young band from the Lawrence Hill area of Bristol called Court Martial. They sent him a demo, which we all liked, and the final decision was made after we saw them play a great gig at their local youth club. The Gotta Get Out EP became Riot 5, and duly reached No.23 on the trusty indie chart in March.

So far, so good, but the crunch came with Simon's next proposed signing for the label. Though most of the Riot City releases to date were more sprightly than the old '77-style punk records, they were not quite hardcore, and on the whole we were still unimpressed with the bulk of the hardcore material we were hearing, but that was a direction that Simon had been wanting to move in for some time. As early as May 1981 he had released Disorder's Complete Disorder EP on the Disorder imprint (Order 1), though whether we objected to them joining Riot City, or they didn't want to come anyway, I honestly can't remember, but it was an argument that was always going to crop up eventually. It came to a head when he insisted on Chaos UK as the label's next release. Beki was the only one of us with much sympathy for hardcore, and history has since proved both she and Simon right and the rest of us wrong - it was the next and only logical step for the punk movement - but at the time we were not happy bunnies. Against our wishes Chaos UK's Burning Britain EP became Riot 6, and sold very well, reaching No.8 on the indie in March, which we couldn't easily argue with, and at that point we became contributors to, rather than partners in, Riot City Records. I agree with Simon, though, that this change in roles wasn't particularly acrimonious: 'I'm sure there was probably a time when you said 'Why are you putting that out?' and I said 'Well, 'cos I'm here doing it and you're not,' I suppose. But we never had a meeting did we? I can't recall anything. And I think that was probably how it was left to be honest; you saw that it worked alright under the way it was done, and that was how it was left.'

Though, as we shall see, Dave and I continued to work with Riot City, at this point Mark chose to have nothing more to do with the label: 'Because it still reflected on us years later, I think we should have kept a bit more control. But at the time I was quite happy to disassociate myself from the whole thing, really, that's not what I was into at all. I was never into the sort of Discharge side of it...my girlfriend Kerry was well into Crass and all the Epping Forrest bit, and I went to quite a few gigs, you know. I went to see Crass a couple of times, and I went to see Honey Bane, and I was much more amenable to that, though I still wasn't keen.'

After a while, though, all the bad feelings cooled a little, and I even came up with a proposed new Riot City release. A guy called Ricky Fox, who hailed from Rothwell, near Leeds, was one of our biggest fans, and travelled far and wide to see us, eventually becoming a good friend. However, when he announced that he had formed his own band, and presented me with a demo tape, my heart sank a little. We were forever having tapes forced on us, and past experience told me that it would almost certainly be a load of rubbish - another valued friend lost. Thankfully, though, this turned out to be the exception to the rule, as it was all good stuff, particularly a number called Dreaming, and Dave and I quickly recommended the band to Simon, who was equally enthusiastic.

Ricky's Vice Squad fixation was so pronounced that he based his own band on our blueprint, leading at least one critic to call them 'The New Vice Squad' (whereas, to be fair, we had once been called 'The New Penetration,' which was equally misleading, and probably pissed Pauline Murray off quite a bit). The band's line-up, therefore, boasted a female vocalist called Joanne 'Jo!' Ball, along with guitarist Tim Ramsden, bassist Craig 'Macca' McEvoy and Ricky on drums. Ploughing the Vice Squad furrow still further, Ricky insisted that the band's debut Riot City recording session should take place at Cave Studios in Bristol, where we had, of course, made our first two EPs.

This proved to be a wise move, even if it did mean that the band had to make a 500-mile round-trip and sleep on my floor for the duration (Dave mysteriously found room for Jo! at his house, but I don't think we'd better dwell on that). The session, which kicked off on 1 February, was supposed to have been produced by Dave and myself, but at the last minute we had to book Vice Squad into SAM studios to record some b-sides, leaving the band to do the job themselves. As SAM was only a brisk five minute jog from Cave, once my drum tracks were down, I was able, when I got my breath back, to stick my head around the door, occasionally, to offer the band advice based on my vast experience of production technique, and they kindly gave me a credit, but of course all the real work was done by our old friend Andy Allen.

Three of the songs recorded, No Life, No Future, Dreaming and What Justice? were chosen for inclusion on the band's debut EP, while the fourth was set aside for a forthcoming Riot City compilation. So far, so good, but disputes then arose over which should be the EP's title track. Naturally, Simon, Dave and I assumed that this would be Dreaming; fine though their other material was, this was easily their best song at this point, and, frankly, we signed them on the strength of it. However, in the first of many bizarre moves that would make our long association with the Expelled, um, interesting they decided to call the EP No Life, No Future. The time honoured ploys of threats, bribes and cajolery were brought to bear, but the stubborn Yorkshire folk were having none of it, so No Life, No Future it was.

As we had predicted, when Riot 8 first appeared, some reviewers concentrated on the title track and the notices were not particularly favourable; but happily most picked up on Dreaming, and the record reached No.16 on the indie in April.

On the strength of this, the band went on the road, supporting the likes of the Exploited, the Business, and Abrasive Wheels, as well as becoming Vice Squad's most regular openers.

A second Expelled EP, Government Policy, this time produced by Dave and I, grandly calling ourselves SAD (standing for Shane And Dave, a minor piss-take of the SAM name, which stood for Steve, Andy and Merv, the studio's owners) Productions, with engineer Steve Street, was recorded at SAM Studios during that summer's World Cup (11 & 12 July, to be exact), but was held back by Riot City until the end of the year. Riot 17 again got favourable reviews, and reached No.15 in December.

Unfortunately, at the end of 1982 it all started to go wrong for the band when Jo! left to get married. She was replaced by Jewelie, who joined the Expelled just in time to record a rather disastrous Peel Session, though once she'd settled in, the live work Jewelie did with the band throughout 1983 was well received.

When Jewelie left the band at the end of the year, for reasons undocumented, she was replaced, briefly, by a girlfriend of Dave's called Penny, who stuck around just long enough to record two tracks with the Expelled that eventually turned up on a couple of Rot Records compilations after the band's demise. And as that demise coincided with the demise of Riot City, we'll look at that at the end of this chapter.

At the end of June 1982, the aforementioned Riot City compilation *Riotous Assembly* (named by me, if memory serves, after the Tom Sharpe novel, though after listening to a couple of the tracks I wondered if *Blott On The Landscape* might have been closer to the mark) hit the shops. The seeds of this release had been sown some time earlier, when Dave and I came up with the idea of a four track various artists EP, along the lines of Heartbeat's 4 Alternatives, to be called Ooh, Aarh - The EP!. I rang Bushell, who obligingly mentioned in *Sounds* that we were looking for contributors to this prestigious project, and the demo tapes flooded in. Simon was so taken with the best of them that the EP quickly expanded into a full album, which also included two tracks from our first Peel Session (Coward and It's A Sellout), the other Expelled track from their Cave session (Blown Away) and a specially recorded track from Dead Katss, who were actually Igor, Bambi and their fellow Fishponds Mental Mob member Mitch, with Kerry on vocals.

The album, which Simon remembers as 'One of the highlights in Riot City's history,' came in a garish red and black leopard-skin sleeve designed by Lloyd Harris, who worked at Revolver Distribution, with photos taken at a big photo shoot outside Virgin Records in Broadmead shopping centre attended by over a hundred brawling punks and skins. When Virgin were celebrating their 40th anniversary in 2013, a photo from the session was posted on their web site, under the heading 'Can you find these punk kids?', and a lot of papers and other media picked up on the story, prompting many of the 'Kids' to write in. Incidentally, you could see me and Mark lurking in the background. Anyway, the record, Assembly 1, was pressed in lurid red vinyl and sold very well, reaching No. 9 on the indie Chart.

One track in particular, the album's closing number, intrigued Simon greatly, and he enthused about it at length - a one track demo by Swindon hardcore band Chaotic Dischord, called Glue Accident. The tape hadn't come from the *Sounds* batch but, as we explained, had been passed to Dave and I by the band themselves. They were serious hardcore activists, with a deep mistrust of the music business, but we had won their trust, and if Simon wanted any more of their material all transactions would have to be conducted through us. Under no circumstances would the band consent to any meeting with a corporate mogul like Simon Edwards. This shroud of mystery just intrigued him all the more, and before the album was even released he commissioned an EP from the band.

By now the joke had gotten out of hand, and things were getting complicated. When, during an earlier argument with Simon over the merits, or otherwise, of hardcore, we had claimed that we could knock up something similar in ten minutes flat, and he had laughed, we had left it at that. It was a bold claim, made in a fit of bravado, and to be honest we weren't sure that we really could do it. We resolved to try, though, and at the end of a Vice Squad b-side session at SAM, Steve Street set the stop-watch, and Dave and I (Pox and Evo Stix), with Igor (Ampex Oxo-Box - named after the first two things he saw walking into the studio control room) on bass and Bambi (Ransid Rotten Idol) on vocals, knocked out Glue Accident. Ten minutes later the track was written and recorded and, to our surprise, it sounded quite authentic; but there was surely no mistaking Bambi's voice or my and Dave's playing to anyone who knew us, so our original plan of trying to persuade Simon that it was a real band seemed to be out of the question. However, having gone this far, we decided to give it a try. To give our ruse some credibility we took the precaution of sending the tape to a girlfriend of Dave's in Swindon, so that she could send it back to us and we could present Simon with a package postmarked Swindon, and if he had had any reservations this simple device dispelled them - he fell for it hook, line, and sinker.

We booked two days at SAM, 2 & 3 March, for the EP (with dire threats that should he come anywhere near the studio the band would immediately return to Swindon), and also suggested that at the same time we would produce the Dead Katss track for the album and, time permitting, a track by our splinter group Sex Aids. The reasoning here was, from our point of view, perfectly sound: with a little chopping and changing, all these bands were principally the same people, and if one Dischord track took ten minutes an EP should be done and dusted in about half an hour. Of course, we couldn't explain these things to Simon, and he doubted if we could achieve all this in two days that were to include over-dubs and mixing. Actually, he was right; we didn't have time for the Sex Aids track, but that was only because we spent a lot of time on a theatrical beginning to the Fuck The World EP. For this our mate Paul Riddell played the part of a judge sentencing bassist Ampex Oxo-Box to 'life on earth' for 'trying to fuck the world,' and his lengthy speech (which he took hours to get right) was followed by a rather spectacular bout of vomiting into the SAM toilet by Mitch from the Dead Katss. Steve spent considerably longer miking up the bog than the band, but it was certainly worth it.

Simon was more than pleased with the finished product, and housed in a sleeve with a glued-up mohican on the front and a few dead bodies on the back (by yours truly, I'm almost ashamed to admit) Riot 10 entered the indie chart at the end of July and reached No.14.

Fuck The World got glowing reviews in the hardcore fanzines, particularly *Maximumrocknroll* (though Richard Butler of Psychedelic Furs also played his part by describing it as 'Awful' and 'Terrible' in *Melody Maker*), and soon fan mail and offers of gigs began to flood in. Bambi became fully immersed in his Ransid Rotten Idol persona and answered all the mail by screwing up the letters and returning them together with the contents of an ash-tray, some scraps of toast, a fetid tea bag, or whatever came to hand. As for the gigs, he just agreed terms, arranged dates, and we never turned up.

While all this was going on Dave, Igor and I were touring America and Canada with Vice Squad, intending to record a follow-up on our return, but the first person to greet us off the plane in September was a rather irate Simon Edwards, whose first words were 'You fuckers! You cunts!' It turned out that our old 'friend' Taff, formerly of the X-Certs and mod band the Review, but then (and now) a member of hardcore band Disorder, had stumbled across our shameful secret and dobbed us in to teacher like the girlie swot he was. Just wait till we got him in the playground...

I think it's fair to say that Simon wasn't terribly amused by our little prank, and it took quite a time to smooth his ruffled feathers. But after a while (and after checking our sales figures) he eventually saw the funny side and decided to commission a second Dischord EP as soon as Vice Squad's schedule would allow.

The rest of 1982 was taken up with an exhaustive bout of touring to promote the State Of The Nation EP, and it wasn't until May 1983 that a positively panting world was treated to another dose of Dischord in the shape of the Never Trust A Friend single (Riot 23). By then even *Maximumrocknroll* had cottoned on, and it must be said that Dig, in his 'UK' column in issue #5 of the mag (March/April 1983) was pretty magnanimous about the whole thing, though naturally the late, great, 'Tim Yo couldn't resist a further dig (as it were):

> 'I suppose you know by now that Chaotic Dischord are really Vice Squad without Beki. Yes, it's another Rock and Roll Swindle (England seems to be full of them...). I can't help but admire the audacity of this one tho, and I must admit it fooled me at first. Anyway, Vice Squad recorded it incognito in order to show how "generic" the thrash sound is, and as a way of ridiculing fellow Bristol bands Chaos UK and Disorder. In issue #1, Jeff Bale reviewed Vice Squad's Stand Strong... EP with the words 'a band that's really deteriorated'. In #2 J.B. reviewed Chaotic Dischord as 'capable of producing 1st class thrash'. (Editors note; it is ironic that V.S. sound better on their "joke" record than as themselves). So I think Jeff ought to eat a little humble pie for being fooled, and you too Tim! But anyway, I think the lessons to be learned from this one are (1) don't judge

anything by first impressions, and (2) remember that thrash punk can be just as generic, clichéd, etc, as the '77 style punk, OK.'

Actually, with skills like those Dig could have walked into a cushy job with the Diplomatic Corps, and no questions asked, as the mood of most people was better summed up by Aphid of The Amebix in the letters page of the same issue:

> 'I was glad that we (Amebix) got a good review for our first EP in issue #2 (which we got from MDC while they were here). But am somewhat pissed off with "along with Chaotic Dischord, one of the few UK bands to break the mold". Their Fuck The World EP has had a great deal of success here in the UK, although unknown to 90% of the people who bought it, Chaotic Dischord is in fact a band made up of members of Vice Squad to take the piss out of Disorder and Chaos UK, financed by Riot City Records. They also plan to bring out a "hardcore" album, no doubt using the proceeds as spare change to mess about with in their hotel suites (cunts).'

Huh! As if we could be bothered with fiddly small denomination currency. We left tipping the waiters, chambermaids and doormen to Igor, as befitted his lowly status.

Anyway, it was obvious that a lot of people now knew our guilty secret, but as Never Trust A Friend was already recorded, we thought we might as well bung it out. We'd actually recorded it way back on 4 January, at SAM, and it was decided to tease folk a little by partially admitting our involvement without stating it outright. For a start, it was credited as an SAD Production, and the cover photos came clean with both Igor and Bambi appearing as their alter egos, but my and Dave's parts were played by Ricky from the Expelled and Mitch from the Dead Katss respectively. Further clues were provided for the particularly brain-dead by the facts that I designed the sleeve, and Simon, who was now well known to have never met the band, took the photos.

Why Never Trust A Friend was listed as a single rather than an EP I'll never know, because like its predecessor it boasted three tracks, with the songs Are Students Safe? and Popstars on the b-side. The first was a sarky dig at a poster campaign by students from St Matthias College in Fishponds, who were getting a tad fed up with the Mental Mob beating the shit out of them all the time, while the second was a very cheeky steal from Attila The Stockbroker. Attila actually wrote Popstars as a poem or rant, but Bambi just copied the lyrics from either *Punk Lives* magazine or *Noise!* and we put our own 'tune' to them. To our surprise, despite our secret being exposed, Never Trust A Friend sold very well; though Riot 23 only made No.30 on the indie chart in this country, foreign sales were more than healthy, and that proved to be the shape of things to come for Chaotic Dischord. Anxious lest we should let down Aphid Amebix, our next move was obviously a full Dischord album, though our manager, Ken Lintern, had some misgivings. Apparently EMI had come to terms with some of the plot, but of course not all of it, and were starting to make noises about 'contractual obligations' etc. Partly for this reason, and partly to see how much further we could cloud the issue, it was decided to just brazen the whole thing out and persist with the notion that Dischord were really a genuine hardcore band from Swindon, and that Dave and I were merely their chosen producers. After all, it would hardly have helped the record to have 'Dave Bateman and Shane Baldwin appear courtesy of EMI Records' on the sleeve, now would it?

While we were pondering on just what shape the album was to take, we had a chat with our mate Lloyd Harris at Revolver Distribution, who had developed a theory based on his professional experience. In terms of foreign sales, he said, hardcore records with the word 'fuck' in the title, and/or a mohican on the sleeve, sold in significantly larger quantities than those lacking these factors. With this information in mind we decided to call the album *Fuck Religion, Fuck Politics, Fuck The Lot Of You!*, and I designed a sleeve with a nine photograph 'picture story' depicting a mohican (a member of the Mental Mob whose name, naturally, escapes me) attempting to fire-bomb Fishponds Conservative Club. This gave us three 'fucks,' nine mohicans, and a bit of anarchic political content, which we reckoned should do the trick. It certainly did that, and then some.

Coming up with a whole album of material (even a Dischord one), needed at least a little forward planning, so we settled down with a selection of fine ales and a pile of music papers and newspapers, to draw up a list of targets for the lyrics. These were then split equally between the four of us and off we went, staggering somewhat, to summon our muse. To keep the thing in The Dischord Spirit, the music, if you'll pardon the term, would still be written in the studio (SAM) as we went along. This became our working method for all the Dischord albums, even though the bulk of the lyrics used tended to be Bambi's - just what was going on in that man's sick mind I had no idea, but it was just the sort of thing we were after.

All went well at first, but as the session progressed, we encountered a small problem that we hadn't anticipated. Six songs per album side was the norm at the time, and we therefore went into the studio with the required twelve sets of lyrics. However, we had forgotten that 'hardcore' songs are, by their very nature, quite a bit shorter than even 'normal' punk songs. The problem arose from a music industry ruling that albums had to last for a specified length of time to be classified as such - around forty minutes, if I remember rightly - and our twelve tracks fell well short of that total. In the time honoured tradition we resorted to shoddy covers, butchering the Lurkers' Shadow, the X-Certs' City Claustrophobia, and even Rodgers & Hammerstein's *Sound Of Music*, but engineer Steve Street's stopwatch still showed us to be short of the mark. Bereft of ideas we repaired to the pub, and I then went home, hoping that a spot of Nature's Sweet Restorer (that's sleep, to you) might provide some inspiration for the only time we had left in the studio, a couple of hours the next day for mixing.

I returned to SAM at the appointed hour a little despondent, the little light-bulb above my head having totally failed to illuminate, but found the others already there, and seemingly in good spirits. This was explained when, with some glee, Steve sat me down and played me a tape that to this day remains one of the funniest and most disgusting things I have ever heard. Apparently, after the pub had closed, the boys went back to the studio for one last attempt at the final track. It then occurred to them that they had no drummer, and anyway, after three hours in the pub no one was capable of playing a note. However, it was noted that, as was his habit after imbibing a few, Bambi was a little, shall we say, effusive, and this could be put to good use. He was placed in front of a microphone, armed with only a bottle of Cinzano (the only alcoholic beverage to hand at that time of night) and left to burble any nonsense that came into his head. As the bottle emptied and Bambi's ramblings became more and more deranged, Steve played excerpts from his collection of BBC sound effects records over the top, which puzzled Bambi no end. In his befuddled state he began to react to these strange noises, and this culminated in the track's final line 'And there wuz cows?!', which became its name. We all agreed that this was by far the best track on the album, and I used the line on the back of the sleeve.

The album, which was recorded in just two days (plus the aforementioned mixing session), unsurprisingly got an almighty panning from most critics, though Attila The Stockbroker, writing as his alter ego John Opposition in *Sounds*, seemed to get the picture:

> 'OK TRIBAL fashion punk clone, the joke's on you - again. What McLaren didn't manage with 'Swindle', Chaotic Dischord set out to achieve with this monster. The Monty Pythons of punk hit back... Just think, there are people who'll not get the joke (the otherwise excellent Maximum Rock 'n' Roll fanzine didn't: CD are hardcore's finest at the moment) but for every dedicated buyer of put-a-mohican-on-the-front-and-it'll-sell-anything compilations, this album is essential listening. Put it on before you go to bed! Do-it-yourself brain surgery!'

Hmm, he must have been talking to Lloyd. Anyway, the review continued in a similarly complimentary vein which fair made us blush (and a little uneasy when he got too near the truth), and he topped it off with a full five star rating, something we wouldn't achieve with Vice Squad until much later.

The album sold very well indeed, reaching No.6 on the indie chart, and No.12 in *Sounds*' 'Best Of 1983' punk chart ahead of the Damned, Anti-Nowhere League, Angelic Upstarts and Southern Death Cult. Bizarre.

Shortly afterwards I got a call from another *Sounds* journalist, Bev Elliot, requesting a Dischord interview. She too had obviously got the nub or gist of the situation, but I kept up the pretence and promised her a written set of statements, by the band, which she could then fashion into an interview-type piece in any way she chose. Here are some excerpts from her piece which appeared in the paper's *Punk And Disorderly* section:

> 'YOU CANNOT be serious! (And other McEnroe-ish sentiments). But, as deeper delving into the history of Chaotic Dischord reveals, thankfully they're not like the Brat - at least not 100%! Hailing from Swindon, and going under the dubious names of Ransid-Pox-Ampex and Evo Stix (guess who's the drummer!) - there's something highly

suspicious about the whole set-up, which seemingly revolves around the brainchilds of this motley crew - Shane and Dave from Vice Squad.

Their track record - as told in the words of vocalist Ransid - should give you the general ideas as to the sincerity of this hilariously brilliant outfit (bearing a close resemblance to a rejected Young Ones script!).

"Chaotic Dischord were formed fuck knows when," (about the beginning of '82 actually) - "when we all lived in a crusty squat in Swindon. We were all very drunk and we decided to make a noise 'cause we hated the people next door. They told the police when we chopped up their front door for fire wood - well, it was cold.

"We stole our amps and guitars, but we never stole a drum kit, that was a bit hard. Evo Stix used to hit boxes and biscuit tins. The first thing we recorded was I'm A Glue Accident.

"We then recorded Fuck The World EP. By then we were tired, so we went to sleep, and when we woke up we moved to Bristol.

"We hope to play around the country sometime this year. We are not Vice Squad!" Really? Hum! At least they admit to Shane and Dave as being the "sort of producers of the album".

If you haven't suffered (!) the experience of hearing them yet, buy the album NOW! The furious, thrashing music is quite highly passable 'noise', though you'd be forgiven for not noticing on the first hearing - the entertaining lyrics crease you up so much you have to exercise your concentration to catch their tongue in cheek renditions of all the boring old cliches and digs that they manage to cram into every track!'

Bev concluded:

'Instead of waiting for the next repeats of The Young Ones or splashing out to see the latest Monty Python film, just whack Chaotic Dischord on to the turntable - it's all there on platter.'

Perhaps the grammar leaves little to be desired, but still, that's high praise indeed as far as I'm concerned.

As we shall see later, most of 1983 was taken up with launching a new line-up of Vice Squad after Beki's departure, and it was well into 1984 before we were able to find time for the next Dischord release. By now we had decided that the joke had gone far enough, and the plan was to kill off the 'Monster' we had created by coming clean, lyrically, on one final record. While we were mulling over the best ways to approach this, Dave and I had a chat with Alvin Gibbs from the UK Subs, who came up with the idea of bowing out in style with an all-star Dischord line-up. He naturally put himself forward, and gave me 'phone numbers for Captain Sensible and Rat Scabies of the Damned, and Knox of the Vibrators. This seemed like a pretty good plan, and when approached all three readily agreed.

Gratified that such luminaries of the punk scene were willing to play on our record (and I would like to point out that none of them mentioned a fee), I then set about trying to organize the thing, which proved to be a logistical nightmare. These were all busy people, particularly the Captain, who, of course, by this time had a successful solo career as well as working with the Damned. At first I tried to set up sessions at SAM Studios in Bristol, but no matter how I juggled with the participants' schedules, there never seemed to be a convenient time when all could make it. Eventually, Captain suggested a studio called RMS in Norwood, London, which was just around the corner from his place, as it happened. As the idea of recording in Bristol seemed like a non-starter by now, however obliging our celebrities were trying to be, we had a chat with Simon, and though the blood drained from his face, and his hand shook visibly as he signed the cheque, he stumped up the cash for a London recording session and even chucked in some dosh for essential expenses. Those being petrol, beer, food and fags, obviously, and not necessarily in that order.

The dates on which this auspicious recording session took place have, of course, been lost in the mists of time, but it was a weekend, and H drove us there early on the Saturday, with all the gear, in his trusty Transit. As it had been recommended to us by a Major Recording Star (ie Captain Sensible) we rather expected that RMS would be a little more plush than a small room in the back of a rather seedy-looking shop, but the engineer, Andy Le Vien, seemed pretty cool, so we began setting up the equipment.

The plan was to record a single, with the a-side being a version of the Pistols' The Great Rock 'N' Roll Swindle, which seemed apt, if a little presumptuous, backed by a cover of the Damned's Stab Your Back, so we rehearsed these for a while as we awaited the arrival of our honoured guests. After a couple of hours, no one had showed up, so we began phoning around to see what was keeping them.

The early calls were dispiriting to say the least. Alvin, since we last spoke to him, had apparently packed his bags and moved to California (if he didn't want to work with us, he only had to say so); Rat was working elsewhere and had made no mention to the folk back home of turning up at our little get-together; and the whereabouts of Knox and The Good Captain were unknown.

By mid-afternoon we were panicking more than a little, when, joy of joys, Knox showed up. Knox is, as you probably know, one of the nicest chaps on the punk scene, and didn't turn a hair on finding that none of his promised fellow celebs had deigned to put in an appearance. Encouraged by his enthusiasm, we got on with the backing tracks with H playing guide bass.

It was of course hoped that at least Captain might have appeared by the time those were completed, but there was still no sign of him, so out of desperation we had a prolonged and very enjoyable jam session. One of the fruits of this was a riff that Dave came up with, following a drum pattern that I'd cooked up out of sheer boredom. Knox liked it, and encouraged Dave to write some lyrics for it, which he did that very night, and the song eventually became the title track on the record, Don't Throw It All Away.

For want of anything better to do we sent H out for some beers and fish & chips, and a packet of cigs for Knox (which he insisted on paying for, despite our protestations), before reluctantly calling it a day.

As we drove into London, giving Knox a lift, I noticed that Dave's old school bag, into which he had packed his smalls and a vast array of Rock 'n' Roll drug taking paraphernalia, had 'The Vibrators' written on it in a juvenile scrawl, and he hastily covered it up. Not cool.

We dropped Knox off at his place, more than a little surprised that he seemed keen to join us again on the morrow, then made our way to our old pal Keith Dunn's joint, where we spent a drunken, if slightly subdued night. Things were not going to plan.

I forget if storm clouds were gathering over Norwood as we drove back on Sunday morning, but if not, they should have been. The whole thing was looking like a wash-out, and early calls to Captain's abode from RMS did little to alleviate our sense of gloom. Still no sign of our hero.

To pass the time we worked on Don't Throw It All Away, with Knox providing an excellent lead vocal, not to mention some fine guitar tracks, but once that was finished we were stymied. We mentioned to Andy, in passing, that Captain had suggested another local punk hero, Johnny Moped, that might be roped in for our project, but he'd failed to come up with a contact phone number or address. It turned out that Andy had, at one time, known Mr Moped, and was able to furnish us with a list of addresses that the man had, at various times, been known to call his humble abode. It was all a bit vague, but we were desperate, so H and I jumped in the van and began what would later be referred to as The Quest For Moped, Johnny.

I don't suppose there are many people that can say they have spent an entire afternoon trekking around the wilds of Norwood and Croydon, knocking on doors and asking if Mr Johnny Moped is at home, and on the whole I wouldn't recommend it. At best you get a puzzled look from the householder, and the suggestion that you may have got the name wrong. At worst you get a Pakistani family who are utterly charming and keen to help in any way they can, while obviously of the opinion that the pair of you should be decanted into a padded cell at the earliest opportunity. So, no Moped.

When we got back to RMS, even Knox had had enough and left, so the only sensible option seemed to be to spend the rest of Simon's money in the off licence, then head for home and worry about how we were going to explain this expensive debacle to him at a later date.

As the last cans were being drained, we began to listlessly pack up the gear, when who should drift nonchalantly in but The Good Captain. Hallelujah!

It turned out that he'd got the dates all wrong, thinking we'd booked the Sunday and Monday, but seemed more perturbed by the fact that he had missed the chance to take the piss out of Knox than the more pressing fact that we now only had a few hours to complete his part of the job. Naturally, with this unexpected 11th hour reprieve, we just wanted to wheel him in front of the mic in an attempt to snatch victory from the jaws of defeat, as it were, but Captain took an altogether more relaxed approach to the situation. First, he asked to listen to the stuff we had recorded, with self a little embarrassed at my drum track for Stab Your Back. I'd had plenty of time to perfect it, of course, but try as I might, I just couldn't get it as fast as Rat Scabies' original, as I explained. On hearing the offending item, Captain just laughed and told us that Scabies had, in fact, never played the song as fast as the released version; the producer, Nick Lowe, had simply speeded up the tape before Vanian's vocals were added. How I laughed.

As for the rest of the material, he seemed quite impressed, but reckoned that the lyrics to Rock 'N' Roll Swindle and Stab Your Back needed a bit of pepping up, and suggested that we retire to the pub to work on them. Apart from the fact that we were rapidly running out of studio time, this seemed a good idea, until we remembered, guiltily, that we were now totally out of funds, despite our earlier promises that no one involved would be expected to put their hand in their pocket come drinkie time. However, he cheerfully pointed out that he was now a Major Recording Star, implored us not to worry, and paid for all the drinks in the pub, plus a new supply of cans for back at RMS. Chap!

Once the revised lyrics were completed, we returned to the studio, and soon saw why Captain had been so calm while the rest of us were practically having kittens at the thought of our rapidly dwindling studio time. For all his oafish stage persona, in the studio he was the consummate professional, putting down both his lead vocals in one take, then adding some dazzling lead guitar to all three tracks without breaking into a sweat. It was all done and dusted in the blink of an eye, then he casually pointed out that if we got our skates on, the pub was still open. Chap!

At closing time, apparently, he was even so kind as to invite us all back to his place for a night-cap, but the tension of the weekend, not to mention the alcohol, had taken its toll on your humble scribe, so the others politely declined and bundled me into the van.

In fact, I don't think anyone can have been firing on all cylinders by the end of the night, because the first thing that struck us the next morning was that we had left the tapes behind. This could, of course, have been highly embarrassing when we reported back to Riot City HQ, but when I spoke to Andy on the phone he suggested that we let him work on the tapes, for free, during the week, then report back to RMS on the following Saturday afternoon for a preliminary mixing session, thereby saving time at a later date.

Yes, the other thing we had to confess to Simon was that, though we had eventually managed to record plenty of material in London, none of it was actually finished. Andy's generosity gave us a small trump card, and with some misgivings he coughed up for a train ticket for me, and some studio time at Cave to finish the job.

Pausing only briefly to buy our Clay a Crystal Palace FC programme for his collection (I had to pass their old ground en route to the studio just as the programme sellers were setting out their wares), I made good time, and met Andy and Knox at RMS to give our work a sober listen. On the whole, it sounded pretty good, though I agreed with Andy that some ill-advised late night backing vocals by Dave and myself should be hastily erased, and felt quite a bit happier about the whole thing when the mixing was completed.

The day finished on a rather bizarre note when, at the tube station, Knox suddenly remembered something he'd read somewhere about tube trains carrying large magnets under some of their carriages that could erase tapes. It seemed unlikely, but having gone this far I was taking no chances, so we spent several minutes stooping and inspecting the nether regions of the carriages, before deciding on one that looked relatively safe. This all made sense at the time, but once on the tube, I noticed that no one seemed keen to stand next to us. I wonder why?

For the Cave session Knox travelled down from London to put the finishing touches to Don't Throw It All Away, and we also managed to rope in John Perry, formerly of the Only Ones, who was living in Bristol at the time. John played bass on The Great Rock 'N'Roll Swindle and Stab Your Back, but it was unanimously agreed that H's guide bass on Don't Throw It All Away couldn't be bettered, so we kept it, and John instead contributed a fine piano track. Looking back, it seems madness that we had secured the services of the man that had played the god-like guitar solo on Another Girl, Another Planet, only to get him to play bass and piano, but he didn't seem to mind, and proved to be a virtuoso on both instruments.

For the massed ranks of backing vocalists required, we drafted in friends, relatives and every local muso we could think of to read the lyrics from Dave's carefully prepared idiot-boards, then allowed Bambi to roundly insult everyone involved on some of the intros and outros; after all, it wouldn't have been the same without him. We were mighty pleased with the finished mixes, and after thanking one and all for their efforts, went home thanking God that the cursed project was finished, and vowing never to undertake such a thing again.

But that wasn't the end of the matter, oh no. A couple of days later, Simon phoned to say that he'd been doing his sums (he seems to have spent most of the 80s totting up figures) and wasn't happy with the outcome of his endeavours. Much as he admired the three tracks we'd delivered, by his reckoning we'd spent the Riot City equivalent of the national debt of a substantial third world country, and the bottom line was that we couldn't even cover costs with an EP. The only answer, he said, was to record six more tracks, hastily and cheaply, and make the thing a mini-album.

Somewhat wearily, we put this to Sooty, who we knew had recently supervised the building conversion, equipment buying, and installation of a new studio in Somerset. Sooty, who had also helped out in no small way at the Cave session, agreed that, though relatively cheap 'n' cheerful, Frome Musical would be easily up to the task of recording some half-baked drivel in the old Dischord vein, so we booked ourselves in.

Just for once, we decided that this part of the operation was to be brisk and business-like, so on the first day only Dave, myself and Sooty entered the studio, along with the resident engineer (and Sooty protégé) Steve. By this time Dave and I had been working together for so long that we could turn out backing tracks (basic punk ones, anyway) at a fair lick, with no guide vocals or bass, and Steve, for one, was fairly impressed by our work-rate. Sooty disillusioned him (and me) a bit by pointing out that it was all just crap, and if we hadn't got our acts together by now, there would have had to have been something wrong with us. But still, the now renowned (stop sniggering) hardcore classics Sausage, Bean & Chips, Who Killed ET? (I Killed The Fucker), 22 Hole Doc. Martens, Anarchy In Woolworths and Batcave Benders Meet The Alien Durex Machine were in the can in just a couple of hours, with Sooty later adding bass, as well as co-engineering. The next night Bambi was allowed in for his vocal tracks, and a truncated version of the Cave Backing Vocal Ensemble were dragged in from the pub around closing time, before an all-night final mix.

In my more perverse moments, those six tracks seem to me to rank among the best we ever recorded, Vice Squad included, though I was inordinately fond of the whole finished release. They were certainly among the funniest, and judging by the mail we received, the spontaneous, supposed throw-away tracks proved at least as popular as the recordings that we had spent so much time and money on. A lesson there, perhaps.

When Simon began sending out publicity material for the album, I was a little surprised to receive a call from Spike Sommer, of *Sounds*, requesting an 'expose' of what was surely the worst kept secret in punk. Of course I obliged, bless his little cotton socks, and even chucked in some off-the-cuff nonsense about a non-existent live album, supposedly recorded during a secret series of gigs in America. The short piece appeared in the paper's *Punk & Disorderly* column, along with a photo of Dave and I by Simon Archer taken outside the Full Moon in Stokes Croft, with the cringing headline 'Chaotic Disquad.' We naturally assumed that the article, if you could call it that, would be the only publicity we would be getting for our humble project, apart from the expected scathing reviews, but help was at hand from some unlikely quarters.

As I've said, by the time the record was released, Beki had left Vice Squad and formed Ligotage, taking Igor with her to London, thereby severing his links with Dischord. Now, Beki had slightly resented not being invited to take part in the early Dischord sessions (as had Mark, to a lesser extent), but we pointed out that: a) the thing had not been planned, had just evolved naturally, on the spur of the moment, and once formed it would have been pointless to tamper with it, and: b) if we had Beki singing and Mark playing bass it would just be Vice Squad playing bad hardcore. At the time Beki seemed to accept these arguments, reluctantly, but just as the final preparations were underway for the release of Don't Throw It All Away, we began hearing some distressing rumours. The gist of them was that Beki and Igor, along with members of Ligotage, were planning a 'spoiler' Dischord album, for release on Syndicate. Of course, at first we were less than pleased by this turn of events, but as Garry Johnson wrote up the 'on-going Chaotic Dischord debacle' as a sort of punk soap opera in successive issues of *Sounds*, the resulting publicity did no harm at all. It was also heartening to be told that the Syndicate record, Fuck Off You Cunts, What A Load Of Bollocks, was as humourless as the title suggested (to this day I've never got around to listening to it), and that they seemed to have missed the point (whatever that actually was), altogether.

There was one further stumbling block, this time with the artwork for the record. Dave and I shamelessly ripped-off the garish 'soap packet' design of the Clash's Cost Of Living EP, but decided to incorporate photos of all the participants, and thereby hung a problem. Captain had consulted the powers that be at his record label, A&M, and been told that though he was allowed to play on our masterpiece, he could under no circumstances be directly named in the credits, nor could any photo of his glorious visage be included in the artwork. This stumped us for a while, but eventually we got around the problem by crediting the erstwhile Ray Burns as Capt. Sen*i*le, and dressing up my ten year old brother Clay in a white sailor's shirt, round sunglasses and a beret, for the photos. As Captain's former bandmate Brian James once famously said: 'Punk Rock? It took years off you!'

When the record first appeared in the shops, it seemed that we had been too clever for our own good. Everyone now had us firmly pegged as wind-up merchants, and there was many a knowing nudge and wink in the pub as people grudgingly admitted 'That bloke you got on vocals, he really does sound like Captain Sensible. Who was it really?' Sometimes, you wonder why you bother.

CHAPTER 11

BACK TO THE PLOT, then, which finds us still in May 1982, Friday the 7th to be exact. We were of course pleased to learn that we had been granted another interview in *Sounds*, but a little concerned that the scribe was not to be Comrade Bushell but Betty Page, the paper's champion of all that New Romantic malarkey that was prevalent at the time, and close pal of Spandau Ballet, not to mention our buddies Duran Duran.

However, when we met her in the George & Railway she turned out to be a perfectly pleasant sort, and if she had any reservations about spending the afternoon with a bunch of uncouth yobs like us, showed no signs of it. In fact, when the interview appeared, while being quite honest about the fact that, at first, she had no time for our music, she was almost enthusiastic after listening to the album: 'For the benefit of this exercise, I ventured perilously close to their new elpee, sure to find a rabble-rousing noise - but no dice. Got listenable pop-punk with thoughtful lyrics and (shock) a tuneful voice.' According to Betty, Beki was '…much prettier in the flesh - a striking, tall figurine, charismatic and street-wise. A throaty, knoworrimean chuckle constantly bursts from her lips'; Mark was the 'strong, silent bassist'; Dave 'ruddy-cheeked guitarist/tunesmith'; and self a 'small but wiry drummer.' Among many subjects, the interview covered the Falklands war, American politics, the state of the punk scene, and, apparently, 'a nasty operation performed on drummer Shane's mate's testicles,' the latter of which I have no recollection. Spread over two and a bit pages, it was a very pleasing piece, and Betty concluded that: 'Maybe the time's ripe that they were seen as the West Country's answer to Tony Benn - Concerned Young Bristolians Speak Out…Punk may not reach my turntable, but if its views are as spiced as Vice, I'll listen too.'

Blimey, I think we can safely chalk that up as a result.

Sooty's and Mark's diaries inform us that an interview took place with Lynden Barber of *Melody Maker*, at their office, on 23 March, and we were not only given a decent page-and-a-half piece, entitled 'Vice Squad Report,' but a very nice colour photo of Beki, by smudge Tom Sheehan, graced the front cover of the 15 May issue. The thing I remember most about this article is the photo shoot, which also took place in a room at the *Melody Maker* office. Two make-up girls were on duty to make us look presentable, and embarrassingly, it was noticeable that the girls spent considerably longer on my make-up than on cover star Beki's, in an attempt to shield the public from the full horror of my advanced acne.

The 'Vice Squad Report' was a curiously structured piece, the bulk of which merely quoted us under a series of headings like 'History,' 'Eating Habits' and 'Politics,' with little editorial comment, seemingly leaving us to sink or swim with our own words. The verdict came at the end:

MUSIC

Kind assessment: A marked improvement on most of the "new punk" groups playing at the moment. Most of these sound like a chainsaw put through an echo chamber with a prison warder shouting inaudible slogans over the top.

   Vice Squad songs have recognisable structures and lyrics covering such topics as vivisection, war and the press. Their singer has a strong voice.

Harsh assessment: Of limited interest. Most of their songs have a tendency to sound like Siouxsie and the Banshees' "Love In a Void". Their lyrics are well-meaning but poorly expressed.

   There are no signs that they have the ability to add to, extend or comment on the music produced by the original punk groups. At their worst - as on their version of the Sex Pistols' song "EMI" - they sound like a Family Favourites Punk Group.

   "On one track on the new album we tried for a day rehearsing stuff that sounds like the Banshees" - Dave Vice Squad.

   "I wanted it to have a Cure feel 'cos I wrote it while I was listening to the Cure" - Beki Bondage.

PERSONALITY

Vice squad are nice people and are sincere about what they are doing.'

So, we were well-meaning chumps, then. Fair enough.

The *Melody Maker* piece may have appeared in the Saturday 15 May issue, but it was only on sale in London on that day; we in the sticks wouldn't have seen a copy until the following Tuesday. So, on the 15th we were still blissfully unaware of its contents and happy enough to meet Paul Morley on that day in the George and Railway for an *NME* interview. The *NME* was always decidedly sniffy and sneery about all this New Punk lark, but on the whole, as we've seen, they'd been fairly kind, if a little condescending, to us, and we had no reason to expect any more or less from this interview.

After a drink in the George and Railway, we, with Suzi Rome, Morley, and photographer Peter Anderson moved camp to Sooty's parents' house in Bedminster. It was a big house by the park, so the plan was to conduct the interview in the house, then all pile over to the park for the photographs.

We were all interviewed separately, with Dave, Mark and I ('the three bland blond boys in the group'), billed as:

SHANE / DRUMS / AGED 20 / SAD EYES / MEDIUM LIPS / BLOTCHY SKIN / LONG NECK…QUIET, FAIRLY CONFIDENT VOICE…

MARK / BASS / AGED 20 / NERVOUS EYES / THIN LIPS / SHINY SKIN / MEDIUM SIZED
NECK…SLOW, DRY, UNSURPRISED VOICE…

DAVE / GUITAR / AGED 20 / DOPEY EYES / THICK LIPS / RUGGED SKIN / SHORT
NECK…SLOW, BORING VOICE…

To be fair, he let us have our say, and reading our comments now, what we had to say
seems reasonable enough, but Morley was unstintingly contemptuous. At first, he seemed
to be fairly taken with Beki, 'The boys are plain; the girl is wildly patterned,' but at the end
even Beki copped it. And it was the end that rather rankled. When the interviews were
over and the photos were taken, Suzy was preparing to drive Morley and Peter back to
London, while we were discussing what to do for the evening. On hearing that we were
merely planning to head for Fishponds for a game of pool, and a few beers, Morley asked
if he could come with us. Now any politician would tell you that we were incredibly naïve
here, as we assumed that, the business of the day over, this was to be a purely social event,
so we welcomed him along, and Suzi didn't mind, assuming we'd won him over. I think the
politicians' maxim runs something like 'Always treat a microphone as if it's live and
remember you're always on duty in front of a reporter,' but as I say, we were just too naïve
in this instance. Now Morley got nasty:

> 'After the interviews are over we go to a nicely austere pub [the Full Moon] in the
> Fishponds area of Bristol where the group live, for a Saturday evening drink. On the pub
> TV it's Higgins versus Reardon. A round of drinks for the group will consist of two pints
> of Bass draught, a pint of Bass special and a pint of lager for Beki.
> In their almost listless offstage way Vice Squad represent the folksy traditionalism that
> there is inside today's punk: beneath the frantic surface, aside from the vulgar
> yearnings, there's a very quaint Britishness, more especially an Englishness. To talk of
> challenge inside the punk context is to talk nonsense; this Englishness is all embracing
> and today's punk is trapped by it.'

Not sure what the Exploited or Partisans would make of that, not to mention Dead
Kennedys or Bad Brains, but anyway. He goes on:

> 'The Sex Pistols weree [sic] city dwellers; Vice Squad are villagers. Harmless and
> charming where the Pistols were harmful and charmless, artless and hearty where the
> Pistols were artful and heartless.'

Served us right for not coming from the mean streets of Shepherd's Bush. What did we
expect? Bastards. Still, he had a nice turn of phrase, I'll give him that.

He concluded with a rant at Beki, 80s punk in general, and even a nearby chip shop that,
he was disgusted to note, wasn't even able to call itself a real McDonalds. My god, until he

pointed it out, I hadn't realised that we were living on the very outskirts of civilisation; a barren, lawless, windswept wilderness. I nearly moved to London the next day, I really did. At least they'd have had a proper McDonalds there.

> 'Beki herself is sat caressing her pint, and she seems to be sulking. The last I see of her is when I'm leaving the pub, driving up the High Street, past 'Curry 'n' Hurry', to buy some chips at a cheap, local version of McDonalds. A vegetarian who's thinking of becoming a vegan yet who wears little other than leather, with brightly coloured hair, tatty tights, studded boots, yards of chain. It could only happen in England. Orwell's nation of "flower lovers and stamp collectors, pigeon fanciers, amateur carpenters, coupon snippers, dart players and crossword puzzle fans" is not disturbed in the slightest by Beki Bondage The Aberrant Character and her punk rock.

Quoting Orwell. Classy, eh?

19 May was a busy day for interviews, so we had to divide them up. If I remember rightly, Dave and I were working on something in SAM that morning, so we did an interview with local listings magazine *Venue* in the afternoon, while Beki and Mark got the train to London for interviews with *Record Mirror*, *Zig Zag*, and Radio 1.

Once the press interviews were over, Mark headed home, but Beki stayed in town to appear on Radio 1's *Rock On* show. Unfortunately, the interviewer's name is lost in the mists of time. She was introduced onto the 25 minute segment, slightly puzzlingly, as 'The band's lyric writer and song bird Beki Bondage, although that's not her real name and I'm not going to tell you what her real name is.' His opening question was: 'Beki Bondage, you seem to be a band with a lot of firm beliefs. I can tell this because all over your leather jacket are written various poems and slogans. What actually are they? Are they by anyone particularly famous?'

Beki: 'Yes, this one's by Vi Subversa of the Poison Girls called Abort The System and it's a pro-abortion song. It's just a couple of verses of that, and this one's part of a Crass song. I can't remember which one it is but it's against all the factory farm meat you get in the supermarkets. So I sort of shoved it on, so there's bit of feminism on this side and a bit of vegetarianism on the other side.'

And asked about her favourite punk bands, she replied, succinctly: 'I like the Exploited's music and I like Crass's lyrics.'

He opined that: 'You seem to be a lot more sensitive, really, than the original first school of 1977 in regards your lyric writing, and you're also vegetarian, I think,' and they went on to discuss vegetarianism, the fact that she was considering veganism, and also vivisection, war, and work:

Beki: 'I worked for the Department of the Environment, I was a clerical assistant…I had to make up planning appeals, ha ha ha! It was really boring, I had to sit there filling out all these little forms all day.'

And, predictably, he asked about her name. 'Beki, the very name Bondage seems to be one that gets you in a lot of trouble, because I think you seem to be regarded in some areas of the press as being some sort of sex symbol. Is that something that sits easily on your shoulders?'

Beki: 'The name Bondage was really meant as a joke, because you know how women are pushed around a lot by blokes? I took the opposite view, 'I'm gonna push them around', you know, the whip and all that. And of course everybody totally twisted that round, so now I'm the sex object. So I don't carry the whip any more!'

He also played Stand Strong, No Right Of Reply, Humane and Propaganda from the album, and after the latter said: 'Propaganda, Vice Squad, from *Stand Strong and Stand Proud* [sic]. Excellent album, well worth lending an ear to.'

So, nothing too controversial, but Beki acquitted herself well, the questions weren't as inane as they could have been (he'd obviously taken the trouble to at least do some research) and it was invaluable exposure on prime time national radio.

Around the same time (The date is now…etc.) Beki also appeared on another, rather bizarre, Radio 1 show. Hosted by DJ Andy Peebles, it was called *Honesty Quiz*, and in his introduction, Peebles summed up the show's remit thus: 'There are many aspects that make up your personality, so which ones make you a good person? That's tonight's main question.'

In this massively pointless show, the questions were set by Peebles and Reverend John Peck, and, he said, 'We have very wide variety of personalities for you. Delighted to welcome firstly Leslie Ash, Simon from Jimmy The Hoover, Beki Bondage, it's got here 'Sometimes known as the queen of punk,' how do you feel about that as an assessment Beki?' 'In punk,' she said, patiently, 'there's not meant to be any kings or queens or leaders, so it's a rather silly term to give me.' He went on with his introductions: 'Liz Powell is the Youth Club Member of the Year, from the Birmingham region of the National Association of Youth Clubs, Christopher Lee, not the one with the teeth and the Dracula relations, but the Gold Award Winner of the Duke of Edinburgh Award which he won in March this year, and my friend Robert,' who was apparently 'on parole.'

I'll spare you the full tedium of this show, and just give you a taste of the first round to give you the idea:

Question 1. Whether you would ride your bike on a No Cycling path. (Beki: '[Yes, but] I'd probably slow down at the end…so people don't walk into you. It's more a question of morals than law.'

Question 2. Whether you would illegally tape records or radio programmes (including a po-faced statement on the subject by Bob Montgomery, General Director of the Mechanical Copyright Protection Society).

Question 3. Whether you would drink if you were still underage.

Leslie Ash scored 5, Liz Powell 7, Beki 4 ('I reckon the law's a nuisance as far as you're concerned!' laughed the Reverend), Simon 3 ('You really find the law an ass, don't you!'), Christopher Lee 9, (Peebles: 'What shall we do with him, send him to the Palace for tea with HRH?') and Robert 4.

Again, Beki (4) acquitted herself well, coming across as a decent person, without being a priggish girly swot, like, say, Christopher Lee (9), and also displayed great patience in the face of such astonishing banality.

For the *Venue* piece we talked to Dave Massey and did a photo session with Phil Hill, and they gave us a nice full page piece, though Massey couldn't resist using Morley's 'bland blonde boys' crack in his introduction. It was also a bit confusing, as he quoted Mark, who wasn't even there, several times, though he might have been referring to Sooty, who was there but naturally, as manager, didn't actually say anything. Still, it was a positive piece, which was pleasing as *Venue*, and its predecessor *Out West*, had sometimes been rather disparaging in the past. He said that 'One of the more heartening aspects of the resurgence of punk is Vice Squad's success when compared to some of the more neanderthal units that grace the pages of the music press. Vice Squad write songs that are intelligent and articulate and are prepared to ring the changes in the standard 'rock' format of the group. It's not altogether surprising to discover that (for example) Dave left school with 3 'A' levels (Maths, Physics and Economics) and that the individual members of the group are prepared (and able) to discuss serious matters without resorting to sloganising or sub-cultural sectarianism.' Yup, we always said, from the start, 'None of that fuckin' sloganising or, especially, sub-cultural sectarianism.' Only a complete bastard resorts to sub-cultural sectarianism. Whatever it means.

Of course the gigs still piled up, and on May 9th we were back at the Lyceum. For the first and only time we got to headline the place, but sadly, only by default. Discharge were given top billing, but had to pull out, and though this was known some time before, we were sworn to secrecy, as presumably it was thought that ticket sales would dwindle if the news got out. This was probably true, but a bit unfair on punters travelling to see Cal's mob, and I can't honestly remember why we went along with the shameful scam. But we did, and on the night we were supported, rather impressively, by GBH, the Insane, the Defects and the Dark.

Back in chapter 5 I bored you with the fact that I'm a great fan of the Sherlock Holmes stories, and time on the road had given me plenty of time to catch up on my reading. Having noted on previous visits that the backstage area of the Lyceum seemed to have altered little since Victorian times, once the gear was piled in, I took myself off to a corner, Sherlock book in hand, to have a read and soak up the atmosphere. I must have got a little carried away, because some time later a rather glam-rock-type bloke teetered up to me in high-heeled boots and asked if I was Shane from Vice Squad. I said 'Yes' - it would have been futile to deny it - and he kindly informed me that our soundcheck was well overdue and that the management were issuing dire threats if I didn't get down there pronto. I thanked him, of course, and legged it, but I never got the chance to speak to the teeterer again. That was a real shame, as his name was Razzle, the new drummer with the Dark, who of course later went on to greater fame with Hanoi Rocks. Sadly, as you probably know, he died in a car crash in California, in a car driven by a member of Motley Crue. I got to tell this story a few years ago in a piece in *Sherlock Holmes - The Detective* Magazine, as, as I said earlier, the Lyceum is actually mentioned in one of the Holmes stories, *The Sign Of The Four*, though what the students of Victorian literature made of it I can't imagine. The editor, David Stuart Davies, seemed happy anyway.

On 25 May, at a 100 Club show with the Expelled, we were bemused to find that we were scheduled to be interviewed for *Musicians Classified* magazine. Even if you can't remember it (and frankly, I doubt we'd ever heard of it before the interview) you can imagine from the title that this was an extreme muso's mag, and not therefore our sort of thing at all. The interviewer was a nice chap, and he began with a few cursory questions about the album, but it obvious that he just wanted to talk about gear. Now when people ask me about how I chose my drum kit, I usually say something glib like 'Well, I just kept buying drum kits until I found one that didn't fall apart when I hit it,' but in fact that's pretty much the truth. And that pretty much went for Dave and Mark as well. The best we could do for the bloke was to inform him that I preferred Zildjian crash cymbals, Beki had her own Electro Voice microphone to avoid sharing with other singers, and Mark, given the choice, favoured Orange amps. Thin pickings for the poor chap, but he did his best and turned in a nice little piece, though sadly I can't find a copy of it now.

Incidentally, after the gig we all stayed as the 100 Club was kept open for Charlie Harper's 38th birthday party.

In the 5 June issue of *Record Mirror* someone called Sunie contributed a sneery one page article, peppered with inaccuracies, headed 'The Big Softie.' It began:

> 'Who'd have thought it? There I was expecting to meet a sullen punkette and instead
> I'm presented with this plump, laughing Avon maid, who looks as if she'd be more at
> home in a milkmaid's smock than in today's hot and heavy get-up of leather and studs.

With her cheerful, forthright manner and pretty buxom looks, little Miss Bond of Bath - Beki Bondage to you - is a wholesome and bawdy, rather than bored, teenager.'

Like several writers of the time, Sunie's gripe seems to have been more about the relevance of punk in general at this point in time than a direct stab at us, though she was still lukewarm about us at best:

'If only by reason of Beki's heartfelt but simply expressed lyrics, Vice Squad appear far more interesting than their contemporary spikey-heads to this observer, who loved the first Clash LP as much as anyone but is hard pushed to see the relevance of "punk" in 1982. Why channel your energies and talents into punk, then Beki?

"I dunno - punk's about energy, really, innit? It's something spontaneous between the audience and the band, that feeling of excitement. That's what I like about it."

Hmmm. It might be supposed that that sort of connection is not impossible to find outside the realms of ramalama dog-collared rock; but if Beki's chosen musical cause is suspect, then her devotion to it isn't. She's been a devotee since the heady days of 1977, in spite of the fact that she was barely a teenager in those apocalyptic times.

"You should have seen me - I used to have black eyeshadow, a ponytail with shoe polish at the front and cochineal at the back, a little mini-skirt with fishnet stockings and stilettos. Just like the London girls really," she adds, though if I ever saw anyone running around the capital with their barnet smothered in boot-black and pink food dye, the memory escapes me.'

You get the picture. Luckily, by now we were getting used to this sort of sniping and were developing thicker skins. And in this instance it also helped to reflect that, as far as the music inkies were concerned, it was mostly a straight fight between the yob-friendly *Sounds* and the pseudo-intellectual, student-based *NME*, with the occasional muso-type who favoured *Melody Maker*, but no one ever owned up to reading *Record Mirror*.

Over the next few months we played around a dozen one-off gigs, the only notable one being the Zig Zag Club on June 22nd, part of a weekend mini-festival that was set up, so they said, to rival the Rolling Stones' current stadium tour. On the 21st the Adicts took the Zig Zag fest top slot, and the night we headlined, the Stones packed out Ashton Gate in Bristol. I bet Mick Jagger was shitting himself.

The afore-mentioned *Zig Zag* interview that Beki and Mark had done with editor Mick Mercer for the magazine appeared in the June issue, which also carried a full page advert offering readers the mouth-watering prospect of a copy of the *Stand Strong* album for 'just a quid' if they took out a subscription.

The two page article had the interview and a couple of black & white photos on one page and a colour photo of Beki on the other, and oddly, though Mercer took lots of photos of our dynamic duo at the interview, only stock photos were used in the piece. This despite the fact that he's since included his photos in books and offered prints for sale on the internet.

It was a pleasant enough chat that he began by describing his horror at hearing the 'ghastly' *No Cause* '…where highly promising songs lay hidden under a filthy layer of grim draberama.' He went on to praise *Stand Strong*, saying that ' I was particularly impressed by three songs, 'Out Of Reach,' 'Rock 'n' Roll Massacre' and a cover of an old Bowie number, 'Saviour Machine.' One of the most interesting parts of the interview was when Beki said 'I didn't write 'Rock 'n' Roll Massacre,' Dave did, it's his tribute to the dead,' before going on to explain what she saw as the difference between his writing and hers:

'He writes his lyrics coldly, I get all emotional…like 'poor Janice died of a heroin overdose.' I mean I could write a whole song about her, because I read her life story and really got into it, really affected by what she went through…but he's much more conservative about it, which is good cos it's a contrast to the way I do it. I just go heading into it, writing emotionally. I like giving a piece of myself to the song, in a way that other people understand as well.'

With all this attention, by now we were getting a bit cocky, and moaned at Sooty and Ken that it was about time we did some serious touring instead of all this buggering about with one-off gigs and short runs. They took us at our word, and planned out a relentless schedule for the rest of the year.

The main event, that we had nagged for incessantly, was a US tour, and one was duly booked to take place in August and September, to be followed by a huge UK tour in October, with some European dates fitted in where possible. And in case we had any plans for washing our hair, trimming our nails, or spending time with our loved ones in the foreseeable future, we were packed off to Cave Studio on 20 July to begin work on a new EP, entitled State Of The Nation. The idea was that we would conquer the US and Canada, promoting *Stand Strong* over there in the process, then return home with a new product ready and waiting for the folks back in old Blighty. This sort of forward thinking we just weren't used to, but it made a welcome change.

Once the EP was put to bed, as it were, we all began to gee ourselves up for the US jaunt, but before we went, Beki got a rather surprising call. Some crusty, a representative of the impressive-sounding Wet Paint Theatre Company, invited her to partake of the thespian arts. Avoiding any obvious Carry-On style jokes, she was offered a part in a play called *Plastic Zion*, and fair play to her, despite no acting experience, she decided to give it a go. If nothing else, the venture generated plenty of publicity. The June 17 issue of *The Stage and Television Today* impressively announced that: 'Punk star Beki Bondage is being given the chance to score as an actress through the enterprising scheme of a fringe theatre company.' The writer went on to reveal that the company, founded by playwright Chris Ward, was ambitiously attempting to mix music and theatre, performing extracts from their plays before gigs by the likes of UK Subs and the Wall. The piece also revealed that Ward 'first mixed drama and music when he put Richard Jobson, bass player with the

Skids, into his 'Demonstration of Affection' at the Cockpit Theatre' (bass player?!).

Bushell did a nice interview with Beki in *Sounds* to promote the endeavour, and the play, which took place at the Finborough pub theatre, Kensington, opened on 25 July, getting a good notice in The Times, no less.

Unfortunately, the play, which was scheduled to run for a for two weeks, was pulled by the resident theatre group The Good Company Touring Theatre after just four performances, with ourselves apparently the villains of the piece.

Naturally, clad in our best evening suits and clutching opera glasses and bunches of flowers, we had turned out to support our Beki, but as a piece in *Sounds* reported, it all ended in tears. Good Company manager Mike McCormick told the *Jaws* column that 'The important issue is that the theatre is situated in the pub by Whitbreads (the owners) simply to pick up trade for bar takings - and the problem was that on Wednesday, one of Vice Squad came to see the show and was apparently smoking cannabis. I say apparently because I wasn't there at the time, but it was reported to the bar manager by several customers, who were also upset at punks swearing at some elderly customers.'

Well you'll have to believe me, friends, when I say that there was no truth in the accusation. In fact, none of us were in the habit of smoking the stuff, our indulgences lying in other directions.

Wet Paint representative Maggie James told *Jaws* 'Well - they just freaked out when they saw Vice Squad, and anyway there were hardly any pub customers there - most people had come to see the play.'

It would be impressive to think that the mere presence of me, Dave, Mark, Sooty and Igor had been terrifying enough to close a play, but on the whole, I think an earlier quote from Maggie was nearer the mark: 'They're just prejudiced against the audience; they don't like punks.'

CHAPTER 12

THE US/CANADIAN TOUR turned out to be the highlight of what we laughingly refer to as our 'career.' We didn't realise it at the time, of course. Having talked to people like Charlie Harper and Mensi, who by 1982 already regarded a lengthy jaunt around the US in August and September as a regular, annual event, we rather assumed that we'd fall into the same rather lovely pattern. As it happens, we never got to do it again as a band, and to this day I've never been back. As I say, at the time we had no inkling that this would be our one and only shot at the US, but I do remember Mark saying to me at one point: 'Well, whatever happens from now on, the bastards can't take *this* away from us.' So perhaps it was in the back of our minds after all. Or perhaps Mark is psychic? Spooky!

No, he just knew our fuck, fuck, fucking luck.

If our preparations for what was to happen after the tour had been meticulous, quite a lot for the tour itself was left dangerously late. According to Mark's diary, we only got medical insurance sorted out on 3 August (strange that, as I remember that while we were over there he had to have some dental treatment that cost about £70 - a week's wages - so we'd considered letting the sod suffer) and also a carnet. A carnet was, and I think still is, a legal document that you need to carry equipment into another country for work purposes without incurring tax. When you leave you have to prove that you are carrying out the same equipment that you brought in and have not sold any of it or bought new stuff. Or, like in *The Hitchhiker's Guide To The Galaxy*, they surgically remove the weight of anything not listed on the carnet, from your body, to preserve the equilibrium of the country. And that's true.

Again according to Mark's diary, the next day we were still trying to obtain one, and presumably succeeded as it's not mentioned again, but for some ridiculous reason we didn't actually get around to sorting out the most important thing of all, the visas, until the day before we left. Madness.

This meant driving to the American Embassy in London and hanging around for bloody hours, cursing furiously, but of course we only had ourselves to blame. Or our managers. Yes, our managers, it was their bloody fault!

No, that didn't help. In the end we got our visas, which were H1, the genuine ROCK STAR classification, same as Rod Stewart and that. My mum was impressed, I can tell you.

Unfortunately, but not unnaturally had we stopped to think about it, the American Embassy informed us that they couldn't furnish us with Canadian visas, so we'd have to cross that bridge when we came to it, as it were.

A day or two before we left, a load of us got together at the Swan for a lunchtime farewell drinky, or several, and rather touchingly, My Kind Of Town (Chicago Is) and New York, New York, were placed on the jukebox in our honour. At chucking out time, which in those days was 2.30, we headed for the Hanham Abbots School playing fields, and held a prolonged and increasingly vicious football match, which left me, at least, covered in bruises, and with muscles that ached for the first few days of the tour.

Sooty's diary entry for Tuesday 10 August is as poetic as you might expect a manager's to be:

Depart Heathrow
Must be at Airport 10.30am (BST)
Terminal 3. Intercontinental Panam, Boeing 747
Polar Route
Flight: Panam 232
Distance 5,580 miles
Av. Altitude 39,000 Feet
Flight Time 10 ½ Hours
Boarded 12.45pm (BST)
Take off 1.15pm (BST)
Landed LAX 11.45pm (BST)
Left Airport 12.30am (BST)

Arrived 3.45pm LA Time

Mark's diary reveals that we flew over Greenland, Baffen Island and Canada. Same route as the Beatles then. Oh, you remember, it was in A Hard Day's Night: Reporter: 'How did you find America?,' Lennon: 'Turned left at Greenland.' Oh well, please yourselves.

The flight, though uneventful, was of course a great adventure, as I'd only flown once before, on a cheap package holiday to Malta with Mandy a year earlier, and I don't think any of the others had flown at all.

We had the expected hassles at LAX customs (spiky hair, leather jackets and tattoos were still pretty taboo in 1982, especially in a country as conservative as America), but got through eventually. As Beki recalls, though, our own officials had been just as stringent, if not positively prejudiced: 'I even had trouble at Heathrow because of my bullet belt, they wouldn't let me on the plane with it and I had to let them put it in the hold. In those days you could smoke on planes (I'm glad that you can't any more) so we basically smoked and drank for the duration of the flight to LA.'

And the first thing that struck us, leaving the airport, was something that will sadly mean nothing to Brits arriving in the US today, and that's the police car sirens. Now they sound the same, all over the world, but back then, British police cars made a boring 'Nee, Naw, Nee, Naw' sound, while American police cars, in TV cop shows like Starsky and Hutch, made that much more exciting 'Weeeer!, Weeeer!, Weeeer!' noise. Somehow it seemed strangely exotic.

A taxi driver took us to our hotel by the scenic, rather than the shortest route, but I'm sure that was just because he could tell we were anxious to see the sights and that he had no thought of ripping us off.

The hotel in question was an excitingly famous rock 'n' roll dive, the Tropicana Motel, 8585 Santa Monica Boulevard. Today, the first hit on Google throws up pictures of Bob Marley, Joan Jett, Blondie and Tom Waits staying there, and we heard at the time that people like Alice Cooper, Iggy Pop and Jim Morrison had also frequented the joint (more of Jim Morrison later, incidentally). So, pretty impressive stuff to yokels like ourselves.

It was a sprawling place, with palm trees, astro turf and a pool, though the pool was murky and filled with God knows what. It was just nice for lounging by in the California sun and thinking how much the anarcho punks back home would hate us if they could see us.

Predictably, though, when we first arrived we found that our contact with local promoters Goldenvoice, the bizarrely named Chip Quigley, hadn't booked us in. No, we never did quite get over his name, and as Beki remembers, 'We called him Shit Quickly,' but eventually we managed to keep a straight-ish face. Anyway, we 'hung out' (we had to get used to using such terms. When in Rome and all that) on the steps outside the hotel, but when it became clear he wasn't going to show up we gave in and paid for two rooms ourselves. Not a good start.

But hey ho, here we were, and as there were no signs of our old friends Chron Gen, who were also staying there and who we were to play a week of dates with, we decided to buy some cans of beer and 'hang out' by the pool.

Incidentally, the way these tours were set up meant that they worked as a relay, with one band beginning on one coast, playing for a week with a band that were about to return to the UK, then they would spend four weeks driving to the other coast to meet a band that had just arrived, play a week of dates with them, then return home, ad infinitum. All the bands would play the major coastal and central cities, but alternately one would go down and play some dates in the South, then the next would go up into Canada, so those living in the extremities only got every other tour. Chron Gen had drawn the South, we had drawn Canada. Got that? Good. Anyway, back to the plot.

We bought lots of cans of a beer called Schlitz, stretched out on sun beds, and set about getting bladdered. Some time later, we realised we were belching like crazy but stone cold sober, at which point Chron Gen wandered in. They took one look at the mountain of discarded Schlitz cans and our distended bellies and burst out laughing, then told us a home truth. The fact was that, in 1982 (I don't know about now) American beer was so pathetically weak, almost like that shandy you can buy in newsagents over here, that it was a complete waste of time drinking it. I've never been a big spirits drinker, but on that tour there was no other option, and if there was beer on the rider we often added a splash of vodka to it, much to the amusement of watching yanks. In restaurants, the waiter would take our order, then ask what we wanted to drink. One of us would order a pitcher (a large jug) of beer and the waiter would start to walk away, thinking it was for all of us, as was customary, until he was made to understand that we wanted one each. It really was that weak.

We finally got a call from Chip at 1.30 in the morning, and he finally showed up the following lunch-time.

We were also, at some stage, introduced to a new member of our happy throng, as Igor remembers: 'Pepe turned up, he turned up cos he was going to be our tour manager, and he was pissed out of his head!' Pepe, as it turned out, was a Scottish nutcase, agreeable enough, but permanently off his head on vodka, which he swigged out of a bottle in a brown paper bag, even while driving us around. As we'll see his tenure was a short one. At some stage which has also disappeared into the mists of time (you were wondering where that had got to, weren't you?) we also met up with the wonderful but crazy BYO crowd. BYO, as I'm sure you know, stood (and still does stand) for Better Youth Organization, a label that had just been set up by the Stern brothers, Shawn, Mark and Adam, who had their own band, Youth Brigade. They had just put out their first release, a compilation album of US bands entitled *Someone Got Their Head Kicked In*, and were about to set out in a battered yellow school bus on a massively ambitious national tour with another outfit called Social Distortion.

When I started writing this book, I had it in my head that we played some shows with Social Distortion and Youth Brigade during our week in LA, but research now proves that though we met at that time, we didn't play together until some time later, as we will see. I think my confusion is down to a memory I have of when, as we were about to depart LA on our respective tours, we said goodbye to the BYO crowd with handshakes, manly hugs and exchanged gifts. I still have my copy of *Someone Got Their Head Kicked In*, but sadly some girl half-inched my Social Distortion single.

To be honest, we'd never heard of either of them, and only much later did we learn that that they, along with a few other local bands, could actually pack out the Hollywood Palladium. If we'd known that, and the fact that Youth Brigade and BYO would thrive and be respected all over the world to the present day, and that Social Distortion would be one of the biggest and most influential punk bands to emerge from the US, I'm sure we'd have pooped ourselves at the idea of following them onstage. But ignorance is bliss, and though we were of course aware that Youth Brigade were a fine street punk band, and Social Distortion were brash and earthy, with some excellent songs written by singer Mike Ness, our arrogance was such that we weren't unduly worried.

The next day, Wednesday 11 August, we were playing the Whisky A Go Go, just down the road on Sunset Boulevard, which like the Tropicana, was steeped in rock 'n' roll history. Janis Joplin, Led Zeppelin, Frank Zappa, Alice Cooper and the Doors were just some of the famous names that had played there. When H heard that we were to play there, as a massive Doors fan, he nagged me to nick a toilet seat, as 'Jim may have sat on it,' and I resolved to do so. Unfortunately, the toilets had been recently refurbished, so unless Jimbo had made a ghostly jaunt over from Paris just to crap in the Whisky, it was unlikely that he'd made any contact with the shiny new seats. I had to settle for nicking H a bottle opener and some other paraphernalia from the place. Shame that. I had, however, borrowed Jerry Hopkins' and Danny Sugerman's biography of Jim Morrison, *No One Here Gets Out Alive*, from Chron Gen bassist Pete Dimmock, and used it to spot more Doors sites and connections as we moved around, such as the fact that Jim had lived at the Tropicana for a while. He also regularly breakfasted at Barney's Beanery, on Santa Monica Boulevard, where we too often partook of eggs and hash browns of a morning, so I bought H a Barney's Beanery shirt. Incidentally, in the second episode of *Columbo, Ransom For A Dead Man*, Peter Falk eats chili in Barney's Beanery, and returns to the place in several other episodes.

As I remember it, though we were suitably impressed to be playing such an important venue, come gig time we weren't really at the top of our game, such as it was. I for one was suffering from jet lag and the consequences of our Swan leaving do/football match/drunken brawl and ached all over. When we got to the venue, the kids were friendly and seemed keen to talk to us, but the gig itself seemed a bit subdued to me. Perhaps that was just me though, as local fanzine *Flipside* were happy enough. Reviewer Frank H said that:

> 'I arrived at around 8:00 and it was unusually uncrowded, but this was just a case of everybody being fashionably late. Anyway, it filled up quick and after a short while Vice Squad came on led by the Sexy Punk Godess Beki Bondage. They were really good except that the drums weren't loud enough and the guitar player needs more powerful amps. But these were minor flaws in a really fun set. Beki even let the crowd sing in on some of the hits. Coward, Last Rockers, Humane and Resurrection were the high points of the night. They also did a good version of the Sex Pistols song EMI.'

The fine chap went on to give Chron Gen a nice write-up as well, concluding his review with: 'This was an exceptionally great and fun show, I for one want more.' He was right about the bloody drums as well.

One thing he somehow failed to mention, though, was a huge riot outside the venue after the show. If we thought the relationship between punks and the police was sometimes a little fraught at home, we had no idea of the brutality that Californian punks suffered at the hands of the local gendarmes. I've since read of many incidents of gigs by the likes of Black Flag being broken up by armed police, but at the time it came as an unexpected shock. It was Igor who ran up and said 'Come and have a look at this!' I went outside and could hardly take in what I was seeing. It was a full scale riot, with police sirens going off, missiles flying and even helicopters with searchlights hovering overhead. I couldn't take it in and just wandered back into the club in a daze.

The incident was reported in *Sounds* thus:

> 'Stand Up For Your Riots: The same night Billy Idol was drunk and sort of disorderly at the Roxy, the Los Angeles police were screaming down the road to the Chron Gen/Vice Squad show. Seems a combination of seeing punters in black leather and studs and hearing some tip-off that an LA punk band was playing there, brought the boys in blue out in force. When an excitable youth took it into his head to use a police car bonnet as

a trampoline, half a dozen cops pinned him down and the riot squad was called for. The result: yet another ban of punk at the Whisky and rumours that all but MOR acts will be turned away at the doors.'

A few weeks later, the paper had even more distressing news for LA punk and rock fans:

'The Whisky isn't just banning punk and HM shows, it's doing away with live rock altogether. The famous Sunset club closes its doors next week, though we hear that after remodelling it will emerge from the ashes as yet another new wave disco-dance club.'

Yes, those pesky new wave disco-dance clubs, you couldn't move for the bloody things in Hanham. So, a fairly historical event in rock history, though of course the club did re-emerge as a live music venue and continues to this day. However, much as I would like to, I can't really believe that it was due to the 'excitable youth' and his pals being whipped into a frenzy by Chron Gen and ourselves. We just happened to provide the venue. The next day, the riot was on the front page of the local paper, but unusually for me, the hoarder, I didn't keep a copy. Quite honestly, if it wasn't for the *Sounds* reports and most of the others in our party recalling it, I'd think I just imagined the whole thing.

Beki, however, says 'I don't remember a riot. I do recall that we sounded pretty awful though! I played at The Whisky again a few years ago, it reminded me of the Wardour Street Marquee as it has a similar size stage and everything's black.'

Another fairly minor point is that I've always said over the years that although we were billed to headline all our four shows together, as Chron Gen were mates, we agreed to alternate with them, working it out so that they got to take top place at the San Francisco show, their last before flying home. And though it's hard to be certain, again the evidence seems to indicate that we didn't alternate after all. We were certainly happy for them to close the Whisky show as we were all jet-lagged, and a Flipside review of the next gig at San Pedro gig also lists Chron Gen as top of the bill. An LA Weekly advertisement listed us as headliners at Olympic Auditorium, and as I say, Glynn and the boys certainly closed in San Francisco. Oh dear, senility is a terrible thing.

The next day, Thursday 12, Mark's diary tells us that we 'Went to bank & cruised Sunset. Went to SIR for drums. Sat around pool & went to Barney's Beanery. Went to boring night club on Sunset.' Which reminds me that the promoters had provided me with a ghastly, awful-sounding, aesthetically-displeasing wood-finish drum kit that, as Mark says, I took back to the hire company and traded for a better kit. Unfortunately, it turned out that SIR had shops in both LA and New York, and that the bloody woody thing was from the New York shop and had to be returned, so I was bloody lumbered with it, as it were.

And yes, it was a boring night club. Three days into the adventure of a lifetime and we were already blasé.

We were bemused to find that on Saturday 14 August, at 1.00pm, we were booked, along with Chron Gen, to make a personal appearance at the Vinyl Fetish record store, to 'meet the kids' and, hopefully, sign some records, though we didn't really expect much of the latter. There had been a plan at EMI to release a 'Best Of' compilation, only for release in the US, to coincide with the tour, and they had had the bizarre idea of a sleeve depicting two policemen snogging. We had had our doubts about the wisdom of that part of the plan, but agreed that it would have been a good idea to have some product for sale other than extortionately priced import albums. In the end, though, for reasons now lost in the mists of time, the plan had come to nothing. Thankfully, a few kids with deep pockets took pity on us and bought records for us to sign, so it wasn't a total embarrassment, and we had a good time chatting to a decent sized crowd. A girl called Kim even gave Beki a big bunch of flowers, which was sweet.

That night we played the aforementioned San Pedro show, at the exotically named Dancing Waters club on 14th & Pacific Avenue, with Sin 34 and Discords also on the bill, which, if I remember rightly, had real running water for a backdrop. All Igor remembers of the day is that 'We went to San Pedro, and we went to a pier, and there were lots of Mexicans fishing on the pier, and John Greenhalgh was with us by then, and he told us not to talk to them cos they would probably kill us, cos they hated gringos. But I can't remember the gig.'

Thanks for reminding me Igs, I should have mentioned John earlier. John Greenhalgh had joined our happy throng when he took over as driver and road manager from mad Pepe, who was clearly out of control, and was great fun from the start. He led a strange life, driving one punk band from one coast to the other, then immediately picking up another and going back the other way, ad infinitum. In 1991, when I was working as a promoter at the Fleece & Firkin in Bristol, I booked GBH, who had just returned from a US tour, and they told me that John had been their driver. He was still there, going back and forth, punk band in tow! Perhaps he still is?

The aforementioned *LA Weekly* advertisement appeared in the 13-19 August issue, a big half page job announcing the Summer Slam '82 at the Olympic Auditorium on Sunday 15 August, along with a mention of our Vinyl Fetish appearance. The doors opened at 5.00, and as well as us and Chron Gen, the impressive bill included Wasted Youth, Channel 3, Battalion of Saints, Circle One, Aggression, Lost Cause and Deadly Reign, all for the princely sum of $9.00. It was a massive venue, which you could often see on the tele back home when it held top-flight boxing matches, usually with commentary by Harry Carpenter.

Here things get a little confused on the driver/road manager front. As Igor says, John was with us by this time, but for some reason Pepe was at the Olympic show, albeit briefly. In a disturbing incident that made us seriously worried about the American psyche, as we were loading the gear into the venue, Pepe collapsed and had some sort of fit or seizure. His eyeballs rolled back and he was thrashing about on the pavement, having convulsions. Several passers-by rushed over, we assumed to help him, but, in fact, they just produced cameras and began taking photos of him! Exit Pepe, who was rushed to hospital, though he would crop up again much later.

As for the show itself, this is how Igor remembers it: 'The Olympic Auditorium sounded horrible didn't it? That's the one where Sooty got in a strop, because I asked him at the sound check why Chron Gen sounded much better than you did, and he said 'It's because they can play better.' It's true! And I said well, no, it's because the guitar sounds crap. Their guitars sounded good, and Dave's just sounded like ZZZZZZZ! And Sooty started saying 'What are you saying, are you saying that I'm a bad mixer?' There was something absolutely bloody awful about the sound. There were loads of people weren't there? 6,000 people or something like that, all slamdancing.'

And Beki agrees that the sound left something to be desired. 'I remember playing some huge gig but it seemed half empty to me because it was so big with seating all the way around the arena. The sound was just horrendous, it's extremely hard to get a decent sound in a place like that but to be fair we did make a racket, Dave had a really distorted guitar sound and I could never hear my voice above the band so I used to just shout over the top of it. It was very punk rock though, there was nothing polished about us.'

Igor brings us onto another point when he says that 'I can remember that girl in the leopard skin dress, who had also been at the first gig.' As Mandy and I had sadly split up recently, this was my first tour as a single bloke, and I'd been rather looking forward to taking full advantage of the fact. Unfortunately, the in-flight magazine on the way over had had an article about the latest sexually transmitted disease, herpes, that was apparently sweeping America, and if you got it, according to the article, or at least our interpretation of it, yer knob dropped off. So, to my utter disappointment, we all swore a solemn oath that we would remain celibate for the whole tour. If anyone was spotted talking in anything like a flirtatious manner with a member of the opposite sex, a cry of 'HERPES!' went up.

Dave, as was his wont, lasted about three days before succumbing, becoming something of a pariah. The weather, as you can imagine in California in August, was sweltering, and we only kept going by constantly passing cans of cold fizzy drink around the van. Cruelly, Diseased Dave was not included in the round and only left the nasty, warm, spitty dregs at the end, as no one would drink from a can after him. Even more cruelly, as most of the rest of us also succumbed, one by one, having seen the treatment meted out to Dave we kept schtum while he still suffered. On the subject of 'the girl in the leopard skin dress,' Igor continues 'She was really cute, a typical cute American blonde, and she really, really wanted it. And I was scared to do it in case she had herpes. I think I asked her, ha ha! That was the end of that relationship for the night.'

He also reckons that 'One thing I do remember, when we were in the Tropicana, I remember Beki had two lesbians up in her room, do you remember that? There were these two lesbians in bed, snogging and things, and I actually stayed to watch!' Beki, however remembers it differently: 'That was two blokes dressed as ladies pretending to be lesbians, I'm not into girls in a sexual way.' Whatever Igor was drinking that night, I don't want any.

On Tuesday 17 we drove the 400 miles to San Francisco and checked into the Canterbury Hotel. After a meal, I went with Beki, and Pete and Floyd from Chron Gen, to radio station K.V.S.F. for an interview. It was nothing remarkable, apart from the fact that I persuaded the DJ to play Frank Sinatra's Strangers In The Night on a punk show, and his assistant Mitzi to let me nick the rare early DJ copy into the bargain. She eventually agreed, on condition that I put her on the guest list for the next night's show, which I did. She wrote her name on the sleeve to make sure I didn't forget, and I still have the record, but sadly Beki sat on it a few days later. Still plays though, despite the crack. I could have put that better...

When we got back to the hotel we found out that there had actually been a small earthquake in our absence. The radio station was housed in a new building that had been built to withstand earthquakes, so we hadn't felt a thing, but back in the old hotel building the thing had made its presence felt to the others, even if there was no real danger. I was quite sorry I'd missed it.

The next day we played the Old Waldorf, a really nice venue with a great crowd, and as we were on first we were able to do our bit then get drinking early while Chron Gen did the rest of the work. When they came back on for their encore, the inevitable Living Next Door To Alice, they dragged us all onstage for backing vocals, Glynn bellowing for Mark when he was reluctant to join in, and 'The Squad Sisters,' as he called us, made a truly terrible din. Embarrassingly, the set was taped and released as an album by the Picasso label three years later. Actually, despite the embarrassment, I still keep a copy as a memento of a great night.

After the show, for reasons now lost in the mists of time, I was given a tour of San Francisco's night life by two very nice lesbians, and in one of the first clubs we visited I was pleased to find that Social Distortion were not only there but already on stage, and bloody marvellous they were too. Shawn from Youth Brigade confirms that I'm not just imagining this: 'The first show of the tour was in San Francisco at the On Broadway, us and Social Distortion, so it's likely that's the show you came to.'

Thursday 19 we took Chron Gen to the airport, then set off for the next gig, two days later, in Seattle. As Mark's diary says, we 'Drove into the Rockies and stayed in a motel in Weed.' Someone piped up 'Ha! Weed, California. Find that in yer fuckin' Doors book, Baldwin!' I dutifully recited 'Jim Morrison's wife Pam was born in Weed, California, on 22 December 1946...' at which point they tried to beat me to death with a bass pedal. Mark also says that we 'Went for a drink and got a warm reception.' That was a biker bar that we'd entered with some trepidation, but desperate for a drink, and as Mark says, once they got over the shock we had a fine evening with the assembled hairies.

Next day, after breakfast, we continued the trip to Seattle, but somehow, at some point now lost in the mists of time, we learned that the gig had been cancelled, so headed instead for Portland, Oregon. It had been arranged that we would stay there in the house of a nice couple called Freddie and Ronnie Seegmuller before the next scheduled show in Eugene, Oregon, on Monday 23 August.

I can't remember who Freddie actually was, but he seemed to be quite a mover on the local scene. He had a huge record collection and piles of local fanzines, and he gave me quite a few, which I still have.

By this time Dave and I had acquired one of those big outsize bottles of whisky, the sort often used when empty to collect coins for charity, but our mission was to drink our way through this bugger. However, we couldn't just drink all the time, so Freddie offered to set us up a low-key local gig the next night, Saturday 21, in place of the Seattle show, in the Cafe Oasis. It really was a cafe, with just the tables and chairs pushed out of the way, and we played on the floor, but it was great fun and we were glad of the diversion.

Sunday 22, according to Mark's diary, we 'Went to Columbia Creek. Swam in the river & saw second highest falls in the USA. Had a big pizza.' Well I remember the pizza, of course, it was a beauty, but the rest is lost in the mists of time.

Monday 23 we headed to Eugene for the show at a picturesque venue called BJ Kellys. As I remember it, it was a big wooden building that looked more like a family restaurant, situated next to a lovely flowing river that we sat next to, on a veranda, in the sun, after the soundcheck, with cooling drinks.

The gig itself, however, was rather more traumatic. The punks in the audience seemed to be outnumbered by rowdy locals intent on causing trouble, and eventually someone was actually stabbed. We were all for calling it a day, but were advised that the best way to keep the peace was to keep playing, so reluctantly, we did. The gig was recorded on a cassette tape from the mixing desk, which Igor kept, and it was released as a live album in Link Records' *Live And Loud* series in 1988. You can hear the point where we start playing noticeably faster and that's when the stabbing happened. We couldn't wait to get off and away.

As early in the tour as this, tempers became a little frayed, and we even indulged in a little uncharacteristic rock 'n' roll destruction. Talk of the BJ Kelly's gig prompted this exchange between Igor and Beki. For what it's worth, I thought Dave blew up the TV, but I could be wrong.

Igor: 'After one of these, I think it was BJ Kelly's, they had a party for us out at a big house in the countryside, and it was something to do with the promoter. They had this big house, this like proper big American house. And I had a fight with Mark, didn't I, does he remember? Cos I had a fight with all of you, didn't I, at one stage or another. I had a fight with Dave in Canada, and you hit me when you poured the orange juice down the back of the TV.'

Beki: 'Oh yeah, the orange juice down the back of the TV, I think it was vodka and orange actually. We had a big plastic bin in the van filled with either vodka and orange or Black

Russian minus the coke, and we'd just dip our cups in. There was some Jerry Lewis charity fund raiser thing on TV all day and we got totally bored watching it so decided to blow up the telly. This was the night we told the promoter Igor was gay and he made a pass at Igor, I think we locked him out of the motel room, and we were sniggering as we listened to him trying to politely get away from the promoter.'

Or something like that...

Our next gig, in Calgary, Canada, wasn't until three days later, but on Tuesday 24, for want of anything better to do, we drove the 500 miles to the border anyway, arriving, I learn from Sooty's diary, at 3.30pm. And it was just as well we did, because it turned out that our visas weren't in order and we were turned back. We headed for Seattle, checked into the Seal Hotel, and went for Italian food.

Next day we got the visas sorted, and a few years ago, Sooty remembered an incident that occurred afterwards and sent it to me on a postcard:

'Shane!
Picture this...We've just come out of the Canadian Consulate in Seattle after sorting our entry visas to Canada. The day before we were turned away, remember?
Neatly placed under one of the wiper blades is a piece of paper which reads:
"HI THERE!! JUST A SHORT NOTE TO SAY THAT YOU FOLKS HAVE GOT TO BE THE LARGEST COLLECTION OF ARSEHOLES I HAVE EVER SEEN IN ONE PLACE BEFORE. THE PURPLE AND BLUE HAIR IS A NICE TOUCH, BUT DID YOU KNOW THERE'S A LEASH LAW IN THIS CITY?
SIGNED: THE AMERICAN KENNEL CLUB."

Talk to you soon Soot X'

Marvellous stuff, thanks Soot! We then played tourists, visiting a fun fair and the Space Needle, before having another crack at the border. This time they let us in, but only after we paid $400 duty on the equipment and left our stocks of t-shirts, supposedly to be reclaimed later. This never happened for financial reasons, and for a while afterward you could tell which Brit bands had been touring over there because they'd be wearing our abandoned shirts. I recall that the next time I saw the Upstarts they were all wearing them. As Beki remembers, though, it was still a struggle to get through: 'When we first crossed the border from the US into Canada the customs officials wanted to take our studded jackets, belts and wrist bands off us as they were 'potential weapons,' they let us keep them in the end when we persuaded them that the studs were part of our act. There was a car in front of us and the customs men opened the boot and it was full of bags of weed, there must have been thousands of dollars' worth of it stashed in this car.'
Through at last, at 1.30am we finally pitched up in Merritt and booked into the Douglas Motel.

Thursday 26, Mark's diary reveals that we 'Left Merritt at 9.30 & drove very fast across the Rockies, saw lots of snow & glaciers & it rained.'

That night we played Calgary University, a lovely venue up a picturesque snow-covered hill that had to be approached up a very long and steep road. Wandering idly outside, looking down I saw in the distance an old fashioned yellow US school bus, coughing and wheezing its way up the hill agonizingly slowly. Oh no, BYO were coming!

Yes, unbeknownst to us Social Distortion and Youth Brigade were also on the bill, and it was great to see them again. Their tour was much more ambitious than ours, and on an even smaller budget, so it was hard going for them. The organizers had kindly provided a chilli for our rider, but as Igor remembers, though it was a shade too rich for us lily-livered Brits, the BYO crowd were made of sterner stuff: 'They gave it to us for tacos, and we put a little bit in the tacos and went '*Ooh no, it's too hot!*' 'cos we were wusses, and their Mexican roadie went 'Watch this,' and he just drank the whole lot.'

The whole BYO tour was being filmed, and was eventually released as a documentary on video as *Another State Of Mind*. As all concerned are happy to admit, some parts of the film were faked and/or filmed later, but it remains a fascinating document and a great tribute to a massively impressive venture, as well as two great bands. The sad thing is that we were also filmed at several gigs, but weren't included in the finished movie, a fact that the Stern brothers complain about in their commentary on the DVD release. You can see my horrible wood-finish drum kit though. Incidentally, when we were putting together our Vice Squad DVD (which we will cover later) I asked Shawn if we could get hold of any of the footage of us from the tour, and he told me that it does exist but all the footage from the tour is owned by the bloke who manages No Doubt and Social Distortion, and he apparently refused to part with any of it. Shawn couldn't even get his own stuff, so we had no chance, which was a terrible shame. Apart from anything else I would have liked to have just seen it.

Though it may well have been asking for it, I asked Shawn what he'd thought of us, and here's his reply:

'What did we think of you? Hmm, well everyone thought Beki was pretty hot, well I thought she was okay, but some of our friends drooled over her. The thing is we were also promoting shows in L.A. and we met a lot of English punk bands during these years. My opinion was that the British music papers, *NME*, *Sounds* and…shit, I can't remember the third one, were instrumental in building up bands and then as soon as they started to get popular it seems they'd trash them and bring them down. I know that the headlining bands would treat the new bands like shit and there was a lot of rock star attitude when they came to L.A. We didn't put up with that shit, punk rock in L.A. was totally DIY and whether a band was headlining the show or just opening, they all used the same stage, drum riser, p.a. etc. We had some bands come over and try to force us to set up in front of the drum riser, only use the remaining 6-8 spots on the p.a. board, so nothing would be moved from their sound check, and we thought that was total bullshit.

It seemed younger bands, Chron Gen and Anti Pasti in particular, didn't have so much of this attitude, but we also met them when we were promoting this club Godzilla's at the end of '81 and early '82. The Damned were always nice guys as were GBH. I think most of the English bands after coming to L.A. and seeing how huge the scene was and becoming friendly with a lot of us, that stopped them copping any attitude.

My hands were pretty full on the '82 tour, it was our first and I had booked it all myself and we were financially dealing with it. We had tried to get on more dates together with Vice Squad since we were routed the same, but the NY agent you guys had wasn't really interested, but that was typical. You guys seemed okay, kinda quiet. We only did the four or five shows together which isn't always enough time to get to know a band on the road. I do remember you guys came to party in I think Calgary or Saskatoon and our roadie Marlon was off in a room with Beki doing what we don't know! Ha ha! I did like the band, it's a shame we didn't get you into the *Another State of Mind* movie or do more shows together.'

Friday 27, we headed for Edmonton to play at the Villa Vesuvius and stayed at the Pan Am Motel. Again we were joined by the BYO crowd, and we learn from Mark's diary that on arrival in Edmonton we 'Got stopped by Mounties & had visas checked. Had a real PA. Had a big Lasagne. Good gig followed by a good party.' As no one now remembers any of this, I'm glad someone was taking notes.

Not much is remembered about the next night's gig in the Memorial Union Building of the University of Saskatchewan, Saskatoon, promoted by *Rhythm* Magazine. Shawn Stern has some memory of the evening, though: 'I know we were there, maybe we didn't play but my brother Mark remembers we did. It was at the University and the kids put some funky blue dye in their hair and the sweat made it drip all over their faces and necks.' Mark's diary is less than enthusiastic: 'Got up early & drove to Saskatoon. Got stopped for speeding. Crap gig but we had some cups of tea.' Tea? *Must* have been a bad night. Next day, Sunday 29, was taken up with the drive to Brandon, Manitoba, near Winnipeg, where the next show was to take place. We stayed at the Colonial Inn, and according to Mark's diary 'Watched *Minder* on TV.' Rock and bloody Roll!

Monday 30 we played at Monterey Furdey Hall, Winnepeg, with a band called the Stretch Marks, though, of course, the details about this momentous event have been lost in the mists of time. Mark's diary, however, reveals that we 'Had a very cheap Italian meal & went to party afterwards.' He also informs us that we 'Got back' to the Charles Hotel '@ 5AM,' so it must have been some party. And that, incidentally, was written years before the '@' sign became fashionable.

Tuesday 31 we took an hour's drive back into the US through what Mark describes as 'A massive thunderstorm' to the Viking Hotel, Alexandria, Minnesota. And we apparently had a Mexican meal. I hope you realise how massively cosmopolitan all this foreign nosh was to a bunch of Bristol kids in the 80s. We thought pizza was fancy and prawn cocktail the height of sophistication.

Wednesday 1 saw us storm the stage of the Upper Deck Club, Minneapolis, described in Mark's diary as a 'Crap place' with a 'Stupid promoter,' where we did '2 interviews,' though who with is not made clear. It was also a 'Shitty veggie place.' Pretty damning stuff, I think you'll agree. Poor old Minneapolis. And if you're taking notes, we apparently stayed at a Best Western Motel.

Thursday 2 we made our way to Chicago and checked into the Spa Motel in readiness for a show on the next day at the C.O.D. club with the BYO boys billed on the posters as 'Special Guests,' and why not.

Just to give us a flavour of good old Chicago tradition, Igor remembers that 'When we got to Chicago, those gangsters were fighting, weren't they, in the parking lot, and then the police turned up.' Yup, guns firing, baseball bats swinging, police cars everywhere. And that was just the hotel car park. Mark also recalls that 'I remember getting out to get some postcards in Chicago, and there were some kids on the street corner with home-made guns, which were probably more likely to kill them than me I think.' Nice place.

Mark describes the show as an 'Excellent place' with a 'Boring crowd but good gig.' Not so boring for Youth Brigade and Social Distortion, as Shawn remembers that they '...got in a big fight with the security that ended outside in the street. Cops came and our bus was escorted to the city limits. Then we went around the corner and drove over to Articles of Faith's house for a big party.' I remember that I met a rather personable young lady from Boston, a student at Chicago University, who I invited to my room to look at my etchings, but perhaps we'll draw a veil over that. Especially as John Greenhalgh was sleeping in the bed next to us and I had to scrounge a green condom from Igor that I knew for a fact had been festering in his wallet for at least six months. She probably sticks in my mind as she had a cute New England accent. But I digress...

The main thing that the others remember about Chicago, strangely, is a pizza restaurant. They also confirm my verdict on the spineless nature of American beer:

Igor: 'We went in the same pizza place twice didn't we, and they gave us free beer the second time, which was a mistake, instead of giving us free pizzas. We were there for two days, and we went back to the same pizza place. Because I'd never had pizza before I don't think, and that was the first time I'd ever sat in a restaurant and had a pizza!'

Mark: 'I think by then we'd worked out that the only way to get pissed on American beer was to drink about three gallons of it.'

Igor: 'And the waiter was giving it to us in big jugs wasn't he? A pitcher each.'

Beki: 'Oh yeah, the beer! We must have been serious piss heads back then as we'd drink several crates of American beer and be barely tipsy, we were used to several pints of strong lager plus shorts a night, so the American beer didn't affect us. I always tried to 'keep up with the boys' which was daft as women don't metabolise alcohol as easily as men do. I have to say that keeping up with the boys was a lot easier than keeping up with Girlschool!'

Our next event was on Saturday 4, in Detroit, an eventful trip, as Igor remembers: 'We got lost didn't we? Cos we drove up, and it was big thunder storms, and we were listening to Ku Klux Klan radio, do you remember? For some reason we put it on, and it was all about this Ku Klux Klan shit. We were driving to Detroit and then we got lost. And we went to that garage and the guy said 'Get back in the van, shut all the windows, turn around and don't stop until you've done, like, twenty blocks that way.'

Mark: 'He said something like 'Hit the freeway for five miles then ask somebody else.' 'Man, you're in the wrong part of town,' I think he said.'

Me: 'That's where the Eminem film was set.'

Mark: '*8 Mile*, yeah. I think that was the road we had to get on wasn't it?'

Igor: 'Yeah, we drove into 8 Mile Road. Not a good place. Well Detroit's not a good place! Where the Motown Museum is, it's fine to go there in the day, but if you go there at night you'll be dead. Cos Detroit's a city that just empties in the middle at night. Everyone lives in the suburbs, all the Ford workers and all the GM workers and all that, and Detroit is just absolutely dead. It's like a ghost town at night.'

Beki: 'There was definitely a black/white divide, though I found black people were fairly tolerant of us because we were foreign and had dyed hair. I think that if we had been white Americans we would have got our arses kicked.'

Igor: Detroit we had to have armed guards when we did the load-out, cos we were next to a soul club weren't we? We loaded out onto the back alley, and there was a gunnery place, and next door was a black soul club, and we had armed guards with shotguns while we loaded the van up.

Mark: We missed all this.

Igor: You wouldn't have been there, you'd have been relaxing in the dressing room with champagne and cocaine and all the groupies, eating grapes.

Before all this fun and games, we had booked into the Leland Hotel for a wash and up before our gig at the City Club. Dave Betteridge, one of our booking agents, and his wife, were on holiday (I think) in the US at the time, and they turned up at the show. It was nice to see some faces from home.

The BYO boys were on the bill, and as usual, had problems with the yellow bus, as Shawn recalls: 'I know we broke down on the way to Detroit but I believe we were never on that show. I think we did make it to watch you.' Mark's diary, however, states categorically that 'The BYO turned up and played,' so it looks like they made it eventually.

Next morning, Sunday 5, was decidedly unwholesome, according to Igor.

Igor: 'We went off in the van in the morning, and John wanted to get some dope, and we wanted some vodka. They took us to an off-licence, like I never saw again until I moved to Liverpool, where you walk in and it's all metal bars, all metal grills, and we bought some vodka, then we got back in the van. Then John saw some drug dealers on a corner, so he got out to do the deal, and this black bloke said he wanted to kill me because he thought I was the devil. He came up and started waving a gun through the window. And you were all, like, moving as far away from me as you could on the back seat!'

Beki: 'John and I were doing 'coke' every day, I think most of it was talcum powder because I always managed to sleep. I didn't get addicted to it, and when we came back to the UK I just stopped taking it. It must have been talcum powder and Ajax. I remember him telling you all to shut up or get out when we went to a veggie restaurant because you were all taking the piss out of the food, I thought it was good of him to stick up for me but looking back it was probably because I was his talcum-snorting partner in crime. I'd like to make it clear that I don't take drugs now, in fact I find them boring, they are no substitute for Rock and Roll!'

We now move to a much more pleasant but thoroughly un-punk part of our trip. Later on Sunday 5 we drove to Port Clinton, Ohio, for two days off, staying in Phil's Inn, Restaurant & Hotel. As Mark's diary says, on the first night we 'Went out on the town. Very friendly people.' Indeed they were.

Monday 6 was Labor Day in the US and Canada, and after a lie-in we caught a ferry to South Bass Island, arriving at the literally-named Put-in-Bay. Wikipedia tells me that 'South Bass Island is a small island in western Lake Erie, and a part of Ottawa County, Ohio, United States. It is the southernmost of the three Bass Islands and located 12 miles (19.3 km) from the south shore of Lake Erie. It is the third largest island in the Lake Erie Islands. The island is a popular recreation spot.'

As it was a holiday, it was busy, but the tiny island was beautiful, and the weather wonderful, so we hired bikes and rode over most of it. According to Mark's diary we also 'Went to Capt. Bill's Pizza House and Urb's Bar.' A really lovely day that I remember vividly. For some reason, now lost in the mists of time, Dave and I had instigated a Revolting Breakfast competition, and while in Port Clinton I found somewhere that served Lake Erie Perch - freshwater fish in batter - for breakfast, which was, yes, as revolting as it sounds.

This took poll position for some time, until eventually Dave found somewhere that did frog's legs for breakfast, at which point I conceded.

The next day Mark's diary tells us that we 'Drove to Pittsburgh. Worst place in the world. Worst gig of our lives at the Electric Banana. Got paid $136 & couldn't find a motel for miles.' Ah well, swings and roundabouts. Igor doesn't remember it in quite so desperate terms though: 'It was all normal people, there were no punks there at all. But people danced.'

The venue was run by a gangster called Joey Banana (I kid you not) and as Mark remembers 'We reckoned we broke the percentage, and he said 'No, no, no. Anyway I've got the contract up in the office, come on up.' So we get up there and we're stood in front of his desk, he sits down and opens the drawer and there's a big 45 Magnum.

'Oops, sorry boys, wrong drawer.'

''Yeah yeah, we'll go!' We weren't going to get any more money out of him were we?'

We eventually found rooms at the Lakeview Motel, Sandy Lake, and probably cried ourselves to sleep.

Wednesday 8 we drove to Buffalo, booked into the Sheridan Park Motor Hotel, then as Mark's diary gloomily tells us, we 'Tried to get visas and failed again.' We then 'Went to Niagara Falls & stared at it for hours.' And why not, it's a bloody impressive sight. In today's insanely Health & Safety-conscious world, the fencing around the Falls is no doubt on a scale to be compared with Fort Knox or even, possibly, the Glastonbury Festival, but then it was just a few bits of rusty metal that you could just jump over. You could then stand on a bit of crumbling rock and give yourself vertigo, getting wet from the spray in the process. Great fun and only mildly life-threatening.

In this instance, heading for our next destination, London, Ontario, crossing the border at Niagara Falls made geographical sense, but we had tumbled long ago that even if it meant going hundreds of miles out of our way, it was always worth crossing the US/Canadian border there if possible. This was because, as it was a busy tourist spot, the guards simply didn't have time to strip-search us and take the van apart, which they would undoubtedly have done otherwise.

Thursday 9 we finally got the visas, did indeed cross the border, with little fuss, and in London checked into the Hyland Motel. Our gig was at the Fry Fogles Tavern, a show which elicits no mention in Mark's diary beyond the fact that one of the amps packed up, though he does now recall that it was 'The gig where we banged through the whole set in about 35 minutes, came offstage thinking it was a good gig, and then were told we were contracted for an hour. Probably why we managed to break the amp. Definitely the only gig I ever managed to break a bass string.' Must have been a blinding evening. The only thing I remember is that Sooty had told us that he had a cousin in this city, and that she would be coming to the gig. Well, when Sarah Wilson walked into the dressing room, Dave, Mark, Igor and I were delighted to see that she was a very attractive young blonde, but Sooty swiftly put his foot down. 'Don't. Any. Of. You. Even. Fucking. *THINK ABOUT IT!!!*' he bellowed as we swarmed enthusiastically toward her. But seriously, she was a sweet girl, and it was cool to meet one of Soot's relatives in such a remote (to us, of course) spot.

Mark and Sooty's dairies both tell us that on Friday 10 we drove to Toronto to pick up some money, but just what money this was and why we had to go to Toronto to collect it are facts now lost in the mists of time. While there, Mark proved he was getting a bit too into the spirit of things by purchasing a baseball bat and glove. Glorified bloody girls' school rounders if you ask me.

We crossed back into the US via Niagara again, 'Had excellent meal somewhere,' Mark's diary tells us, and pitched up at the Albany Motor Inn. Again thanks to Mark, we can see that next day we 'Drove to Long Island, through Harlem, Brooklyn, Yonkers, Manhattan, Bronx, Fillmore. Went to Long Beach with Sooty.' We checked into the Long Beach Motor Inn and that night played at the Fillmore Club, Long Isand, NY, supported by the Nihilistics, who provided the only noteworthy aspect of an otherwise perfectly good natured but unremarkable show. Sounds reported that Nihilistics singer Ron said that he:

'…approached Beki "Just to introduce myself and say hello" during soundcheck, only to be given a quick and unprovoked "Piss off!" by the Bondaged One before he could barely open his mouth. "I could almost understand it if there had been anyone else around that she wanted to impress with that attitude," Ron reported, "But there was no-one at all nearby."'

Hmm, and that also means, of course, that there were no witnesses to the alleged incident. Certainly, when we later read this nonsense, we remembered no contact with the band beyond saying the usual 'Hello, how are you?' on arrival and things like 'Is that case in your way?' while setting up. I dunno, some people, eh?

Sunday 12 it was back up to Canada, though unusually, this time we crossed the border on Highway 87, heading for the Polish White Eagle Hall for a show with Black Flag and our old pals Discharge. Billed as the 'Montreal First Hardcore Blitz!!', this was clearly not an ideal show for us to be part of, but, surprisingly perhaps, we went down reasonably well, and over the years a few people, including the Sub Pop band Eric's Trip, have mentioned that they were there and enjoyed our set.

If I may digress a little at this point, Igor remembers that by this time we had discovered a new drink:

'Yeah, we started getting into Black Russians didn't we? That was John Greenhalgh wasn't it? But it wasn't Black Russians like they sell now because it didn't have Coke in it did it. It was just vodka, Tia Maria and ice, and that was it. Because the first time I had Black Russian with Coke I thought it actually tasted nicer, because the Coke actually makes it more of a drink doesn't it?'

Mark: 'In Montreal, the first gig we did with Discharge and Black Flag, Cal came up, I was fiddling around restringing me bass or something, and he came over and said 'Can I have a swig of your Coke mate?' I had one of those ice buckets, full of like a pint of Black Russian, and he took a massive gulp and nearly puked!'

All I really remember of the show is walking into the dressing room and, observing the, at the time, long-haired Henry Rollins, asking 'Who's the hippy?' I must have been feeling somewhat suicidal that day, and why he didn't just deck me I don't know. He'd have been fully justified.

Actually, we must all have been feeling a bit off that day, as later events at the Hotel Colonnade demonstrated. Igor recalls that 'I had a fight with Dave in the bar [at the hotel], and we took those girls off Discharge. Dave was being really snotty, and he must have been being snotty at Beki, cos the only times I ever had a fight with Dave was normally when he was being snotty at Beki, and I smacked him.'

At the same time, I had bought a tray of glasses of vodka and orange to take to my room with one of the girls, but the barmaid wouldn't let me take them out of the bar. We got into an argument, the drinks somehow ended up on the floor, smashed glass and Screwdriver everywhere, the barmaid burst into tears, and there's Dave and Igor rolling about on the floor, knocking over tables and chairs, trying to kill each other. Discharge just stared at us. 'Oh Igor, my hero!' laughs Beki. 'Alas I don't remember this either. Discharge's van broke down on the way back to the US and we had to tow them, I think they ran out of petrol! It was funny being with them as we'd been out there longer and were all tanned whereas Discharge were all pale blue and wearing leather jackets in the sweltering heat. I think we even had cowboy hats by then, which must have looked odd on a set of spiky herberts.'

Igor continues: 'And then I went to bed with one of the girls, the groupies who were with Discharge, and I woke up in the morning, and Mark had woken up first, and thought that I'd had my head cut off and someone had put a head with pink hair on me. Because he was so pissed! He thought that I was in bed next to him and all he could see was this girl's pink head. Then she woke up and said 'I think this is the same bed where I slept with Magoo,' so I went 'Eeurgh! Fuck off!' Magoo out of the Anti-Nowhere League! So we kicked her out. They were French, they couldn't speak English could they?'

Yes, I did later wonder what my chat-up line could have been, cos I don't speak a word of French, but hey ho, it seemed to work. Ahem, sorry, disgraceful behaviour.
'I thought all of you were gay,' scoffs Beki.

Next morning, to make amends, I got our out-sized bottle of vodka out of the van and poured a liberal dose into everyone's breakfast orange juice, whether they wanted it or not.

Then, we were off to Toronto, where we were to play the Coronet Club with Discharge and the Effigies. On the way, as Beki says, Discharge did indeed break down, though

Mark's diary tells us that they had blown a tyre. Either way, we had to help them push the bloody van for miles. Same night, we crossed the border at Buffalo and there checked into the Sheridan Park Motor Hotel.

We now had just one more gig scheduled, in Washington DC on Thursday 16. However, the promoters contacted us to say that Discharge's problems went further than transport troubles. They were due to support Bad Brains in New York on Saturday 18, but as their papers weren't in order, they either couldn't leave Canada or enter the US, I forget which, and as it would take some days to sort the mess out, they'd have to miss the gig. We were asked to stay on a couple of days to fill in, promised wealth beyond the dreams of avarice, and a few bottles of vodka, and agreed, though Mark wasn't keen. So, as we'd have some time to kill, it was agreed that we'd base ourselves in New York and drive back up to Washington. Tuesday 14, then, we drove to New York, to check into the Hotel Iroquois, another famous rock 'n' roll dive. It was built in 1899 and an issue of the Hotel Gazette, published in 1936, states: 'All through the dreary years of depression The Iroquois has gone on its tranquil way, never allowed to deteriorate, kept in the pink of condition, and always with a good house count of people who appreciate a quiet, refined, well-kept hotel.' Later, James Dean lived there, and though the place was indeed always well kept (today it looks super-posh) as time went on it acquired a more, shall we say, raucous reputation.

We'd first heard of the place when the Clash mentioned it in an interview, so when we couldn't find it, we joked that we should just look out for a hotel with Joe and Mick stood outside. And when finally we found the place, between 5th and 6th Avenues, there were the Clash, standing outside, hailing a taxi. Would you Adam and Eve it? We were so excited it was pathetic.

As well as the Clash, Chelsea and Brian Brain from PiL were staying there, and rumour had it that Lou Reed was occupying the whole of the top floor, but the first person we encountered, asleep on a bench in the lobby, was bloody Pepe! Oh, you remember, the drunken driver we'd last seen on his way to hospital in LA. I forget what he was doing there, but we were just relieved (and, frankly, surprised) to see him alive. Boy, could that man drink.

We saw the Clash around the place several times, and I was always too awe-struck to speak, except for late one night when we got back to the hotel, and I was so drunk that when Strummer walked past, wearing some perfectly inoffensive head-gear, I apparently shouted out that he had a 'Stupid hat.' When they told me about it next morning, I was mortified.

Igor had more luck, however: 'When we ended up in the Iroquois, there were those girls with Harley Davidson knickers, from Atlantic City. We were in that big horrible room, and they were nearby, and they took me to Joe Strummer's room. Cos I've still got the 'Good luck Beki Bondage,' signed copy of Should I Stay Or Should I go. I wonder what it would be worth now? Because it's genuine isn't it? Should I Stay Or Should I Go, American import, 'Good Luck Beki Bondage' signed by Joe Strummer. Quite unique really. I should give it to Beki, cos it's 'Good Luck Beki Bondage,' so she should probably have it really shouldn't she? But then why should I give it to her, ha ha!'

'Yes, give it to me Igor,' shouts Beki. 'He obviously wanted me to have it!' Before a punch-up starts, we'll move on...

That night we went to see Chelsea at the Peppermint Lounge, where I met up with a girl called Samone that I'd met last time we were in New York. She was surprised to see me back in town, and after I'd explained the change of plan, she asked what everyone was laughing at. I told her that the girl Dave was chatting up claimed to be one of the famous Fonda family, the silly moo. Samone said 'Yes, that's right. She's Bridget Fonda and her dad's Peter.' She went on to explain that Bridget was a drama student at New York University and the Lee Strasburg Theatre Institute. Interesting.

Later in the evening, I noticed that Dave was talking to another girl, who he subsequently disappeared with. Next morning, I asked him what happened to Bridget. 'Well,' he said, 'I thought her mate looked more likely to fuck. And I was right.' What a charmer!

The gig itself was quite eventful, with singer Gene October throwing a wobbly, storming off stage and refusing to come back on. No one knew what had brought this on, but he was never the most stable of people, as I was reminded a decade later when I booked Chelsea for a gig at the Fleece in Bristol. Anyway, the upshot was that guitarist Nic Austin sang for the rest of the set and played a blinder. The story was reported in *Sounds*, and the fact that we were in the crowd was even mentioned. Gosh, what celebrities!

Wednesday 15 September we spent the day shopping for presents and seeing the sights, the only business in hand being an interview and photo session for a magazine whose name has been lost in the mists of time. The plan had been to do the photo session on the Statue of Liberty, but, just our luck, it was closed for refurbishment.

Far more importantly, when I went out with Samone in the evening, I asked her to take me to the one place in NY that I really wanted to visit, the birthplace of US punk, CBGB's, in the Bowery. To my horror, she told me that that too was closed for the week for refurbishment. Knowing the famous venue's reputation for squalidness, that sounds strange, but as I made her drive me there so I could at least see the place and stand outside it, I can vouch for it being completely closed. These days the Bowery has been shamefully gentrified, and the CBGB's building, 315 Bowery, is, at the time of writing, a branch of men's fashion design store John Varatos To make up for the disappointment, we went to the Mudd Club, just cos the New York Dolls used to play there.

Next night we loaded the van and headed up to Washington DC for a show at the original 9.30 Club, already famous by then as a hardcore venue. We didn't know much about the local DC hardcore scene at the time, but if the locals were really more interested in Minor Threat and the other Dischord Records bands, they were kind enough not to show it.

We had to play two short sets, one early evening and one late-nighter, so when we found out that one of our favourite bands, the Lords Of The New Church, were playing a club up the road, at the end of our first set we all piled in the van.

This is one of my favourite stories from our US trip, as anyone I've bored stupid in the pub with it will tell you, but it's a truly special memory, so bear with me.

The Lords were, of course, a sort of punk supergroup, comprising of Stiv Bators from the Dead Boys, Brian James from the Damned, Dave Tregunna from Sham 69 and Nick Turner from the Barracudas, and we loved the Lords as much as we loved their original bands, so it was worth giving up our fag break to catch their set.

A lot of our crowd had the same idea, which can't have pleased the 9.30 management too much, but as, at the end of the Lords' excellent set, a lot of their crowd came back with ours for our second set, they were presumably mollified. We'd met the Lords a couple of times before, once in a club in Manchester I seem to remember, but we were still hugely flattered when we found out that as well as a lot of their audience, the boys themselves had actually made their way down the road to see us!

Carried away, we hurriedly decided to open our second set with the introduction to the Dead Boys classic Sonic Reducer, in tribute to Stiv, but made an embarrassing hash of it. Still, we played a decent enough set, went down well, and a fun night was had by all, I think. The only thing that troubles me is that we have no note of who supported that night. It was probably some Dischord band that are now living hardcore legends, and if that's so, sorry to leave you out.

After a post-gig drink or several, we finally headed out of DC and back to NY, and were soon fast asleep. As we drove into New York the dawn was rising over the city and the Statue of Liberty loomed in the distance, a breathtaking sight as the mist settled and the sun rose majestically, casting colour-drenched shadows over the still-quiet city. Mark gently woke me and pointed at this beautiful scene, a view never to be forgotten. I blinked out of the window, muttered 'Ahh, fuck off,' and went back to sleep.

Friday 17, after a lie-in, we learn from Mark's diary that we 'Went to in Chinatown & had meal. Saw Lords Of The New Church at Hitsville in New Jersey.' Sooty elected not to go on the latter trip and have a quiet few beers in the Iroquois instead, despite us all calling him an antisocial git. As it turned out, though, he had the last laugh. He hadn't been in the almost empty bar for long when Strummer walked in, and they were soon chatting. The booze flowed, and eventually, with Strummer at the piano, the pair of them held a drunken sing-song late into the night. When we heard about it next morning, we were green with envy.

Incidentally, I interviewed Joe for the *Bristol Evening Post*, when he was doing the Class War Rock Against The Rich tour with his band Latino Rockabilly War in 1988, and for some reason he mentioned the Iroquois, and I told him about us being there when the Clash were, and to my amazement he remembered. Well, he remembered who we were at least, as he said 'Yeah, I remember. Last Rockers, Beki Bondage…' Also incidentally, he was the best interviewee I've ever talked to. Every quote a potential headline and he even fixed my tape recorder when it broke down; a real professional and a very nice bloke. I was so sad when he died.

And so to our final US date, on 18 September, in New York, at 285 Broadway, formerly known as the Rock Lounge. Interestingly, a quick search on the internet turns up not just the 'Bad Brains & Vice Squad' gig flyer, a copy of which I still have, but also one for the gig that never happened, 'Bad Brains & Discharge,' almost identical except ours had purple writing and theirs was yellow.

As we've seen, so far on this tour the American bands had allowed us to headline the shows, despite many of them being popular in their own right, probably just out of politeness and hospitality as we'd travelled such a long way. So, we were mildly surprised to find that we would actually be supporting Bad Brains. We'd heard of Bad Brains, but didn't really know much about them, so when we turned up for the soundcheck we were intrigued.

Even in the soundcheck, they were one of the most awesome live acts I've ever seen, with the band belting out the fastest, hardest, loudest, most brutally precise hardcore, and singer HR running around the venue, round the hall, over the stage, round the dressing room, back on the stage, all the time screaming his head off and smoking an enormous spliff.

When the dust finally settled, Dave paused for a long while, staring dazedly into the middle distance. Then, slowly, he turned to me and said 'Well, I don't know about you mate...but I'm fucking glad we haven't got to follow that!' I heartily agreed.

'Ah the Bad Brains gig!,' chuckles Beki. 'Those guys smoked so much weed I was off my head on the fumes, seriously. Their dreadlocks were green from all the weed they smoked, I'm amazed that they were so aggressive on stage, if I'd smoked that much I'd have been in a coma for days.'

Igor: I remember the last gig, with the Bad Brains. That's the one where we trashed the whole stage at the end.

Mark: Dave started early didn't he, cos he tore the machine heads off his guitar.

Igor: And you kicked the drum kit over.

Me: It was a hired kit and I hated it.

Mark: I only had one guitar so I wasn't going to break that!

Igor: They were very good, weren't they, Bad Brains. I didn't like them for that reason!

As well as being a staggeringly good hardcore band, Bad Brains were also, of course, dab hands at dub reggae, making them a unique phenomenon. Some of their beliefs have been questioned over the years, but we found them to be a sound and friendly bunch of guys. They even complemented me on my drumming and gave me a handful of Bad

Brains badges, a couple of which I still have. When they played the Bierkeller in Bristol the following year (which at that time was part of the Dingwalls chain), we were touched when we walked in and the band immediately shouted out 'Hey, Vice Squad!' and came over for a chat. It pissed off a lot of the local hardcore merchants as well, ha ha!

Sunday 19 September, according to Mark's diary, we: 'Went to Greenwich Village then to JFK airport @ 3pm & boarded @ 7.15. Flight left @ 8pm.' From Sooty's diary we also learn that we were again on a 'Boeing 747, Flight Panam 002, Av. Alt. 35,000 Feet.'

We arrived back at Heathrow at 7.00am BST, which was probably just as well as according to Sooty's diary our US visas expired at 12.00 midnight that day.

We were met at the airport by Ken and Simon, in their respective cars, but as I explained earlier, our homecoming wasn't quite joyous as we'd expected due to Simon finding out that Dave, Bambi, Igor and I were in fact Chaotic Dischord. As I also explained earlier, this little tiff soon passed, but it did cast a pall, and the next few days were also less than jolly.

When I got home, I was put out to find the house empty, and with no key I had no way to get in. For want of anything better to do, I walked down to the newsagents, collected six weeks' copies of *Sounds*, and sat down on my dad's work bench in the back garden. When the old folks returned, we had a properly joyous reunion, at least until we got into the house. The first thing I saw was a very small, very cute kitten, rolling about on the floor, and the sight of it was a massive blow. I instantly knew what this meant. Yogi, my beloved pet cat for all the 20 years of my life, had died. Worse was to come.

I was then told that Sam Williams, father of my old boss Mike, was dying. Next day I walked down to Sam's place, next to the workshop, and spoke to Mike. He told me that Sam was too ill to speak to anyone, but he'd tell him that I'd visited. Next thing I heard was that Sammy had died.

At the funeral I met up with my old workmates, who all asked about our Great USA Adventure, but I naturally kept it brief. Some homecoming.

CHAPTER 13

AFTER BEING AWAY SO LONG (by our standards, anyway; no doubt seasoned road-hogs like the Subs and Motorhead would snort derisively at a mere six weeks), it was difficult to settle down at home again. If Mark's diary reflects the period for all of us, then the next two weeks (roughly) were spent in pubs, having our hair cut and dyed, in pubs, and visiting arboretums, though that last one was probably just Mark.

On the business front, Mark's diary shows that we held a good many meetings with the management planning the State Of The Nation Tour, our most ambitious yet, three solid weeks around England. A three week tour without even touching Wales, Ireland or Scotland, mark you.

When I saw the itinerary, I thought it was mad, particularly the Yorkshire dates. How could you play Leeds, Bradford and Keighley on the same tour? Sometimes when we played in Yorkshire, I swore if you stood on tip-toe and squinted you could see the place we'd played the previous night. As it turned out, I was wrong, and not only were all the Yorkshire dates well attended, it wasn't, largely, the same people at all the gigs.

On 21 September, Mark's diary says that he 'Picked records up from Shane,' which presumably marks the arrival of the State Of The Nation EP. The EP's three tracks were Citizen, Scarred For Life and Faceless Men, all decent enough songs, though Citizen, the a-side track, was a bit scuppered production-wise, and I have to put my hands up for this one.

With its chorus chant of 'Upright Citizen! Upright Citizen!,' Dave and I had the idea of putting our Swan drinking buddy Bill on the cover, his neatly-trimmed moustache, blazer and regimental tie making him ideal, and the fact that he was actually such an old reprobate made for a delicious private joke. The idea was that our 'Upright Citizen' would be photographed, blithely reading the Times, at a bus stop surrounded by a scene of desolation. On the day, we saw a headline in another newspaper, and glued that to the front of the Times, and if you look at the sleeve carefully, you can see that the glue is still wet. Unfortunately, I can't now remember what the headline actually was, it's not clear on the sleeve, and I can't find the original photo. The parts that I can see appear to say 'God Save **** Anthony' or possibly 'Anthem' but I've no idea what the asterisked part said or what the whole thing meant. It obviously seemed a good idea at the time though.

Another thing that seemed like a good idea, after meeting Bill and his mate Emerys in the Swan, was to fill the car with bottles of Natch cider to drink on the way to the photo shoot, which took place at a bus stop in, I think, the Totterdown area of Bristol, possibly near what is now the Thunderbolt music venue. The upshot of this was that we drunkenly decided that Bill and Emerys must now sing backing vocals on the record, and once the photos were 'in the can' we repaired to SAM, where Steve dutifully recorded their drunken bellowing. The results weren't good, but Steve and producer Sooty made the best of it, and though low in the mix, we insisted that as the boys had made the effort, they had to be on the record. The result was a muddled compromise which didn't really work, but all three songs were enthusiastically picked up by the fans and went well live. In *Sounds*, Bushell said: 'Vice Squad are as good as ever. A-side Citizen displays all their myriad strengths: thinking lyrics, Beki's big, powerful, umm, vocal attributes, the band's compact power and solid command of hooks. But sadly I fear this won't be the one to set the charts alight. Nice try though.' Which, as ever, was very fair of him, not to say lenient.

The last preparations for the tour were a photo session at EMI on 1 October, more meetings, answering more fan mail, the purchase by Mark of 'Aubergine Crazy Colour & dumbbells' (?), and finally, on 6 October, a single, solitary, pre-tour rehearsal at Biggles. And now we were off.

But first, I must reluctantly tackle one of the few things that we, as a band, were responsible for, that I've always quietly regretted, the manner in which we recruited tour support band Flowers Of The Past. Igor introduces the subject:

Igor: They thought they were Theatre Of Hate didn't they, and they bought onto the tour.

Me: I've always felt badly about that.

Igor: That was to do with Sooty and Ken wasn't it? Ken probably more than Sooty.

Me: We shouldn't have allowed it.

Igor: They were nice lads, weren't they? They had this scam with the guest list. They were asking for places on the guest list, but they were asking for funny names like Horse Head and Slag and things like that, and it turned out they were selling them outside. But there was a bit of comedy about that, because the person had to turn up and we'd say 'Who are you on the guest list?,' 'I'm Slag' or 'I'm Horse Head.' And I cottoned on after about the third gig, because they were asking for the same names. I said 'Who are these people that are following you around? Because I've not seen them.' And then the penny dropped and then they told me what they were doing. So we used to give them three guest list places a night so they could make, like another £10 or however much.

The least we could have done, I'd have thought. I mean, buying on to tours was, and probably still is, common practice, the argument going that it simply helps cover the cost of the PA etc, and eventually, after much debating we allowed ourselves to be talked into it, but in our hearts of hearts we knew it was wrong. When we did our first bit of touring, a few dates supporting the Subs, dates that any punk band in the country would gladly have paid for the privilege of playing, they not only didn't charge us, but paid us £100 a night. So, they set an example to us, and to my shame we failed to follow it.

Probably to assuage our guilt, whenever possible we sneaked the lads (singer Gary, guitarist Lee, bassist Martin and drummer Kevin) into our B&B or hotel rooms rather than have them kipping in the van, and when we found that they had a self-released single, The Fuhrer, out, on their own Memorial Records label, with no distribution, Dave and I arranged to release the remaining copies through our Resurrection Records label and Revolver Distribution. Big of us, eh?

'What is this Resurrection Records that thou doth speak of Shane?' I hear you ask, anxiously and all aquiver. Yes, I should have mentioned this earlier. As it happens, I recently wrote about the label for a sleeve note for a Lunatic Fringe compilation CD, so out of sheer laziness, I'll just reproduce it here:

> 'I can't now remember why Dave Bateman and I decided to set up our own label, when we already had Riot City. Just a whim, I suppose. We borrowed £1,000 from Dave's uncle to finance the venture, and our label office was 38 Tudor Road, Hanham, Bristol - the council house that Dave shared with his mum and dad.
>
> We told Garry Bushell about our idea, he gave us a plug in Sounds requesting tapes from up and coming punk acts, and they literally flooded in. We were astonished at how many arrived. We were also astonished at how bad most of them were. In the end, we decided that the best tape was a cover of the Human League's Don't You Want Me Baby, by a band called Oi Polloi, which was at least funny. But no, we didn't really think so.
>
> I also can't now remember why Lunatic Fringe were never signed to Riot City. They were on our *Riotous Assembly* compilation after all. For whatever reason, they weren't, so as a prominent band on the local scene, as yet unsigned, we snapped them up. I seem to remember a meeting in a pub in Old Market, possibly the Coach & Horses. It wasn't a long and protracted negotiation. We said 'Wanna make a record?,' they said 'Yeah, alright,' and we had a drink on it.
>
> We recorded the single at SAM Studio (annoyingly, despite trawling through a couple of diaries I can't pin down a recording date) and as always when Dave and I were credited as producers, we really just helped set up the gear and, effectively, held the spanners for engineer Steve Street who did all the real work.
>
> We were pleased with the result, especially Age's wonderfully camp 'Fares please!' in the intro to Omnibus (Bristol Buses), and despite a disparaging review by Bushell, the record did reasonably well, making No.50 on the indie chart in August 1982. No one made any money from the project, and it turned out to be the only Resurrection Records release (apart from helping a band called Flowers Of The Past, who supported us on a UK tour in October 1982, by putting their self-released single through our distribution with a Resurrection Records sticker). However, it did break even, Dave and I were able to pay his uncle back, and as we all had fun making the record, we were perfectly happy. In December 2014 Mark Hambly and I attended a Lunatic Fringe show at the Exchange in Bristol, and had a great evening, and I was especially pleased, and a bit proud, when the band played Who's In Control near the end and it got a massive cheer.
> Shane Baldwin, January 2015'

First date of the tour was 7 October, in Bradford, but for the first part of the tour we had decided to base ourselves in what had become a sort of home-from-home by now, the Hunter's House Hotel in Sheffield. After checking in and a quick drink at the Droitwich Pound Hotel we made our way to Bradford

We were to play Bradford University Union, on Richmond Road, but the first thing that happened, on entering Bradford (on the first date of the bloody tour, mark you), was that Sooty crashed the van into a Cortina. No, not that sort, a car. Oh well, it can't have been that serious, as his diary says that we 'Paid £10 cash as settlement.'

As Mark's diary says, it was an 'Excellent gig 'til the riot. Nothing got very broke.' Well that's alright then. Actually, I do remember that the evening ended in a relatively serene manner, as the venue had the very wise but rarely used idea of making sure that the bands finished in time for people to get the last bus, but keeping the venue open for a couple of hours afterwards with a disco for anyone who wanted to hang around for a late drink. A damned handy arrangement for the bands, too.

I also remember, at this one, early in the evening Mark and I chatting up a couple of girls, who clearly didn't believe that we were in the band. They were quite shocked when, at the appointed time, we downed our pints, got onstage and kicked off. Didn't get us anywhere with them though! Ah well, win some lose more.

Next day, exhausted from enduring a whole day on tour, we had a day off, and Mark's diary says that we 'Went to Marples for dinner.' Presumably he means lunch. I always said it was a mistake allowing the working classes into punk.

Apparently he then 'Went to X-Clothes & bought a Meteors t-shirt. Went to 2 local pubs - Porter Cottage & The Lescar. Crazy Coloured hair.' This is really very worrying indeed. Back on 4 October, as I'm sure you remember, he bought Crazy Colour. Is he now proposing to dye his hair again? So soon? Or did he just buy the dye four days earlier and is only now using it? After a solid day roaming South Yorkshire boozers? Either way, it'll result in split ends, you mark my words.

Saturday 9 October we drove across Snake's Pass to air our wares at Manchester Polytechnic, which we learn from Mark was a 'Good gig but got out of hand - met Scots loonies.' No surprise on either count there, then.

By now thoroughly shagged out, we had another day off, during which we drank in the Porter Cottage lunchtime and evening, and Mark 'Had a bath all afternoon,' the lazy bugger.

Monday 11 October saw us at the unlikely-named Keighley Funhouse, though Mark does say that it was a 'Good gig except for the get-in.' The day's tragedy was that, when he went to Sheffield market to buy some boots, it was closed. Into each life some rain must fall.

More luck next day, another day off, when he did indeed get dem boots, and also, apparently, visited the Leadmill and Limit clubs in Sheffield. Coincidentally, my eldest son Jake was at Sheffield University from 2008-2012, and when visiting him, I passed the Leadmill, a place I've never been to. In 1982 the club had only recently opened, and I remember the others deciding to check the place out, but I elected to get a lift with Ricky Fox to see SLF in Hull instead. Presumably this is that night. Also coincidentally, while Jake was in Sheffield, no less than five books on the South Yorkshire music scene were published, by two authors, Tony Beesley and Neil Anderson, and we are mentioned in some of them. A section from this book, quoting Dave's thoughts on Sheffield Marples is included in the last of Tony's trilogy of books covering the punk and mod scenes in the area, *This Is Our Generation Calling*.

In other news, Sooty's diary tells us that on this day our press officer, Suzie Rome, rang about a 'School days article' with Beki for *Smash Hits*, which I don't recall ever seeing. Shame that, as I was quite diligent with me scrap book. He also says that Suzie and someone called Tony Mitchell (whoever he was) would be joining us for the Brighton and Isle of Wight dates later in the tour.

Wednesday 13 October we were at the Liverpool Warehouse, though this wasn't the first time we'd played there - that was the Absolute Disaster Tour, back in Chapter 8, remember? At that point in our torrid tale I'd forgotten to explain the history of the venue, so let's do it now. The Warehouse had previously been Eric's, run by Roger Eagle and Ken Testi, a famous venue that played host to many early punk gigs by the likes of the Pistols, Clash, Banshees, Slits and so on. And as if that wasn't enough, it was situated on Matthew Street, opposite the original Cavern Club. A pretty cool place to get to play then.

Igor reminded me that one of the shows we did in this venue (he can't remember which one) was so packed that the kids at the front were wedged against a crush barrier and unable to move away, so when the call of nature became too strong, they just pissed through the gaps in the barrier. Unfortunately, our open flight cases were directly in their line of fire, so Igor had to hastily drag them out of the way.

Afterwards, we repaired to the Orrell Park Hotel on Orrell Lane, where we were to spend the next two nights.

Thursday 14 October, after Mark had done his laundry, apparently, we made our way to another Warehouse, this time in Preston. Unfortunately, once the gear was unloaded, we realised that we'd left all the merchandise back at Liverpool Warehouse, so the poor deprived people of Preston would be denied the right to purchase a State Of The Nation tour shirt. Grown men wept in the streets.

Worse was to come. Preston was always a good gig for us, though the kids were, if anything, a trifle overenthusiastic. There was always an immediate stage invasion, which we didn't normally mind, but as the stage in this venue wasn't particularly large, things tended to get accidentally trashed.

The organizers had clearly given the matter some thought this time round, but their solution was far from ideal. The stage was of the type with an expanse of wall a few feet wide running parallel to the front of the stage on the left and right of it and also above. This makes it a sort of square box set into the wall, if you follow me. Anyway, the organizers' bright idea was to get some of that metal fencing used on building sites - thick metal rods, welded together about 6 inches apart, criss-cross, to make large sheets of wide, heavy mesh, forming lots of squares about 6 inches by 6 inches. They got some large lengths of 4" be 3" and used six inch nails to construct a cage that stretched across the stage from left to right and floor to ceiling.

Ingenious? Oh yes. Fucking stupid? Absolutely.

After a couple of songs, the kids began tugging at the fence, eventually managing to drag down the top part while the bottom remained nailed to the foot of the stage. This meant that there was now a row of potentially lethal spikes facing back into the hall that the kids being pushed forwards began to get impaled on. Soon the whole construction was dragged down and trampled underfoot, but not before a few kids were hurt and some blood was spilled. We stopped the show for a bit to make sure no one was seriously injured, and when we carried on it was stage-invasion-as-normal. Bizarrely, someone filmed all this and approached us with the idea of releasing it on video. All you could see was the fence being dragged down, then the audience piling on each other's shoulders to form a solid wall of bodies, after which you couldn't even see us until the end of the set, not to mention the severely muffled sound from that point on. We said yes and took the money. Only joking.

We issued a grovelling apology to the music press praying that no one would sue, and luckily no one did.

To round off this fabulous evening's entertainment, we headed back to Liverpool Warehouse to collect the merchandise, have a few drinks, and what Mark describes as an 'Amazing kebab.'

Friday 15 October we again made our way over Snake's Pass, pausing only to take in the majestic splendour of Glossop and confirm that it was as breathtaking as it had been two days earlier when we'd stopped off for a bite to eat on the way to Liverpool. Our destination this time was the trusty Retford 'Slaughterhouse' Porterhouse. It was a good show, as ever, but as I've said before, the stage time of midnight was a drag, particularly on a Friday, as experience had taught us not to imbibe more than a few pints before a show.

My humour wasn't improved when I met up with the girl from the pea factory that I'd 'got friendly' with last time we'd played there in June, to find that she'd got herself a boyfriend. My god, aren't women fickle? Just because I fly off to another continent and don't ring for four months, she considers herself a free agent! Pah!

It's interesting to note, in Sooty's diary, that we were paid £350 for the Retford gig and £300 for the previous one in Preston. Now, as I've said, at first we were only able to pay ourselves, for a brief while, was £70, and don't get me wrong, it was wonderful to be paid for doing what we loved and not have to worry about work, and we knew how lucky we were. I mention this because around about 2003 an excellent ska-punk band called Jesse James got an awful lot of bad-mouthing on the scene for having the almighty gall to charge £250 per gig. I don't need to point out that this was 21 years after the period we are covering here, so the impossibility of the maths as far as sustaining a working band is obvious, especially when you consider that there were seven of them. But this attitude on the punk scene of the time, that seeing five bands for a fiver was reasonable, resulted in a great ska-punk scene collapsing with the loss of class acts like Lightyear, the Filaments and Five Knuckle who understandably decided, eventually, that slogging it around the toilets of the UK for wages of £2.50 a day (literally, the drummer from Five Knuckle told me that) was no way to live. And sadly, that attitude towards paying bands (or rather, not paying them) persists to this day. Ahem, sorry, rant over. Back to the plot.

After Retford we'd returned to the famed Hunter's House Hotel, for one night, before making our way to Middlesbrough for a gig at the Cavern on Saturday 16 October. Some of us, however, made a detour...

We were sat in the Hunter's bar when Ricky Fox turned up for a lunchtime drink. While reading a newspaper, he noticed that Bristol City were playing Hartlepool United, in the old fourth division, on that very day. How could we pass up the opportunity to witness such a glamorous fixture? Dave and I downed our pints and we piled into Ricky's van, instructing him to get a bloody move on. He drove as fast as his dodgy motor would allow, but traffic was bad, and by the time we got to the ground and made our way into the away end, which consisted of a steep, muddy, uncovered hillock, it was half time, and if I remember rightly, City were already 2-1 down. From the internet I'm reminded that City definitely lost 3-1 in the end, and the crowd was just 1,449. These were indeed grim times for Bristol City FC. Still, it was an interesting diversion, and the looks on the faces of our old footy mates, who we hadn't seen for some time, was a picture when we casually strolled in at half time in that god-forsaken place.

By the time we got to the gig, we were well late and less than popular, and worse was to come. As Mark's diary states, it was a 'Good gig but trouble with support.' Now, FOTP singer Gary was an agreeable soul for most of the time, but he was prone to flare up now and again, and this particular night, during their set, he got into an altercation with some drunken yob in the audience. The ruck was over almost as soon as it started, and no one thought any more about it, but the yob in question wasn't about to let it lie.

When FOTP came offstage, Gary went to help Ricky behind the merchandise stall. Meanwhile, the yob had rounded up his mates, and the next thing we knew they'd charged at the merchandise stall, giving Gary and Ricky a good slap and scattering t-shirts, records and badges hither and yon, before the security woke up and quelled the disturbance. A nasty end to a quite strange day.

Before we move on, I should mention that before the tour, Beki had done a couple of

those full page Q&A things, one appearing in the 16 October issue of *NME* entitled 'Portrait of the Artist as a Consumer,' in which she revealed that, among other things, she'd just read *Slaughter of the Innocent* by Hans Reusch, and she liked 'buttocks.' In the other, in an unidentified and undated magazine's Profile section, she put:
'Height: Six foot, three inches! *(I don't think you're taking this seriously enough - Ed)*.
Weight: Two Grammes *(Come on, play the game - Ed)*.' Good girl!

Sunday 17 October, a day off, we 'Slept all day,' according to Mark, in the Pendelphin Guest House, Proprietor Mrs G. Phripson, then 'Went to see The Wall. Went over pub. Then had a Chinese meal & watched *Lord Of The Flies*.' A packed and, I'm sure you'll agree, confusing day, that I can't be bothered to try to unravel. I am of course assuming that he's referring to Wallsend band The Wall and not some piece of local architecture, but you can't be sure with Mark. Ahem, onwards…

Monday 18 October we had a show at Leeds University, where we met up with Suzie and Winston Smith, the latter to interview us for both *Sounds* and *Noise!* The 30 October issue of *Sounds* (35p) boasted an eye-catching photo of Beki, naked from the waist up, back to camera, that naturally caused plenty of comment, as did an inside shot, facing forward, again naked, with arms strategically crossed. Some feminists got a little uppity, perhaps understandably, but as the whole idea was cooked up by Beki herself and photographer Laura Levine it was no good their trying to play the sexism card. And, of course, it was all done in the best possible taste, as that Kenny Everett character would have said.

For his two page article, Winston spoke to a number of fans, including Steve, from Derby, who was '…an enthusiast with a capital 'E'. He's already taken one entire week off 'sick' to see Vice Squad play at Keighley, Liverpool, Preston, Retford and Middlesbrough, and a warning has been given; if he wasn't at work today he'd be fired.
He wasn't at work today.
He'd be fired.
But unfortunately, he won't know if he's lost the job for quite a while yet, because tomorrow, along with his good friend D.R., Steve is off hitching down to Brighton, and the day after that the Isle of Wight; to see Vice Squad…'
Immensely flattering of course, and we valued the support of people like Steve and D.R. more than I can say, but for someone to risk losing their job, particularly in that period of massive unemployment, just to watch the likes of us, was a bit disturbing and made one feel more than a bit guilty. Nice to see the guys getting a well-deserved mention though. And, indeed, in the interview we covered our rapidly expanding guest -list of travelling fans, as well as the US tour, animal rights, sexism, the chaotic live show (he thought, quite rightly, that we tended to play too fast) and lack of radio airplay for punk, among other things. A nice, fair, article.

Winston also did a double page spread for the 11 November issue of *Noise!*, beginning his piece with: 'Vice Squad have just returned from America. America will never be the same again...' A much more lurid piece, in keeping, I suppose, with the nature of the magazine, this time he concentrated on our US jaunt, including this quote from Dave: 'In Hollywood, Sunset Boulevard, I was sick for two miles out the van window, all the way along it. There were all these pimps, prostitutes and pushers, the lot right, and there was all my sick falling on their heads. Which wasn't nice. I won't say why I was sick...' You get the idea.

However, one rather right-on female friend of mine, despite criticising the scurrilous nature of most of the article, and our actions described therein, did concede that one part of it did give us at least a small measure of hope. Dave: '...we went to like total tourist-spots like Niagara Falls and the Empire State Building, and we also made our driver drive us round all the slums as well; like downtown Chicago, and in New York the Bronx, Harlem, Queens and all of that. It was really good. Well...I wouldn't like to live there, but it was very interesting...'

As for the gig itself, we had some problems early on when we popped out for a post-soundcheck beer and returned to be confronted by crowds of disgruntled fans. Bizarrely, the Student Union had ruled that only SU members would be admitted to the gig, ruling out the vast majority of our fans. In the end, the matter was only resolved when we flatly refused to play, regardless of the financial implications, unless everyone was allowed in. Whether the presence of the press had anything to do with this unusual show of bravado, I honestly can't remember.

Anyway, the show did indeed go on, and as Winston pointed out in his *Sounds* article, it got a bit boisterous to say the least:

> 'Down the front, everybody is going crazy. Loony after loony climbs over the ample stage-defences, struggles past the security, and ends up on the boards with the band for a few fleeting moments before he finds himself hurled over the barriers and back into the crowd where he joins the queue, to end up doing the same thing all over again...'

Unfortunately, later things took a more serious turn:

> 'Someone is pulled out of the lunatic crowd. It's D.R., and in the middle of her 37th Vice Squad gig, she's been crushed against the barrier, and her nose is engulfed in a sickly layer of bubbling blood. Beki holds up the show to tend to her wounded follower, and the invaders carry on invading...'

Blimey, dramatic stuff, eh?

Many years later, when working in admin' at the University of the West of England, I noticed that one of the lecturers, David Lown, kept staring at me in a puzzled way. Eventually, this started to get on my nerves, and I started wondering 'What's he fuckin' looking at?' Eventually, he came up to me and said 'Did you used to be in Vice Squad?'

'Yeah.'

'Ah, I thought so, I saw you at Leeds University. You must remember it, there was a massive fight afterwards and the place got smashed up.'

'Hmm, no, you'll have to do better than that.'

Next morning, 19 October, we left the trusty Hunter's and drove down to Brighton, via London, checking in at Nash's Hotel on the sea front. A memorable day for Igor, it seems: 'I can remember I had a bath in Brighton! We were in a big old hotel, and I got in much later than you lot, and it was the first time on that tour that I had a bath.'

'Actually it was the first time that year,' laughs Beki.

The gig itself, at the X.Treems club night at the New Regent, now sadly elicits no memories from anyone, other than the fact that some of the Test Tube Babies turned up to say hello.

A more interesting event was the 20 October trek across to the Isle Of Wight for a gig on Shanklin Pier. Mark's diary says that we: 'Left Brighton late & got 2.30 ferry. Drove to Shanklin & booked into excellent hotel opposite pier. Excellent gig & spent hours chatting to bikers. Loaded PA down pier & got weed on.' I think, and indeed hope, that the last bit was a reference to the inclement weather.

Mark's mention of the bikers reminds me that in a way this was an odd booking for us. It became very clear quite quickly that this was essentially a biker venue, staffed mainly by bikers, so why we were booked was a puzzle. The hairies were polite enough, but obviously not exactly thrilled by our presence, so the evening boded dodgy.

In desperation, we wondered if it might be a good idea to soundcheck with a song we'd been playing just for fun in rehearsals, Motorhead's White Line Fever. We tried it, and made a right hash of it, but the fact that we'd had a go seemed to endear us to the bikers, and they were on our side from then on. In fact many of them caught the ferry to Portsmouth the next day to see us there, which was both unexpected and flattering.

The Isle Of Wight show itself was, as Mark says, excellent, the punks and bikers rubbing along together nicely, not always the case in an era when the factions existed in quite jealously guarded bubbles. There was little in the way of crossover in those days.

The fact that the weather was so awful, with wind and rain pounding down on the pier, seemed to bring out that old Dunkirk spirit, and there was a great atmosphere.

We were booked into the Osborne House Hotel, Esplanade, a very nice place indeed, so this was turning into a very enjoyable trip. One thing that especially impressed us with the Osborne was that in the bar, the serious drinker could order beer in quart, or two pint, glasses, which we naturally did. Frequently.

So impressed were we that, when we later came to record the Sex Aids single, for one of the b-side tracks we wrote a song called The Amazing Mr Michael Hogarth after the hotel's proprietor. In the song we referenced the large breakfasts served, Mr Hogarth's moustache, and, of course, the fact that 'He serves beer/In a two pint glass.' We sent them a copy, but I don't recall if they ever wrote back. Strangely, I still have one of those little matchbook-type packets that you used to get in hotels with needle and thread from the Osborne. God knows why.

I was very sad when I heard that the pier had been destroyed in a terrible storm in 1987.

On Thursday 21 Mark's diary says that he 'Went to the Castle in Sandown.' This must have been an interesting trip, as, according the internet, Sandown Castle was demolished in 1631, and now, 'Although nothing remains of the castle, its possible foundations can be seen at low tide.' Ah, Mark and his bloody snorkel again.

The castle's loss was a terrible tragedy, because, as you all know, 'This was the earliest fort in England to have been built with an arrow-headed bastion.' And where would we be without our trusty arrow-headed bastions?

Ah, no, hang on, I see there's a boozer on the Isle of Wight called the Castle, so, prosaically, that's probably what he's referring to. Shame, I liked the image of Mark exploring the murky depths in frogman gear, like a moist Tony Robinson in the *Time Team* TV programme.

At 3.30 we caught the ferry back to Portsmouth for a show at the Polytechnic, which was well attended, the audience bolstered, as I've said, by a large contingent of the Isle Of Wight biker chapter.

At this point, Igor brings up the subject of one of the most unpleasant aspects of this tour: 'In Portsmouth Alan lifted me up over the balcony, I'm sure it was in Portsmouth, and there was a balcony, and we were, like, talking in the afternoon, and he just grabbed hold of me by me jacket and lifted me right over the balcony, and then pulled me back. And that was really funny apparently.' As this was a hefty tour, Beki persuaded us to let her boyfriend Del and his mate Alan roadie on the tour, and as Igor says 'That ruined that whole tour didn't it, I think, the pair of them being there, to be honest.'

Well it certainly didn't help, that's for sure. At one date, I forget which, we met up with Discharge in a bar, and for absolutely no reason, Alan walked up to Bones and emptied an entire pint of beer all over him. We were mortified, bollocked Alan and apologised profusely, but Bones was livid. In fact he was still extremely frosty when I met him, briefly, at a Holidays In The Sun festival in Dublin in 2002.

After the show we drove back to Bristol, as for the next leg of the tour it was practical to base ourselves at home.

Friday 22 we left at 3.00 for a show at Leicester University, described by Mark as an 'Excellent gig - loads of people - amazing rider.' Sadly, I can find no details of this remarkable repast. Oh, or the gig.

Saturday 23 we popped down the road to play Bridgewater Arts Centre, with our friends Intensified Chaos added to the bill. The show was reviewed in an unknown local paper by one Brian Smedley, who said that Intensified Chaos '…released a mix of energy and frustration akin to the current "oi oi" style of punk rock which seemed to appeal to the skinhead section of the audience in particular.' He also declared them '…an entertaining starter for the evening.'

'Flowers of the Past,' he said, 'added a degree of menace to the punk sound, drawing on such contemporary influences as Theatre of Hate.'

He then opined that 'Vice Squad's success is due, to a large extent, to their fusion of influences within the new-wave format, drawing on heavy rock patterns within the music and adding that accessible edge through their stage presence.' So that's what we were doing. I thought we were just making it up as we went along.

He went on to report that Beki '…displays incredible staying power with her vocals, maintaining a constant "scream pitched" shout for the full set which lasted almost 60 minutes.' And as if that wasn't enough, 'Her aggressive posturing at the front of the stage incited the vast throng of punks at her feet to leap about in the wildest display of punk-pogo dancing yet seen at the arts centre.' Well, that's if you don't count the previous month's Henry Moore retrospective.

The nice man went on to say that 'The gig was a joint promotion between the arts centre and local promoters, Sheep Worrying Enterprises, demonstrating to all present that a West Country band can succeed in the music business without selling out its ideas.' A very, very, nice man.

By contrast, all I can tell you about the next night's show, at Plymouth Top Rank, is that a bad tempered entry in Mark's diary says that we 'Left late in Sooty's car - boring gig. Got home @ 4am again.' Ah well, swings and roundabouts.

Monday was a day off, the highlight being, according to Mark's diary, he and Kerry going to see *Bladerunner*, which the bastards didn't invite me to. They knew I wanted to see it.

We were actually a bit nervous about the next gig, a Bristol show at Trinity Church on Tuesday 26. By this stage, in some towns and cities we were playing venues the size of Bristol's Anson Rooms or Locarno, but we weren't able to do that in our home town, which was a bit sad really. The Granary would have been too small, but the local backlash against us signing to EMI was such that we weren't able to progress to the bigger venues, so Trinity was a compromise. And even then, we were far from confident that the people who did turn out to see us would dance rather than chuck bricks at us.

After the soundcheck we went to Radio West, by the docks, to be interviewed on the early evening show by Johnnie Walker. The former Radio 1 DJ had been sacked in 1976 for, among other things, slagging off the Bay City Rollers, then moved to the States. By 1982 he was back in the UK presenting Radio West's *The Modern World* show, and we were quite honoured to meet him and appear on it. And, of course, plugging the gig and new record didn't hurt either.

Walker was another nice man, with a long history in music, and eventually rejoined the BBC at Radio 2, where he remains to this day. He was also a consultant on the 2009 movie *The Boat That Rocked*, drawing on his early years in pirate radio.

Back at Trinity, we were relieved to find we had a good-sized, good-natured turnout. Interestingly, I've always had it in my head that only my parents out of all the band's parents, ever came to our gigs, but as so often while writing this book, I find I'm wrong. Mark's diary says that it was a 'Good gig & the whole family came.' Then, in Rich Braybrooke's review in *Venue*, he reports that '...even Bekki [sic] Bondage's mum seemed to be enjoying herself.'

It was indeed a good gig, and my most vivid memory is of Igor, who had been given the task of setting off some strategically placed flash-bombs that we'd purchased to impress the locals. The idea was that we'd set them off as part of our hugely impressive finale, but as the kids began invading the stage, Igor decided the bombs would be better used trying to blow up the marauding hordes. I think he caught Jase Stallard, later of Onslaught fame, a good one in the nether regions, but I could be wrong.

As a result, the thunderous explosion that was to have brought Last Rockers to a devastating end turned out to be few feeble pops, but it didn't really matter.

Friend Braybrooke (presumably, now I stop to think about it, the bass player in Court Martial) takes up the story:

'Chants of 'Vice Squad, Vice Squad' and into the encore - another of their earlier hits, 'Resurrection'. And to round things off with a nice touch of nostalgia, they gave us a version of the old Pistol's number 'E.M.I.'

They finally left the stage amidst an ecstatic crowd invasion, well, more of a road crew invasion actually - either way it looked great! It was good to see Vice Squad playing so well. Dave Bateman has finally got his guitaring together and Bekki's vocals were almost spot on throughout the set.' Another nice man! With dodgy spelling and punctuation!

All very nice and flattering, of course, but the verdict we awaited most, with no little trepidation, was that of Merv Woolford. As I've said before, despite having some grudging respect for our having achieved some level of success with the band and label, he was always scathing in his appraisal of our musical abilities, or rather lack of them. So, once the dust had settled a little, Dave, Mark and I wandered over to Merv and Steve Street who were propping up the bar. 'Well, Merv. What did you think?' He paused for a few long seconds, as if in pain. Eventually, he said 'You know, boys, there were times out there tonight when you almost sounded like a real rock band.' We were over the moon.

Next day, Wednesday 27, we set off for Lancaster, for a gig at the polytechnic. As I've said, universities and polytechnics could sometimes be very generous with their riders, so after we had been on the road for some time I hungrily (or more likely thirstily) asked Sooty what we could expect on this occasion. He couldn't remember and told me to look at the contract in his case. I did, and became puzzled.

'Soot, where are we playing tonight?'

'Lancaster Poly.'

'It says Lanchester here.'

'Whaaat?'

Everyone else: 'Where the fuck is Lanchester?'

It is, of course, near Coventry, and is, I believe, where the Specials played some of their earliest gigs. We hastily changed course. Unfortunately that's the most memorable part of what Mark describes as a 'Horrible gig in a massive hall.' If I remember rightly, the problem was that the poly employed their rugby team, all in red t-shirts, as somewhat overzealous security, which rather soured the atmosphere.

After a fun-filled night at the Rochelle Guest House in Coventry, we emerged bright and early (but not too early) and set sail for Cambridge and a show at the good old Sea Cadets Hall. We'd played here back in May and enjoyed it, and according to Mark's diary the return engagement didn't disappoint: 'Really good gig & broke percentage.' However he continues: 'Tried to find party & wandered round Cambridge for hours. Slight mental breakdown.' Boy, he must have really wanted to go to that party.
Sooty's diary, as ever, sticks to the cold, hard facts. We stayed at the Lensfield Hotel, Lensfield Road, Cambridge, so there.

Another old favourite on Friday 29, the Gala Ballroom in Norwich, with audience right round all four sides of the stage and scrummy chicken-in-the-basket on the rider. Mark reckoned it a 'Pretty good gig but too hot & much too tired.'

No worries, you lazy sod, we've got four nights off before the last date of the tour. For some reason it took some time for our agent to book a London date. A Sounds news piece said sniffily 'Vice Squad finally confirm a London date for their current tour. It's at Hammersmith Klub Foot on November 4. Support will be provided in the form of Brutal Attack and Flowers Of The Past.'

By the time *Sounds* ran this piece an advert for the gig was placed alongside it, revealing that Urban Dogs had been added to the bill, taking the stage immediately before us. Why we agreed to this I'll never know. Now don't get me wrong, I love Charlie Harper and Knox very much, two of the very nicest men in punk, but both of them, in the same band, playing the greatest hits of the UK Subs and Vibrators? How the hell do you follow that? We sat in the dressing room and whimpered, pathetically, as they cranked classic after classic. Still, at least we can now say that we got to play at the Klub Foot, the hallowed home of psychobilly.

After four days off, which Mark mostly seems to have spent repairing his motorbike and, sadly, splitting up with Kerry (though you'd hardly notice as she keeps popping up in his diary) we headed off for our second 'European Tour,' a massively expanded jaunt compared to our first trip, now comprising of four dates in Holland rather than three. Why did we only ever play Holland? Did the rest of Europe really hate us that much? I really can't remember.

Anyway, on 9 November Mark's diary tells us that he 'Cleared up garage. Rang Kerry for 1 HR [told you - Shane]. Got picked up @ 4pm, drove to Harrow then Harwich & just caught ferry. Watched leaving England then sat in the bar.'
Next morning we 'Docked @ 8am, drove to Amsterdam & slept for 3 HRs then went on boat trip.' My god, that boy lived for pleasure alone.

I can only assume that at this point Beki was staying with Del in Harrow, hence the detour. The Amsterdam show was at the Paradiso, a picturesque old church and a very historic venue, that had, in the 60s, played host to the likes of the Rolling Stones and, interestingly, was where Glen Matlock played his last show with the Pistols (well, until 1996, obviously). It's still going today, and among many other famous names to grace its stage are Nirvana, Bowie, U2 and Pink Floyd. I think the high point of the show for us, however, was that an old friend of ours from home, Roy Savage, turned up.

11 November saw us back at Groningen, but this time at a venue called Simplon rather than the Club Vera that we'd played last time. Mark reckoned it a 'Crappy gig but quite good PA.' And for some reason he 'Went for a cycle & drink after the gig.' Who the hell goes cycling after playing a gig? Weird.

12 November we drove to Vlissingen, for a show at a venue called De Piek, blowing out a tyre on the way, a recurring feature of this trip, according to Mark's diary. He also reveals that we 'Had a horrible meal in a T.I.R. restaurant. Good gig & very good PA. Met a kid from Manchester & a bloke from London.' Yes, I remember the 'kid from Manchester' very well. I think his name was Steve, but I am certain her name was Poppy, a local girl, and we were most concerned as she pogoed enthusiastically throughout the gig, despite being heavily pregnant. Neither of them seemed at all bothered by this, and in fact were amused

at our concern. They were a nice couple, but seemed terribly young to be starting a family.

By now we were getting more than a little concerned about DR and her crew, who, with Dave's ex Penny also in tow, had set off at the same time as us to hitch their way over (though how they had planned to tackle the ferry I can't remember). Three days in, still no sign of them.

Happily, just as we finished the last song of the encore, in they trooped. Naturally, we squeezed in one more song, just for them.

13 November we were off to Leiden for a show at another quite famous venue, LVC, at Breestraat 66. The 600 capacity venue had opened in 1969, but as I write, in March 2013, it is sadly due to close down at the end of the month.

Mark describes it as a 'Good gig - really packed & good fun. Minor ruck afterwards. Funny little hotel nearby.'

Next day Mark says we 'Got up late & drove to Hoek Van Holland. Went in bar on beach then bar full of drunken English & dart boards.' Hmm, I don't recall any drunken dart boards. I'm sure I'd have remembered.

Monday 15 November we 'Got to Harwich @ 7am, stopped in transport café then dropped Beki. Got home @ 2pm then had a bath.' I should think so, Mark, you were beginning to niff a bit.

Over the next few weeks Mark seems to have spent most of his time fixing his bike or with Kerry (no change there, then), though we (Mark, Igor and self) did get the coach to London on 2 December to see the Subs at the Marquee and stay with Beki and Del for a few days. I also met a girl called Caroline, from North Acton, at the gig, and went out with her for some months afterwards.

Sooty spent some time recording local band Choice Treats For Children at his brother Dave's studio in Cotham and on 9 November went to a gig in the Midlands with Shiva, an excellent rock/metal band also managed by Ken, who were supporting the Michael Schenker Group.

22 November, Me, Dave, Igor and Bambi went into S.A.M. to begin work on the aforementioned Sex Aids single. The idea of recording a drinking song had begun with a loose-knit collective of young reprobates from the Swan and Maypole, whom we dubbed the No-hopers. At first the idea was that the lads from the pubs would actually play the thing, but in the end it seemed much simpler if, effectively, Dischord played it and the lads came in for backing vocals and the sleeve photo-shoot.

The idea for the main song came from some awful old hippy or folk record that Sooty had called Back On The Road Again, though the exact identity of its perpetrator is now lost in the mists of time (ah, there you are, wondered where you'd got to). In our hands, drastically rewritten, it naturally became Back On The Piss Again.

B-side track The Amazing Mr Michael Hogarth I've already explained, and for the other b-side we plumped for a cover of Motorhead's We Are The Road Crew. The reason for this, if I remember rightly, was that the only major difference between Dischord and the Sex Aids would be that Bambi wouldn't do lead vocals. We all had a go and were found wanting, with my own attempts being particularly woeful, and in the end Igor was judged to be the least worst. Igor was the roadie…road crew…geddit? Although, come to think of it, so was Bambi, occasionally, so that doesn't really work, does it? Alright, I don't know why we chose it. Does it matter? I don't know why you even brought it up. Let's just get on, shall we? Thank you.

I'm writing this almost exactly eight years after Merv's untimely death, from heart problems, on 27 March 2005, aged just 49. As we've already seen, Merv was a real character, and he was in full flight during the recording of this single. He was fairly disparaging about the whole project, which was, admittedly, highly self-indulgent, but when we came to Road Crew, he began to get angry, pointing out that we were playing it in the wrong key. We admitted that we hadn't noticed this, but it seemed to suit Igor's vocal range, so what did it matter? 'No,' he said, 'I'm not allowing you to record it in that key.'

'Um, Merv. No offence, like, but we are paying for this session. We are a paying, not to mention regular, customer. Surely it's, like, up to us what we record?'

'No, this song is in the wrong key. You cannot record it in that key. I will not allow it.'

And so on and so forth, until we finally gave in. We recorded the song in the correct key, Igor gave himself laryngitis putting down the vocal track, and Merv played an utterly fantastic lead guitar solo on it. What a chap. A legend, as he often said himself, in his own lunchtime.

The photo shoot for the sleeve (which for some reason didn't take place until 21 January 1982, according to Sooty's diary) was also great fun, with as many mates as possible crammed into the tiny King Charles pub, not far from SAM. Possibly due to the laryngitis, but most likely due to the constant barrage of insults that Igor received from Merv, who took a perverse delight in winding him up for some reason, Igor took this opportunity to get his own back. There was a slightly raised area in the front window of the pub, which meant we could photograph two tiers of people apparently having a joyous, drunken, pub singsong, and Igor chose his moment of entrance carefully. Once Merv and a group of his mates were in place in the back tier, he came in, stood at the front, then when the photographer was ready, took off his jacket to reveal a home-made 'Merv Is A Fat Cunt' t-shirt. Sheer genius.

It looked great on the cover, and Merv took it on the chin, speechless for once.
Incidentally, American band Defiance covered Back On The Piss Again for their literally-named European Tour 1995 EP on the Consensus Reality label, and did a jolly good job. It was certainly faster than ours, anyway.

14 December we went to St Matthias to see Wilko Johnson, and were amused to see that the stage we had constructed from building site pallets and school desks, covered in planks and held together with six-inch nails back in 1979 was still achieving the unusual feat of being so rickety and full of holes that it was difficult to stand on, but at the same time so firmly nailed together that the students found it impossible to dismantle. As Dave later said, 'We had great fun watching Wilko 'treading the planks' of our makeshift stage, and often losing his footing down a hole.'

Our final gig of 1982 was a Christmas show at the 100 Club on 21 December. A news piece in *Sounds* informed readers, rather grandly, that we would not be appearing at a Christmas On Earth gig with Discharge at the Lyceum on 26 December '…because their guitarist will be out of the country at the time.' I know Dave, flush with a publishing cheque, went back to America on holiday with a mate from football around this time, so this is probably what they were talking about.

It's interesting to note that a 100 Club advert, also in *Sounds*, promoted, as well as our 'Xmas Bondage Party' and Christmas shows by the 4-Skins and GBH, one by Skrewdriver. Amazing to think that they were still operating as just another punk band as late as December 1982, though as Mark says, rumours of their, or at least singer Ian Stewart's, dodgy leanings had been rife for some time.

A few years ago I went back to the 100 Club for the first time in decades, for the *Big Cheese* magazine 100th issue party, and was appalled at the state of the place. It was clean and tidy, light and airy, when once it had been dark and dingy, reeking of tobacco smoke, stale beer, sweat, glue, Boots hairspray and piss. Now, the paintwork shone and the walls were tastefully adorned with framed photos of the great and good that had graced its tiny stage since it opened in 1942. I was slightly surprised to see that there was no photo of me, but that was obviously just an oversight that would soon be corrected by the management. Actually, Liam Gallagher was probably the least famous person to be included!

Despite the fact that we hadn't played for a while, the show went well. Flowers Of The Past supported, and it was good to meet up with them again, there was a nice party atmosphere, and it was a pleasing way to round off what had been a really brilliant year.

It was also the last gig we ever played with Beki.

CHAPTER 14

WE APPROACHED THE NEW YEAR in a mood of optimism. We had worked hard throughout 1982 to make amends for that terrible first album and prove our worth. *Stand Strong* had been a good album, selling reasonably well and getting decent reviews. We'd toured a lot, done all the press, fanzine and radio interviews asked of us, and generally done everything we possibly could to move the band forward. If we were ever going to achieve real success, 1983 was surely the year it would happen.

We weren't trying to be pop stars, we just wanted to be a good, honest, respected, and, yes, solvent working band.

The plan was simple. With the Christmas and New Year festivities out of the way, we would settle down to write and record a new album, then tour the arse off it off it for the rest of the year, hopefully returning to the US and taking in more of Europe and who knew where else? The huge markets for punk that exist now in places like Germany, Spain and South America hadn't really happened by then, or at least not to the same extent, but more of the world was opening up to punk all the time.

For some reason the Sex Aids single wasn't completely finished until backing vocals were added on 6 January, and after a band meeting with Ken on 11 January we began writing and rehearsing the new Vice Squad material at SAM on 17 January.

At this time, Beki was living with Del in London, and didn't seem keen to leave him just yet, so in the meantime, we hit on a compromise. Dave would write the music, then arrange it with Mark and I, and tapes would be dispatched by post to Beki, who would send down her lyrics also by post. Unorthodox, perhaps, but no different to bands today who have members living in different cities, or even countries, simply sending their parts in files over the internet.

However, it now seems incredibly naïve of us not to have smelt a rat. As Mark says, 'She wouldn't come to the studio, there was always an excuse not to…'Oh, Beki'll be here Tuesday next week.'

As Sooty says, though, the alarm bells really began to ring when Beki's lyrics arrived. 'Beki gave me, and I've still got them, I photocopied them, a bunch of what you could call songs, but it was a bunch of scribblings. Mostly about animals having their fur ripped off, stuff like that. Every song was like another Humane. Which isn't a bad thing, but I thought, 'Hmm, yeah, not a lot of variety going on here.' But Crime And Passion was in there, that was a good song, eventually, once it was sorted out and produced. I've got that first sheet with the very beginnings on. I took them to Dave, and we just thought 'God, what are we going to do with that lot?' I got the feeling that Dave wasn't being given anywhere near as much as he used to be given by Beki. We were dead worried about it. I remember going out one night to Frampton Cotterell to chat to her and think about the next step, and it all seeming…not like it used to be, you know? She was gearing up, I think, to go.'

That meeting must have taken place some time around 2 February, as Mark's diary reveals that not only was Beki back by then, but that 'Beki decided to leave but wouldn't tell anyone and practiced anyway.'

Now, he says that 'Beki pulled me to one side in the King Charles and said...I may be making this up, but this is a faint recollection...and she said 'I've been offered [whatever] and I'm going to stay in London'...and she asked me if I wanted to go with her. Cos I'd always got on [with her] probably better than you and Dave did. Slightly. You know, we all took the piss out of each other immensely, but we got on. And I said 'I'll think about it,' with no intention of leaving Bristol, you know. I wouldn't have come back and said 'Look, Beki's about to leave,' that was for her to say.'

This is news to me. The first I heard of it, I remember, was when I was sitting at home watching TV one evening (the Courage brewery must have burnt down or something) when Mark rang and gave me the news. I was so shocked I burst into tears, I just couldn't believe it.

At first I felt betrayed and sad. We'd been through so much together and I'd always, rather romantically, thought of us as mates first and a band second, a sort of gang. Then, when I thought about how hard we'd worked to get the band going in the first place, and then how hard we'd worked to pull things round after the No Cause debacle, I got angry. It seemed so senseless.

We had several meetings with her, in Bristol and London, but she refused to budge. When reminding her of the above points made no difference, we tried pointing out that we were, at that stage, as likely as we were ever to be of having a proper hit record. Also, (and I just had a head-scratching half-hour poring over the contract, and I think this is correct) if we had delivered the next album we would have moved into the third stage of the contract and been paid £30,000. Not to be sniffed at today, for sure, but enough to buy a small South American country in 1983. Surely, if she was determined to go through with it, she would be better equipped to embark on a solo career with a hit record under her belt and a cut of 30 grand in the bank? After all, it only took Vice Squad a month to write, rehearse and record an album. Guns & Roses we weren't. And as several songs had already, by this time, been written, we could probably have finished in as little as three weeks. For 30 grand.

When she still said no, it just got nasty, and there was no point in further discussion. It was over.

So, where did we go from here? Well, we were determined to complete the new album, at least, and as the new songs were proving a little more complex than our older material, we asked Sooty to join on lead guitar. His diary says that he 'Joined lads as semi-member, 19th of February.' He was perhaps being cautious by calling himself a 'semi-member' at this stage, as Ken had jumped ship as soon as Beki had left (taking Igor with her, incidentally), leaving Sooty as sole manager, so now he had to juggle two roles. Effectively, though, he was a full member of the band from this point on.

We knew that Beki had already been offered a solo deal by EMI, but our standing with the company was only made clear when Sooty, in his managerial capacity, was summoned to Manchester Square. The fact that Ashley had recently left EMI was more than a little worrying, and when Sooty returned to Bristol with the bad news, we weren't unduly surprised. 'I had to go and see Hugh Stanley Clarke, he was the A&R guy who took over from Ashley Goodall, and it hurt terribly,' he says. 'I was booked to go in the office at EMI, and I went in to see him, and he said 'Right, Sooty, there's no point me pitching a comment about the music and stuff because I'm in no way interested in carrying on signing Vice Squad. As far as I'm concerned you're absolutely free to go, there will be no more recordings with EMI.'

And with that cleared up, we decided to worry about finding a new label later, and for now concentrate on finding a new singer. This was an unusual process for us, to say the least. Beki was the only member of the band who hadn't already been known to us before joining, but, as I've said, at that time it was purely a question of whether she'd agree to join a bunch of nobodies like us. While hardly rock giants, it's true to say that we did, by this time, have some small status, so this would be an entirely different situation.

As we were now seeking a singer, and Beki now was seeking a band, it was painfully ironic that our respective adverts, in the same issue of *Melody Maker* were so nearly identical that I cut both out and kept them in my scrap book:

NAME FEMALE
Vocalist with major contract
seeks young experienced
London based guitarists
bassist and drummer for
Dolls/Heartbreakers type punk
band. Image essential write
stating details.
Box No 226 B120

FEMALE SINGER
Urgently required by major
recording band for immediate
recording, future international
touring commitments. Extrovert
performer with strong voice to
compliment N.Y. Dolls, Joan Jett,
Sex Pistols, Slade, type image,
photo preferred.
Box No 227 B168

Looking through the documentary evidence with the others, we are now quite surprised how quickly the audition process was put in motion, credit for which must go to Mr Sooty. He began contacting applicants on 20 March, and auditions began soon after. Soot's diary mentions one interesting (and cheeky) early applicant called Dale: 'Turned out to be a bloke, but good voice.' You'd think the name would have been a bit of a giveaway, wouldn't you, but that's Soot for you. As he leafs through his diary, he gets all nostalgic for what was, in a way, nice work if you can get it: 'All these different people, look, Karen, Tracey, Wendy, Kathy…Tracey Coleman - evening…Susan, Jade, she was a fantastic singer, that girl Jade, Kaz. Yes, 'Phone Tracey Coleman for possible audition.'

But still, as Mark says, 'It was a really odd situation for the three of us to be in, you know, girls coming from all over the place to try to impress us, you know, it was funny.'

I remember one in particular that looked absolutely stunning in her photo, so much so that Steve stuck it over the SAM mixing desk, but when she turned up, though nice looking and a very nice girl, she didn't really live up to the photo, much to our disappointment.

Yes, as Mark remembers, predictably, our attitude to the situation wasn't always as professional as it could have been: 'We weren't necessarily the best judges I don't think. I think Sooty was a little bit more objective than us. There were several, I seem to remember, who couldn't necessarily sing, but 'Fancy coming for a drink?' Ha ha!'

As it turned out, though we had applicants from all over the place, in the end we went for someone who'd been practically in front of us all the time. Enter, the mighty Julia 'Lia' Rumbelow.

I asked her about her family background: 'Fairly bohemian I suppose, is the best way to describe it,' she says. 'My dad was a freelancer for television and worked as a TV dresser, worked in theatre, my mum also used to do odd jobs for the BBC and not get paid much for doing it in the 60s and 70s. Dad was quite arty, mum used to do up houses, and interiors…always very broke, but they kind of got by. I went to I suppose what you'd call a very good school, La Retraite High School, a Catholic girl's school run by nuns! My sister went there as well, and my brother went to Cathedral School. We all got in on bursaries cos my parents were a bit broke, TV didn't pay well then at all, and dad was always off filming, trying to make some money. We lived in Clifton in lots of different flats, then bought a small house in the 70s, and kept moving until we got bigger and bigger houses, and that's really how my parents made their income, by buying and selling their houses.'

So, a posh school, eh? Was she a girly swot or a St Trinians-style rebel? 'I did alright at school, but I got involved with the music scene very early on, cos I knew the Cortinas, they were neighbours. My best friend was Daniel Swan, who was the drummer, Jer Valentine and I were mates, Nick Sheppard and I were really good friends from the age of three. These boys who were in the Cortinas, and other bands that were around too, were just around me. The brilliant thing was that in Daniel's house there was a basement, it was a big crumbling house in Cornwallis Crescent in Clifton, and his parents let them all play in the basement, so everybody rehearsed there.'

But the big City soon beckoned: 'I left home and got a proper job, which didn't last. I went travelling, came back at nineteen. Then I had a phase in London. I was very good friends with a guy called Rob Marche, who played for the Subway Sect. My mates Sean, Chris Bostock, Rob, and Dave Pollard, they all moved up to play in Subway Sect and we all kind of followed them, en masse, a friendship group, so I did spend a very, very enjoyable three years in London, virtually living in the Wag. So I was very lucky early on to meet people like the Clash, because we shared a recording studio space, Star Studios in Camden Lock, run by Bernie Rhodes. Because of Subway Sect I was privileged enough to meet these people that you wouldn't normally meet. I knew Bernie Rhodes really well, for my sins! He was actually affable enough, you know, a bit sort of dodgy. And also, this is the best bit, I lived next door to the Camden Palace, in a little terrace flat. So when I first went to London it was fab! It went a bit wrong at the end, but never mind.'

And so Julia returned to Bristol. I believe the first time we became aware of her was when, to our surprise, Steve and Merv announced that they were recording their own single, under the unlikely name Affairs Of The Heart. And guess who the singer was? So tell us about it, girl: 'Waterloo Sunset, on Heartbeat Records, that was 1983. And so I did this single, and we had to get permission; for some reason Ray Davies had full control. Although it was published, there was a caveat that he had to approve of any cover artists. So we went up to London on a very grey March day, me, Steve Street and my friend Steve Miles who was living up there, so we met Ray Davies in this dingy café somewhere in Victoria. This guy in a cardie, literally, this old man's cardie, patched sleeves, and he shuffled along. We had an English breakfast and he joined us a bit later. He wanted to meet me for some reason, he'd heard the record, we were about to do the first pressing, the test pressing, at Virgin Townhouse. He said 'Oh yes, I've heard the record,' and we were thinking 'He doesn't like it, it's a disco version,' and he said 'It's great.' Phew!'

So how, I wondered, did all this come to be? 'Simon [Edwards] asked Steve and Merv, cos he liked my voice. I was just pootling around SAM studios, guesting for people like the Rimshots, Fear of Darkness and various other people. If they couldn't hit the right notes I would go in and sing for them. I was getting paid a small wage by Steve, helping keep the studio clean, answering the phone, and doing session stuff. At one point I was earning good money, because I was doing these radio commercials for which you got the huge sum, then, of sixty five quid an hour. That was a lot. Well it's a lot now! They would take about fifteen minutes, cos you'd hear it, go through it, Steve's engineering and I could do it first or second take, not a problem, cos it was quite straightforward. And Simon had heard, I think, the Fear of Darkness stuff, and he said 'I really think Julia ought to do some singing of her own,' and Steve said 'Sure, but we can't fund it,' cos he was just making ends meet. And Merv said 'Why don't we do a cover that we all like,' and it was Simon's idea, he'd always loved that song, so he went 'Could you do a cover of this?' and I went 'You're joking, the Kinks, oh my God, Ray Davies will hate it!' And Steve said 'Isn't there something a bit more, you know, girly?' But it sounded, actually, quite good. It was alright.'

My own view of their version is that the original demo, which ended up on the b-side, was great, but that Steve flogged it to death coming up with the over-produced a-side. Julia agrees: 'He became obsessed. He messed it around too much when he didn't need to, but that was his kind of Chic-obsessed disco thing. I said to him 'Look, please don't put all these overdubs on,' and Merv had a word with him as well, but he was insistent.'

It did okay, though. 'It got quite a lot of airplay,' she says. 'Janice Long liked it, Kid Jensen,

Gary Davies. There was this plugger, I can't remember who it was now, and he got it onto the Gary Davies show on Radio 1, and it was quite newsworthy for a while. It was big news, then littler news, and then it sort of dropped down. But by that time I'd joined Vice Squad!'

I was quite astonished to learn that, despite plenty of experience singing in studios, Julia had never performed live before. 'I had been asked to join a band called Fishfood, I did rehearse with them, you probably remember them from *The Bristol Recorder*, and there was also talk of me doing some singing for Circus Circus, but it didn't actually happen. So no, my first time actually singing onstage was with Vice Squad.'

You lucky, lucky girl. 'I was one of the last people to audition,' she says. 'Cos I saw you guys at a gig at St Matthias, and I said 'Oh I'd really like to do that,' just off the cuff. Cos I'd met you down at SAM before. And I remember Mark saying 'Yeah, just speak to Sooty about it. Let him know, cos we're doing auditions now.' You didn't seem upset about the fact that she [Beki] was going.'

She continues (you try stopping her!): 'According to Sooty, when he phoned me up, cos I was working at Window Graphics, as a graphics assistant doing windows and stuff, and he phoned me up there, he got my number from Steve Street, and he said you'd had 400 responses from around Europe and Britain. He said there was somebody you liked who'd come over from France, who was quite promising.' Sadly, the 'promising' mademoiselle has disappeared into the mists of time.

But had Julia ever actually seen us? 'Never, no, I'd never seen the band play. But I'd gotten to know you over time and it was about…probably a year before Beki left, just because you used to come down and leave your gear at SAM, or just rehearse there, and because I knew Steve [Street] I used to be calling in all the time. But I'd heard, on John Peel I think, Last Rockers, and thought what a brilliant song it was, really liked it, an absolutely brilliant record. And then, after one particular rehearsal you had at SAM, got introduced to Mark, and then there was the St Matthias gig soon after.'

She recalls that the audition took place at 'Sooty's brother's house, with that studio in the basement. I was just larking about, Sooty made me laugh, then I listened to The Pledge and liked it, and that was the audition song. I sang a few actually, there was another one that had nothing to do with Vice Squad that he got me to sing, but I can't remember what it was. So I was singing that, the best I could, and I just remember thinking 'I'm not their kind of singer, I know I'm not,' ha ha! But I thought 'I'd really like it, it would be great, and I know they're doing good things.' By that point, what was interesting was, was that the earlier reputation had gone, and suddenly the band were serious contenders among local music. Because Vice Squad had had that real 'Trouble' tag earlier, wherever you played there was trouble, not necessarily generated by you, but there was always a fight…or five!' Even now, she seems uncertain why we chose her: 'I think Sooty played the audition tape to Dave and you, wasn't it? I didn't seem the type of singer that would be right, but because I can sing, I suppose it was adequate, I don't know.' As I said to her, in response to this, 'Honestly, when we all sat down and listened to it, we all just thought 'Why didn't we just ask her in the first place? It's bloody obvious.' And so it was.

However, the audition proved to be the easy bit for our new chanteuse: 'What was actually quite hard for me, was as soon as I got accepted, I remember being delighted, and then thinking 'Now the hard work starts.' I was presented with 43 songs, straight off. Sooty got me round once again to his brother's house and he just had song list after song list, all these lyrics, and he went 'You've got to learn those!' And I said 'Oh, right, how long have I got?' and he went 'A couple of weeks?' And that was actually quite a tall order.'

CHAPTER 15

SO, WITH THE NEW LINE-UP IN PLACE, it was time to move on, but we now entered a somewhat hazily remembered phase of what we laughingly refer to as our 'career.' I've always thought that the reason we played no shows in 1983 was because of on-going legal problems with Beki, but the reasons for this possibly imagined scenario are, now that I come to think of it, unclear.

Does Sooty blame legal problems for our stage-dodging stance? 'Yes, but that didn't affect us creatively. I just don't think we managed it very well on reflection, it took too long. It was ridiculous, January 1984 to do the next gig? Forget the new material, we could have just done the old set with a new singer! But you can't go back, Shane…'

True, but it's also quite possible that by now delivering the third Vice Squad album had become something of an obsession, because we spent the rest of the year writing, rehearsing, and recording. Not that we'd turned into Genesis, but simply because lack of funds meant that a lot of the work had to be done using scraps of cheap studio down-time. However, even after being dropped by EMI, according to Mark finance wasn't an immediate problem: 'Who was paying for the rehearsals? EMI paid a bit, didn't they, and was it Polydor? Polygram? We were getting lumps of money from record companies who were sort of courting us, to keep us practising. We were getting lumps of money down which was keeping us going.' Really? This seemed highly unlikely to me. Why would EMI keep giving us money after dropping us? And why would other labels give us money for work on an album that they held no legal rights to? However, at the time of writing I've just read *Post Everything* by Luke Haines, the bloke from the Auteurs and Black Box Recorder, and he confirms that it was common practice, in the days when the labels were still coining it, to do just that, even with bands they'd just 'let go.' In fact it seems that by scooping up no-ties hand-outs from various labels, including the one they'd just left, he was able to finance the recording of a whole Black Box Recorder album, which was then owned by the band themselves. The music industry didn't need the internet to kill it off, it was doing just fine by itself.

Sadly, we weren't as clever as Luke, but this strange industry practice did at least give us some breathing space.

Gratifyingly, as Mark says, various labels were showing an interest, and I got very excited when Sooty told me that Bronze Records, home to Motorhead and Girlschool, were interested. I can't tell you how much I would have loved that. Sooty had dinner with the label's A&R man to talk it over, apparently, but they then went off the idea. God knows what he did. Ate the wrong end of his asparagus?

Eventually, in the absence of anything concrete in the way of a proper deal, we decided to take up Cherry Red on their offer of a one-off single. Why not? At least it would get us 'out there,' and we were confident that the song we had in mind, Black Sheep, was a belter, even if it was 'Off the peg.' 'It was a song I'd done before, in a different key, in Vitus Dance,' says Sooty. 'It was one of the ones I'd solely written in Vitus Dance, and Dave was song-hungry, so I said to Dave 'I've got this song,' and played it to him, and he said 'Yeah, we'll have *that*.'

Yet another 'fact' that I've misremembered over the years is that I thought all the records released from this point were first recorded as demos at SAM with overdubs and mixing done at Crescent, but it seems that in the case of the tracks on the Black Sheep single, at least, I was wrong, as Julia remembers and a look at the sleeve credits confirms. 'No, we did [b-side track] New Blood at Crescent,' says Julia. 'You had a major drum session at Crescent. You got really annoyed cos you kept breaking sticks, and in the end you refused to play any more. You went round to the Bell on Walcott Street, you stormed off, and we had to come and find you Shane. You were so grumpy! I was really grumpy that day, it was one of those days that didn't really work very well at all. And I'm surprised I did the vocal track, because I was dreading the day, cos it was the day that David Lord [Crescent Studio owner and engineer, working at the time with Peter Gabriel] was going to be there, and I just kept thinking that if Peter Gabriel comes it would just be so embarrassing and horrible, I was really worried about it. And Mark and I had rowed...I was in a really bad mood, Sooty was in a bad mood, Dave was normal but hung over, jovial but hung over, and you weren't too happy about being there at all. Cos you kept saying 'I could have done this at SAM or Cave.'

I've somehow managed to forget all this. So what was my problem? Julia continues: 'David Lord is quite a hard taskmaster, and he wanted you to do overdub after overdub, and your sticks kept breaking, and you got so pissed off that you threw them down and said 'I'm fucking going to the pub!' Sooty said 'That's alright, don't worry, Shane will be fine,' and we had to come and find you. But it worked, because there's a much fuller sound, actually. I was listening to it the other night, and I actually really like New Blood, and I like it more, in a way, now, than I have before, the more I listen to it. It's very well produced, very well produced. It's now sonically aged by the Simmons and stuff, so you know it's an 80s track, but you know, that doesn't detract, it's fine. The timing of the drums is really good. It's kind of back-line heavy, I like it, I really like that sound. And it's a good song!'

The single was recorded over three days, 26 - 28 September, just before, incidentally, Simon Edwards married my sister Trayci on 1 October. It was a big church wedding in Hanham, and Dave and I were nominated as ushers, but us being us, by the time we'd got out of the pub and rounded up our girlfriends, we ended up being the last people in the church.

The reception was in a big sort of manor house in Willsbridge, and the whole event was very formal, a top hat & tails job, though thankfully at Trayci's request Dave and I were allowed to turn out in our customary black jeans and leathers. Eventually, Dad got bored, and when the speeches had gone on long enough led an 'Escape Party' to the Queen's Head down the road. Chap! In the evening, Ken's band played, then Cold, who at that time actually had their own drummer, Mark Ernest. Next day, someone congratulated me on my performance when I got up and played drums on Riders On The Storm with them. I said 'But I don't know how to play Riders On The Storm!' God, I must have been really pissed.

At this time Simon was hosting a programme on Radio West on Thursday nights called, naturally, *Punk And Disorderly*. A DJ called Chris Bull played the records and did the engineering, while Simon brought along the records, talked about them and read out requests. While Simon and Trayci were honeymooning in New York for two weeks, I was roped in to take his place, and apart from being very nervous it was great fun. I played everything from The Terrible Twins' Generation Of Scars from *Oi! - The Album* to Hanoi Rocks' Malibu Beach and ended the first show with Frank Sinatra's I'm Gonna Live Till I Die and the second with Madness' Return Of The Los Palmas 7, just to show how wacky and eclectic I was. As it was a commercial station, it was a quite bizarre to play some obscure punk track then have an advert for Pampers Nappies, the TSB bank, or *Do It Yourself* magazine come obtrusively crashing in. Quite amusing though.

I also, at Chris' request, played the SAM demo versions of The Rest Of Your Life and You'll Never Know and talked about the new line-up, and played a track from the first demo by Onslaught that Dave and I had just produced at SAM, the snappily-titled Thermonuclear Devastation Of The Planet Earth. Chris, despite my warnings, underestimated how ear-splittingly loud it was and had to hastily crank the faders down when it came thundering out of the speakers.

Local radio stations gauged audience figures by numbers of responses to competitions or people phoning in, and it was gratifying that my girlfriend at the time, Mel, and her friend Maria, who were manning the phones, were quite inundated, though I did tend to mess up the requests quite a bit, like dedicating one meant for the Cwmbran skins to the Cumbrian skins. How far did I think Radio West's transmission area extended? Ah well, it was all good fun. And no, since you ask, I never did run into Eddie Shoestring. He was in the morning slot.

The Black Sheep single, with b-side New Blood, was released by Cherry Red's punk subsidiary label Anagram on 9 December as a 7" (ANA 16) and 12" with an extended mix of New Blood and an extra track The Pledge (12 ANA 16). It was engineered by Glenn Tommey and Steve Street, and produced by Sooty.

I designed the sleeve, with Ken Lush's photos - one night we had waited until Ken's flatmates had gone to bed so we could use their kitchen for the cover shot. The idea was that we all lived in the same house, like the Monkees, and the kitchen would be decked out with debris that reflected us and our position. Or something like that. Anyway, we scattered the table with photos, music papers, tape reels, fags, beer, lyrics, and, slyly, a piece of Anagram note paper with '£810 Max!!,' the paltry rehearsing, recording and artwork budget we'd been allocated, written on it. It was a black and white photo, that I added colour tints to on an overlay, an idea I nicked from the back of Paul Simonon's sleeve for the US release of Should I Stay Or Should I Go.

Julia says that 'They [the critics] had knives out and were waiting for a crap debut and they didn't get it, they got a good first single. So that was good, job done.'

In fact, the reviews veered from gushingly positive to sneeringly vindictive. As the release of Black Sheep coincided with the debut single by Beki's new band Ligotage, Crime And Passion, in *Sounds* Garry Bushell reviewed both together under the heading 'Not Bad.' As that suggests, he took the middle view of both. He was moderately positive about Crime And Passion, which was, we all agreed, a good single, but concluded that '...it's a shame the lead guitarist stayed in the pub when they were recording.' He continued: 'Perhaps they should have nicked Vice Squad's, who reels off some hot licks (man) over a powerful little punky pounder. New crooner Lia's got plenty of promise and the band have got more punch than a nob's ball.' Ah, if only he could have left it there. Sadly, he went on: 'If they find some tunes they'll be well away.' Ouch.

Surprisingly, perhaps, Ian Birch at *Smash Hits* liked it. This appeared in their 5 - 18 January 1984 issue:

> 'This might come as a surprise so make sure there's a chair handy. The new Vice Squad (without Beki Bondage) sound uncannily like Blondie in their early days. Fast, noisy, dog-eared and good fun.'

Tony Mitchell, who for some unknown reason reviewed it again in the 10 December issue of *Sounds*, had slight doubts:

> 'The new look Vice Squad, post Beki, have got it half right with the acquisition of the youthful and pleasantly voiced Lia. Now all she's got to do is get rid of the rest of them, bring in some people who can match her vocal talents with their writing and playing, and they'll be laughing. As it stands, however, it's totally devoid of guts.'

Have I used 'Ouch' yet? Oh yes, so I have.

Undoubtedly, the best notice came from Ben Fleet in *Punk Lives* magazine:

> 'Yes, Vice Squad, complete with new guitarist Sooty and vocalist Lia. The big question is obviously how do the line-ups compare? Simple, there's no contest, this is easily the best Vice Squad. Not only is Lia more pleasant to look at than Beki, but is a far better singer, and in some places reminds me of Debbie Harry. And to complement that, the group have progressed sensibly. EMI should have dropped Beki and signed this lot up. Don't be surprised if these, like the Toy Dolls, have a hit.'

How kind. But don't let him advise you on any Stock Exchange investments.

Actually, the record did very well, thanks in no small part to the fact that David 'Kid' Jensen picked up on Black Sheep and gave it heavy airplay on his early evening Radio 1 show. And while the kudos were always with getting on the John Peel show, the fact remained that he had the 10.00 to 12.00 slot, whereas David Jensen was on from 7.00 to 10.00 (the slot once occupied, as mentioned earlier, by Richard Skinner), when 'normal' people, as well as more serious music fans, were still listening while driving home from work. Potentially, it offered a more mainstream audience.

Of course, whether many of the 'normal' people were actually interested in hearing us is open to question, and in fact some of Jensen's colleagues were even bemused. I remember hearing his fellow Radio 1 DJ Steve Wright, who for some reason was in the studio while Jensen was doing his show, spluttering, after hearing Black Sheep, 'Who the hell are Vice Squad anyway? Why don't you play some decent music like George Benson?' A fair question, I suppose.

Nevertheless, thanks to David Jensen and the largely positive press, Black Sheep went into the indie chart on Christmas Eve and rose to No.13, staying on the chart for 9 weeks. It sold around 15,000, which Cherry Red were more than pleased with. The Ligotage single sold the same number, suggesting that our loyal fans bought both, but as, unlike Cherry Red with us, EMI had spent a considerable amount of money on a video and extensive advertising, they were less than pleased and the band was dropped soon after, which even we thought was a little harsh after just one single.

Right, that was the easy bit. Now it was time to get out there and finally play a gig.

We'd been rehearsing a live set for some time at SAM, Frome Musical, Impulse and the Arches at Temple Meads, and Sooty's diary tells us that he had discussions with various venues about possible dates, including the Marquee and 100 Club, but for our first outing we decided on the good old Granary. We had finished the aforementioned Chaotic Dischord mini-album *Don't Throw It All Away* on 1 and 2 December 1983 at Cave, and on 8 December Dave, Sooty and I had a meeting with Les to discuss dates. We plumped for 4 January, a sort of New Year, new band show, which was a nice idea, but the short notice was a bit scary.

The first thing that I had to sort out was that, as Julia mentioned earlier, we had bought one of those new-fangled Simmons electronic drum kits - you know, the ones with drums shaped like 50p pieces, that went PING!!! all over many records of the time. I'd had my doubts, but Sooty had assured me that they didn't have to go PING!!!, that was just the sound they came automatically programmed with. The kit included a big console on which you could change the sound of each drum, and punch in different combinations of sounds for different songs. It was just a case of working out all the settings for each song and remembering which buttons I had to press before each one. We spent many hours programming the thing, and I spent many more trying to remember all the different combinations, but I got there in the end, and had to admit that, yes, it did sound pretty good. In retrospect, of course, although the drums didn't go actually PING!!!, they still didn't really sound like drums, and do date the tracks we recorded with them quite a lot. However, as I still used an ordinary snare and bass drum, it wasn't quite the culture shock it could have been, and the toms were very easy to play. They were solid so it was like bouncing the end of a pencil on a table top - you could do really fast rolls with hardly any effort.

What with it being our first show for a year and Julia's first show ever, nerves were naturally a little fraught, but we needn't have worried. A decent sized, enthusiastic crowd turned out, and once we had a couple of songs under our belts, we relaxed and actually began to enjoy ourselves. The gig was given a half page review in the 14 January issue of *Sounds* by Dave Massey, under the predictable headline 'Porn again!,' and apart from a reference to '...the decision of the management to exclude a lot of Squad fans (on whatever spurious grounds they used),' of which I have no recollection, he too was enthusiastic. He went on:

> 'But the band were undaunted, blasting into their set with a buzz-saw blend of the twin guitars of Dave and Sooty, giving the ears a healthy dose of punk that was fresh, alive and contemporary.
>
> Vice Squad have always done more than virtually any other punk band to take a wider view of the boundaries within which they operate: that's been apparent right from 'Last Rockers'. With the new line-up the horizons have broadened still further and the band are now able to travel a route that crosses the borders of punk and hard rock. If they play their cards right, the American market is wide open for them because the ingredients - instrumental toughness, rough commerciality, youth rebellion and an attractive singer - are just right.
>
> The new singer, Lia, is a more than adequate replacement for Ms Bondage. She's a tough cookie who will stand on her own merits, although the one minor foible is that her voice recalls the throaty urging of Pauline Murray. But the effect is good, cutting straight through to the listener, crisp and clear.'

As foibles go, let alone minor ones, I think we were all, Julia included, happy to go along with that one. He concluded:

> 'Above all, it was a gig which brought all round enjoyment. The group were obviously glad to be back playing 'live' - even the normally po-faced Mark's face lit up on a couple of occasions, and Sooty enlivened him further by his antics at the back of the stage. Here's hoping that high spirits lead to big rewards, because for Vice Squad it's now or never.'

And with a couple of good photos of Julia by our old friend Simon Archer, it was far more than we ever expected to come back to. If a year is a long time in politics it's a fucking lifetime in rock and roll. Hey, that's quite a good line, I must make a note of it and put it on a t-shirt or something.

The same day that the review was published we did a photo session with Simon Archer, and the following day, 15 January, another one, and an interview with Dave Massey. Of the interview Mark only remembers that 'I don't remember a great deal, cos I'd been at the

Dug Out until about half past two the night before. I remember Julia having to put make-up on me because I had no eyes whatsoever. So with the ridiculous hair I do look a bit of a tart [in the photos]. Massey was being a pain in the arse, I remember, us having to chase him, because it was a Sunday.'

I probably should have mentioned by now that virtually as soon as she joined the band, Julia and Mark became a couple. She'd taken over Simon Edward's flat, 4 Melrose Place in Clifton, back when he married my sister, and Mark soon moved in with her. Julia, that is, not my sister. Not as far as I know, anyway.

I suppose it seemed a bit odd, making for a different dynamic to when Beki was in the band, but then everything was different now, so it was no big deal, really.

Anyway, back to the plot. Yes, as Mark says, when we went to Dave Massey's house at the appointed time on Sunday morning, we had considerable trouble rousing him from his slumbers as he, too, had been hitting the sauce the night before. I can't remember the condition of the rest of us, but with interviewer and at least one interviewee suffering from monumental hangovers, this wasn't shaping up to be a great flow of soul and feast of reason.

In fact, once strong black coffee and a cattle prod had been utilised, it went quite well, though the interview appeared under another cringingly punning headline: 'Vice of the People.'

After first explaining our recent history and current situation, Massey then quoted Sooty as saying that 'We did 'New Blood' as the 'A' side and spent a lot of time on it, but at the last minute the record company changed the songs round. They didn't consult us, they just quoted the contract to us, said that as they had the master tapes they'd go ahead, regardless of what we thought.'

This seems odd to me. As it was only a one-off single deal, why would we have signed a contract giving them the right to do that? And also, we put together our own finished artwork, with Black Sheep clearly listed as the a-side. I guess whatever that was all about is now lost in the mists of time…

He then told a slightly garbled version of the Kid Jensen/Steve Wright/George Benson story, before moving on to something else that I probably should have covered earlier. Along with a photo of the band, the feature was accompanied by a photo of Julia, captioned 'LIA: sweet but not sixteen,' as in the piece he said that 'One other marketing ploy that annoyed the group was the Anagram press releases sent out which depicted Lia as a 16-year old (she is in fact 22). It's part of the pop process which doesn't treat people as 'real', mucks them about and doesn't consider the consequences.'

Actually, we were being a little disingenuous here, as the idea of portraying Julia as a 16-year old was all Sooty's idea, and one which displeased Julia, but we all went along with it, so minus several credibility points all round.

Later, Dave Bateman refuted Dave Massey's possible inference that we may have been deliberately aiming at the US market with our new material: 'A lot of people have been picking up on what you said in your review and perhaps the potential is there, but we didn't deliberately set out to set out to write songs in that vein. It was more a question of reforming, being in debt and having to come up with material so we could start paying the bills!

So in the end we wrote songs for ourselves, not the American market. If it comes to it we probably won't ever make it to the States again - we probably won't even make it as far as Swindon!'

Dave Massey, however, was more optimistic: 'Perhaps the group don't totally appreciate the undoubted attributes they have between themselves. This time I think they've got luck and the right timing of their campaign working very much in their favour. The message is clear and simple, and best expressed by Shane - 'come and see us, listen to our records, and make your own minds up.'

Likewise the sentiments and ambition which will get Vice Squad where they want to go is direct and to the point.

Sooty: 'All of us, as human beings, want it to be "now or never", because we're not interested in sitting around and saying we could make it in four years time.'

Mark: 'Basically we've been through all the shit, spent a long time working ourselves to death while we had full time jobs, so now we want some reward for that effort.'

The tune might change, but not the song. May perseverance triumph.'

On 21 January we met up with Spike Sommer at the George and Railway for an interview for *Punk Lives*, though I don't recall it ever making it into the magazine, probably due to it folding shortly afterwards, and on 6 February Dave and Julia appeared on the *6 O'Clock Rock* show on Radio Bristol, interviewed by our old friend Al Reed. More rehearsing and recording followed, then we tentatively headed out on the road once again.

We'd been keenly looking forward to our first London gig with Julia, at the famous Dingwalls, in Camden, on 28 February, but, as you'll be completely un-staggered to hear, it didn't quite go to plan. The big problem was that there was a total bus and tube strike on the day of the gig, but surprisingly, Dingwalls didn't want to cancel, so under the terms of the contract we had to go ahead with it. One of the first people I met when we got there was an ex-girlfriend of mine, Caroline, and when she told me how much trouble she'd had getting a taxi to the gig from North Acton, not to mention the extortionate fare, the alarm bells started clanging loudly.

To make matters worse, Julia also remembers that: 'There was that weirdy London support band [Cry Of The Innocent] who thought they were brilliant. They were really up themselves.' However, the crowd, though fairly sparse, was quite enthusiastic, and the evening did have one massive compensation, as Julia again recalls: 'I loved it,' she says, 'that's when Lemmy turned up! People don't believe me. I'll name-drop only if people are going on and on and then they say 'Have you met anyone famous?' And you think 'Oh no, no,' because it really does piss me off. But it did crop up when one of my girls said 'You know Motorhead? Mum's only met the singer,' and everyone's going 'No way!' And I had to say 'I'm delighted to say that he came to see us play, actually, *and* bought us a drink!''

As you can imagine, I was flabbergasted. My flabber, as Frankie Howerd used to say, had never been so gasted. Lemmy lived right next to Dingwalls at that time, so probably turned up there any night he wasn't working, and probably, more often than not, had a drink with the band. But when he introduced himself and we began chatting, it was obvious from what he said that he really did know who we were and what our history was, which was hugely flattering.

I was terribly impressed when he casually pulled out several bank notes, handed them to Dave, and said 'Get everyone a drink son, mine's a treble Jack Daniels and Coke.' Class! We all sat around for a long time after the gig, drinking and chatting with Lemmy - the staff were probably anxious to close up and bugger off home to bed, but didn't like to chuck us out as long as he was there, but we did eventually relent and say goodnight.

Not long after, H and I went to see the Vibrators at the Marquee, and I saw Lemmy at the other end of the bar. As I say, I assumed that he drank with all the bands that played at Dingwalls, so that didn't mean he was suddenly my best mate, so I decided not to say anything. I figured he probably wouldn't have remembered me anyway. But as soon as he caught my eye he waved and walked over. We had a bit of a chat, then I had to visit the little boy's room. When I got back he gestured to H, who by now was well pissed, and said 'You're alright son, but if your mate doesn't shut up I'm gonna belt him.' I never did find out what H had said to the man, but it can't have been as bad as all that, as for a while afterwards I bumped into Lemmy now and again at London gigs, and he always stopped to say hello. Which was nice.

After the show I am reminded by Mark's diary that we stayed at Sooty's brother's house in Watford, though future historians will be frustrated to learn that he doesn't specify which of Sooty's brothers owned the house. Not Dave, who as we know lived in Cotham, so possibly the remarkably named Daisy, but as Sooty's from such a large family it's hard to tell. I suppose we'll just have to try to learn to live with it.

Next day, 29 February, once it became clear that no girls had been waiting for just this opportunity to propose marriage to any of us, even Julia, we headed up to Leeds for a gig at the trusty Bierkeller, supported by Uproar, the Fiend, and possibly Pagan Idols, though there's a question mark by their name in Sooty's diary.

The show, promoted by our old friend Nick Toczek, may well have been a barnstorming rock 'n' roll event, with rabid punters tearing the place up, after all, we always went well in Leeds, but the fact is that the most exciting thing recorded about it, in Sooty's diary, is the fact that someone stole his plectrum tin. In the diary he makes vaguely accusing noises about the support bands, but the evidence is flimsy to say the least, so let's not reopen the police files on the case just yet. And as if that wasn't enough excitement for one night, Mark's diary reveals that we broke down near Sheffield on the way back and didn't get home until 9.30am.

Undaunted by Steve Wright's scathing words about us, Kid Jensen invited us to record a session for his show, which we were more than pleased to do, and on 4 March we made our way to Studio 5, Maida Vale, to begin recording at 2.00pm. Like our earlier Richard Skinner session, the producer was Dale 'Buffin' Griffin, of Mott The Hoople fame, and as Mark remembers, he was much more enthusiastic about working with us than last time: 'Yeah, Simmons kit, more complex songs, and he was *very* interested in Julia I seem to remember. He kept ringing her up for weeks afterwards.'

And he wasn't the only one making more of an effort. 'I think, certainly you and I spent a lot more time involved,' says Mark. 'Normally you and I were done in an hour weren't we? Get the fuck out and go and have a beer. But I remember I was much more interested in the production side, because I'd spent so much time at SAM. I sort of saw myself doing that after the band, sort of thing…but it never quite happened. But I remember staying in the control room a lot more that time.'

We recorded four songs, Saviour Machine, You'll Never Know, Rest Of Your Life and Scarred For Life, the idea being, I think, to include two new songs and two old, Beki-era songs - Saviour Machine and Scarred For Life being not-too-obvious choices and also ones that showcased Julia's vocal abilities particularly well.

The session, which was first broadcast on 14 March, turned out rather well, if I say so myself, was well received, and repeated several times, which was very gratifying. And as Mark says, it was good to work with Dale again (though we still didn't have the nerve to call him 'Buffin'): 'He's a real, proper hero, you know? And he was very positive, it was great, it was nice to have him there.'

Most of the rest of March was taken up with recording and rehearsing at SAM. On 7 March Sooty took the train to Utopia for a cutting session for our next single You'll Never Know, and I delivered the artwork to Cherry Red on 20 March. The same night I had already arranged that I, along with my parents, would travel to London in the Crazy Trains' van to the Venue in Victoria, where they were playing with the Adicts and Vibrators.

Bristol band The Crazy Trains were singer John McLean, guitarists Paul Grudzinski and Barry Cooper, bassist Jon Chilcott and drummer Neil Mackie, formerly, of course, from the X-Certs. The band played an excellent blend of rock 'n' roll, punk and rockabilly (but definitely not psychobilly) and soon built a big local following, eventually signing to CBS subsidiary Spellbound for two singles and played many high profile shows, even supporting Tina Turner! I became really good friends with Jon Chilcott (and recommended Neil to him when they were looking for a new drummer), spending many hours drinking with him in the Dug-Out and many other watering holes.

My parents knew Jon and the Trains well by this stage and used to regularly go to their shows, so there was nothing terribly unusual about them hitching a ride in the van. I arranged to meet them at the gig, and made my way to Cherry Red. When I told them about the gig, they got on the phone and arranged a guest list for me, so outside the venue I asked a group of lads if any of them wanted to buy a ticket. Now, human nature is a curious thing. When one of them asked me how much I wanted for the ticket I said £3.50, or whatever the face value of the ticket was. He immediately became suspicious and decided it had to be a forgery. It took some time to convince him, and even then he only believed me when one of his mates recognized me. If I'd just said '£10 to you guv' in the first place he'd have paid up, no questions asked, and been well pleased.

The recording and rehearsing continued into April, but on the 11th we played at the Level 3 club in Swindon, and as Sooty recently remembered, it gave us the chance to work with an old friend again, as the PA for the gig was provided by Pete and SKAN PA Hire. I was shocked to hear from Sooty that Pete died not long ago. I'd last met him when he did the PA for a Fields Of The Nephilim gig at Bristol Locarno in the early '90s. 'Oh yeah, yeah. Aww, a lovely chap. You know SKAN PA Hire is absolutely massive now. He did that business where he just started to grow and then he slowly started to sell his bits of it, and the company that he started now does, like, the O2 Arena in London and Justin Bieber, stuff like that. He started that. Pete sold his interests off bit by bit, you just get too old for it, but now SKAN PA are absolutely massive and I'm so proud of him, he started this huge company.' Well that's nice to know, anyway.

The support band at Swindon were the remarkably-named Colonel Kilgore's Vietnamese Formation Surf Team. The band had been formed by our old mates Mitch, Lee 'Flea' Edwards, Neville, and Mark O'Neil, who was often working for us as a driver at this time, but for obvious reasons, not this particular gig. It is also notable as Dave's girlfriend at the time, Dreena, was one of the backing singers.

As you may have deduced from the name, the concept of the band was based on the film *Apocalypse Now*, with the band all dressed as US soldiers in the Vietnam War. Their brilliant stage show was meticulously choreographed, with the members, up to nine of them, going through drill routines during the songs. As the stage set got more and more elaborate, there were even full size surf boards, on jointed stands, that allowed the band members to surf on stage in time with the music. I actually played a gig with the Kilgores, at the Turntable Club in Temple Meads, when Flea was arrested for driving his car through a caravan. In fact, his car had been nicked and the thief had driven it up over a roundabout and right through the side of a caravan, like something out of James Bond, but it took some time to prove his innocence. They rang me at the last minute, and not unreasonably, I protested that I didn't know their set. They pointed out that the actual songs were mainly punk and New York Dolls covers, and that even the original material was in the same vein, so Mitch and Neville could cue me in and nod the time changes to me. As a clincher, they all also promised to buy me a pint each after the show, so I agreed. Luckily, H's dad had recently finished building a Kit Car yellow jeep, so I was able to arrive at the venue in something almost in keeping with the theme of the evening. The gig went surprisingly well, and at the end the band kept their promise, but when confronted with nine pints of Blackthorn cider to consume before closing time, I began to see the flaw in my plan...

As an unfortunate footnote, not long after this Dave and Dreena had planned to get married, with me as best man, and Dave, his dad Terry, and I, even got measured up at Moss Bros for the old top hat and tails, while mum had measured up Dreena for her wedding dress, but at the last minute Dreena ran off with Mark O'Neil, which caused some serious ructions, believe me.

Next night, 12 April, we headed down to a gig at Plymouth Sound City, situated at 59 Union Street. The latter part of that line is important, as it led to our being reacquainted with an old friend, Dave Pritchard, the guy from BBC Bristol that had interviewed us for the *RPM* TV programme in 1981. At this time Dave was about to find fame and, presumably, fortune as producer and onscreen foil for chef Keith Floyd. The duo's first TV series, *Floyd On Fish*, would be aired in 1985 to great acclaim, but for now, Dave was gainfully employed by BBC Plymouth. He was making a documentary about Union Street, a street well known as a red light district and, presumably because of this, a favourite haunt for sailors on shore leave in the port. The street was also packed with pubs and clubs, hence our presence. We just happened to bump into Dave and his film crew in the street, and when we told him our reason for being there, he decided to film our entire show for use in the documentary. To this day I've no idea if any of the footage was used, as none of us ever saw the documentary, but I would still like to get hold of the film, if it still exists.

I also met another old acquaintance that night. You've probably forgotten by now, but back in 1978 I'd got disillusioned with TV Brakes and answered an advert looking for a drummer. This was the bloke who looked a bit like Marc Bolan, with the druggie-looking girlfriend who I'd met again in 1979 when she was with Feargal Sharkey at an Undertones gig at the Bristol Locarno. Yep, God knows why - if she told me the reason then it's lost in the mists of time - but here she was again, like the proverbial bad penny. It's a small world. Oh and I dimly remember that, though the audience was strangely un-punk, perhaps because of the location, it was still a good show.

Our next port of call was Hereford Market Tavern, New Market Street, on 13 April. We got there fairly early, so pulled into a pub on the outskirts of the town for a couple of pints. For some reason we hadn't arranged anywhere to stay, just planned to find a hotel in town, but when we mentioned this to the landlord, he said that the pub could also provide accommodation. As you can imagine, we were far from averse to residing in a public house, so we took him up on his kind offer. It would turn out to be a fortuitous move in more ways than one.

The show was a good one, with a big, enthusiastic crowd, but as Julia recalled, when I sat down with her and Mark, there had been some friction between us and some of the locals. 'Do you remember, Mark, that young guy was chatting me up, and would not leave me alone, and that really got on your nerves. It was the closest I've ever seen you to literally getting really physical because he would not leave me alone. So I was trying to be polite, and then trying to have a laugh, but he was just getting far too close, and in the end you almost literally removed him. You just said 'Shut up, you've gotten far too personal, now leave her alone,' and shoved him aside. He didn't like it. But it was actually quite a good gig.'

And things just got worse. Mark recalls 'Driving through Hereford having to drag Shane in the van by his collar as he's getting chased by irate boyfriends, as usual.' Flattering as that may sound, actually, as far as I remember, this is the only occasion on which such a thing happened. Dave and I had got together with a couple of the local girls, who, it turned out, were the girlfriends of a couple of members of some sort of local gang. Unfortunately, one upshot of this was that, when the girls finally left the venue, the boyfriend of the girl I'd been with broke her nose for her, though I didn't hear about this until some time later. Even more unfortunately, as far as I was concerned, when I finally left the venue, said gang were gathered outside baying for my blood, and as Mark has said, I only got away as Sooty screeched up to the door in the van, the others dragged me in, and we sped off with the nutters chasing us down the road.

The rest of the story only came to light as Dave stayed in touch with the girl he'd been with, and visited her for some time afterwards. Apparently they shared the same taste in certain sexual practices, which we won't go into here. Oh come on, there could be children reading. Unlikely, I agree, but you never know.

Anyway, it seemed that all the bands that played Hereford stayed at the same hotel, where we would no doubt have ended up if we hadn't stumbled across the pub, and she told Dave that the local thugs had laid siege outside the hotel all night waiting for us, while we were safely, and smugly, tucked up in bed in the pub a couple of miles away.

A gig at Oddy's Club, Oldham, on, if Sooty's diary is to be believed, Boner Street, on 14 April, turned out to be a tough one, 'The worst pit we have ever played,' according to Mark's diary. Our old comrades the Expelled supported, but that seemed to be the gig's only highlight. The audience were almost all purist anarcho and hardcore fans, and seemed to have turned out, and paid good money, with the sole intention of not liking us. Aren't people strange?

As we slogged doggedly through the set, it occurred to me that this was the first real test, as far as gigs were concerned, that Julia had had to face. Until now the crowds had been kind and supportive, but these bluff northerners were determined to give us a rough ride, and as the front person, Julia was firmly in the firing line. As the set progressed, and they stood there, motionless and stoney-faced, I could sense her confidence wavering. Finally, though, something seemed to snap inside her, and she took the gig by the scruff of its neck, strutting the stage, leering into the crowd and belting out the songs with gusto. They were a bit shocked and uncertain at this sudden change of attitude, but gradually, reluctantly, they loosened up, and by the end of the set were dancing and cheering like mad. We even squeezed a couple of encores out of the miserable buggers. Julia sums it up succinctly: 'It was horrific, but we did win them round.'

I'm unable to put a date to the release of our next single, You'll Never Know, as, depressingly, it never even grazed the indie chart, but I'm guessing it must have been at about this point in our story. I thought it was a good single, and still do, but it aroused no interest at all. I can only find one review, and a disparaging one at that, in, judging by the typeface, Sounds, which complains of Julia '…singing in a horribly US of A voice.'

The You'll Never Know 7" (ANA 22) and 12" (12 ANA 22) both had another favourite new song of mine, What's Going On as the b-side, and the 12" also had a new version of The Times They Are A'Changin'. For the latter, in '80s 12" single style, Sooty added a swirling, sort-of-orchestral synth ending that built to a big crescendo, before the original end of the single kicked back in, which I thought worked really well. Sooty had first played it to us all a while back at a party at Dreena's house, and people loved it, so we thought we were on a winner. Ah well, back to the drawing board.

CHAPTER 16

FOR SOME REASON, gigs at Gillies in Manchester and Liverpool Bierkeller, on 15 and 19 April respectively, had fallen through, but no matter. A little treat was coming up. Our agent had received a call, out of the blue, from a chap called Jose Silva. Jose had just set up a swanky new club in Lisbon called the Rock Rendezvous, and was wondering if we would fly over and open the club, playing the first two nights on 24 and 25 April. He would pay our usual fee, plus - and this where it got even better - he would pay for our flights, hotel bills, and any other expenses, and we would be on free drinks in the club for the whole duration of our stay. Naturally, we bit the bugger's hand off.

We also insisted that we had to bring our own sound engineer. This was patently untrue, as Sooty always set up the desk himself, then just gave the resident sound man detailed instructions on what to do while he, Sooty, was onstage. It had simply occurred to us that as Steve Street had been putting in serious amounts of unpaid work on the album, it would be nice to take him on the trip with us to say Thanks.

The night before we left for Portugal, H and I had the ludicrous idea of loading up the aforementioned yellow jeep with bottles of beer and driving to Weymouth. As when we got there we just had a few more drinks, bought some breaded mushrooms in garlic sauce from a chip shop, then jumped back in the jeep and drove all the way back, I don't know why we bothered. Anyway, the upshot of this inadvisable night out was that when I met up with the others at the bus station next morning, 24 April, for the 7.15am coach to Gatwick, I was feeling more than a little tender.

Flight BA 432 left for Lisbon at 11.55am, and was largely uneventful, but as we all felt that this little trip seemed like some sort of reward for all the work we'd been doing, under quite difficult circumstances, there was a definite party atmosphere to the proceedings.

And happily, the Rock Rendezvous crew, both staff and punters, were also in a party mood, it seemed. As the first show was that night, we only had time for a quick wash and brush-up after checking into our very nice hotel, before heading down to the club. We were encouraged to see that it was a very professional, well set-up operation, with excellent facilities both in the bar décor and stage and PA set-up. We were also encouraged to see that the club's patrons (the bar was open all day, we weren't in bloody England now) were also very easy on the eye indeed. We got chatting to some of the girls at the bar, and I eventually hooked up with a girl with an unpronounceable name that I dubbed Rio, for convenience sake, while Dave seemed unable to make up his mind and had a few of the girls in tow, just in case. When we got to the dressing room, we asked the club manager about the rider, which confused him a little. At first he seemed to think we were asking for prostitutes, which he was happy to provide until we told him that wouldn't be necessary. He did, however, provide, as well as plenty of booze, quite a mountain of cocaine. I thanked him for his generosity, it would have been rude not to, but gave my share to Rio. I could be insufferably self-righteous at times.

Both shows went well, even if Mark's diary tells us that on the first night 'Dave was too pissed,' and we attracted a sizeable crowd both nights, which at least justified our outrageous bar bills to some extent.

Several incidents that took place on this trip are now remembered, but not the actual day on which any of them occurred, so I'll just give you a few at random.

One day Dave and I set out to explore a bit of Lisbon, and went into a little café/bar in a back street, run by two little old ladies in traditional Portuguese dress, for a beer. Unlike all the local kids we'd met, these two ladies, though charming, spoke no English, and instead of beer, kept bringing us tiny mugs of very hot, very strong coffee. We tried to explain for some time that we actually wanted beer, but in the end gave up, drank the rather expensive coffee, paid, thanked them and left. I have this vision of the two ladies, after we left, laughing and saying, in perfect English, 'Bloody tourists, gets 'em every time!'

Mark and Dave also had a similar experience, says Mark: 'I remember being very confused by Portugal because it was so cheap. I'd never been abroad on holiday, so didn't know that southern Europe was a bit of a bargain. Dave and I - you were doing your soundcheck - so 'Right, beer?,' 'Yeah, him banging away on that fuckin' bass drum for half an hour…,' so we went over the road for a beer. And they had these really flash bottles of Carlsberg lager, with big foil tops. We went 'We'll have a couple of those please,' and it was, like, 19p a bottle. And you could tell by their body language that they were ripping us off, cos we were obviously tourists. We drank them and went up and got some more, and we said 'We know you're ripping us off, but it's so fuckin' cheap we don't care, we'll have another two please!' Then *they* were confused!'

We also, naturally, repaired to the beach several times, once with nasty consequences for Steve. 'He nearly died,' says Mark. 'Remember that on the beach? It was April, but cos it's so far south the Atlantic's quite warm, so we're in up to our knees or whatever, just chatting in the shallows, Steve and I, and all of a sudden 'Ooh, look at that wave' - BANG! I get flattened and he's gone. And he comes up about 20 yards off-shore, bleeding, because he's been knocked over and dragged along the gravelly bottom. I got out and I'd swallowed a lung-full, and I came up to you or Dave and said 'Give us a swig of that,' to get rid of the taste of the salt, and it was that fuckin' wine that you'd bought for about 9p a litre. I think I went back in to rinse me mouth out with sea water again!' Yes, we'd thought that wine was a bargain when we bought it on the way to the beach, but it was completely undrinkable, worse than vinegar. As a jape we poured some over Sooty's head, but it was so acidic it burnt his eyes quite badly [see photo]. How we laughed.

'I can't remember the exact details,' says Mark of another occasion. 'But I thought we were going out one day, and I came down a bit late, and everyone had disappeared. Including Julia, which pissed me off cos I was sharing a room with her. So I just got a cab into the centre, there was some big fiesta going on, quite an impressive square with great big marble steps, and a Land Rover comes in with these guys on the back of it, and they're lighting rockets, big, six foot high rockets, with like, a broomstick as a handle. I'm thinking 'Wow, that's very continental.' Whoah, up it goes! And of course it's lunchtime, and it goes out, doesn't explode, and you think 'Oh fuck,' and you're shoulder to shoulder there, and I thought 'I am not going to get speared to the floor in Lisbon,' so I shuffled me way out of the crowd before they killed anybody. It was just one of those Latin things I think. Great lumps of wood going 200 foot in the air, then 'Now what? Oh yeah, gravity!' So I got the hell out of there and made my way back I think.'

While we were there, the Rock Rendezvous held a daytime competition for local bands to get up and do their best Siouxsie and the Banshees impersonation, and we were nagged to take part. To be fair to us, we had no notice, and just knocked something together quickly in the dressing room. The song we did is now lost in the mists of time, but I do remember that we were easily the worst contestants, which was pretty embarrassing, even if everyone was too polite to say so.

Rather oddly, but very flatteringly, a local newspaper heard of some of our wild and depraved rock 'n' roll antics (Ozzy Osbourne, Motley Crue and GG Allin had nothing on us, believe me), and printed a strip cartoon about us in its pages. Who did these people think we were?

When we finished the last show, Jose promptly paid us, and once we had the money in our hands, a thought struck us. Apart from a few dirt cheap beers in local bars, we hadn't had to put our hands in our pockets once on this whole trip, and as everything was so cheap, we worked out that we could stay in the hotel for another week or so, and still go home with money in our pockets. Good plan. The only problem was that we were booked to play Woods Leisure Centre, Colchester, on 27 April. We called our agent, explained the situation, and asked if he could rearrange the gig for a later date. He said no, absolutely and definitely not, and no amount of nagging, cajolery, begging, bribery, blackmail, sobbing or threats would budge him. The unfeeling swine, thinking about some innocent promoter and our fans rather than letting us have a good time. Some people are just self, self, self.

So, on 26 April, somewhat dejectedly, we bade Jose and the Rock Rendezvous crew a fond farewell and got flight BA 433 back to London, arriving at 20:35, according to Sooty's diary.

The plan had always been that H would load the gear into his van and pick us up at the airport. We would then stay in a hotel in London that Sooty had booked and drive to Colchester the next day. For obvious reasons we were already in a bad mood, but when H failed to show up tempers became seriously frayed. For want of anything better to do, I began swigging out of a bottle of vodka that I'd bought in duty free, and that only served to make me even more belligerent.

When he finally turned up, several hours late, it turned out that he'd simply got the time wrong, but we were in a less than forgiving mood.

To make things worse, when we got the hotel, it turned out to be the worst hovel we'd ever stayed in. Sooty had obviously chosen it simply on the grounds that it was, presumably, very, very cheap. After we'd checked in, the 'porter,' or rather the fat, sweaty bloke in flared jeans and a heavily-stained and evil-smelling white shirt that did an impersonation of one, tried to show us to our rooms, but continually got lost in the maze of corridors. We traipsed around and around, up and down stairs, getting more and more irate, until, finally, he found our rooms. We soon wished he hadn't.

My room was filthy and smelly, and there were even used syringes in the bathroom. Mark's was even worse: 'They were in my bedroom! There was twin beds, and then the sink, and both beds touched both walls, so you had to climb over the beds to get to the sink, and watch where you were stepping.'

Why we didn't just walk out and stay somewhere else, I don't know. Possibly by then we were just so tired and pissed off that we didn't care any more. Next morning, we went down to breakfast, which consisted of stale croissants and lukewarm coffee, and got chatting to some of the other people staying there. It turned out that they were mostly homeless families, people just out of prison, and other people that just couldn't afford to go anywhere else. A desperate place.

By now, we all had what we termed Galloping Portuguese Gut-Rot, presumably due to that dodgy wine on the beach, and anxious to avoid the hotel toilets at all costs, we jumped in the van and headed for Cherry Red. We all trooped in, said 'Hello' to the receptionist, used their toilet, said 'Goodbye' to the receptionist and all trooped out again. She just looked puzzled and blinked a lot.

As we set off for Colchester, despite having sore bums, we tried to look at things in a positive light. We'd done the right thing. We'd come home because duty called. The show must go on. We wouldn't let our fans down, no siree. Some of the others, those with no moral fibre, had wanted to stay in Portugal, but not me, oh no.

When we got to the Woods Leisure Centre it looked strangely deserted. Not only that, the doors were all locked. We started to get a bad feeling. Eventually, we found a janitor, who seemed very surprised to see us. We started to get a very bad feeling. Okay, you're ahead of me. Yes, the bloody gig had been cancelled and we'd come home from what could have been a lovely holiday for nothing.

As you've read, though on the whole we did try to behave reasonably decently, there are several incidents which we should feel thoroughly ashamed of, but this is certainly the worst. I honestly don't know what we were thinking. Mark's father, Colin, had recently died at the tragically young age of 48, and as if that wasn't enough for the poor bugger to cope with, his relationship with Julia was in the process of falling apart. We sensitively responded to this by sacking him. Even more shamefully, Julia remembers that 'Mark and I split up, remember. But I had to say that the band had decided he ought to leave, which I thought was absolutely outrageous.'

He was showing up at rehearsals less and less, but that was because he'd had to find a job: 'I was working at the time. I had a job at the garage at the top of Blackboy Hill because we had no money,' he says.

For some time Dave and I had been working on a side project called Sweet Revenge, with Jon Chilcott from the Crazy Trains on bass and vocals. As I've said, we'd become great friends with Jon, and when we discovered that all three of us were big fans of Johnny Thunders, we decided to put together a set of Heartbreakers and NY Dolls covers and play a few local gigs, just for fun and beer money.

Jon was great fun. He shared my birthday, 5 July, but he was four years to the day younger than me. You wouldn't have known it though. Despite being just 17 years old, he lived in his own flat, could booze with the best of us, and was already hoovering up speed like it was going out of fashion.

He began to socialize with us more than his own band, and would turn up at our rehearsals and recording sessions, waiting for Dave and I to come out to play. Presumably, as Mark was so seldom there, that's why we got the idea of bringing Jon into the band, but it was a horrible thing to do. He said yes straight away and went off to inform the rest of the Trains, straightforwardly and honourably, while we got a girly to do our dirty work. Oh, the shame.

There is some slight mitigation (very slight) when, when I sat down with Julia and Mark, they had this exchange:

Julia: But you were really unhappy about being in the band, you really were, and you'd expressed that unhappiness.

Mark: I can understand that I can be a pain in the arse when I'm not enjoying something. And things weren't necessarily good at home at the same time. Partly my fault, because coming home from SAM, I'd be going 'Right, what's for tea?' and 'Let's get over the pub.' And Julia was 'Oh, what do you think of that song?,' 'What do you think of such and such,' 'Do you think we should change...' And I'd think 'Oh shut up.' It was far more exciting for you than it was for me at that stage.

Julia: Well it would have been. My first crack of the whip, as it were. But also, I was very, very into the music at that point. I knew Steve very well and I did know the recording process quite well, and I got very, very into recording songs for the album, I enjoyed singing those songs.

Considering how shamefully he'd been treated, Mark's reaction to the situation was dignified and reasonable. He shunned us for a couple of weeks, then began to come and drink with us again in the Dug-Out, but the hurt was plain to see.

At least partly as a guilt-assuaging move, though it may have struck some people as odd, it occurred to me that, as the Trains were now short of a bass player, why didn't Mark join them? I mentioned the idea to Neil Mackie, and he thought it a good one. If it worked out,

I would then, hopefully, be on reasonably good terms with both the Trains (who had naturally not been best pleased about us poaching their bass player) and Mark again. If it didn't, well, I didn't want to think about that. As it happened, it turned out to be one of my better ideas. Mark says that: 'My recollection is that I left, or was told to leave, Jon came in, leaving a gap, and I thought that makes some sense. And then thinking [when starting to play the Trains' songs] 'Fucking hell, he was quite good wasn't he? Ow!'' While Julia's recollection is that: 'I do remember, Mark, that you were quite happy to be playing with the Trains, you really did enjoy it a lot. I remember you saying that there was a different energy about it, a very different band, very different status and everything, but you had a good time.'

I saw Mark play with the Trains often, including an appearance at the Ashton Court Festival, which none of the rest of us ever got to do, and yes, he really did seem much happier, much to my relief. Here's how he remembers it: 'The Trains, I really enjoyed. It was quite tough, because obviously Chilcott was quite a good bass player, so to step into his shoes...I don't think I ever did, but I got away with it, eventually. And I quite liked playing sort of twelve-bar runs, they're fun for a bass player to play. Whereas I think ours was a lot more precision, I think you and I had to work very hard to make it work, cos if we wandered it was shit, wasn't it? Cos it was so fast, a lot of it. I think you and I got it in the end, that we could cover pretty much anything that Beki or Dave threw at us, and sort of make it back into a song. We were pretty tight. I think we realised 'We've got to work as a unit, otherwise, there's no chance. Those two are a bit free-style, so something's got to be solid.''

Jon's first duty as an official member of our happy throng was not actually with Vice Squad. Dave, Bambi and I had hit on the idea of recording a Chaotic Dischord live album, *Live In New York*, though of course it wouldn't really be live, or, for that matter, in New York. We were booked into Cave on 29 and 30 April, and asked Jon to play bass. Bill Ferrier engineered the session, and we explained to him our detailed plans on how to fake the album. We had a copy of Simon and Garfunkel's LP *The Concert in Central Park*, which we used to make a tape loop of constant crowd noise, and we had a couple of BBC sound effects records of assorted crowd noises, things like 'loud cheering,' 'mild applause,' 'loud applause,' 'angry shouting,' things like that. The idea was that we would record banter between the songs, and bring in the appropriate crowd responses, over the S & G tape loop, at the appropriate times, often overlapping each other. With the technology of the time, as Bill patiently explained, this could be a very complicated process, and so it proved.

Recording the music, a mixture of old Dischord favourites and new songs, was easy, of course, as was the between song banter, song introductions, and bad jokes delivered by Bambi, Dave and Jon. Fading the appropriate crowd noises in and out, however, was something of a work of art, with various bits of tape running off reels and round pens stuck upright in lumps of blu-tak when we ran out of tape machines, and everyone in the room following a complex written plan, pushing faders up and down in unison. These days you'd programme a computer to do the job and it'd be a doddle, but with 1984 technology it took a very long time, and frankly, it would have been much easier to just play a bloody gig. It did, however, sound reasonably authentic, so us being us, we deliberately sabotaged it by having Bambi tell the crowd to shut up, at which point all the crowd noise stopped abruptly and completely, before coming crashing back in a few seconds later. Mild mannered Bill even got to appear on this one, playing acoustic guitar and amusingly impersonating a hillbilly on You're The Ugliest Thing I've Ever Seen before Bambi incites the crowd to 'Cut him into little bits.'

For the front cover photo, we used Bambi's front room, which had an entire wall done up as a Caribbean island, as a backdrop, with us in sunglasses on the 'beach' and my sister Trayci and a mate of hers, Julie, posing as waitresses, serving us drinks. I've no idea what any of this was supposed to have to do with New York.

When the album had its only CD release to date, in 2001, the lovely Dave at Punkcore Records in New York coupled it with a Dischord compilation album that we put together as Riot City was winding down in 1985, called *Now! That's What I Call A Fuckin' Racket* (Vol.1) on Not Very Nice Records. I'm pretty sure it went through the books as a late Riot City release, so I'm not sure why we used a different label name. We probably just thought it was mildly amusing, which indeed it was. Very mildly. The album title was of course nicked from the Virgin Now!... series of appallingly successful chart compilations that began in 1983 and continue to this day. As we were only putting the thing out to squeeze the last few quid out of the cash cow, the cover art budget had been tiny, so I just put the title in big white letters on a black background, much as I would have liked to have done a proper parody of the real Now! sleeve design. For the Punkcore reissue, Dave Bateman wrote a great sleeve note with a 'Glossary of Terms' for the benefit of our American cousins, including:

BUSTING A BOLLOCK - To apply undue haste.
SCROTE - From Scrotum - Term of endearment.
FUCKWIT - Less intelligent than a halfwit.

I'm sure they found it helpful. And better still, after all those years, Dave Punkcore agreed to my earlier idea of spoofing the Virgin Now! sleeve design (the Now! series was by then up to Now! 50). He'd never heard of it, but my young sons had a few of the latest ones, so I sent one over to him. He and his art department did a fantastic job. At first glance it looked completely authentic, until you realised that the background was leopard-skin and in the bottom right hand corner a tiny Bambi was gurning out at you. We were all very pleased with the CD until Virgin served writs on Dave Punkcore and Simon for infringement of copyright and the record had to be withdrawn from sale. Hmm, I hadn't thought of that…

Sorry Dave.

According to Sooty's diary, we began rehearsing with Jon at Cotham on 2 May, and work continued on the never-ending third Vice Squad album at SAM on 14 and 15 May. On 16 May, Jon made his Vice Squad live debut at Leeds Bierkeller. It was a fairly disastrous event for two reasons, neither of them Jon's fault.

The support act were our old pals the Expelled, and after the soundcheck and a couple of drinks, everyone in the Vice Squad camp but me decided to find our hotel, guided by Ricky Fox, as we hadn't checked in yet. We'd played Leeds Bierkeller many times, of course, and were used to going onstage around 10.00, with the support strutting their stuff at about 9.00, so those of us left in the venue were a little surprised when the promoter began chivvying the Expelled to begin their set at 8.00. For some reason, at this point in time, Leeds Bierkeller had to run all their gigs through early, but we hadn't known that. It was probably in the contract, but no one had noticed it. As time went on, the promoter got more and more agitated, so in the end, out of desperation, it was decided that, as the Expelled were drummer-less, I should go on and begin their set and hope that Ricky wouldn't be too long. The set had to be hastily rearranged, putting the songs I knew best first, and we gave it our best shot. It didn't go too badly, but I was mightily relieved when the rest of Vice Squad and Rick got back. The look on his face when he saw his band already onstage, with me on drums, was a picture.

Looking back now, I can see the funny side, but to this day the memory still pains Sooty: 'It wasn't funny, it was a disaster. You didn't let me down off that for a very long time and you had every right not to. Imagine the shame I felt, I was the manager. And that guy Paul Twemlow, the guy who ran it, we later found out was a kind of gangster type figure who ran all the punk gigs. 'Can I go on now?' 'Yeah, you go on now son, but you're in deep trouble with me,' completely threatening the shit out of me. And then he ducked our money down on some of the other gigs. I got it back in the end, but I was forever ringing him for the money.'

To make matters worse, the Upstarts had originally been booked to play this date, but had to cancel, and the promoter hadn't publicised the fact that we'd been brought in to replace them. Now, obviously lots of skins who followed the Upstarts would also go to gigs by the likes of us, there were always plenty of skins in our audience, but they were understandably more than a bit miffed to have been shafted in this underhand fashion, and they made the fact very clear, as Julia remembers: 'It was really scary because they wouldn't applaud, nothing, for the first three songs. It was his [Jon's] first gig, and it was really scary for him. Although they weren't hostile, they were indifferent. I just thought 'This is Chilcott's first gig and this is awful.' I remember you, Shane, saying 'It's not always like this!' And they did warm up, actually, they were alright in the end.'

We now come to a dark and sinister passage in our story. On Saturday 19 May, we headed up to Blackpool for a show at the Bierkeller, and after the soundcheck, and after the doors had opened, we all sat around a table in the Bierkeller having a bier, sorry, beer. Looking across the room, I could see a group of girls sat around another table, having a drink and horsing around, one of which had cropped blonde hair, shaved at the sides, and was very cute indeed. I kept looking over, wondering how I could get to talk to her without her mates getting in the way, when someone at our table asked me a question. I took my eye off the ball, as it were, for a moment, to answer the question, and the next thing I knew, the brazen hussy had crossed the room, sat on my bench, and slid up close to me. Very close. She said 'Hello, I'm Jo, what's your name?' Quick as a flash, I said 'Hello Jo, my name's Shane.' I almost always get that right. She said 'Have you got a knife I can borrow? I've got a splinter in my finger.' Still a bit taken aback at this sudden turn of events, I had a stab at suavity by saying 'David, this young lady has a splinter, could we borrow your knife please?' When he clocked Jo, Dave also tried moving into Cary Grant mode, making a flashy exhibition of flipping open his football hooligan-issue butterfly knife before handing it over.

This spot of minor surgery completed, I said 'I'm going for a drink, do you want one?' and she did. When we'd been chatting for a while she said 'You're not from round here, are you? Where are you from?' I'd assumed, I suppose, that this was a groupie situation, but now alarm bells began ringing. It got worse when I replied 'Bristol,' and she asked 'Oh, are you up here on holiday then?' I said something snooty like 'Well actually, I'm in the band that I suppose you've paid to see,' but she explained that no, she wasn't a Vice Squad fan at all. It seemed that a couple of times a year, she and a group of friends from Dewsbury, Yorkshire, hired a coach and went to Blackpool for the weekend, taking over a B&B owned by a couple who were friends of one of her mates' parents. Four members of this group of friends had a band called the Legion, and when they saw we happened to be playing a weekend when they would be in Blackpool anyway, they phoned the promoter to see if they could blag the support. He told them that Broken Bones had already been booked, but when they explained that they would be bringing a whole coachload of people, he agreed to let them open.

After this decidedly unpromising start to the conversation, we actually got on very well, so much so that we were gone much longer than I had planned, as Julia remembers: 'I know you disappeared, and we couldn't find you, and we got panicky about it. And Sooty was saying 'He's bound to have gone off with that girl,' and I was saying 'Well not necessarily,' and Dave was going 'What? *Yeeess!*''

When we got back, H, who was driving us to all these gigs, informed me that we were due on any minute, so I arranged to meet Jo after the show and quickly headed backstage. I was desperate for the toilet, but had no sooner sat down than H began getting agitated, or as agitated as it was possible for the Jeeves-like H to get, so I gave up, ran upstairs to the stage and got behind the kit just as the intro music was fading out.

Happily, for the rest of us, of course, but especially for Jon, it was quite a good show, though he did amuse me with a story he told me afterwards. He said that for most of the gig, Helen, the attractive bass player from the Legion, was stood in the crowd, right in front of him, so when, as he was playing, he felt someone caressing his balls, he thought his luck was in. Unfortunately, at the end of the song, he looked down to see a large, ugly, skinhead bloke grinning up at him. Ah well, even cutie Jon couldn't win 'em all.

When it was all over, the security were very officious about clearing the venue quickly, so I only saw Jo briefly, but she said that they were having an all-night party back at the

B&B, and she'd written down the address if we wanted to go along. We had a quick meeting and it was decided that H would drive Sooty and Julia back with the gear, and Sooty gave us some cash so that Dave, Jon and I could go to the party and get a coach back the next day.

It was a raucous party, which did indeed go on all night, and we were all particularly impressed when next morning Jo elected to give me her breakfast and have a pint of Tetley's bitter instead. As we were about to leave, she wrote her address and phone number on a beer mat for me, and after we'd gone for our bags, next thing we saw was Jo being carried onto their coach.

Yes, dear reader, that inebriated girl is now my wife, and we have two grown-up sons to show for it. At the time of writing, early 2015, Jake, 29, has recently completed a masters degree in International Relations at Ritsumeikan University, Kyoto, Japan. He married a local girl, Tomomi, in 2013 and they are expecting their first child in July. Also in 2013, Louie, 26, got his degree in English Language and Linguistics at the University of the West of England, where, incidentally, I've been working in administration for nearly twenty years, and got engaged to his girlfriend Phuong.

We're tremendously proud of them both. God knows where they get it from, certainly not me.

On 22 May David Jensen repeated our session, then on 25 May we had a show at Cambridge. The venue is, unusually, unrecorded in Sooty's diary, though he now reckons it was at the Boat Club. One thing sticks in the memory about this one. After the soundcheck, as it was a lovely sunny day, we sat at a table in the garden of a pub near the university. The garden was a large one, with a lot of tables and bushes, and around a table on the other side of the bush next to ours, we could hear a group of students congregating. When what sounded like a substantial group had gathered, a new bunch of arrivals were cheered loudly. When the noise had subsided, one of them asked 'What are you all doing tonight then?' and the reply was 'Well, we *were* going to see Vice Squad, but we're not going to bother now.' We looked at each other, thought for a bit, then burst out laughing. It was either that or burst into tears.

The next night, 26 May, we played Liverpool Bierkeller, about which nothing is now remembered by anyone, which is a bit of a shame as it turned out to be the last ever Vice Squad gig! The exact reasons for this are now lost in the mists of time. It's true that Sooty was spending a lot of time engineering at SAM (He would eventually take over when Steve left) and Dave, Jon and I were more and more busy with Sweet Revenge, but it seems more likely that we decided to just concentrate on finally finishing the album.

We certainly got a (small) cheque from Anagram on 4 June, and the next day carried on working on backing tracks and guitar overdubs, which continued, sporadically, thereafter. Incidentally, on the finished album Mark played on five tracks and Jon on four, with Sooty playing bass on the other two. Money was, as always, a big problem, and as soon as the drum tracks were finished, we sold my Simmons drums to Merv to pay for more studio time - like breaking up the coaches to stoke the steam engine to finish the journey. Or something like that.

The final mix down began on 15 August, a laborious process that continued until 26 August, when Sooty at last spliced together the third and final Vice Squad album.

The album was preceded by a single from it, a cover of Teenage Rampage by the Sweet. We were all fans of Brian Connolly and co., but when we began to dissect the song and attempt to play it, they went up even further in our estimation. It was a very complicated arrangement, and a right bugger to play, as Mark recalls: 'I remember doing Teenage Rampage at Oasis, that caff we used to practice in. 'Cos we couldn't get that half a beat in the middle, and we did end up throwing things at each other. We were driving each other round the bend. Dave and I would get it then you would fuck it up, then I'd cock it up, and it went on for about three days I seem to remember. We just could not get it, then suddenly it just clicked and we thought 'What was all the fuss about?''

To replicate the intro to the original single we used a tape of the crowd at Manchester Mayflower chanting 'Vice Squad, Vice Squad,' recorded by Mandy, bolstered by a crew of Dave's City Service Firm mates who also provided footy-terrace chants for the fade-out, and we were all very pleased with the finished track.

Sooty's diary says that the single was cut at Virgin Townhouse at 5.00pm on 11 September, and as the album tracks and side timings (side one, 18.46, side two, 18.50, fact fans) are listed in the same entry, I assume the album was cut at the same time.

On 23 September we met up at midday in the Shakespeare Tavern for a photo session for the single cover, which again was a bit off as Mark actually played on the track and not Jon. Again, I'm not sure what we were thinking, as two days later, 25 September, we met up in Bath at 1.00pm for a photo session for the back of the album cover, with everyone that played on it, including Mark. As we were a five-piece band, with two bass players, Glenn who played piano, a chap called Terry who played some brilliant lead guitar, and Steve and Merv who both contributed vocals and more besides, that made us ten in all. To get us all in shot, Ken Lush had to stand so far back you could hardly see our faces, so he had to stand closer, take two photos, and splice them together afterwards. Looking at the finished photo, I suggested we change our name to The 1966 England World Cup Squad. Actually, the 1970 one or any subsequent bunch of England losers might have been more appropriate.

The single was released on 10 December, and at first, as Julia remembers, the signs were good: 'Janice Long played Rampage [on her Radio 1 show], it was her Single of the Week. And she liked it so much that she extended it for another week. I remember hearing, actually hearing it in a restaurant. I was eating a meal and it was on a radio in the kitchen. And the guy I was with, Steve, went and said 'Excuse me, I just have to say that my companion here is singing on that record!,' and the bloody chef came out! I was so embarrassed!' But of course, it couldn't last. 'It was weird, it was gathering a kind of momentum, and I don't know why, but nothing more went forward after that. But people were starting to actually come up to me and say 'Oh, I heard your single,' so it was kind of getting a buzz. But I don't know what actually stopped it getting any further.' The main problem was that Janice Long, bless her, was almost a lone voice in the media. I can only find one review, and that a poor one, from *Sounds* judging by the typeface, calling it 'cliched,' among many other insults.

Even after all the Radio 1 airplay, it only made No.44 on the indie chart, and just to rub it in, a month earlier, 10 November, Chaotic Dischord *Live In New York* had gone into the indie top 20 at number 18. I could have stamped my little feet.

We now come to yet another example of a story I've been telling anybody who cared to listen (and a good many who didn't care to listen) for years, not in fact being true. For the sleeve of the album, that we had by now decided to call *Shot Away*, an expression we were using more and more to describe our condition after yet another night in the Dug Out, I'd had the idea of extending the concept I'd first used for the Black Sheep sleeve. This time, the room on the sleeve would be that of a hit man, out to kill us. We had plenty of new band photos, and I bought some targets from a sports shop and punched 'bullet' holes in them. I had the whole idea sketched out in some detail and I've always said I couldn't finish the artwork as we were on tour, but obviously that can't be true. The reason why I was too busy to finish the thing is now, naturally, lost in the mists of time. Anyway, from Sooty's diary it's clear that we had several meetings with Jim Phelan, the resident artist at Cherry Red, and explained the idea to him, as well as supplying him with everything needed to put the sleeve together. Sooty takes up the story: 'I wasn't at all happy with that chap. All the artwork went up to be done, we did all those photos with Ken and that, for some nice fancy artwork, and behind our backs he got together with Theo and they made the decision to do that yellow and black thing, 'Oh no, slash the budget, instead of four hundred quid I want it done for fifty.' They just put it out in that awful cheap cover. Dreadful. And all he could do was shuffle his feet, cowering, and go 'Well Soot...the thing is...Theo...' and all that type of thing.' The finished sleeve used a band photo, given a negative effect to make it a black blob, on a nasty yellow background, with the band and album names in a tacky stencil typeface. It looked like a can of supermarket own-brand baked beans.

Now discouraged even further, we awaited the reviews with trepidation. Dave, Jon and I were actually soundchecking for a Sweet Revenge gig at the Western Star Domino Club in Bristol when my sister Trayci came in excitedly clutching the 2 February 1985 issue of *Sounds*. Staggeringly, they gave *Shot Away* the maximum five stars, the first and only Vice Squad album to achieve such a thing. Oh, the irony! Under the yawningly punning (and strangely familiar) heading 'Porn Again,' the fragrant Spike Sommer wrote:

> 'The three singles from the resurrected and revamped Vice Squad that preceded '*Shot Away*' suggested it was always going to be one mighty fine album, but they never hinted that it was to be as good as it's turned out to be.
>
> As the needle drifts through the opening 'New Blood', it's clear that this is one quality piece of vinyl. The pounding rhythms and atmospheric landscapes of that piece still sound as fresh as they did on the 'Black Sheep' EP but even this classy number is

outshone by the bright 'n' breezy 'Take It Or Leave It', a racy rocker and first rate anthem.

'Out In The Cold' sees a slower, almost jazzy side to Vice Squad and 'Nowhere To Hide' takes the show back into driving rock 'n' roll before the side one closer, 'You'll Never Know', a meaty, memorable melody that deserved to do so much better than it actually did as a single.

The second side is as good as the first, taking in six stunners with no let-ups or disappointments among them. 'Rebels And Kings' bears a great chopping motif with Lia's vocals as close to perfection as you can get. The other five ride along well enough, with 'Killing Time', 'Playground' and 'What's Going On' being the best of the bunch.

With 'Shot Away', Vice Squad have laid down the law that they're now a force to be reckoned with. No longer can they be dismissed as another punk band - they've transcended the trappings of that category most impressively by moving towards an appealing rock 'n' roll style of their very own. Five stars is not enough.'

Aww shucks, Spike, stop it. You're making us blush! Sadly, it did no good, though, and the record failed to even make the indie chart. Strangely, though, over the years, several people, hearing me say that the album sold nothing, have replied 'Well, I bought it,' including Neil Anderson, co-publisher of this very book. And when our paltry royalty checks come in, in recent years we see that sales of the CD of *Shot Away* seem to be growing. Not massive numbers, you understand, but it's heartening to find that, say, 52 people in the US, 30 people in Canada, 13 in Japan and 3 in Sweden have bought it recently, and I'm just glad, and grateful, that after all the hard work, at least some people are now listening to it. And yes, I do still think, despite the dodgy drum sound, that it's a good album. Still a shit sleeve though.

And that turned out to be the end of Vice Squad, though as Julia says, there was never a formal split, just a tacit agreement that we'd reached the end of the road: 'You were doing Sweet Revenge, yes, but I don't remember a defined split, or why, or if there was one. It's very muddy. There was never a moment when we said 'Shall we call it a day?' There was no band meeting saying 'Well that's it, we should go our separate ways,' nothing like that. So there we are, we're still technically together, ha ha! I knew there'd be a way, Shane!'

Dave, Jon and I continued with Sweet Revenge for some time, with Sooty sometimes coming in on second guitar or filling in if Dave was absent, but he always refused to join the band. We released a 12" single, called Nothing Ever Goes (The Way It's Planned), on our own Revenge Records, with Simon, and played a lot of local shows and a few in London. As we were skint, for the London shows we ran coaches from the Old England pub and charged people for the trip, thus giving ourselves free transport to the gig. We also got Mike Darby's brother Neil's band, Fear of Darkness, to do the supports, so that we could just turn up and use their gear.

Tim Galley joined on lead guitar for a while, before spectacularly leaving the band mid-song during a gig at the Granary (all our fault, the drink and drugs were getting out of hand), a chap called Rich Lacey also played lead for a while, and we eventually brought in a great rockin' singer called Andy Rope. We had a great time as Sweet Revenge, but after about a year Jon and Andy decided to move to London, and I found out that I was about to become a daddy, so that, too, ground to a halt.

And that, we thought, was that. But at that time, the reissue market was tiny, so we had no idea how huge it would become.

As I've said, Link Records issued our *Live And Loud* album in 1988, then in 1991 Abstract released *Last Rockers: The Singles Collection* on vinyl and CD, our first release on the new-fangled format. Our two EMI albums were reissued by first DOJO in 1993, then Captain Oi! in 2000, and there have been numerous reissues since, on various labels, on both CD and vinyl. Anagram reissued *Shot Away* on CD in 1994.

There have also been many, many compilations, three of which are, I think, worth noting. In 1997 Anagram released *The BBC Sessions*, for which I contributed sleeve notes and Dave did the artwork, though, you'll not be surprised to learn, Anagram ruined it by cutting down the colour overlays to save money. It's mainly notable for the first Peel Session, still, for my money, one of the best things we ever recorded.

In 1999 Captain Oi! issued *The Rarities- All Unreleased Versions*, again with sleeve notes by myself and artwork by Dave, with various Vice Squad demos including the Trinity Tape, which was pleasing as the VS version of the TV Brakes song Spikey Hair at last got an outing, giving H and Ian a writing credit. There were three tracks from the first ever VS gig, at the Anson Rooms, and the Sweet Revenge demo versions of two of the single tracks, which meant that Tim Galley made an appearance, which was nice. Best of all, though, was that here the TV Brakes finally got their first ever record release. The original TV Brakes version of Angry Youth, recorded in H's dad's garage, sounded great, and was declared best track on the album in a review in *Record Collector*.

In 2000 I compiled and did the sleeve notes for *The Very Best Of Vice Squad*, for Anagram, Sooty did all the mastering at Channel House Studios, Bristol, and Dave did the artwork. We were able to do the whole job between us, 'in-house,' as it were, and send the complete package direct to the factory. Not that we didn't trust Anagram or anything...

In 1994 Visionary released *Vice Squad: The Movie* on VHS, with live tracks filmed in Cardiff and Preston and the Granary live footage and the Swan interview from the BBC RPM programmes. Sales were minimal, so when, in about 2003, Cherry Red decided to put out a Vice Squad DVD, I wondered if we could improve on it. A mate of mine from work, Dave Spiller, told me that he and a friend of his, Andy Bray, had made a number of short films, including one that had appeared at a film festival at the Arnolfini in Bristol. We talked about the Vice Squad DVD, and came up with a plan. We decided that the best idea would be for he and Andy to film new interviews, and clips from these, along with scans from my scrapbooks and audio from tapes I had of John Peel and Richard Skinner talking about us on Radio 1, would be slotted in around the grainy live footage, to give us a proper sort of movie. And in keeping with the format, we'd also include some previously unreleased live audio tracks from Plymouth Top Rank and a photo gallery.

For some reason, Cherry Red weren't keen at first, but gave in in the end, and gave us a budget of £500. Knowing that when we all got together, we'd be yapping away ten to the dozen, but immediately clam up once a camera and microphone were pointed at us, I asked a mate, Ian Glasper, bass player with, among others, Stampin' Ground, and music journalist and author, to conduct the interview, which he graciously agreed to do.

As we couldn't afford proper lighting, on the day, Dave Bateman and I drove around various people's houses, collecting all the lights and lamps we could find, and took them, along with a crate of beer and some water for Ian, who doesn't drink, to my mate Dave Lown's house, he being the only person we knew without a noisy family or ferocious dogs. Now most people, knowing that film crew are coming to their house, would tidy up a bit, but not our Dave. He let us in, showed us into the kitchen, where Dave Spiller and Andy were already setting up, and went out to do his shopping, not at all worried that his dirty washing was directly behind where we would be filming.

Me, Dave, Mark, Simon and H took part in the interview, and as Ian had recently interviewed Beki for a magazine article, I asked him to ask her if she'd like to take part, even if she'd rather film her own contribution in London. She politely declined, but asked him to wish us all the best with the project.

Dave and Andy did a great job, and when the DVD was released in 2005, we were all really pleased with it. It also got decent reviews, the first pressing of 1,000 sold-out straight away, at full price, and it has sold steadily ever since.

And that would have been pretty much the end of our story, but for two tragic events that I'm going to have to share with you. On the advice of a friend, Dave Patton, I wrote these accounts just after these events occurred, and have decided not to go back now and edit them.

Tuesday 11 December 2007

I got into work at about 9.00am, but with other work to do, I didn't sit down at my desk until 10.00. Opening my emails, I found one from Steve Grice, the drummer from Onslaught, an old friend, which said simply 'Please call me.' Wondering what it was all about, I did just that. He told me that Dave had died. I went cold with shock and swore several times, unable to think straight, even when he told me that he and Steve Summerhayes, another friend, were heading straight over to see Dave's mum. Shaking, I went outside and smoked a cigarette, then pulled myself together a little. I rang back and asked them to pick me up.

Dave's mum, Eileen, seemed bewildered but holding up remarkably well, as we took her to a nearby pub for lunch and to discuss arrangements to get to the funeral, which was to be held in Spain the following Saturday.

Dave had moved to Fuengirola, Spain, four years before with his wife Jenny to open a bar. All had gone well at first, but recently he had lost the bar and Jenny had left him for another man. When I'd spoken to him on the phone over the previous weeks, he'd tried to put up a brave front, but he hadn't sounded at all well. At this stage, the details were sketchy, and if anything, they became more so, and all we could be sure of was that he'd had a fall after leaving a bar while celebrating his 46th birthday on 5th December, been taken to hospital with head injuries, and died on the 11th.

Steve G booked the air tickets for seven of us, Eileen, of course, himself, me and Steve Summerhayes, Sheps, Pete Walker and Ian Westaway, with Colin Huntley and Pete 'Blitz' Silvester making their own arrangements but taking the same flight. These were all friends of Dave's from music, football and rugby.

On Friday I spent the day in Newport waiting for a new passport, mine having expired just before, and after an hour's sleep, the two Steves picked me up at 2.00am Saturday morning to round up the others and collect Eileen. We arrived at Bristol airport at 4.00am, met up with Colin and Blitz, and headed for customs for the first of many trials and tribulations.

Given that we were made up of rugby players, football fans, rock drummers and a 74 year old woman, who do you think attracted the attention of the customs fascists? Yes, you've got it, Dave's mum. The others passed through without incident and headed for the bar, because, of course, you need a beer at 5.00am, while I went through with Eileen. They took her luggage to pieces, rifled her medication and toiletries, and generally made things as unpleasant as possible for her. When we tried to repack her bag, it was such a mess that I offered to let her put some of her stuff in my half-empty bag until we could sort things out later. Unfortunately, she elected to pack a skirt in my bag, which of course provided the others with a standing cross-dressing gag at my expense for the whole weekend. Oh well, I like to see people happy.

After an uneventful flight we reached Malaga airport at an ungodly hour, to be met by Maggie and her bloke, friends of Dave who also owned a bar in Fuengirola, nine or ten stops away on the train. Maggie, who is originally from Swindon, had actually been at the hospital when he died, and it had been she who had phoned Eileen with the news, but as she had been visiting family back in Swindon when the accident actually happened, she knew little more than hearsay.

Eileen stayed with Maggie for the weekend, and luckily for us, Pete happened to own a very nice villa up in the hills of Fuengirola, so at least accommodation wasn't a problem. After a quick beer, and wash and brush-up chez Pete, we donned suits and headed back to Maggie's bar, the Bow Belles, where local friends were meeting up before the funeral. Given the circumstances, it was, of course, a little awkward when Jenny turned up, but Dave had assured me the split was amicable, and I'd always got on fine with her, and after all, she was still his wife. One thing that made me laugh was when Steve G and I were sat at the bar watching football on the TV, shortly before heading off for the funeral. Jenny came up and handed me a folder that she'd found among Dave's stuff, and she said she thought I ought to have it. Steve and I looked at it, then burst out laughing, cursing our old mate all the while. You see, Dave had run his own small graphics company, Resolution

Now! for a while, and when Vice Squad stuff was reissued on CD, he often did the artwork while I did the compiling and sleevenotes. When he lost interest in all that, Steve, who runs a proper graphics company, took over for a series of Riot City CDs for Step One Records. He kept asking Dave for photos he could use, but Dave always insisted that I had them. Things got desperate, and we had to make do with the few we could find, but I was bloody sure I'd given them to Dave, and there they were. However, I was curious as to why he'd taken a folder full of photos from our youth with him to Spain when he'd given me all his records after selling his house. I like to think it was sentiment, but I'll never know now.

As is the Spanish custom, I suppose, there was a viewing of the body, but I think only Pete went to that, the rest of us were too squeamish. Then it was off to the funeral in a fleet of taxis - Dave made a lot of friends in his short time there.

The crematorium was up in the hills, a big picturesque building that we were surprised to find included a bar, of all things. Only in Spain, we reckoned. For some reason the crematorium was doing unusually brisk business, so the ceremony was uncomfortably brief, though we were pleased, and again surprised, that the vicar conducting the service was from Bristol.

Eileen and Jenny led us into the service, and I sat next to Steve G at the front, both of us trying to retain some dignity, but looking at the coffin, draped in a Kingswood Rugby Club flag and other mementoes, including Dave's garden gnomes painted in Kingswood Rugby Club colours, it truly came home that that was our mate in that box, fuck it.

The vic did his best, but due to unruly people outside waiting for the next funeral, could hardly be heard, and with nerves already strained, we got a bit agitated, especially Steve G, who muttered dark threats if the offenders didn't belt up. Fair play to him.

Steve S then got up and gave a very touching speech about how much Dave meant to him over their long friendship, and amazed me with an equally moving poem.

Then the vicar pressed the button on a portable CD, and we filed out to White Man In Hammersmith Palais. This was chosen by me as 11 years before, Dave narrowly missed my Dad's funeral, typically driving up as we were leaving, just in time to go to the pub with us, where I told Dave the music we had played, in that case Motorhead, Bob Marley and some steam train records. In the pub on the following Sunday, we had a drink with his mate Chewie, and I told the tale again for his benefit, and Dave stated that White Man was what he wanted played on his demise. For some reason, I never forgot that, and I'd rather not think about why that should be.

Of course, as we were sitting at the front, we had to file out first, and never got to hear anything after 'Darren Wilson, cool operator.' Other people said they enjoyed it though.

Outside, we just stood around not sure what to do next, feeling the pain. When I hugged Eileen, she was shaking, the only time she seemed close to breaking down, and who could have blamed her if she had, but she was obviously determined to stay strong, probably for the benefit of the rest of us.

As ever, it was attending to mundane matters that got us through it, namely ordering a fleet of taxis back into town, and this went well until just the two Steves, Pete, Sheps and self were left. Our bugger never turned up, so we resolved to walk back, not minding the idea of a bit of solitude - at first, anyway. Walking down the dusty road gave us all time to reflect, and talk to our inner self, or summfink. However, the novelty soon wore off, and as the still dusty road stretched into the distance, talk tailed off and people drifted apart, walking in single file, though Steve G did strike up a stimulating conversation with some goats by the roadside.

Happily, we hit civilisation again about halfway back into town, and reckoned we deserved a beer in the bar of a rather posh-looking hotel. Pete ordered five beers, but ten turned up, as we were informed that it was Happy Hour. So, we took this as an omen and set up camp, placing the Bateman Gnomes on a table among the beers, and draping the Kingswood Rugby Club flag across the front for a photo. Taken, of course, by a woman drinking in the bar who just happened to be from Bristol. We were getting used to this sort of thing by now.

A couple of pints each was quite sufficient to destroy our hiking ambitions, and we later headed back to Fuengirola in a taxi.

I think the original plan, at this stage, was that we'd be going back to Pete's place to change our suits, eventually, but after more beers at the Bow Belles, that rather went out of the window. We met up with Ian, Colin and Blitz, and for a while tried to get more information from locals about what had actually happened to Dave, but again got nowhere definite.

After a while, we decided to move on, and the evening degenerated into one that Dave would definitely approved of. Bars, beers, clubs, beers, Italian restaurants, beers, kebabs, beers, not to mention frayed tempers and the possibility of a fight breaking out any minute. He'd have loved it, especially when in one bar, Blitz, attempted to physically remove a covers band from the stage, his idea being that Steve G and I should get up and play a few ditties. The fact that two drummers were hardly likely to put on much of a show didn't seem to curb his enthusiasm.

We got back to Pete's place at about 4.00 Sunday morning, naturally the worse for wear (I calculated that by then I'd had about one hour's sleep since Friday morning) and gratefully hit the sack. Ian kindly offered to let me swap rooms with him, as his apparently contained a wardrobe full of Mrs Pete's frocks, just in case the cross-dressing mania had still to leave me, but I declined his kind offer.

Next morning, we rose in better condition than we had any right to expect, shaved, showered and packed, and took a brisk walk into town. But not that brisk, to be honest.

After a quick beer at the Bow Belles, where we stashed our bags until departure time, we decided to venture further afield. Colin and Blitz had departed by an early flight, but we weren't due to leave until 7.30pm, so having made sure that Eileen was still happily settled, off we went. First we had a look around a Christmas market, which was pretty enough, but disappointingly reminiscent of one that I'd visited in Bath only a week before, so we...went for a beer.

With a long day ahead of us, food seemed a wise idea, and Pete suggested that we repair to a seafood restaurant that he was in the habit of frequenting, right on the beach. We did so, and it wasn't a bad idea at that, though I must admit I blanched a little at the prices. Still, you can't let the side down, as it were, so I just tried not to wince as Pete ordered copious plates of Sea Bass, Sea Bream, King Prawns, pilchards, tuna, potatoes, vegetables, wine, beer, and I forget what else. Unfortunately, as our fishy friends were brought to the table, heads intact, Ian displayed a delicate side to his nature that I was previously unaware of. Those sightless eyes staring up at him was just too much, and he departed rapidly, preferring a plate of egg and chips elsewhere. A shame, as it was an excellent meal, over which the talk naturally turned again to Dave. Not for the first time, we reflected that he of all people would have enjoyed the weekend more than anyone, though as Pete wryly pointed out, he certainly wouldn't have liked shelling out good beer money on a meal like the one we were consuming. And it must be said that a lot of the talk centred around the fact that, while we all loved him, we were all angry with him for letting matters come to this sorry state. Anyone listening in would have got entirely the wrong impression at the harsh words exchanged, but the fact is that if we hadn't cared so much, we just wouldn't have bothered saying them. It was a way of trying to come to terms with it all, but having Dave's mum on the trip with us and seeing her suffer, just made us that bit more bitter.

After hitting a few more bars, we headed back to the Bow Belles to collect our luggage, (and Eileen) and say our farewells to the locals before getting the train back to Malaga, and thence the plane back to dear old Blighty. Nothing much to report there, other than an amusing quip from Pete, while we were waiting for a taxi in a freezing cold and foggy Bristol Airport: 'I want to be there when they read the will. I want to know which of his debts he's left me.'

Later, the two Steves arranged for a charity night in Dave's honour, at, of course, his old stamping ground, the Plough in Kingswood. The charity nominated was Paul's Place, whose worthy function was providing help for adults with learning difficulties in South Gloucestershire. Onslaught had played a benefit for them a while previously, and Dave had expressed his approval, so it made perfect sense. The event took place on Friday 29 February 2008, and the original plan was that I would meet the Steves in the Plough at 1.00pm to start setting things up. This seemed a little foolhardy to me, as we were to be in the role of hosts for the evening, and meeting this early in the day must surely involve some imbibing of potent fluids, but I thought that if we just had a couple of pints, no real harm need be done.

As it happened, at 11.00am on the day, Steve G rang me, and said 'Are you out of bed?'

'Yes.'

'Are you dressed?'

'Yes.'

'Have you spiked your hair?'

'No.'

'Well, get on with it, we'll pick you up in ten minutes.'

Oh God. We drove out to a pub in Kelston, which is between Kingswood and Bath, had a couple of drinks, swapped reminiscences of Dave, then drove some more searching for a shop that could sell us some buckets for the charity collection. That was really the whole excuse for the early drink.

We never found any suitable receptacles, so after picking up the posters and photos of Vice Squad that Steve G had blown up for display, we headed for the Plough. I went round sticking up the artwork, while the Steves checked out the pub's CD and DVD systems. The idea was that the Vice Squad DVD would be shown early on, then two CDs of Dave's favourite music that I had prepared with my son Jake would take up the rest of the evening. As it happened, neither they, nor anyone else at the pub could get either system working. As the afternoon wore on, things began to look desperate. Eventually, Steve G solved the DVD problem by simply unplugging all the Sky TV stuff and plugging the DVD player straight into the pub's biggest screen. The CD, though, still refused to work. In the end, after frantic phone calls, a disco system with speakers was located and installed, and we were set. I got home at about 5.30, with a belly already full of beer. Oh well.

Fed, scrubbed up, and with my wife, two sons and mother in tow, I headed back to the pub at the appointed hour. The place was already filling up, and Eileen looked a little bewildered at all the attention, but I think was relieved to see my mother, and they spent the evening together. The two Steves kicked things off with a few brief words over the PA system about the reason for the evening, then we played the DVD.

I hadn't been sure how well the DVD screening would go down, as many of those present were Dave's friends from football, rugby, and ordinary Plough regulars, but a lot of people seemed interested and watched it all the way through. I then went down to the bar to mingle, and if the night was always going to have more than a touch of melancholy about it, it was at least good to meet up with so many old friends. Some I'd expected to see, of course, like Sheps, Ian Westaway, Colin Huntley, Blitz, Matty Isles, Mark Hambly, Sooty, Julia, Bambi, H, Steve Street, Mike Darby and his wife Barb, my mate Dave Lown, in whose kitchen the DVD interviews were filmed, and local band and old friends the Bolsheviks, but also some that I hadn't. These included Brian, Phil and Tim, the notorious brothers from early gigs and football mentioned earlier in this book, Mike Nutt from school days and, again, football, Jase Stallard from Onslaught...suffice to say, it was a great turnout, and like the funeral weekend, I couldn't help thinking that Dave, of all people, would have loved to have been there.

After the DVD, I noticed that the Clash CD that we'd put on as people were coming in was just playing in rotation, and remembered our carefully prepared compilation CDs, but could only get the thing going with the help of Sooty. After that, time to wind down a bit and get some more ale down.

Toward the end of the evening, I noticed that, unconsciously, Julia, Sooty, Mark and myself had sort of grouped together, and as Mark said, 'If Dave was here, we could do the show right now!'

By the end of the night, we were all a bit worse for wear, and as Steve Grice was a bit wobbly on his pins, me and mum went out with him to wait for his taxi. After a while, he loudly whispered 'Shane! Your mum is holding my hand!' 'If she didn't you'd fuckin' fall over!' I replied.

Some time later, I met up with Steve again for an afternoon beer, partly to have a chat, and partly to hand over some contributions to the charity that had been sent and handed to me. Cherry Red had chipped in with £100, Igor had sent a cheque, and a mate of mine in work, Dave Patton, had made a donation.

After the inquest, some more details had come to light about Dave's death, and I'd heard some of them from Eileen, but Steve filled me in properly. It seemed that in fact, Dave had been diagnosed with cancer and only given a few weeks to live, but had concealed the fact from us all. So, even the small crumb of comfort that we'd consoled ourselves with, that he'd died happy celebrating his birthday, was taken from us.

No happy ending here.

Three years later, more awfulness. I was doing some housework one night in February 2011 when my brother Clay rang. He told me to sit down, he had bad news. He told me that Jon Chilcott had died. By this time I had lost so many friends and family members that I knew from experience that it would take some time to sink in, so I just took a breath and asked if he knew how it had happened. He'd hung himself. This was awful on so many levels. First and foremost, because Jon had a wife, Heather, and two children, aged just 10 and 13. He'd had some demons in his past, but he'd fought them and built up a successful construction business as a welder, even building sets for the likes of Robbie Williams - impressive stuff.

I hadn't seen him for a few years, since we met by chance at a Motorhead gig, and though we'd arranged a couple of meetings, they somehow never worked out. I'd got his new phone number from a mutual friend just before Xmas 2010, and meant to ring, but never got round to it. These are the things that haunt you, aren't they?

The mutual friend was Andy Bretta, former singer with Jesus Bruiser, who had recently been working at the university in the post room, and on the day of the funeral, mum and I picked him up from work and she drove us to the crematorium at Canford.

Canford has both a crematorium and cemetery, and as we walked up the long drive, and saw the large crowd of people milling around, I assumed there must have been two funerals being held at the same time. But no, they were all there for Jon.

They were a colourful crowd, as one might have expected, and I actually felt a bit out of place in my formal suit and black tie. We soon met up with H, then Trayci and Simon, and I wandered over to talk to Mark and his wife Ali and Julia and her husband.

The crematorium was packed with people, and I heard later that when they couldn't cram any more in, a large crowd stayed outside to listen on a tannoy. There were no hymns or prayers. Touchingly, Jon's children had made a running order, headed 'Set List,' gaffa taped it to the side of an amp, draped a guitar lead over it and photographed it, and this was presented on a glossy card with Jon's grinning photo on the back.

The funeral guy, or whatever they're called, did a decent resume of Jon's life, but a more personal, and brilliantly delivered speech came from his friend Pete.

At the end, Mike Crawford, in a bright pink rock 'n' roll suit, turned and said 'Ladies and gentlemen, a round of applause for Mr Jon Chilcott!' and the crowd went mad like it was the end of a gig. It was the moment that broke most people up.

Afterwards there was 'Tea Cake & Comfort' provided at the South Bank in Bedminster, but thankfully that was a euphemism. There was a bar and I needed a beer and I wasn't the only one.

On 29 March there was a tribute/family benefit night at the Fleece and Firkin, with the Crazy Trains reforming for one night only. This felt particularly weird as I'd been a promoter (as part of Red Guitar Promotions) at the Fleece from 1989 to 1992, and had put on the Trains when they reformed in the early 90s, by which time both Jon's younger brother Jay and veteran Bristol muso Mike Crawford had joined the band. They were supported by all-girl late-80s band Scouting For Boys (again reformed just for the night) and another band opened, with Julia getting up to sing Last Rockers.

Unfortunately, I missed this, as me, H, his stepson Steve and my mum had elected to get a drink next door in the Seven Stars first. In there we met up with Mark Hambly, Bambi and his new missus, Mark O'Neil and Tim Galley, who I'd rarely seen since he left Sweet Revenge all those years ago. We decided that with two of our number gone in just three years, and a depressing number of other friends from the old days now departed, it was time to bury the hatchet.

When we got into the Fleece it was pleasing to see such a good turn-out. It was good to see both bands again, and especially touching to see Jay get up for a few songs - he really is very like Jon in his gestures and mannerisms. We met up with Simon and Trayci, and Julia, among others, and like everyone else tried to make it a celebration of sorts. But of course, due to the manner of his passing, it wasn't easy to carry off.

During the evening an old friend, Mark Vickery, gave me DVDs of two Sweet Revenge shows, which I had had on VHS years ago but had mislaid. I was especially pleased about this, as we rather stupidly had never recorded our set, so only the single that Simon released and some photos exist. Mum and I watched them when we got home, and I enjoyed it at the time. I really think Sweet Revenge was a good band, and it was nice to see Dave and Jon interacting on-stage. Predictably, though, the good mood didn't last. I'm typing this a few weeks later, and it still seems impossible that I'll never see either of them again. I just feel very, very sad.

Alright, you can stop blubbing now, you big girl. Happily, I can end this on a bit of a high note.

Some time ago, Beki decided to start using the Vice Squad name for her rock band, the

Bombshells, which as you can imagine, didn't please me one bit. We had re-established contact at one point, but fell out again over that. When Dave died, after a gentle prod from Mark Brennan, I rang Beki to tell her the bad news, and we had a long talk. She was very nice about it, put nice things on the 'Vice Squad' web site and sent Eileen a card, and we've stayed in touch, by phone and email, ever since. Well, obviously, otherwise she couldn't have contributed to this book!

Anyway, what I'm leading up to is that in June 2014, I went down to Sand Bay Leisure Resort, near Weston-Super-Mare, to review Inkfest for *Vive Le Rock* magazine, and who should be playing on the Sunday evening but 'Vice Squad.' I rather dreaded it, but in fact the new band is so far removed in style from the original band that I felt completely detached from it. Though having said that, after a while, I went to the toilet, and while splashing the porcelain, heard the intro to Last Rockers, and for a split second had a panicky feeling that I should have been somewhere else. When I got back my friend Sam told me that while I'd been in the toilet, they'd dedicated the song to me, which seemed very Vice Squad somehow.

After the show, Beki came to our table and we hugged and had a drink together for the first time since 1983, and it was lovely to meet her again. We talked about Dave and our other losses - her mother had sadly passed away not long before, and my little brother Clay had died the previous January, but we also reminisced on the good times, of which, as I think you can tell from this book, there were many.

A final footnote: In December 2014, Mark and I went to see the reformed Lunatic Fringe at the Exchange in Bristol, and towards the end of the evening a chap came up to me and said 'Hey, Shane, do you know what the best thing about Inkfest was this year?'

No, what?'

'Seeing you and Beki together again.'

Aaw, ain't that sweet!

Thanks for reading.

THE END

VICE SQUAD GIG LIST

By **Mark Hambly**

1979   VENUE   WITH

Date	Venue	With
12/04/79	**Bristol** - University Anson Rooms	Crisis, Iganda, X-Certs
Unknown	**Bristol** – Swan Inn, Hanham	
17/06/79	**Bristol** – Locarno	The Damned, Ruts, Auntie Pus
24/06/79	**Bristol** – Trinity Church, Old Market	X-Certs, The Numbers
Unknown	**Bristol** – Trinity Church, Kingswood	Under-Fives
11/07/79	**Bristol** – Summit Youth Club, Kingswood	S.O.S.
03/09/79	**Weston Super Mare** – Flanagan's	
14/09/79	**Trowbridge** - Town Hall	Angelic Upstarts, The Wall
15/09/79	**Cricket St Thomas** - Wildlife Park	Joe Public, the Review, Double Vision, The Groove, etc.
27/09/79	**Clevedon** – Youth Club	X-Certs, The Review
Unknown	**Sea Mills** – Youth Club	X-Certs
05/10/79	**Portishead** – Youth Club	X-Certs
11/11/79	**Bristol** - Fishponds, St Matthias College	Under-Fives, Pus Trams
14/11/79	**Warminster** – Athenaeum Arts Centre	Rupert & The Dufflecoats, Stupid Humans, The Mental (Stalag 44 were billed but may not have played)

1980

Date	Venue	With
16/02/80	**Bath** - Trinity Church	The Mental
24/04/80	**Weston Super Mare** - Bourneville Community Centre	Red Alert
12/07/80	**Bristol** - Trinity Church, Kingswood	Under-Fives
16/08/80	**Bristol** - The Crown, Old Market	
23/09/80	**Bridgend** - Sports Centre	
26/09/80	**Bristol** - Trinity Church, Old Market	Demob, Zyklon B
04/10/80	(**London** RAR Rally - Cancelled)	

1981

Date	Venue	With
13/02/81	**Birmingham** - Cedar Ballroom	
18/02/81	**London** - Bridgehouse, Canning Town	4-Skins, Anti-Establishment
20/03/81	**Malvern** - Mount Pleasant Hotel	The Samples
21/03/81	**Gloucester** - College of Arts & Technology	Demob, Icon
02/05/81	**Bristol** - Swan Inn, Hanham	Blue Turks
05/05/81	**Bristol** - Berkeley Centre	Angelic Upstarts
21/05/81	**Malvern** - Unknown	
06/06/81	**Manchester** - Mayflower Club	Varicose Veins

1981	VENUE	WITH
05/07/81	**London** - Lyceum Theatre	The Damned, Anti-Nowhere League, Ruts DC
01/08/81	**Manchester** - Mayflower Club	The Insane
10/08/81	**Bristol** - Granary	Court Martial
23/08/81	**London** - Lyceum Theatre	The Exploited, Anti-Pasti, Zounds
01/09/81	**London** - 100 Club	The Dark
12/09/81	**Manchester** - Mayflower	Blitz
14/09/81	**Sheffield** - Marples	Debar
18/09/81	**Retford** - Porterhouse	
03/10/81	**Grimsby** - Central Hall	
04/10/81	**Stevenage** - Bowes Lyon Hall	Erazerhead
05/10/81	**Bristol** - Granary	Lunatic Fringe

UK Subs Endangered Species Tour

10/10/81	**Cambridge** - Corn Exchange	UK Subs, Long Tall Shorty
16/10/81	**Birmingham** - Digbeth Civic Hall	UK Subs, GBH
17/10/81	**Manchester** - Polytechnic	UK Subs, The Fits
23/10/81	**Weston Super Mare** - Burnbeck Pier	

Anti-Pasti Six Guns Tour

29/10/81	**Leeds** - Bierkeller	Anti-Pasti, Chron Gen
30/10/81	**Birmingham** - Cedar Ballroom	Chron Gen
31/10/81	**Manchester** - University	Chron Gen
01/11/81	**Rotherham** - Civic Hall	Anti-Pasti, Chron Gen
02/11/81	**Blackburn** - St Georges Hall	Anti-Pasti, Chron Gen
05/11/81	**Derby** - Assembly Rooms	Anti-Pasti, Chron Gen
06/11/81	**Retford** - Porterhouse	Anti-Pasti, Chron Gen
07/11/81	**West Runton** - Pavillion	Anti-Pasti, Chron Gen
10/11/81	**Cardiff** - Top Rank	Anti-Pasti, Chron Gen
11/11/81	**Bristol** - Granary	The Stranglers
14/11/81	**London** - Rainbow Theatre	Anti-Pasti, VS, Angelic Upstarts, Chron Gen, Charge, Splodgenessabounds, Chelsea, Honey Bane, The Wall, The Insane, Erazerhead, The Case
15/11/81	**Portsmouth** - Top Rank	Anti-Pasti, Chron Gen
20/11/81	**Newport** - Polytechnic	Death Patrol, The Fits

First British Tour
(Oi! The Absolute Disaster Tour)

30/11/81	**Birmingham** - Cedar Ballroom	Death Patrol
01/12/81	**Sheffield** - Marples	

1981

	VENUE	WITH
02/12/81	**Liverpool** - Warehouse	
03/12/81	**Carlisle** - Market Hall	
04/12/81	**Hull** - Tower	
06/12/81	**Middlesbrough** - Crypt	
08/12/81	**Huddersfield** - Cleopatra's	Mayhem
09/12/81	**Leeds** - Brannigans	Mayhem
10/12/81	**Manchester** - Mayflower	Mayhem
12/12/81	**Worksop** - Sports Centre	
20/12/81	**Leeds** - Queen's Hall	The Damned, The Exploited, UK Subs, Chron Gen, VS, Anti-Nowhere League, Black Flag, Chelsea, The Outcasts, Trockener Kecks, Charge, GBH, Lama, The Insane

1982

15/01/82	**Bradford** - Queens Hall	
	First Holland Tour	
22/01/82	**Appledoorn** - Gigant	Cheap 'n' Nasty
23/01/82	**Zandaam** - Dreiluit	
24/01/82	**Groningen** - Club Vera	
26/01/82	**London** - 100 Club	The Fits
05/02/82	**Newcastle** - University	
27/02/82	**Lancaster** - University	GBH, The Insurgents
28/02/82	**Glasgow** - Apollo	The Exploited, Anti-Nowhere League, Infa-Riot, The Threats
28/3/82	**London** - Lyceum Theatre	The Damned, Peter and the Test Tube Babies
01/04/82	**Preston** - Warehouse	The Expelled
13/04/82	**Plymouth** - Top Rank	Decontrol
20/04/82	**London** - 100 Club	Lunatic Fringe
22/04/82	**Hull** - Tower	
23/04/82	**Norwich** - Gala Ballroom	Abrasive Wheels
09/05/82	**London** - Lyceum Ballroom	GBH, The Insane, The Defects, The Dark
25/05/82	**London** - 100 Club	The Expelled
27/05/82	**Cambridge** - Sea Cadets Hall	
28/05/82	**Exeter** - St George's Hall	Lunatic Fringe
29/05/82	**Nottingham** - Union Rowing Club	
11/06/82	**Retford** - Porterhouse	The Expelled

1982	VENUE	WITH
22/06/82	**Brighton** - Xtreems/New Regent	Flowers of the Past
26/06/82	**London** - Zig Zag Club	Charlie Harper's Urban Dogs, Dead Man's Shadow, Special Duties
13/07/82	**London** - 100 Club	Soldiers of Destruction, Intensified Chaos
14/07/82	**Manchester** - Drifters	The Expelled, Crash
16/07/82	**Norwich** - Gala Ballroom	Dogs of War
	USA and Canada Tour	
11/08/82	**Los Angeles** - Whisky a Go Go	Chron Gen
14/08/82	**San Pedro** - Dancing Waters Club	Chron Gen
15/08/82	**Hollywood** - Olympic Auditorium	Chron Gen, Wasted Youth, Battalion of Saints, CH3, Circle One, Shattered Faith, Aggression, Lost Cause
18/08/82	**San Francisco** - Old Wardorf	Chron Gen
21/08/82	**Portland** - Oasis Café	
23/08/82	**Eugene** - B.J. Kelly's	The Rats, Punishment Farm
26/08/82	**Calgary** - University	Social Distortion, Youth Brigade
27/08/82	**Edmonton** - Villa Vesuvius	Social Distortion, Youth Brigade
28/08/82	**Saskatoon** - University	
30/08/82	**Winnipeg** - Monterey Furdey Hall	Stretch Marks, Social Distortion, Youth Brigade
01/09/82	**Minneapolis** - Upper Deck	Social Distortion, Youth Brigade
03/09/82	**Chicago** - C.O.D. Club	Social Distortion, Youth Brigade
04/09/82	**Detroit** - City Club	Social Distortion, Youth Brigade
07/09/82	**Pittsburgh** - Electric Banana	
09/09/82	**London, Ontario** - Fry Fogles	
11/09/82	**New York** - Filmore Club, Long Island	Nihlistics
12/09/82	**Montreal** - Polish White Eagle	Black Flag, Discharge
13/08/82	**Toronto** - Coronet Club	Discharge, The Effigies
16/09/82	**Washington, D.C.** - 9:30 Club	
18/09/82	**New York** - Rock Lounge	Bad Brains
	Second British Tour (State Of The Nation Tour)	*Support on all dates:* Flowers Of The Past
07/10/82	**Bradford** - University	
09/10/82	**Manchester** - Polytechnic	
11/10/82	**Keighley** - Funhouse	
13/10/82	**Liverpool** - Warehouse	
14/10/82	**Preston** - Warehouse	
15/10/82	**Retford** - Porterhouse	
16/10/82	**Middlesbrough** - Cavern	
18/10/82	**Leeds** - University	

1982

	VENUE	WITH
19/10/82	**Brighton** - Xtreems/New Regent	
20/10/82	**Isle of Wight** - Shanklin Pier	
21/10/82	**Portsmouth** - Polytechnic	
22/10/82	**Leicester** - University	
23/10/82	**Bridgewater** - Arts Centre	+ Intensified Chaos
24/10/82	**Plymouth** - Top Rank	
26/10/82	**Bristol** - Trinity Church	
27/10/82	**Coventry** - Lanchester Polytechnic	
28/10/82	**Cambridge** - Sea Cadet's Hall	
29/10/82	**Norwich** - Gala Ballroom	
04/11/82	**London** - Klub Foot, Clarendon Hotel	+ Urban Dogs, Brutal Attack

Second Holland Tour

10/11/82	**Amsterdam** - Paradiso	
11/11/82	**Groningen** - Club Simplon	
12/11/82	**Vlissingen** - De Piek	
13/11/82	**Leiden** - LVC	
21/12/82	**London** - 100 Club	Flowers Of The Past

1984

04/01/84	**Bristol** - Granary	Kiev
28/02/84	**London** - Dingwalls	Cry of the Innocent
29/02/84	**Leeds** - Bierkeller	Uproar, the Fiend, Pagan Idols
11/04/84	**Swindon** - Level 3	Colonel Kilgore's Vietnamese Formation Surf Team
12/04/84	**Plymouth** - Sound City	War Toys
13/04/84	**Hereford** - Market Tavern	Foreign Legion
14/04/84	**Oldham** - Oddy's	The Expelled

Portugal

24/04/84	**Lisbon** - Rock Rendezvous	
25/04/84	**Lisbon** - Rock Rendezvous	
27/04/84	(**Colchester** - Woods Leisure Centre - Cancelled)	
16/05/84	**Leeds** - Bierkeller	The Expelled
19/05/84	**Blackpool** - Bierkeller	Broken Bones, The Legion
25/05/84	**Cambridge** - Sea Cadet's Hall	
26/05/84	**Liverpool** - Bierkeller	